UNEVEN DEVELOPMENT IN THE THIRD WORLD

Also by A. S. Bhalla

BLENDING OF NEW AND TRADITIONAL TECHNOLOGIES
    (*co-editor*)
ECONOMIC TRANSITION IN HUNAN AND SOUTHERN CHINA
TECHNOLOGY AND EMPLOYMENT IN INDUSTRY (*editor*)
TOWARDS GLOBAL ACTION FOR APPROPRIATE TECHNOLOGY
    (*editor*)
NEW TECHNOLOGIES AND DEVELOPMENT: Experiences in
    Technology Blending (*co-editor*)
SMALL AND MEDIUM ENTERPRISES: Technology Policies and
    Options (*editor*)

Uneven Development in the Third World

A Study of China and India

A. S. Bhalla

St. Martin's Press   New York

First published in the United States of America in 1992

Printed in Hong Kong

ISBN 0–312–06821–2

Library of Congress Cataloging-in-Publication Data
Bhalla, A.S.
Uneven development in the Third World: a study of China and India
/ A.S. Bhalla.
p. cm.
Includes bibliographical references and index.
ISBN 0–312–06821–2
1. India—Economic policy—1947– 2. India—Economic
conditions—1947– 3. China—Economic policy—1949– 4. China–
–Economic conditions—1948– I. Title.
HC435.2.B449 1992
338.951—dc20   91–24074
                                                      CIP

To Arman, Praveen and Ranjan

Contents

Contents   ix

List of Figures

List of Tables

List of Abbreviations

CASS	Chinese Academy of Social Sciences
CGHS	Central Government Health Scheme
CHW	Community Health Worker
CSIR	Council of Scientific and Industrial Research
CSO	Central Statistical Organisation
GDP	Gross Domestic Product
GNP	Gross National Product
GOI	Government of India
GR	Green Revolution
HYV	High-yielding Variety
ICAR	Indian Council of Agricultural Research
ICOR	Incremental Capital-Output Ratio
ISIC	International Standard Industrial Classification
NAS	National Accounts Statistics
NCAER	National Council of Applied Economic Research
NCNA	New China News Agency
NDP	Net Domestic Product
NSS	National Sample Survey
PQLI	Physical Quality of Life Index
PRC	People's Republic of China
SRS	Sample Registration System
SSB	State Statistical Bureau
SSTC	State Science and Technology Commission
SYC	Statistical Yearbook of China

Preface

The major part of the work on this book was undertaken when I spent 1988 as Hallsworth Professorial Fellow at the Department of Economics, University of Manchester, England. Initially this work began as an attempt to empirically test Michael Lipton's hypothesis on urban bias in developing countries as a major cause of poverty. However, as research progressed, I realised how ambitious and difficult this task would be, particularly since the notion of urban bias itself was rather difficult to define and measure. This is all the more so in the context of a socialist economy like the Chinese where urban bias is so closely intermingled with bias of the state apparatus and party/political considerations. Furthermore, there are several statistical problems and a degree of arbitrariness in estimating urban bias. To measure it, one would need the yardstick of an unbiased situation which is difficult to determine in both capitalist and socialist economies alike.

My ambition therefore had to yield ground to the more modest task of an analysis and measurement of uneven development in Third World countries in general and in China and India in particular. The book deals with theoretical concepts like unbalanced growth and their empirical analogues. Alternative development strategies like heavy industrialisation, sectoral balance and economic liberalisation are considered from the point of view of their outcomes in terms of growth, equity and access. Special attention is paid to spatial and class inequalities. Rural–urban, intraregional and interregional dimensions of spatial inequalities are analysed with special reference to China and India.

The first four chapters of the book deal with macroeconomic and sectoral considerations in identifying the process of development and its outcome and impact on growth, equity and access. Chapters 5 and 6 discuss the outcome in terms of growth and equity respectively. Chapters 7 to 9 are concerned with access to technology, health and education, which influences the material, mental and physical well-being of human beings who are, after all, the target and beneficiaries of development. The last chapter – an attempt at summing up – also ventures into the importance of political economy considerations in the achievement of goals of development and equity.

In September 1988, I had the opportunity of visiting China. I spent three weeks in Beijing, Hangzhou and Shanghai. During my stay there I had many opportunities of discussing my preliminary ideas about my manuscript with several Chinese scholars, particularly at the Chinese Academy of Social Sciences. I received very helpful comments and suggestions from many of them.

In writing this book I owe a debt of gratitude to several institutions and individuals. First, I am most grateful to the University of Manchester for the Fellowship award which made it possible for me to pursue my research in a very congenial academic environment. The librarians of the London School of Economics and Political Science, the School of Oriental and African Studies and the School of Hygiene and Tropical Medicine of the University of London also deserve a note of thanks for their unfailing assistance.

For inspiration and moral support, I am grateful to: Professor Michael Lipton of the Institute of Development Studies, University of Sussex; Professor Stanley Metcalfe, Chairman of the Economics Department, University of Manchester, Dr George Joseph of the Department of Econometrics and Social Statistics of the University of Manchester, Dr Athar Hussain of the London School of Economics, Professor Ranjan Ray of the Delhi School of Economics, University of Delhi and Professor Dilip Nachane of the University of Bombay.

The individuals who offered generous assistance in the writing of the book are far too numerous to be all named individually. I am indeed grateful to all those who spent much of their precious time in commenting on various draft chapters and in clarifying concepts and methodologies. In particular, I would like to single out the following: Professor Shu-ki Tsang of Baptist College, Hong Kong; Dr Shujie Yao of the International Development Centre, Queen Elizabeth House, University of Oxford; Professor Hans Singer of the Institute of Development Studies, University of Sussex; Professor Jeffrey James of the University of Tilburg; Dr John Enos of Magdalen College, University of Oxford; Professor Amit Bhaduri of the Institute of Management, Calcutta; Professor Subbiah Kannappan of Michigan State University; and Messrs Ajit Ghose and Salem Sethuraman of the ILO World Employment Programme, Geneva. Any remaining errors and omissions are my sole responsibility.

Mrs Ira Ray, Additional Director-General of Health Services, Ministry of Health and Family Welfare of the Government of India, New Delhi, kindly helped with the supply of health data for Chapter 8. Professor Jacques Silber of the University of Jerusalem gave useful comments on the same chapter. Mr Sun Yonghong of China National Packaging Import and Export Corporation (formerly of Beijing University of International Business and Economics) was most helpful in the collection of unpublished Chinese data. He also answered many queries so willingly. Dr N. V. Varghese of the National Institute of Educational Planning and Administration, New Delhi, read Chapter 9, and Frances Stewart of the International Development Centre, University of Oxford, Chapters 1 and 2, and gave stimulating comments. Dr Ajit Ghose of the ILO, and Christian Peters, a political scientist from Hamburg University and staff member of ILO/SATEP, Harare, Zimbabwe, offered constructive suggestions for the improvement of Chapter 10. To all of them I am most grateful.

A Chinese graduate student at the Department of Economics, University of Manchester, provided most able research assistance during my stay at Manchester and subsequently. My wife, Praveen Bhalla, had the unenviable task of editing the entire manuscript which she did with unflinching enthusiasm.

Finally, I would like to acknowledge the untiring and cheerful assistance of Jean Ashton and Amanda Brereton of the Faculty of Economic and Social Studies, University of Manchester in typing and retyping the manuscript.

A. S. Bhalla

Acknowledgements

In writing Chapters 3, 5, 7 and 8 I have drawn on my articles in *Applied Economics* (with Yue Ma), *World Development, Journal of International Development* and *Science and Public Policy*. I am grateful to the publishers of these journals (Chapman & Hall, London, Pergamon Press, Oxford, John Wiley & Sons, Ltd., Chichester, and Beech Tree Publishing, Guildford) for permission to do so.

The author and publishers also wish to thank the following for permission to reproduce copyright material:

The People's Medical Publishing House, Beijing, for Figure 8.2, from R. Keqin, 'Health of the Chinese People', in C. Yueli (ed.), *Public Health in the People's Republic of China* (1988).

The World Bank, Washington, D.C., for Figure 9.1 and data in Table 8.1, from D. Jamison *et al.*, *CHINA – The Health Sector* (1984) and *World Development Reports*.

Oxford University Press, for data in Table 2.2, from World Bank, *World Development Report, 1987*.

China Quarterly, for data in Tables 3.1 and 5.5, from Kuan Chen *et al.*, 'New Estimates of Fixed Investment and Capital Stock for Chinese State Industry' (1988).

Journal of Development Studies, for data in Table 3.2, from S. Paine, 'Spatial Aspects of Chinese Development: Issues, Outcomes and Policies, 1949–79' (1981).

Journal of Comparative Economics, for data in Tables 3.2 and 6.1, from I. Adelman and D. Sunding, 'Economic Policy and Income Distribution in China' (1987).

Cambridge Journal of Economics, for data in Table 6.1, from A. K. Ghose, 'Rural Poverty and Relative Prices in India' (1989).

Gower, for data in Table 7.6, from I. Ahmed and V. Ruttan (eds), *Generation and Diffusion of Agricultural Innovations: The Role of Institutional Factors* (1988).

Stanford University Press, for data in Table 8.1, from J. Banister, *China's Changing Population* (1987).

Part I

Development Strategies and Concepts

1 Strategies and Outcomes

Development has two important aspects: the approaches for achieving this goal and the outcomes in terms of growth, access and equity. Development planners may adopt unevenness or unbalanced growth as a deliberate strategy or it may be incidental to this strategy. Unevenness may also result from wide gaps between planning and expectations and reality. Development decisions are made on the basis of certain assumptions about the functioning of markets and institutions, the availability of resources and their utilisation which often turn out to be not valid in practice.

A development strategy requires certain policy blueprints and public action before any of its outcomes can be anticipated. Following Anderson a distinction can be made between policy outputs and outcomes.[1] The process of implementation of strategies and policies determines certain policy outputs (e.g. operation of health clinics). However, these outputs give no indication of the outcome – that is, the effectiveness with which the output or institutions are channelled towards social welfare. Furthermore, while some outcomes may be due to policies or strategies, others may be the result of private economic decisions and market forces. In planned mixed economies, it is not easy to isolate market-induced inequalities from those resulting from public policy and action. Nevertheless, special priority to exports instead of domestic production or to heavy industry as opposed to agriculture and rural non-farm production, may result in skewed income distribution. Similarly, a policy of favouring capital cities against small towns and countryside or coastal regions against hinterland, would lead to spatial inequalities.

The adoption and implementation of strategies and policies depends on a number of actors and interest groups at the national, regional and local levels. The interests of these groups may be in conflict and their political power and influence may vary. There are also losers and gainers from the implementation of particular policies and programmes. An effective implementation of strategies, policies and programmes therefore requires support from dominant interest groups. Failure to implement policies may result partly from a neutralisation of conflicting interests of potential gainers and losers.[2] If the above non-economic forces are unimportant, the outcomes of policies and programmes may turn out to be as intended.

3

Thus, the content of policy, the nature of its design, the resources allocated and the political/administrative context in which the policies and programmes are implemented, all tend to determine outcomes. For example, one kind of economic and political regime may be more conducive to even and balanced development than another.

I STRATEGIES: ECONOMIC AND SOCIAL OUTCOMES

Uneven development can be viewed as (a) intrinsic to the development strategy or process, or (b) an unplanned or unanticipated outcome.

Some outcomes, whether they are the result of an explicit strategy or an unplanned process of development, may be either egalitarian or unbalanced. Outcomes which are inegalitarian or unbalanced may stem from (i) shortcomings of implementation or (ii) unforeseen events or exogenous factors over which the strategy has no control. The strategy and the outcome may thus be closely associated or entirely unrelated. Even an unbalanced development strategy (growth without redistribution for example) can result in a greater income equality (as seems to be the case in the Republic of Korea and Hong Kong). Similarly, a balanced development strategy which emphasises proportional growth of agriculture and industry may have inegalitarian outcomes if agricultural development is bi-modal and exclusively favours large commercial farms. Johnston and Kilby have argued that a unimodal strategy – progressive modernisation of the entire agricultural sector – is much more likely to result in egalitarian outcomes.[3]

Our concern in this book is with an examination of the processes and strategies of development in terms of performance regarding growth, access and equity.

1.1 Strategies and Outcomes

Several alternative situations describing the relationship between strategies and their outcomes are summarised in Table 1.1.

In the Third World, three main sets of strategies have been adopted: namely, heavy industrialisation, agriculture-led development and redistributive or egalitarian strategy.[4] As noted above, the implications and outcomes of these alternative strategies tend to vary. For example, the heavy industrialisation strategy followed in

Table 1.1 Strategies and their outcomes

Strategy	Outcome	
	Economic (growth)	*Social (equity)*
Uneven development (Heavy industrialisation or agriculture-led growth)	High/low	Uneven or inegalitarian income distribution and access
Uneven development	High/low	Even or egalitarian income distribution and access
Even development (Redistributive or egalitarian, balance between agriculture and industry)	High/low	Uneven or unequal access
Even development	High/low	Even or equal access

the 1950s and 1960s in most developing countries assumed that rapid growth was the main route to development and that it could be achieved through industrial development, high rate of capital accumulation and capital-intensive technology. The high growth rates were expected to lead to rapid expansion of output, the benefits of which would trickle down to different parts of an economy and among different socioeconomic groups of the population. In practice, in most developing countries this did not actually happen. If anything, in some cases income distribution was skewed in favour of the richer – the so-called saving classes – to raise capital accumulation.

The adoption of agriculture-led and redistributive strategies in many developing countries was a reaction to a negative impact (in terms of its social outcomes) of the growth maximisation strategy. As noted above, an agriculture-led strategy can also lead to uneven outcomes if the pattern of agricultural development is bi-modal where considerable land ownership is concentrated in the hands of a few. To make an agriculture-led strategy compatible with greater equality in income distribution, an appropriate balance between agriculture and industry would need to be achieved. Greater emphasis on agricultural output and employment implies that the agricultural sector acts not only as a reservoir of labour supply but also as supplier of raw materials for industry and a source of demand for its products like agricultural fertilisers, farm equipment, and construction materials.

Redistributive or egalitarian strategies (which have been the hallmark of Maoist China as we shall examine in Chapter 3) are explicitly designed to give economic development a human face. They aim at improving income distribution, reducing income and spatial disparities and promoting employment generation. As we show in this book, the development of the Third World is not simply a question of growth and investment allocation. Amartya Sen's pioneering approach concerning human capability shows that the human and social dimension of development is as important as the entitlements to commodities on which the traditional GNP approach concentrates.[5]

This approach has now gained international currency with the publication in 1990 of the United Nations Development Programme (UNDP) Report on Human Development.[6] A composite human development index of life expectancy (longevity), literacy (knowledge) and basic income for decent living has been constructed. The ranking of countries by this index is often very different from that indicated by GNP per capita which suggests that there is no automatic link between the two indices. Thus the human approach to development which puts human welfare at the centre may at times be incompatible with the objective of growth *per se*.

It is evident that a redistributive strategy would be expected to lead to egalitarian outcomes in terms of equity and social welfare. But it is less evident that its outcome in terms of rate of growth of output would also be favourable. At least in the short run, an egalitarian strategy may lead to a decline in the growth rate owing to a shift of resources from investment and capital accumulation to consumption and subsidies. In the longer run however, equity and growth need not be in conflict. There is no empirical evidence to prove that an objective of equity and a basic needs approach is systematically associated with low investment ratios or investment productivity (reflected in high capital–output ratios).[7] Investments in human capital are likely to accelerate growth. Similarly, consumption by the poor, at low levels of nutrition, has an investment element in so far as it is likely to raise workers' health and productivity and thus human capital formation. Empirical support for the hypothesis that a basic needs strategy can stimulate economic growth is provided by a study which used a lagged-dependent variable model for 46 countries and showed that the Physical Quality of Life Index (PQLI) had a positive effect on GDP.[8]

Clearly there are overlaps between the three strategies discussed above. Furthermore, these strategies have not been followed consistently by developing countries for long enough periods. In many cases only certain elements of a given strategy may be introduced on a trial and error basis before any coherent strategies emerge. And even in the same country, different strategies may have been tried during different time periods. But it is difficult to put these strategies into different watertight compartments. For example, in China and India despite a shift to an agriculture-led strategy, the emphasis on heavy industry continued. Similarly, the introduction of a market-oriented strategy did not replace the important state sector; it simply involved an emphasis on its improvement and efficiency. As we shall discuss in Chapter 3, China and India both followed a heavy industrialisation strategy during the 1950s, both of them shifted to agriculture-led strategies in the 1960s and 1970s; and in the mid-1980s they both introduced liberal market-oriented strategies. The motivation for this shift lay in a desire to achieve more successful outcomes in terms of growth, efficiency and equity.

1.2 Inequalities as Outcomes

Whether growth and equity are compatible and whether there is a relationship between economic development and income inequality are issues surrounded by controversy. Kuznets has observed an empirical link between these two variables: in the past, inequality was greater in countries at early stages of development when incomes were lower, it tended to increase as incomes increased, and fell to its lowest levels after a point of satisfactory development was reached.[9] This inverted U-shape relationship has, however, been questioned. Anand and Kanbur argue that the empirical results are sensitive to the choice of data sets and the measure of inequality.[10] We thus conclude that there is no convincing and necessary relationship between development *per se* and its outcome in terms of income inequality, and that the relationship is indeterminate (see Table 1.1).

Greater equality is much more dependent on the type of development strategy adopted (Chapter 3), on access to productive assets and technology (Chapter 7), on access to health services (Chapter 8) and on the distribution of educational opportunity (Chapter 9) than on the level of income *per capita*. Government policies and actions which affect the output of services and institutional infrastructure will also have an impact on the distributional welfare of the population.

In a large number of developing countries, in the absence of a dominant distributive strategy growth maximisation or heavy indus- trialisation *per se* did not lead to a 'trickle down' or widespread sharing of the fruits of growth. Empirical evidence shows that while growth in many developing countries has been quite reasonable in the past two decades, income inequalities have also grown. In some countries even absolute standards of living of some poverty groups have declined.[11]

Income differentials between sectors and social classes and unequal access to resources and markets manifest imbalances. In this book we examine the following types of imbalances:

(a) *Income inequalities* – within and between sectors,
(b) *Spatial/regional inequalities* – between rural and urban areas and between different geographical regions and provinces, and
(c) *Class and socioeconomic differences in incomes* and access to such goods and services as health, education and technology.

The different types of inequalities noted above are not indepen- dent of each other. Regional or locational inequalities may overlap sectoral inequalities. This point deserves emphasis because of the tendency in dualistic models of development to equate 'rural' with 'traditional' and 'subsistence' agriculture, and 'urban' with modern industry. But modern industry often includes not only heavy industry but also infrastructure and transport. Also the mix of economic activity is much wider in the urban areas while rural areas also show much diversification.

Geographical and sectoral disparities may also overlap class in- equalities, especially when income and occupational stratifications and access factors are taken into account. In the Marxist tradition, the focus is essentially on the ownership of property rights. Bhaduri has further noted that ownership of capital implies not only owner- ship of a physical stock, of a means of production, but 'a social relation embodying property rights'.[12] The structure of property rights determines the distribution of wealth and income assets in a given society. Even more, in the radical economic tradition, the State is not a neutral entity but a vehicle of the dominant class, its support for particular classes being reflected in prevailing policies and pro- grammes. Such bias may be rationalised on pragmatic economic grounds (capital accumulation) or political grounds (the power of the rich farmers and industrialists).

Class analysis has also been used to explain the growth and distribution of sectoral incomes.[13] Ashok Mitra divides society into four classes: the rich farmers, the industrial bourgeoisie, industrial working class and the poor peasantry. Taking the Indian example, he shows how the industrial bourgeoisie and rural oligarchy colluded to manipulate terms of trade, lending and borrowing the taxation and subsidies to their advantage through political influence on public decisions.

The study of social classes and property relations to explain uneven development in the Third World remains an underdeveloped art. This is partly due to difficulties in quantitative disaggregation, and partly to the dominance of neo-classical economics with its concentration on economic aggregates like investment and consumption, and the individual unit as the decision maker. To quote Ashok Mitra: 'Once the neo-classicals and the "marginalists" had made their debut, the issue of an antagonistic relationship between social categories, so much to the fore in classical political economy, was ushered out of the limelight, and a process of atomisation set in: an individual unit of a factor of production became the focal point of analysis, classes lost their erstwhile pre-eminence.'[14]

The goal of planned development is to narrow inequalities within target dates. A development strategy should also identify target groups of the underprivileged and the deprived. In most cases, this would involve providing these groups better access to resources, jobs and public goods and services. But access is a necessary but not sufficient condition due to the dependence of public services like health and education on the availability of complementary infrastructure like transport and communications.

Both neoclassical and Marxist aggregations and dualisms may be flawed, however, unless we have a clear picture of the distributional aspects of income and access.

The heterogeneity of income classes within urban areas and the existence of the urban poor in both the formal and informal sectors further highlights conflicting interests between the urban rich and the poor. The interests of the marginalised urban poor will be in conflict with those of the urban rich but not of the urban workers who may be buyers of their cheap goods and services. Aggregations based on property will also profit by further breakdowns. At least in terms of the income criterion, it makes sense to disaggregate urban, rural or other classes into several categories.[15]

1.3 Biased or Uneven Development?

Writers like Michael Lipton explain biased development and persistence of poverty in developing countries as arising from the neglect of agriculture.[16] Our concern in this book is not so much with this urban bias as with the significance and implications of the rural–urban dichotomy for uneven development and economic/social inequalities.

The determination of urban bias and its quantification presupposes a hypothetical 'unbiased' situation against which any deviation may be measured. What is an unbiased alternative? What would a *laissez-faire* policy yield and would it be optimal? Not necessarily, since an initial imbalance and unevenness may warrant deliberate offsetting steps.

Development calls for movement of labour and capital from agriculture into industry which inherently implies some sort of a bias. Biased development is sometimes measured by the divergence between domestic and world prices assuming that the latter reflect a neutral equilibrium position. However, this is not a satisfactory assumption considering that world prices can also be distorted by the international policies of cartelisation, preferential tariffs and the use of distorted exchange rates.[17]

Perfect equality between sectors (or equal weights attached to them by planners and policy-makers) is neither possible nor desirable. Weights given to different sectors and activities, in determining priorities or allocating resources, reveal the preferences or objectives laid down by the planners. Thus certain elements of subjectivity or arbitrariness in defining uneven development would be unavoidable.

Uneven development may be defined in terms of a departure from a norm. This may indicate special weights or priorities accorded to certain sectors, regions or income classes, or an abstract ideal. An example of the last is the results which flow from an optimal path (e.g. Uzawa's two-sector model or von Neumann's multisectoral model). The ideal can also be defined in political and moral terms, as was done in the case of China's development strategy under Mao. In Chapter 2 we discuss uneven development in terms of imbalance between consumption and investment and between agriculture and industry. Uneven development is also examined in terms of urban bias and unequal exchange in international trade and economic relations. In subsequent chapters, wherever appropriate, political and other non-economic considerations, especially in the context of China, are also examined.

To measure uneven development is clearly a Herculean task, considering the paucity of relevant data and methodological limitations. Despite these problems which we discuss in Chapter 2, a heroic attempt is made to measure unevenness in terms of intra-industry and intersectoral imbalances. This is done mainly by way of illustration of the empirical analogues of the theoretical concepts reviewed in Chapter 2.

II WHY A CHINA–INDIA COMPARISON?

A few words are now in order to explain why we choose to compare China and India to illustrate cases of uneven development. These two countries together account for over 30 per cent of the world's total population, nearly 40 per cent of the population of the Third World and nearly 70 per cent of the population of Asian developing countries.[18] Also both of them have continued to suffer from acute poverty despite over three decades of development planning. Clearly, therefore, solutions to the problems of development in these two countries can have important implications and lessons for poverty alleviation and socioeconomic development elsewhere in the Third World.

One may argue that both China and India are very large and rather closed economies whose experiences are unlikely to have any lessons for small open economies. It is true that diseconomies of small scale may prevent the latter from following the type of self-reliant strategies that were adopted by China and India. The greater reliance of small open economies on exports and foreign markets may be associated with different development paths and degrees of commodity specialisation, and with differences in the way their development plans and programmes are financed. One may also speculate that the problems of uneven development, e.g. inequalities in income distribution, regional disparities and class distinctions, are less likely to be as acute in open small economies as in large economies of China and India.

Notwithstanding the differences in size of countries (a subject beyond the scope of this book), there are clearly some common goals for both large and small developing countries – adequate economic growth, improvement in standards of living and quality of life. Despite the differences that may arise in achieving these goals, the Chinese and Indian experiences could have some useful lessons for the Third World in general.

There are several parallels between China and India which also make a comparison between the two countries useful. Both countries have vast areas and natural resources and big domestic markets which enable them to pursue goals of self-sufficiency and endogenous development. Both are planned economies with strong control and/or ownership of investment resources. Both economies have experienced large domestic savings rates for capital formation (in the case of India savings for the most part are voluntary whereas in China they were forced). High savings rates have considerably reduced the need to rely on foreign capital for financing of development programmes and projects.

The fact that China and India differ in political organisation and socioeconomic systems (one is a socialist economy and the other, a market-oriented mixed economy) makes the comparison particularly interesting. In India, after independence in 1947, a socialistic pattern of society and state capitalism and controls were built on the existing capitalist edifice. In China, the more sweeping Revolution in 1949 replaced capitalism with communism. In the post-Mao period market mechanisms and limited competition were reintroduced but without dismantling the foundations of the socialist structure.

In the late 1940s both countries started at more or less similar levels of development as measured by such indicators as per capita income, life expectancy and mortality rates and industrial development. It would therefore be useful to examine the results of alternative development strategies under two different political systems in terms of growth, inequalities and access. If the outcomes in terms of these indicators were different, was this due to differences in design of strategies and policies adopted, lapses in implementation or the different political and administrative systems in the two countries?

III OUTLINE OF THE STUDY

This study is about development strategies and their outcomes. Uneven development is defined in terms of these two variables. In Chapter 2 we define the concept of uneven development and discuss approaches to its measurement. In Chapter 3 we measure the degree of uneven development in China and India. Explanations are then sought for unevenness in the two countries in terms of the broad development strategies and macroeconomic policies adopted. Chapter 4 is concerned with the measurement of intra-industry and intersectoral linkages and policy measures that may hinder or promote the growth of such linkages. The experiences of China and India are also compared with a selected number of other developing countries to determine whether some generalisations can be made for the Third World or at least for the Asian region.

Chapters 5 to 9 are concerned with the outcomes in terms of growth, inequalities and access. The outcomes in terms of growth of output and productivity and efficiency of investments are discussed in Chapter 5. Chapter 6 examines income, spatial and class inequalities. The issues of the impact and outcome of development strategies and processes in terms of access to technology, health and education are discussed in Chapters 7 to 9. The final chapter speculates about the political economy of development in countries like China and India with widely differing political systems but sharing common economic and social problems.

Notes and References

1. See James E. Anderson, *Public Policymaking*, New York, Praeger Publishers, 1975, p. 134 and Merilee S. Grindle (ed.), *Politics and Policy Implementation in the Third World*, Princeton, Princeton University Press, 1980. Also see Bernard Schaffer, 'Towards Responsibility: Public Policy in Concept and Practice', in E. J. Clay and B. B. Schaffer (eds), *Room for Manoeuvre – Explanation of Public Policy Planning in Agricultural and Rural Development*, London, Heinemann Educational Books, 1984.
2. See Merilee S. Grindle, 'Policy Content and Context in Implementation', in Grindle, 1980.
3. Bruce F. Johnston and Peter Kilby, *Agriculture and Structural Transformation – Economic Strategies in Late-Developing Countries*, London, Oxford University Press, 1975.
4. For a general discussion of alternative strategies, see Keith Griffin, *Alternative Strategies for Economic Development*, London, Macmillan Press, 1989.
5. See Amartya Sen, 'Development: Which Way Now?', *Economic Journal*, December 1983; Amartya Sen, 'The Concept of Development', in H. C. Chenery and T. N. Srinivasan (eds), *Handbook of Development Economics*, Vol. I, Amsterdam, North-Holland, 1988; Amartya Sen, 'Development as Capability Expansion', *Journal of Development Planning*, no. 19, 1989; and Keith Griffin and John Knight (eds), 'Human Development in the 1980s and Beyond', Special Issue, *Journal of Development Planning*, no. 19, 1989.

6. UNDP, *Human Development Report, 1990*, New York, Oxford University Press, 1990.
7. See Paul Streeten, *First Things First: Meeting Basic Human Needs in Developing Countries*, London, Oxford University Press, 1981, ch. 4.
8. Barbara A. Newman and Randall J. Thomson, 'Economic Growth and Social Development: A Longitudinal Analysis of Causal Priority', *World Development*, April 1989.
9. Simon Kuznets, 'Economic Growth and Income Inequality', *American Economic Review*, vol. 65, no. 1, 1955, and 'Quantitative Aspects of the Economic Growth of Nations: V-Long-term Trends in Capital Formation Proportions', *Economic Development and Cultural Change*, vol. 11, July 1960.
10. S. Anand and S. M. R. Kanbur, 'The Kuznets Process and the Inequality–Development Relationship', Discussion Paper No. 249, Economics Department, Essex University, August 1984; and 'Inequality and Development – A Critique', paper presented at the 25th Anniversary Symposium of the Economic Growth Center, Yale University, 11–13 April, 1986. Also see N. Stern, 'The Economics of Development – A Survey', *Economic Journal*, September 1989.
11. Keith Griffin and Azizur Rehman Khan, 'Poverty in the World: Ugly Facts and Fancy Models', *World Development*, March 1978.
12. Amit Bhaduri, *Macroeconomics – The Dynamics of Commodity Production*, London, Macmillan, 1986, ch. 1, p. 9.
13. Ashok Mitra, *Terms of Trade and Class Relations*, London, Frank Cass Ltd, 1977.
14. Mitra, *Terms of Trade*, p. 25.
15. Alain de Janvry and K. Subbarao, *Agricultural Price Policy and Income Distribution in India*, Delhi, Oxford University Press, 1986; and Keith Griffin and Jeffrey James, *The Transition to Egalitarian Development*, London, Macmillan Press, 1981.
16. Michael Lipton, *Why Poor Stay Poor – Urban Bias in World Development*, London, Temple Smith, 1977.
17. John Toye, 'Political Economy and the Analysis of Indian Development', *Modern Asian Studies*, February 1988, and Bhaduri, *Macroeconomics*.
18. Wilfred Malenbaum, 'A Gloomy Portrayal of Development Achievements and Prospects: China and India', *Economic Development and Cultural Change*, January 1990; and Robert F. Dernberger and Richard S. Eckaus, *Financing Asian Development 2 – China and India*, The Asia Society, Lanham, MD, University Press of America, 1988.

2 Concepts and Measurement of Uneven Development

In this chapter we examine the concept of uneven development in terms of three development models, strategies or processes: (i) unbalanced growth, (ii) urban bias, and (iii) unequal exchange in terms of international resource gaps and inequalities. An attempt is also made to look for empirical measures for these theoretical notions.

Uneven development in terms of unbalanced growth (associated with Hirschman *par excellence* but also with Streeten) and urban bias (with Lipton primarily) follows mainly a closed-economy model which corresponds well to the large economies of China and India with their big domestic markets. The interpretation of uneven development in terms of unequal exchange (associated mainly with Emmanuel) is more relevant to the open trading economies.

I UNBALANCED GROWTH

Until the appearance of Hirschman's classic – *The Strategy of Economic Development* (1958)[1] – a widely prevalent view was that countries should adopt a balanced growth strategy to avoid supply bottlenecks especially in the short run. There was no clear agreement, however, on what constituted balanced growth. The concept, which is not unambiguous, has been defined in several different ways: namely, sectoral balance in terms of identical growth rates for different sectors (e.g. between agriculture and industry) as is often assumed in growth models, balance between consumption and investment, between investment and consumer goods and between supply of and demand for industrial goods, etc.[2] Complementarities in consumption demand would suggest investments taking place in a number of sectors simultaneously.[3]

There are some differences between the proponents of unbalanced growth and the critics of urban bias like Lipton. The concept of unbalanced growth (*à la* Hirschman and Rosenstein-Rodan) is

15

premised mainly on rapid growth, key sectors and high linkages which provided arguments for the primacy of industrialisation. The balanced vs. unbalanced growth debate was concerned largely (though not exclusively) with intra-industry balance and not with balance between agriculture and industry. The debate relating to issues of agriculture–industry balance (Lewis, Kalecki, Adelman, etc.) was more to do with inter-sectoral rather than intra-sectoral balances. Lipton's urban bias concept was only partly concerned with a greater role for agriculture; it was more concerned with equalising the rates of return on investment across sectors. These various issues are discussed below.

1.1 The Primacy of Industrialisation

Critics of the balanced growth concept have pointed out that it is not possible to make simultaneous investments in different sectors in developing countries because of the shortages of capital, foreign exchange and skilled manpower. Furthermore, in an open economy framework, trade may offset shortages and surpluses so that balanced development of different sectors may not be necessary. Similarly, balanced development of agriculture and industry is necessary only if food cannot be imported. However, even if food could be imported, foreign exchange constraints and limits to export expansion might often make this alternative unfeasible.

Hirschman argued that the developing countries were short of scarce resources like capital, entrepreneurial and managerial capacity, and decision-making. Therefore, these resources should be economised by concentrating on a few key sectors (e.g. heavy industry) which would induce investment in supplying industries (backward linkages) and user industries (forward linkages). The key sectors would need to be identified on the basis of 'backward' and 'forward' linkages, implying that industries/activities with the highest linkages would maximise growth. The relationship between industry ranking, linkages and growth is illustrated in Table 2.1.

The theory of unbalanced growth and the concept of 'big push-'were formulated at a time when growth maximisation *per se* was fashionable. It was assumed that the benefits of growth would 'trickle down' to everyone. Thus the pattern of growth did not really matter – all that was needed was a high rate of growth.

In sectoral terms, this growth strategy meant a much higher priority to industry than to agriculture on grounds of its greater external

Table 2.1   Linkages, key sectors and economic growth

Linkages	Key sectors	Growth
High backward (B) and forward (F) linkage	Mainly 'intermediate manufacture' industries (e.g. iron and steel)	High
High (B), low (F) linkage	Industries relating to final manufacture (e.g. processed foods)	Medium/Low
High (F), low (B) linkage	Industries relating to 'intermediate primary production' (e.g. mining, petroleum and gas)	Medium/Low
Low (B) and (F) linkage	Agriculture, fishing	Low

economies and more important linkages. Hirschman argues that agriculture lacked 'direct stimulus to the setting up of new activities through linkage effects'.[4]

A number of factors seem to explain the preference of developing country policy-makers for heavy industrialisation *vis-à-vis* an agricultural strategy for development. First, in the 1950s and 1960s when the heavy industrialisation strategy became fashionable, the classical development models of Lewis, Fei and Ranis equated agriculture with traditional low-productivity activities. These activities were supposed to be inferior to modern industry which was considered to be the engine of growth (see below). Agriculture was seen mainly as a 'reservoir of resources' (e.g. food, labour, savings and foreign exchange) for industrialisation. Secondly, the experience of the industrialised countries led to a generalisation that modern economic growth (reflected in increasing per capita incomes) is accompanied by a movement of labour and capital out of agriculture and into industry and services. The work of Kuznets provided a quantitative basis for this generalisation about the structural transformation of the advanced economies. It has been noted that 'historically the rise in the share of manufacturing in output and employment as per capita income increases, and the corresponding decline of agriculture are among the best documented generalisations about development'.[5] These inter-sectoral shifts may be explained by three major factors: demand shifts (Engels' law), trade (changes in comparative advantage), and technology (substitution of processed for unprocessed goods) and productivity differentials.[6]

The declining share of agriculture in GDP (especially under assumptions of closed economy and constant prices) can be explained by the low income elasticity of demand for food and other agricultural products. Due to this factor alone, the gross value of farm sales will grow more slowly than GDP.

The lower income elasticity of demand for agricultural products than for industrial goods means that an optimal agricultural growth rate would tend to be lower than that for industry. Thus, the assumption of equal sectoral growth rates in growth models to define balance is unrealistic. A balance between agriculture and industry is more likely to mean that the former moves in a certain proportion to the latter which is determined by the respective income elasticities of demand for agricultural and industrial products.[7] One can even argue that a developing country may be justified in planning for the growth of industry even faster than the income elasticities warrant. This would be the case particularly if the country was pursuing an import-substitution policy and was interested in switching exports from primary products to manufactures.[8] But it is difficult to determine how far this emphasis on industry should be carried before it leads to adverse results. Both the limited supplies of agricultural marketed surpluses and low incomes in the agricultural sector can slow down the process of industrialisation. For example, in some countries of Africa, chronic shortages of food supplies, droughts and balance of payments crises suggest that industrialisation was carried too far at the expense of growth of agricultural output.

1.2 Imbalance Between Consumption and Investment

An aspect closely related to the primacy of industrialisation is that of an imbalance between consumption and investment. A heavy industrialisation strategy is based on the premise that shortage of capital is the major constraint to a rapid growth of output. This constraint can be relaxed only by raising the rate of savings and capital accumulation. The higher the rate of capital accumulation the lower is likely to be the rate of increase in current consumption. Development models like those of Fel'dman and Mahalanobis, which divide the manufacturing sector into consumption and capital goods sectors, assume that it is indispensable to promote a rapid growth of the investment goods sector in order to achieve a rapid rate of growth of output.[9]

The Fel'dman–Mahalanobis model implicitly assumes that the agricultural sector is completely endogenous to the industrial sector so that it adjusts to the latter's requirements. The agricultural marketed surplus or supply of wage goods is not considered a constraint to rapid industrialisation.[10] Nor is the slow rate of growth of consumption considered a limitation. In a latter four-sector model, consisting of (i) investment goods, (ii) factory consumer goods, (iii) household consumer goods (including agriculture) and (iv) services sector covering health, education, etc., Mahalanobis assumed that consumption growth could be met by sector (iii) and/or it could be controlled.[11] However, the absolute level of consumption at a given point in time may be below socially acceptable limits. Even from an economic point of view, to the extent that a part of expenditure on food and health and other basic needs raises productive capacity, neglect of consumption may slow down growth and may even cause social hardships. These problems were not recognised in either the Chinese or Indian model of development.

As we shall examine in Chapter 3, in China from 1958 onwards, too much emphasis on capital accumulation led to a slow growth of the average level of consumption of workers and peasants.[12] Although during the post-Mao period, attempts were made to improve the balance between accumulation and consumption, the primacy of accumulation has not in fact been abandoned.

In India also, at least during the Second (1956–61) and Third (1961–6) Five-Year Plans, the dominant influence of the Mahalanobis model meant a clear preference for high rates of investment particularly in the capital goods sector. (See Chapter 3.)

1.3   Imbalance Between Agriculture and Industry

One of the main theoretical principles underlying an imbalance between agriculture and industry is the Lewis model of development.[13] It assumed that the traditional sector (subsistence agriculture) was characterised by large surplus labour, low labour productivity and an absence of capital accumulation. In contrast, the modern sector (large urban industry) was the hub of economic activity and capital accumulation. The rate of capital accumulation in the modern sector determined the rate at which rural surplus labour could be transferred to this sector. It is implicitly assumed that full employment prevails in the modern sector and that surplus labour in the traditional sector is almost in unlimited supply at a constant wage which is somewhat above the average earnings in this sector, and which sets a floor to the urban or capitalist wage. With the gradual ductivity differentials in the two sectors will narrow until the entire rural labour surplus is exhausted. Presumably at this stage the dichotomy between the traditional versus modern and subsistence versus capitalist production would disappear.

Lewis's structural approach to problems of long-term development of the Third World countries in a dualistic framework necessitated the use of various dichotomies which would become unnecessary when full employment was reached. The extent to which the Lewis model would be successful in absorbing the surplus agricultural labour depended on a number of assumptions: the rate of investment in the industrial sector, the capacity of the industrial sector to absorb agricultural labour which in turn would depend on the employment elasticity of industrial output and the capital intensity of production techniques employed, as well as the propensity of the capitalist class to invest productively instead of wasting profits in consumption.[14] In practice, in most developing countries these assumptions turned out to be quite unrealistic.

The actual experience of large labour surplus economies like China and India (which are the concern of this book) shows that a smooth transfer of surplus rural labour to the industrial sector (as envisaged by the Lewis model) has not actually taken place. In fact, in both China and India, nearly 60–70 per cent of the population continue to remain in rural areas. In the case of China, the control of rural to urban migration partly explains a fairly high degree of labour stabilisation in agriculture and rural non-farm activities. In India, the share of the rural labour force has remained quite large despite free rural to urban migration. This has been due partly to the high rate of population increase and consequently a high rate of growth of the labour force, low rates of industrial growth and a high degree of capital intensity in the modern sector.

The experience of most developing countries also shows that their per capita incomes have not risen as fast as was expected, and that the shares of output and employment in agriculture are still substantial (see Table 2.2). In most developing countries, the share of agriculture in GDP is over 20 per cent and that of the agricultural labour force is over 30 per cent with several countries showing this latter share above 50 per cent. Yet the share of gross public investment (gross fixed capital formation) in agriculture is in most cases less than 10 per cent.

A note of caution about investment data in Table 2.2 is in order. There are serious problems in estimating capital formation in agriculture.

Table 2.2   Output, investment and employment shares in agriculture (percentages)

Country	Annual GDP growth rate in agriculture		Share of GDP in agriculture		Share of labour force in agriculture		Investment share in agriculture	
	1965–80	*1980–88*	*1965*	*1988*	*1965*	*1980*	*1960–65*	*1980–85*
A. Developing countries								
Bolivia	3.8	2.1	23	24	54	46	3.2	–
Ethiopia	1.2	–1.1	58	42	86	80	4.0	–
Jamaica	0.5	0.9	10	6	37	31	10.9	–
Malawi	4.1	2.7	50	37	92	83	12.0	–
Philippines	4.6	1.8	26	23	58	52	5.7	–
Korea, Rep. of	3.0	3.7	38	11	55	36	10.5	7.8
Sudan	2.9	2.7	54	33	82	71	23.3	–
Kenya	4.9	3.3	35	31	86	81	–	8.0
Syria	4.8	0.5	29	38	52	32	19.1	8.3
Thailand	4.6	3.7	32	17	82	71	17.4	–
Egypt, Arab Rep.	2.7	2.6	29	21	55	46	16.2	–
Tanzania	1.6	4.0	46	66	92	86	18.2	–
China	2.8	6.8	44	32	81	74	–	–
India	2.5	2.3	44	32	73	70	–	19.0
Pakistan	3.3	4.3	40	26	60	55	–	13.6
Costa Rica	4.2	2.5	24	18	47	31	–	8.3
El Salvador	3.6	–1.4	29	14	59	43	–	–
Mauritius	–	4.0	16	13	37	28	–	5.0
Tunisia	5.5	2.4	22	14	49	35	19.9	–
Iraq	–	–	18	–	50	30	–	12.1
Israel	–	–	–	–	12	6	–	–
Trinidad/ Tobago	0.0	4.5	8	5	20	10	2.1	–
Guatemala	–	–	–	–	64	57	–	6.5
Venezuela	3.9	3.8	6	6	30	16	–	3.6
Zimbabwe	–	2.5	18	11	79	73	–	9.4
B. Advanced countries								
Japan	0.8	0.8	9	3	26	11	–	–
United States	1.0	3.2	3	2	5	4	–	2.8
United Kingdom	–1.6	3.4	3	2	3	3	–	2.3
France	1.0	2.3	8	4	18	9	–	4
Italy	0.8	1.0	10	4	25	12	–	6.6
Germany Fed. Rep.	1.4	1.9	4	2	11	6	–	3

Sources: World Bank, *World Development Report (WDR), 1990*, Oxford

University Press, 1990, table 2, pp. 180–81 (for GDP growth in agriculture), table 3, pp. 182–83 (for share of GDP in agriculture) and WDR 1988 table 31, pp. 282–83 (for share of labour force). Data on investment shares are taken from E. F. Szczepanik, 'The Size and Efficiency of Agricultural Investment in Selected Developing Countries', FAO, *Monthly Bulletin of Agricultural Economics and Statistics*, December, 1969; and FAO, 'The State of Food and Agriculture, 1978, 1979', Rome and UN, *National Accounts Statistics:* Analysis of Main Aggregates, New York, 1985 (No. E.87.XVII.11).

Note: Data on investment shares refer to gross fixed capital formation.

United Nations estimates (from the *National Accounts Statistics*) do not include working capital or the natural growth of forests and livestock; neither do they make any deduction for replacement of the existing capital stock.[15]

The bias noted above in favour of heavy industrialisation seems recently to have yielded ground to explicit support for agriculture. This is grounded in lessened faith in the industrialisation model in providing equitable outcomes from growth. Thus Irma Adelman's simulations using data for the Republic of Korea for 1963, show that 'an agricultural demand-led industrialisation programme' would lead to a better distribution of incomes and a higher industrial growth.[16] This would call for greater allocation of resources to agriculture, increase in productivity of small and medium farmers, technological improvements in agriculture and promotion of demand linkages.

II   URBAN BIAS

Lipton has explained the above imbalances in terms of the concept of urban bias in the Third World.[17] For tropical Africa, Bates has shown how, in the past, government intervention in markets for agricultural commodities, urban consumer goods and factors of production extracted rural surpluses in order to finance and promote urban development.[18] As opposed to Lipton's closed-economy framework, Bates examined the African open economies. In the latter, governments derived a substantial proportion of their budgets from export agriculture through state marketing boards. The extracted surpluses were invested in urban, capital-intensive and industrial projects. The prices of agricultural products, including food, were kept depressed, to the detriment of rural producers. Support for the industrial sector at the expense of the rural has also been demonstrated for Latin America.[19] The usual mechanism was an import-substitution strategy which led to the replacement of primary production for export by a heavily protected domestic manufacturing industry.

We now examine in greater depth the implications of this approach for efficiency and equity, focusing on Lipton's model of urban bias. 'Bias' implies a deviation from either efficiency or welfare norms.

2.1 Efficiency Norm

This argues that investment allocations or expenditures between agriculture and non-agriculture are sub-optimal. Investment in agriculture is low in spite of potentially higher returns than those of the urban/industrial sector because prices are 'twisted' by governments against the agricultural sector. This results in a disproportionately large allocation of resources to the urban industrial sector, a low yield on aggregate investment and worsening rural–urban income inequality.

This argument is, however, static and over-simplified. Dynamic efficiency considerations require that account be taken of differentials over time between rural and urban resource allocations. Such differences over time may be significant for several reasons. First, there may be differential rates of depreciation of gross capital and investment. Lipton argues that replacement requirements and maintenance costs are lower in agriculture than in industry.

Urban investments may be justified on grounds of inducements to capital accumulation due to the higher savings rates of profit-earners than wage-earners, and low, or no savings, of small farmers. Lipton challenges this defence of urban bias on both theoretical and empirical grounds.

Even a high consumption by agricultural workers (inverse of low savings) can be defended as potentially productive since it would raise efficiency, especially if the farmers have been malnourished (which is often the case in many developing countries). Furthermore, additional urban investment can lower profit rates (and hence savings rates) through diminishing marginal returns to capital.

Even if urban-biased investments raise the savings ratio, the increase is likely to be more than offset by low returns to urban capital due to low rates of capacity utilisation. Thus, Lipton concludes that dynamic adjustments to the efficiency norm would favour rural investment much more than urban investment. There is evidence to suggest that farm savings can often be quite high if not as high as urban savings.[20]

Lipton's efficiency arguments may need to be qualified or rebutted on two grounds. First, certain rural technological choices open to private and even public investors may be inefficient and yield low returns. For instance, this may be the case in India with respect to *kharif* versus rain-fed areas. Second, the initial distribution of wealth and property may be such that there may be few investments which maximise farm output and profits due to demand or purchasing power constraints.

So far the efficiency criterion has been considered mainly in the context of market-oriented economies, where prices and markets are used to allocate resources in alternative uses, and to balance supply of and demand for goods and services. In socialist economies like that of China (notwithstanding the recent price reforms), prices play a minor role in allocating resources or in clearing the market. Instead directives are used to adapt demand to output targets which are predetermined and are based on certain national goals and overall constraints.

Nevertheless, there is one thing in common between market economies and socialist ones like those of India and China. They both suffer from market segmentation and other imperfections which limit the usefulness of the marginal calculus in the search for optimal efficiency. In India this must focus on reform of existing markets and prices. In China the need is not only to reconcile performance with plan targets but to formulate the latter increasingly in terms of prices rather than quantities. To conclude, whatever the nature of the urban bias, the growth of the economy and of the rural sector is affected by given patterns of resource allocation.[21]

2.2 Equity Norm

The equity argument consists of two propositions: rural investments would be more efficient in generating incomes, and an increment in rural incomes would increase the welfare of a larger segment of the population than a comparable increase in urban incomes. The elimination of urban bias would thus maximise economic and social welfare. The fact that inequalities in rural areas are generally less than in urban areas further strengthens this call against urban bias. Equality may mean (a) equality of opportunity and (b) equality of incomes and wealth. The above equity argument is concerned mainly with (b). However, the poor may not command access to such public goods and services as health or education merely because they have additional income. Income is a necessary but not sufficient condition for equality of opportunity, the latter implying equal access to resources, goods and services, and employment. Both (a) and (b) are no doubt interrelated. Equal or greater access to health and education, for instance, is likely to raise the capacity to earn higher incomes (the investment aspect of educational and health inputs) and vice versa.

The two criteria of efficiency and equity are, in fact, related, in the sense that decisions leading to an increased efficiency of resource allocation to rural areas should also lead to an increase in rural welfare. In other words, equity and efficiency (or growth) need not be in conflict.

Either concept, efficiency or equity, is not unambiguous however. Let us take the case of equity. A transfer of additional resources to rural areas will necessarily achieve this objective only if its effect is not to make the rural rich (large farmers, landlords, etc.) richer, while leaving the rural poor at the same level. Such intra-sectoral bias against the rural poor is an important consideration judging from the experience of the Green Revolution which is alleged to have favoured the larger and richer farmers.

This emphasises that Lipton's concept of urban bias goes beyond the usual critiques of unbalanced growth. Lipton attributes the bias to an urban class and thus provides a socio-political explanation of poverty and imbalance (see Chapter 10).

III UNEQUAL EXCHANGE

The concepts of unbalanced growth and urban bias discussed above can be extended to include an international dimension. For example, foreign influences favouring certain consumption styles, inappropriate products, and urban-centred research, can actually reinforce urban bias.

These considerations are emphasised by the dependency school[22] which argues that the metropolitan centres (advanced countries) withdrew surpluses from the periphery (developing countries) to promote their own development. The unequal exchange can be perpetuated by such means as unfavourable terms of trade and transfer pricing by multinational corporations which facilitate the extraction of surplus on unequal terms.

The concept of 'unequal exchange' derives from inherent inequalities in international trade. Associated with Emmanuel[23] it argues that the exports of developing countries (the periphery) are underpriced in relation to the labour value embodied in them. Their imports from the metropolitan countries are however overpriced in relation to their labour embodiment. Emmanuel assumes that capital is perfectly mobile whereas labour is not. Thus wage differentials persist which account for unequal exchange. This results in the transfer of resources from the periphery to the centre.

Other interpretations can be given to the concept of unequal exchange. The gains from trade may be unequally distributed owing to the differential bargaining power of the trading partners.[24] It may also be argued that the resource gaps between developing and advanced countries widen over time, rendering the exchange progressively more unequal.

Wide technological gaps exist between the centre and the periphery since the bulk of the total R and D resources are concentrated in the former. The periphery countries lack capital, technology and skilled manpower which limits their capacity to compete with the rich advanced countries in trade, industry and services. Therefore, they are forced to concentrate, at least initially, on agriculture, primary production and export of raw materials. But even here they are disadvantaged in several ways. Writers like Keith Griffin have argued that technical change in advanced countries (development of synthetics and dematerialisation of production resulting from the applications of new technologies) reduces the demand for the primary commodities produced in the developing countries. Innovations in the advanced countries are generally labour-saving and create a factor bias against labour employed in the LDCs.[25] Furthermore, subsidies granted to agriculture in the centre result in a loss of comparative advantage of the periphery countries in primary exports.

The concept of 'unequal exchange' does not lend itself to empirical testing. It also suffers from the same sort of limitations as the concept of urban bias. In order to define 'unequal' exchange, one must know what 'equal' exchange would represent. Equivalence of exchange is interpreted as an exchange in the Marxian sense of goods 'embodying' equal quantities of labour time. The products produced by the rich advanced countries may include less 'live' labour, i.e. current input of labour, but more products embodying skilled labour. Therefore, it may not be very appropriate to judge 'unequal exchange' simply in terms of current inputs of labour time embodied in products produced by different countries. A construction of indices to measure the complexities of equivalence is a very difficult task.

Finally, the dependency school must face the challenge that the developing countries as a group have grown faster than the developed. This would have also narrowed the relative income gaps.[26]

IV   MEASUREMENT OF UNEVEN DEVELOPMENT

Having discussed different concepts of unbalanced growth, it is useful in this section to explore if appropriate empirical analogues can be found for these theoretical concepts.

4.1   Intra-Industry Imbalance

We noted above that Hirschman's unbalanced growth concept was primarily concerned with an imbalance between industries within the industrial sector. A measure of such imbalance is the size of backward, forward and total linkages generated by a unit investment or production of gross output. The linkage index enables the classification of industries by the type and size of the linkages generated. Two measures considered by Hirschman are:

(a) percentage ratio of inter-industry purchases to total production (backward linkage); and
(b) percentage ratio of inter-industry sales of total demand (forward linkage).

The above linkages are estimated on the basis of input–output tables in Chapter 4 and the methodology for measuring these linkages is described in Appendix 4.1.

Empirical tests of balanced versus unbalanced growth carried out in the early 1970s generally (i) defined a balanced growth rate for the economy, (ii) estimated an index of imbalance and (iii) correlated this index with overall growth rates. If the correlation was positive, it was assumed that the hypothesis of unbalanced growth was valid; if the correlation was negative, the balanced growth concept received support.

4.2   Intersectoral Imbalance

Imbalance between agriculture and industry and intersectoral imbalances in general have been measured in terms of the deviations of the sectoral from the average national rate of growth of output over a specified period of time.

Yotopoulos and Lau[27] (Y/L) used a modified version of the Pearson Coefficient of Variation to measure the degree of dispersion, so that:

$$\bar{V}_w = \frac{1}{G} \sqrt{\frac{\sum_{i=1}^{n} (g_i - G)^2}{n}} \qquad (1)$$

where $\bar{V}$ is the measure of unevenness, G the average rate of growth of a country over a given time period, and g_i the ith sector's rate of growth.

As $\bar{V}$ does not take account of the relative share of each sector within the economy, equation (1) needs to be modified as follows:

$$\bar{V}_w = \frac{1}{G} \sqrt{\sum_{i=1}^{n} W_i(g_i - G)^2} \qquad (2)$$

where w_i is the share of sector i and $\sum_{i=1}^{n} w_i = 1$. It can be shown that $\sum_{i=1}^{n} w_i g_i = G$.

(Y/L) index above implicitly assumes that, under conditions of perfect balance, $g_i - G = 0$ for all i or $g_i = G$. The degree of imbalance would be measured by the size of the index $\bar{V}_w$ – the higher the index the greater the dispersion of the sectoral growth rates and higher the degree of unevenness or imbalance. A low value of $\bar{V}_w$ would show low degree of unevenness.

If an economy was in imbalance initially, similar growth rates in all sectors would continue or worsen the imbalance, but the Y/L index would be low. On the other hand, if the economy moved towards a

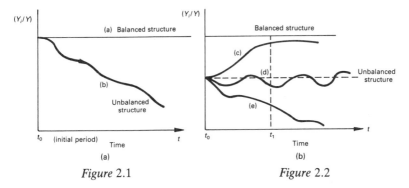

Figure 2.1   Figure 2.2

Balanced vs. unbalanced structure

balanced situation over time, the unequal sectoral growth rates would imply a high value of the Y/L index. This can be illustrated in Figures 2.1 and 2.2.

Figure 2.1 shows that the economic structure at the initial period is balanced. If each sector's development followed path (a), i.e. similar growth rates, then the Y/L index would give a low value. If the economy developed along path (b) unequal growth rates would give a high value of the Y/L index.

Figure 2.2 shows an unbalanced structure of the economy in the initial period. If the economy developed towards a balanced structure along path (c) the Y/L index would tend to be high before t_1 and then tend to be low after t_1. If the economy continued on an unbalanced path along (d) the Y/L index would give a low value. However, if the economy were moving towards a more unbalanced path along (e), the Y/L index would give a high value. These cases are summarised in Table 2.3.

A third version of the Y/L index (in addition to the unweighted and weighted versions given in equations (1) and (2) above) takes account of the income elasticity of demand and is defined as:

$$\bar{V} = \frac{1}{G} \sqrt{\sum_{i=1}^{n} w_i(g_i - b_iG)^2}$$

(3)

where b_i is the total income elasticity of demand which is estimated by regressing the following equation:

Development Strategies and Concepts

Table 2.3 Alternative interpretations of the Y/L index

		Y/L index	
Growth towards →		*Balance*	*Imbalance*
Initial period	Balanced structure	Low	High
	Unbalanced structure	High→low	Low or high

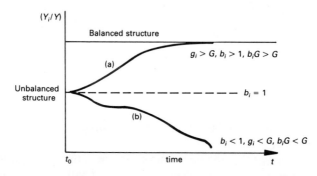

Figure 2.3 Diagrammatic illustration of the Y/L index of imbalance

$$ln\ Y_i = a_i + b_i\ lnY \tag{4}$$

Equal growth rates in all sectors implies that $ln\ Y_i = ln\ \alpha_i + ln\ Y$ where α_i is the proportion of y_i in Y, i.e. the elasticity for each sector is unity.

However, if the economy develops with unequal growth rates in all sectors, the Y/L index will still not be able to reflect whether the economy is developing towards a balanced path (a) in Figure 2.3 or towards a more balanced path (b). To show this, let us recall equation (4) which can be rewritten as:

$$ln\ (y_i/Y) = a_i + (b_i - 1)\ ln\ Y \tag{5}$$

So if the proportion of GDP in sector i is increasing as is Y over time, then $b_i > 1$. Otherwise $0 < b_i < 1$.

Yotopoulos and Lau have tested the Y/L index of imbalance on the basis of cross-sectional data of developing as well as advanced countries. They found a negative correlation between this index and the overall growth rates suggesting support for the concept of balanced growth. However, negative correlation may simply mean that countries with more rapid growth do not experience divergent sectoral growth rates, or in other words, they can correct imbalances quickly.[28] To avoid this ambiguity, in Chapter 3 we use time series data for China and India to measure imbalances in the two countries. The Y/L index is likely to be more useful when sufficiently long span of 30 to 40 years is considered (as we have done) over which the economies have adequate time to adjust.

4.3 Differential Returns on Sectoral Investments

Lipton's notion of equality between rates of return on investments in different sectors corresponds to Lardy's measure in terms of the relationship between investment and output growth. In discussing imbalance in investment allocation between agriculture and industry in China, Lardy considers the relationship between the ratios of the investment shares and the incremental output.[29] However, Lardy's direct concern is not with estimating imbalance but analysing sectoral investment over time. Lardy gives (in a footnote at the end of his book) simple equations to express the condition of balanced growth. He states that balanced growth is achieved when the ratios of investment to increment in output are equal in both agriculture and industry. A departure from this condition is an indication of imbalance. This relationship is expressed in the following equation.

$$I_i/\Delta_i = I_a/\Delta_a$$

where I is investment, Δ output increment and subscripts a and i agriculture and industry respectively.

We generalise Lardy's index for n number of sectors. Let us define the national incremental capital–output ratio (ICOR) as:

$$\bar{R} = \frac{\sum_{j=1}^{n} I_j}{\sum_{j=1}^{n} \Delta_j} \tag{6}$$

where I_j is investment in sector j and Δ_j is incremental output of sector j.

Perfect sectoral balance *à la* Lardy would imply that:

$$\frac{I_1}{\Delta_1} = \frac{I_2}{\Delta_2} = \ldots = \frac{I_n}{\Delta_n} \equiv \bar{R} \tag{7}$$

In other words, balanced growth is defined in terms of equality in the ratio of the investments (or investment shares) in a multisectoral economy and the ratio of growth rates weighted by the ratio of the total outputs of the corresponding pairs of sectors. Essentially, this Lardy index boils down to an equality of sectoral incremental capital–output ratios (ICORs) if investment (I) is equal to incremental capital (ΔK), so that:

$$\Delta K_1/\Delta Y_1 = \Delta K_2/\Delta Y_2 = \ldots = \Delta K_n/\Delta Y_n \tag{8}$$

For purposes of comparison, we construct the modified Lardy index of imbalance or unevenness in an unweighted form as follows:

$$\bar{V} = \frac{1}{\bar{R}} \sqrt{\sum_{j=1}^{n} \left(\frac{I_j}{\Delta_j} - \bar{R}\right)^2 / n} \quad (R \text{ is given in (6)}) \tag{9}$$

and weighted index as follows:

$$\bar{V}_w = \frac{1}{\bar{R}} \sqrt{\sum_{j=1}^{n} w_j \left(\frac{I_j}{\Delta_j} - \bar{R}\right)^2} \tag{10}$$

where

$$w_j = \frac{(Y_j^{1970} + Y_j^{1960})/2}{\sum_j (Y_j^{1970} + Y_j^{1960})/2}$$

Y_j^{1960} is output at 1960 (for China we use National Income, and for India we use Net Domestic Product) for sector j, after taking the moving average for 3 years, i.e.:

$$Y_j^{1960} = \frac{\bar{Y}_j^{1959} + \bar{Y}_j^{1960} + \bar{Y}_j^{1961}}{3}$$

(the $\bar{Y}_j$'s on the right-hand side are historical values).

$$\Delta_j = Y_j{}^{1970} - Y_j{}^{1960}$$

I_j is cumulative investment of sector j over period of 1959 to 1969, assuming one-year time lag between investment and output.[30]

V   CONCLUSION

Above we have considered uneven development in terms of three types of development models and strategies, namely, unbalanced growth, urban bias and unequal exchange. We noted that the three different concepts of uneven development can be reconciled. The existence of sectoral imbalances is common to the concepts of unbalanced growth and urban bias but the latter provides an additional socio-political explanation for sectoral imbalances. In an open economy framework, the concept of unequal exchange has some similarity to that of urban bias – that is, bias in favour of the centre *vis-à-vis* the periphery.

We have also attempted to present measures of uneven development that correspond to the notions of unbalanced growth, agriculture–industry balance and balance between rates of return on investment in different sectors.

Our concern in the following chapters will be mainly with the strategies of unbalanced and balanced development and their outcomes in terms of growth as well as spatial (rural–urban and inter-provincial) and class inequalities. Open economy considerations are relevant to the issues of uneven development but in economies like China and India with a potential for big domestic markets, national considerations would tend to outweigh international ones.

Notes and References

1. Albert O. Hirschman, *The Strategy of Economic Development*, New Haven, Yale University Press, 1958, and Boulder, Westview Press, 1988.
2. For a recent summary and critique of the debate on balanced growth, see Amitav Krishna Dutt, 'Sectoral Balance – A Survey', *WIDER Working Papers, WP.56*, Helsinki, March 1989.
3. P. N. Rosenstein-Rodan, 'Problems of Industrialisation in Eastern and Southeastern Europe', *Economic Journal*, June–September 1943; P. N. Rosenstein-Rodan, 'Notes on the Theory of the "Big Push"', Cambridge, Mass., MIT, Center for International Studies, 1957; reprinted in

Howard S. Ellis (ed.), *Economic Development for Latin America*, Proceedings of a Conference held by the International Economic Association, London, Macmillan, 1961; and R. Nurkse, *Problems of Capital Formation in Underdeveloped Countries*, Oxford, Basil Blackwell, 1953.

4. Hirschman, *Strategy of Economic Development*, pp. 109–10.
5. Hollis Chenery, Sherman Robinson and Moshe Syrquin, *Industrialisation and Growth: A Comparative Study*, Oxford, Oxford University Press, 1986, p. 1.
6. Ibid, p. 349.
7. This argument is based on Michal Kalecki, 'Problem of Financing Economic Development in a Mixed Economy', in Michal Kalecki, *Essays on Developing Economies*, Hassocks, Harvester Press Ltd, 1976.
8. I owe this point to Frances Stewart.
9. P. C. Mahalanobis, 'Some Observations on the Process of Growth of National Income', *Sankhya*, September 1953; and 'The Approach of Operational Research to Planning in India', *Sankhya*, December 1955; A. S. Bhalla, 'From Fel'dman to Mahalanobis in Economic Planning', *Kyklos*, March 1965; and E. Domar, 'A Soviet Model of Growth', in *Essays in the Theory of Growth*, New York, Oxford University Press, 1957.
10. Amit Bhaduri, *Alternative Development Strategies and the Poor*, paper presented at the ILO/SAREC Workshop on the Interrelationship Between Macroeconomic Policies and Rural Development, Geneva, 11–13 December 1989.
11. P. C. Mahalanobis, 'The Approach of Operational Research to Planning in India'.
12. Dong Fureng 'Relationship Between Accumulation and Consumption', in Xu Dixin and others (eds), *China's Search for Economic Growth – The Chinese Economy since 1949*, Beijing, New World Press, 1982.
13. W. A. Lewis, 'Development with Unlimited Supplies of Labour', *The Manchester School*, May 1954; and W. A. Lewis, 'Unlimited Labour – Further Notes', *The Manchester School*, January 1958.
14. Ashwani Saith, *Development Strategies and the Rural Poor*, paper presented at the ILO/SAREC Workshop on the Interrelationship Between Macroeconomic Policies and Rural Development, Geneva, 11–13 December 1989.
15. For a discussion of the nature and limitations of investment data for agriculture, see J. A. Mollett, 'Agricultural Investment and Economic Development – Some Relationships', *Outlook on Agriculture*, vol. 11, no. 1, 1982.
16. Irma Adelman, 'Beyond Export-Led Growth', *World Development*, September 1984.
17. Lipton, *Why Poor Stay Poor* 1977.
18. Robert H. Bates, *Markets and States in Tropical Africa – The Political Basis of Agricultural Policies*, Berkeley, University of California Press, 1981.
19. Markos J. Mamalakis, 'The Theory of Sectoral Clashes', *Latin American Research Review*, vol. 4, no. 3, 1969; and Mamalakis, 'The Theory of Sectoral Clashes and Coalitions Revisited', *Latin American Research*

Review, vol. 6, no. 3, 1971. For a general discussion and critique of the rural–urban concept, see John Harriss and Mick Moore (eds), 'Special Issue on Development and the Rural–Urban Divide', *The Journal of Development Studies*, April 1984.

20. Ashoka Mody, 'Rural Resource Generation and Mobilisation' *Economic and Political Weekly*, Annual Number, vol. XVII, nos 19–21, 1983.

21. Suzanne Paine, 'Reflections on the Presence of Rural or Urban Bias in China's Development Policies, 1949–1976', in Jonathan Unger (ed.), *China's Rural Institutions and the Question of Transferability*, Oxford, Pergamon Press, 1980.

22. For example, S. Amin, *Unequal Development*, New York, Monthly Review Press, 1976; *Imperialism and Unequal Development*, New York, Monthly Review Press, 1977; and A. G. Frank, *Capitalism and Under-development in Latin America*, New York, Monthly Review Press, 1969; and 'The Development of Underdevelopment', in R. I. Rhodes (ed.), *Imperialism and Underdevelopment*, New York, Monthly Review Press, 1970.

23. Arghiri Emmanuel, *Unequal Exchange – A Study of the Imperialism of Trade*, New York, Monthly Review Press, 1972.

24. See George Joseph, *International Trade in an Unequal World – A Survey of Different Theories and their Empirical Potential*, Department of Econometrics and Social Statistics, University of Manchester, 1985 (mimeo).

25. Keith Griffin, 'The International Transmission of Inequaliy', *World Development*, March 1974.

26. D. Morawetz, *Twenty-Five Years of Economic Development, 1950 to 1975*, Baltimore, Johns Hopkins University Press, 1977.

27. Pan A. Yotopoulos and Lawrence J. Lau, 'A Test for Balanced and Unbalanced Growth', *Review of Economics and Statistics*, November 1970.

28. Dutt, *Sectoral Balance – A Survey*, 1989.

29. Nicholas R. Lardy, *Agriculture in China's Modern Economic Development*, Cambridge, Cambridge University Press, 1983, pp. 128–45, and 237.

30. See Sukhamoy Chakravarty, *Development Planning: The Indian Experience*, Oxford, Clarendon Press, 1987, p. 105.

3 Uneven Development in China and India

Having defined the concept of uneven development and its measurement in Chapter 2, in this chapter we measure uneven development in China and India. This is done in Section I using the Yotopoulos–Lau (Y/L) and Lardy indexes discussed in Chapter 2. The measurement of intra-industry and disaggregated intersectoral linkages à la Hirschman is dealt with in Chapter 4.

Once the degree of unevenness is determined it is appropriate to ask whether this unevenness can be attributed to the types of development strategies adopted by the two countries. But first it is important to outline briefly these development strategies and policies to determine whether they are similar or very different. This we do in Section II in a historical perspective starting with the early 1950s. The three main types of development strategies adopted by China and India during different time periods are discussed: the heavy industrialisation strategy, the strategy of sectoral and regional balance and the strategy of economic liberalisation and market orientation.

I MEASUREMENT OF UNEVEN DEVELOPMENT

In Chapter 2, equations (1), (2) and (3) defined uneven development in terms of (i) the dispersion of sectoral growth rates from the national rate of growth, and (ii) the dispersion of the sectoral incremental capital–output ratios (ICORs) from the national incremental capital–output ratio. We use these indices to measure uneven development in the economies of China and India from the 1950s to the 1980s. The process of economic development in these countries is divided into four time periods. Unfortunately, it was not possible to use identical periods for both countries on account of data limitations. For example, for China, investment data are available only for the periods of the economic plans, e.g. First Five-Year Plan (1953–57), Second Plan (1958–62), Third Plan (1966–70), Fourth Plan (1971–75), etc. So for China we take the following periods: 1953–62, 1963–70, 1971–78 and 1978–84. The first period is marked by heavy Soviet aid in China's development and the Great Leap Forward. The second and third time periods refer to the Cultural Revolution and the fourth period corresponds to the post-Mao period of structural economic reforms.

However, for China the period between 1958 and 1962 was particularly unstable and unbalanced due to the Soviet withdrawal, natural disasters, problems caused by the Great Leap Forward and the subsequent adjustments during 1960–2. The agricultural sector was particularly adversely affected. We have therefore sub-divided the first period (1953–62) into two sub-periods, 1953–57 and 1958–62. The former, the period of the First Five-Year Plan, was marked by stability and growth whereas the period 1958–62 was one of turmoil.

In the case of India the periods considered are: 1951–60, 1960–70, 1970–78 and 1978–83. The first period marks the beginning of economic planning. The second period coincides with the spread of the Green Revolution and a reasonably rapid growth of agricultural output. The third period, 1970–78 is characterised by stagnant industrial growth and slow agricultural output growth. The last period is characterised by liberalisation of the economy to accelerate growth and technological modernisation.

The (Y/L) index and the modified Lardy index are computed for China and India and are presented in Table 3.1. The higher the index the greater the imbalance, and the lower the index the smaller the imbalance.

To estimate the Lardy index cumulative investment data were used for different periods. For China, national income data (which is close to net output) is used. For India, to ensure comparability the net domestic product (NDP) is estimated as the sum of the NDP for the five sectors considered: agriculture, industry, construction, transport and trade. For China, investment data are available at current prices. The vexing problem of price indexes could not be solved since there are no data on prices of equipment or capital goods. The recent estimates done by Chen *et al.* relate only to the industrial sector.[1] Under the circumstances, in the absence of anything better, we assume that these price indices are also applicable to other sectors.

The estimates based on the Y/L index and the Lardy index are not always consistent; but there seems to be no *a priori* reason to expect complete consistency between very different measures. In the case of China both the Y/L index and the Lardy index are declining over time although the latter rises slightly for 1979–85. Does this suggest that China has moved from a stage of unbalanced development to that of balanced development? China and India present somewhat

Development Strategies and Concepts

Table 3.1   Indices of uneven development in China and India

Period	Yotopoulos–Lau (Y/L) index		Modified Lardy index	
	v	V_w	VL	VL_w
I. *China*				
1954–58	1.99	1.69	1.47	0.64
1959–63	−0.91	−0.83	−1.79	−2.59
1964–71	0.55	0.77	2.18	1.00
1972–79	0.31	0.43	1.75	0.82
1979–85	0.17	0.10	1.48	0.85
II. *India*				
1951–60	0.66	0.42	0.73	0.45
1960–70	0.85	0.62	0.83	0.56
1970–78	0.66	0.54	0.45	0.37
1978–83	0.40	0.37	0.50	0.58

Source: Based on Appendix Tables A3.1 to A3.4.

Notes: v, VL = unweighted.

V_w, VL_w = weighted. Sectoral output shares at constant prices are used as weights.

divergent situations: while the Y/L index has been consistently declining in China, it has been rising and then declining in the case of India. In other words, the dispersion of sectoral growth rates has narrowed in China and widened in India. Does this imply that the Indian economy has suffered from greater sectoral imbalances and unevenness in terms of performance?

The rising Y/L coefficients for India for 1951 to 1970 are also confirmed by a recent Indian study which decomposed the overall growth rate into sectoral growth rates. It shows that the coefficients of variation for NDP growth rates rose from 1.07 during 1960–70 to 1.4 during 1971–81.[2]

For both China and India, there is some evidence in support of a U-turn for the weighted Lardy index. One explanation for this in the case of China may be the faster growth of agricultural output after 1979 than before, but a decline in its share of investment. Part of the differential in performance can also be attributed to the technology used and qualitative differences in investment reflected in capital waste and variations in technological levels. In the case of India also, the agricultural output growth accelerated after 1977 but so did agricultural investment (see Chapter 5, Tables 5.2 and 5.4). Thus the above Chinese explanation does not seem to apply.

The Lardy index which increased slightly for China during 1978–85 is likely to have increased further since 1985 – the beginning of the second phase of the economic reforms when structural imbalances grew due to excessively high rates of growth, supply bottlenecks and infrastructural constraints.

However, there are some problems with the Lardy index which are associated with the reliability and coverage of investment data, particularly in the case of China. For example, sectoral investment data in China in different periods are not strictly comparable. First, the policies which would affect these outcomes have also been changing. The provisions for the retention of depreciation funds by industrial enterprises have been liberalised. Secondly, agricultural investments during the different periods have varied because of differences in (a) state investment in forestry and fisheries etc. which is included under agricultural investment, (b) collective farm investments and labour mobilisation (which declined after decollectivisation in the post-Mao period), and (c) agricultural price policy and taxation.

We have made a heroic assumption that deflators for industrial investment developed by Chen *et al.* also apply to other sectoral investments. This is not very satisfactory. Chen *et al.* used the following deflator for equipment spending: the ratio of machinery production at current prices to the value of output at constant prices. This deflator does not appear to be very accurate considering that machinery prices have risen much faster during the 1980s than was shown by the Chen *et al.* estimates.

Alternative approaches to the use of investment deflators could have been used if adequate data were available. For agriculture, we were unable to locate a breakdown of agricultural investments into its different components like machinery, land improvement and water conservation projects. Although it is possible to obtain information on the ratio of output calculated at current and constant prices for farm machinery, it does not resolve the problem about the composition of agricultural investments. For transport, perhaps, information about the cost of building a kilometre of highway or railway line might be relevant but even if such data were available the problem of dividing the total investment into construction and equipment would still remain.[3]

From the above it seems clear that at present no satisfactory data or method exists for converting annual investment expenditure at current prices to constant prices. To deflate investment data for China at current prices (taken from SYC, 1986) to 1970 prices, various price indexes provided by Chen *et al.* are used. Specifically, for agriculture, transportation and trade sectors, investment data are deflated by the non-residential industry construction price index; data for industrial investment are deflated by the price index for investment components equipment; construction investment is deflated by the average price indexes of housing and non-residential industrial construction.

The above limitations of our estimation for China need to be taken into account in interpreting the results given in Table 3.1.

II   ALTERNATIVE DEVELOPMENT STRATEGIES

Is the above imbalance and unevenness the result of development strategies and policies adopted by China and India? An answer to this question is relevant since too rapid a growth can cause income disparities and structural bottlenecks with undesirable consequences like inflation. It is therefore necessary to outline the broad strategies and macroeconomic policies of the two countries. It is also useful to trace changes in development performance in response to shifts in development strategy. However, these changes are likely to occur only after a time lag during which the shifts have had time to exercise some influence.

2.1   Heavy Industrialisation

China

A heavy industrialisation strategy of development was adopted in China during the First Five-Year Plan (1953–57). Producer goods industries were given top priority to ensure a rapid rate of capital accumulation and growth of output. (Chapter 5, Table 5.4, shows that the annual rate of growth of industrial output was 25 per cent during 1954–58 and the overall rate of growth, 7.9 per cent.) Agriculture remained rather neglected, its annual rate of growth of output being less than 2 per cent (see Table 5.4.) The share of total investment in agriculture during 1954–58 was only 13.3 per cent compared with 44.4 per cent for manufacturing industry (see Chapter 5, Table 5.6).

Heavy industrialisation in China was motivated by a strong desire to achieve a high rate of growth, to create a sound industrial base for national self-reliance and independence from foreign countries besides providing for a base for sustained agricultural development. But it can also be justified on grounds of military security.

The high accumulation rate needed to implement the strategy was mainly at the expense of conspicuous luxury consumption. At least in the early 1950s, the increase in investment went hand in hand with an increase in per capita income and output of foodgrains[4] (see Chapters 5 and 6).

But many Chinese scholars have argued that the structure of heavy industry was not geared to providing agriculture's input requirements. For example, from 1952 to 1979, only 4.6 per cent of investment in heavy industry was devoted to producing farm machinery, fertilisers and pesticides.[5] The allocations for electricity, power, steel and cement also fell far below agricultural needs.

Heavy industry seems to have been geared more towards the production of consumer durables (than agricultural inputs), the demand for which has been rising rapidly particularly during the 1980s. The industrial base was built well ahead of the expansion of demand leading to severe capacity under-utilisation. Existence of large stocks and useless over-production is a common phenomenon in China.[6]

There was no savings constraint in China for financing the growth of capital goods industries. However, since Mao's death the consumer orientation of the Chinese economy is raising concern among the policy-makers that investment needs are beginning to suffer. (In fact, the adjustment measures introduced in 1988 were meant, *inter alia*, to curb consumption.)

India

The evolution of India's development strategy and its content was in many ways similar to that in China (see Table 3.2). The Nehru–Mahalanobis strategy of development underlying India's Second Five-Year Plan (1956–61) was characterised by a model of unbalanced growth. Influenced by the Soviet Fel'dman model of economic planning, the Mahalanobis model opted for heavy industrialisation and rapid development of a capital goods sector. The Second Plan noted that the development of 'basic industries and industries which make machines to make machines needed for further development' was crucial.[7]

Self-reliance and import-substitution are (or have been) the two cornerstones of the Indian development strategies as well as the Chinese. This was motivated by the importance attached to developing national technological capabilities and an extensive, solid industrial base. These objectives also resulted in high priority accorded to the public sector in both the countries. The effectiveness of self-reliance in a country of the size of India or China depends very much on the extent to which the domestic market (generated largely by the agricultural sector) provides a fillip for industrialisation. This demand constraint does not seem to have been fully recognised, particularly in India.[8]

Much has been written on the high cost of following an inward-looking development path. It has been noted that import-substitution and protectionism led to high-cost industry and discouraged innovation and efficiency owing to lack of competition. The system of administrative controls (e.g. industrial licensing) caused bureaucratic delays and encouraged corruption and rent-seeking.

The influence of the Mahalanobis model persisted until a serious challenge to the planning process emerged at the end of the Third Five-Year Plan (1961–66)[9] and mainly from the dissident states. As Prime Minister, Indira Gandhi subscribed to a strategy focusing on agriculture and populist themes like the elimination of poverty. The agricultural drought of 1967 which led to a decline of agricultural output by nearly 30 to 40 per cent was largely responsible for this policy shift.

2.2 Sectoral/Regional Balance

China

The debacle of the Great Leap Forward (1958–60) led to a reversal of the heavy industrialisation strategy in favour of a balanced development between agriculture and industry.

In many ways, the Mao period was characterised by an explicit attempt to achieve balanced growth and equity. In his 'Ten Great Relationships', Mao identified three important manifestations of uneven development: (i) between city and countryside, (ii) between agriculture and industry, and (iii) between intellectuals and manual workers. He believed that these imbalances could be mitigated through appropriate policy interventions. A balance between city and countryside could be achieved by an appropriate regional development policy which would give special emphasis to the development of weaker and remote regions; that between agriculture and industry (sectoral balance) could be achieved through the simultaneous growth of agriculture, light industry, and heavy industry; and that between intellectual and manual workers, by reducing the gaps between their earnings and standards of living.

It is worth bearing in mind that the Mao concept of balance was different from the Western concept of balanced growth considered in Chapter 2. The latter is based on market principles and profit incentives whereas Mao's concept is premised on political economy considerations of balance between social classes and sectors.[10]

Sectoral Balance. Mao's proverbial policy declaring 'agriculture as the foundation, industry as the leading sector and taking grain as the key link' implied an intersectoral balance. This pronouncement has however been interpreted differently by different scholars. Some writers have explained it in terms of priority given to agriculture as a precondition for industrial development. Others note that it simply meant that agriculture should be developed alongside industry.

The importance of agriculture for industrial development was enhanced after the failures of the Great Leap Forward. At the Tenth Plenum in September 1962 the sectoral priorities in Chinese planning were declared to be agriculture first, light industry second and heavy industry last. Nevertheless, the importance accorded to agriculture remained somewhat ambiguous. Further, the assumption that agriculture was to receive much greater investment allocation was not realised.[11] Nevertheless, the index of agricultural terms of trade has been rising steadily since the early 1950s. Procurement prices of farm products have been rising (especially since 1979) while retail prices of industrial goods sold in rural areas have been fairly constant.[12]

Some Chinese and Western scholars argue that the relative farm prices in China are still well below the market prices. The below-market procurement prices imply a concealed agricultural tax.[13] Furthermore, the state procurement prices were not increased proportionately to the rising costs of agricultural production. According to a national survey, between 1962 and 1976, production costs per hectare for six grain crops grew by 305 yuan, exceeding the gain in output value per hectare of 249 yuan causing the net income per hectare to fall.[14] The rising cost of agricultural production is partly explained by the high price of agricultural inputs (farm machinery, chemical fertilisers and pesticides, etc.) bought by the farmers from the industrial sector. These input prices are known to be well above the domestic costs of production and international prices.[15]

The prices of agricultural inputs were not lowered. Neither were farm subsidies raised. In fact, between 1978 and 1986 price subsidies in China declined from 24 million yuan to only 6 million yuan.[16]

Mao's concept of intersectoral balance implied that both agriculture and light industry should bear the burden of providing surplus resources for expansion of heavy industry.[17] Furthermore, light industry, by relying on unutilised resources, could develop without increasing unduly its claims on resource allocation. It is this that provides a rationale for Mao's strategy of local self-reliance, rural industrialisation and technological balance between capital-intensive and labour-intensive techniques (the so-called strategy of walking on two legs). (See Chapter 7.) Other reasons for promoting local self-reliance included the need to expand rural income and employment opportunities to reduce rural–urban income differentials and curb excessive concentration of bureaucratic power. The lack of an adequate transport network and infrastructure also partly explains a drive towards rural industrialisation based on the use of local resources.

In practice, the promotion of rural small industry often led to competition for scarce raw materials which were often diverted away from large-scale industry which consequently suffered from excess capacity.

Regional Balance.   Inter-regional and rural–urban balance was the second component of Mao's concept of balanced development. Mao noted that there were wide imbalances between town and country and between coastal regions and the hinterland. These imbalances were to be reduced over time by a relatively greater allocation of resources to the deprived regions and areas, and by transferring some of the resources from the advanced regions.

As state enterprises were obliged to hand over practically all their profits to the state, it was easy to use a large proportion of the revenues received from the rich provinces to subsidise the poor and disadvantaged areas. The central budget was unified and included provincial budgets which enabled the central government to manipulate investment allocation for narrowing inter-regional inequalities.

The advanced provinces/autonomous regions like Shanghai, Beijing and Tianjin were required to remit 50 to 90 per cent of their revenues to the central government whereas the least developed provinces, which were exempted from such remittances, received central subsidies amounting to 50 to 80 per cent of their local expenditures.[18]

Poorer regions were also favoured by short-term concessional credit by the State Bank, subsidies on social expenditures (e.g. on health and education), a manipulation of agricultural terms of trade in their favour and a control of inter-industry and inter-regional structure of wages.

A control of labour allocation further enabled the Chinese government to transfer technicians and skilled personnel from coastal areas like Shanghai (which supplied over half a million industrial workers by the early 1970s) to less developed regions in the hinterland.[19]

To promote rural–urban balance, Mao introduced food subsidies and public distribution of health and educational services (see Chapters 8 and 9.) The organisation of communes was also intended to provide a floor to rural consumption and to achieve income equality within the production teams. Although this measure may have induced intra-commune equality, it tended to depress individual incentive.

As we shall examine in Chapter 6, the policy of local self-reliance had the effect of widening income inequalities between localities. The policy of local food self-sufficiency in grains adopted during the Cultural Revolution had a similar effect. Regions well-endowed for efficient production of cash crops like cotton were forced to shift to grain production leading to allocative inefficiencies and de-specialisation production.[20] The motivation for following this policy is not very clear but it may have derived from the need to eliminate foodgrain imports from abroad or reduction of inequalities between rich suburban communes and poor ones in the hinterland.[21] During the early years transport bottlenecks may also have accounted for a drive towards foodgrain self-sufficiency which is also consistent with the policy of controlling rural to urban migration. The labour force kept back in the rural areas needed to be fed and employed.[22] The consequence of foodgrain self-sufficiency has been noticed in a decline in allocative efficiency within agriculture as well as a fall in the per capita consumption of non-cereal foods.[23]

Reduction of Income Gaps Between Professional and Manual Workers.
The third component of Mao's strategy of balanced development consisted of narrowing the income gaps between professionals and

manual workers within and between urban and rural areas. This policy can be related directly to the sectoral balance discussed above, but the need to raise demand for industrial goods was not a major guiding force. There was also a political dimension to the worker –peasant alliance to ensure stable and sustained development. Paine has thus argued that 'the deliberate choice of a strategy to increase mass- and mass rural- living standards was much less inspired by considerations of egalitarianism than by questions of politics and power.'[24]

Despite the above explicit recognition of the importance of balanced development, the Stalinist model of heavy industrialisation and high rate of capital accumulation prevailed in practice. This might have reflected the defence requirements of the military and the pervasive Soviet influence on the Chinese economy during this period. The appeal of heavy industry and industrial autonomy was also independently strong as in the case of other latecomers like the USSR and India. Another plausible explanation is that prior industrialisation was considered an essential precondition for the growth and modernisation of agriculture which called for industrial inputs like fertilisers, pesticides/herbicides and tractors, etc.[25]

Although different policy regimes were followed during the Mao period (see Table 3.2), one can pinpoint the following features of the Maoist development model: a high premium on capital accumulation for heavy industrialisation, a command economy with widespread state controls on the allocation of resources at different levels, granting of a minimum of autonomy to industrial enterprises and an equity-oriented public support system. Within industry heavy producer goods were favoured at the expense of industrial manufactures and agriculture had to walk on the short stump.

Thus, in actual practice, Mao's balanced strategy did not lead to very egalitarian outcomes (see Chapters 6 to 9). Rural–urban and regional differences continued despite the redistributive policies discussed above. What explains this phenomenon? Is it due to a failure of Maoist thought or serious problems of implementation, or some amalgam of the two? Implementation failures are suggested by the lack of support for Mao's strategy of 'agricultural priority' and the exaggeration by the communes of grain output figures. Furthermore, as we note in Chapter 8, opposition to Mao's rural health policies also led to long delays in implementation. It could also be that the initial imbalances in the early 1950s were so great that the heavy industrialisation strategy simply magnified these imbalances. But inequalities might have been worse without the Maoist egalitarian measures.

India

Sectoral Balance.   Unlike Mao's China, India had no clearcut policy towards sectoral balance between agriculture and industry until the end of the Third Five-Year Plan (1961–66) and the beginning of the Fourth Plan (1969–74). There is a widespread belief that price policy in India was biased against agriculture particularly in the 1960s and mid-1970s onwards. Lipton has argued that in the 1960s an additional factor, food aid under PL 480, had this effect. The lowering of food prices and discouragement of domestic food production led to income transfers from agriculture to non-agriculture to the tune of about 4 per cent of total farm incomes. This sum was far in excess of tax revenue from agriculture.[26] Furthermore, under the prevailing high tariffs on industrial imports and rising prices of farm inputs, the farmers had to sell far more agricultural output in exchange for non-agricultural inputs.

However, there is no conclusive evidence to support the assertion that the terms of trade have been against agriculture. The estimates of terms of trade are often sensitive to the base period considered. Kahlon and Tyagi have estimated the agricultural terms of trade for three different periods: (a) 1952–53 to 1963–64 when terms of trade were against agriculture, (b) 1964–65 to 1974–75 when they remained in favour of agriculture, and (c) 1975–76 to 1983–84 when they again moved against agriculture.[27]

In India also agricultural investment was relatively neglected. The share of agricultural investment in the 1960s and 1970s was lower than that in the 1950s and the late 1970s and early 1980s (see Chapter 5, Table 5.4). Many Indian scholars have argued that low public investment in agriculture has been responsible for low rates of growth of agricultural output.

Regional Balance.   Given its political system, India had from the outset emphasised regional balanced development as one of the goals of planning. The initial emphasis was on reducing inter-regional disparities and attention was focused on industrial and fiscal measures. Although regional disparities in industrial growth seem to have received much attention the planners focused on regional agrarian disparities as well. The strategy of industrial location was intended to stimulate growth in backward regions like Bhilai and Durgapur where steel plants were located. Special measures were undertaken during the Second Five-Year Plan, (1956–61) and subsequently, to decentralise industrial production, e.g. location of new industrial enterprises and estates in backward regions, special preference for credit allocation and infrastructural facilities to the small enterprises located in rural and backward areas, and organisation of migration from more to less densely populated areas.[28]

The choice of measures consisted of direct schemes to develop backward regions and areas (deserts), target groups (scheduled castes, small farmers), and low-income activities (rural industries, rural electrification and Basic Minimum Needs programmes). In addition, indirect measures like tax relief, investment subsidies and preferential allocation of raw materials for backward areas were introduced.[29] These measures seem to suggest that the general sectoral investment programmes were not very effective in bringing about a more balanced spatial development.

The policy of industrial location may have led to inefficient production. Projects located in backward areas tended to have higher investment costs and fixed capital per worker than similar projects in the advanced regions. Investment subsidies (between 1980 and 1985, the central subsidy for capital investment increased from Rs.310 million to Rs.1000 million) may partly account for capital-intensive enterprises in the backward areas. Special protective measures in favour of rural small enterprises seem to have discouraged growth of large enterprises. Thus the benefits of economies of scale were forgone.

The overemphasis on promoting an inter-regional industrial balance continued due to political considerations. The federal structure of the country results in different states putting pressure on the Centre to obtain a share of state or private investments. This leads to dispersal of industrial capacity across different states without regard for economic efficiency and economies of scale.[30] However, the expected linkages did not materialise. Industrial investments in backward areas did not lead to the development of many subsidiaries.[31] These investments were thus not adequate enough to reduce regional disparities. Their impact may also have been limited because of the absence of concern for spatial planning. For example, plants of uneconomic size may well be justified under conditions of serious transport bottlenecks and spatial market segmentation. (Indeed, as noted above, this seems to have been an economic rationale for the vertical integration of industry and dispersal of rural industry in China.)

Furthermore, the state governments (and not the Centre) are responsible for the planning and implementation of projects within their boundaries particularly in such sectors as agriculture, health and education. In addition, fiscal measures were also not effective in reducing regional disparities. Investment allocation to the states may also have been regressive. During 1956–77 the five rich states (namely, Maharashtra, Punjab, Haryana, Gujarat and West Bengal) received per capita allocations from central funds nearly equal to the average for 15 states (Rs.774) whereas the four poorest states (U.P., Bihar, Madhya Pradesh and Rajasthan) received 8 per cent less than the average.[32]

To summarise, both China and India followed a strategy of sectoral and regional balances at least during part of their planning process. However, our results show that China succeeded in reducing imbalances more than India. Reasons for this divergence may be manifold, but as we speculate in Chapter 10, the problems of the implementation of declared strategies and their design may have had a role to play.

Unsatisfactory performance in achieving the desired results seems to have put pressures on both China and India to try alternative paths to development, which we discuss below.

2.3 Economic Liberalisation

China

The post-Mao development strategy has departed significantly from the earlier goal of balanced development. While the emphasis on rapid economic growth is not entirely new, the abandonment of egalitarian policies of the Mao period is. The emphasis is on light industry and agriculture rather than heavy industry, on consumption rather than investment and on market socialism rather than a command economy. There has been a limited functioning of the market mechanism and a greater reliance on material as opposed to moral incentives. The thrust of the rural economic reforms – the rural responsibility system and the abolition of communes – has been to link rewards to effort in the interest of efficiency and output growth and to decentralise decision-making. Furthermore, an open-door

policy of liberalising imports of foreign technology and investment
has replaced the earlier policy of local or national self-reliance.

Many of the Maoist policies for the development of coastal areas
have been reversed. State enterprises are no longer required to hand
over their profits to the state. This means a reduced central control
over investment funds and less ability to effect inter-regional transfers. The new scheme enabling profit retention by enterprises has
meant a decline in state revenues. Decentralisation policies also
involve a greater fiscal control by the provinces as is the case in India.
This favours those provinces with a capacity to raise resources but
hurts those provinces which continue to need central support. Presumably this hurts most the poorest provinces that do not have an
industry or other tax base. In 1981 the central government established a fund to finance projects in the backward regions but the
amount is too small to appreciably reduce inter-regional disparities.[33]

The policy of retention of foreign exchange from export proceeds
also tends to favour the coastal areas which specialise in exports and
enjoy overseas connections. The ability of firms to import technology
from abroad is tied to their foreign exchange earnings through the
so-called foreign exchange system which stipulates a certain proportion (varying from 20 per cent to 100 per cent depending on localities,
sectors and time periods) which the firms can retain. In contrast, the
provinces in the hinterland are short of foreign exchange which they
often purchase in the black market.

The export processing zones established in the 1980s are also
located in the coastal areas like Guangdong and Shenzen which have
been the target of attack for exploiting the hinterland. Some efforts
have been made by the coastal industrial provinces to enter into
compensation agreements with the raw-materials-producing interior
provinces. But the benefits to the latter from such agreements cannot
be determined in the absence of adequate data. The effect of this
measure on reduction of inter-regional inequality is likely to be
negligible.

The decentralisation and profit retention schemes noted above
have led to a shrinking of central plan resources. The scope of the
central plan has been reduced a great deal during the ten-year reform
period. The government is thus poorly equipped or unable to implement redistributive measures to alleviate inequalities.

The market and price reforms were stalled on account of fear of
accelerating inflation. Furthermore, the prerequisites of the success
of these reforms – legal framework, a monetary and fiscal base,
transport and communications – were not adequately provided.

The decentralisation of power without concomitant market mechanisms and macroeconomic management of the economy encouraged investments which eluded both the discipline of the market and of aggregate demand. Many short-term quick-yielding projects took off but the needs of slow-yielding and low-profitability sectors like energy, transportation and raw materials were ignored. The result was structural disequilibrium, supply bottlenecks and growing imbalances in the economy.

Deliberate government policy to raise consumption and the standard of living of people (through increase in urban wages and higher grain procurement prices) has had the effect of causing the so-called 'overmaturing of consumption' (*xiaofei zaoshu*) under which most of the resources were spent on consumption and housing construction.

The above circumstances made the 1988 austerity adjustment programmes and recentralised control inevitable. The adjustment programme includes such measures as control of investments and demand through credit squeeze (the growth rates of total credit by banks and credit cooperatives declined from 22.5 per cent in the first quarter of 1988 to just over 4 per cent in the second quarter of 1989), limits to the growth of the private economy and closure of loss-making enterprises. In 1989, the Agricultural Bank of China and Rural Credit Cooperatives were required to slow down growth of credit to rural industry to only 8 per cent which represented a significant decline from growth during the 1981–88 period. A number of private enterprises which are presumably considered to be 'redundant' or 'not able to meet the public needs' are known to have been abolished.[34]

It appears that after the clamp-down on pro-democracy protests in June 1989, the austerity programme of adjustment has been further accelerated. Centralisation of control on resources and investments has also been reintroduced as has been central planning. A 39-point plan of action has been introduced to implement the new policies of controlled prices, strengthening of state enterprises and increased taxes on private and collective enterprises.[35] It is proposed to eliminate the two-tier price system which has been associated with growing corruption and speculation (goods are bought at low state-controlled prices and sold at higher market prices). It is also proposed to strengthen the state's role in agriculture and labour mobilisation for building large-scale irrigation works.

The indirect repercussions of the June crackdown in terms of the condemnation of the Western world and shying away of foreign investments from China are likely to have an adverse effect on the pace of economic reforms if not their direction. Foreign commercial banks are known to have delayed new loans; bilateral donors have frozen grants-in-aid and many foreign firms have postponed decisions on investments. Whether this has long-term adverse effects on economic reforms will depend on the outcome of the adjustment measures as well as on the government's attitude towards political liberalisation.

It is too early to determine the outcome of the Chinese adjustment programme. It is also not clear whether the June 1989 crackdown has strengthened the bargaining power of the central authority *vis-à-vis* the local and provincial governments to enable the former to implement effectively the policy of recentralisation. Some of the provinces, like Guangdong, seem to be politically quite powerful and have enjoyed the fruits of decentralisation. They may be reluctant to give up their autonomy and power easily. Secondly, another question to which at present there is no clear answer is: has the crackdown of June 1989 adversely affected worker morale so appreciably that the efficiency improvements necessary for the success of the adjustment programme might not materialise?[36] There is some indication of a reintroduction of such non-material incentives and mechanisms as political re-education (reminiscent of the Mao period) in favour of discipline and party ideology.[37] These developments seem to suggest that worker morale and motivation may have suffered.

It is difficult to predict the future of economic reforms in the absence of answers to the above questions. But in some ways at least it would seem that the reforms which are backed by both the people and the bureaucrats, are irreversible. Furthermore, the austerity adjustment measures do not seem to have been enforced with full vigour. The measures to control inflation – control of credit, raising of interest rates and curbing of private enterprises – have not been easy to implement. The curbing of private enterprises seems to have been abandoned since it created too much unemployment. Similarly, credit control is said to have been eased because of the hardship it caused to those enterprises which employ a large number of people.

India

Until the 1980s, the Indian development strategy was characterised by the predominance of the public sector and administrative controls over the private sector (e.g. licensing and import allocations). The nationalisation of such industries or activities as life insurance, banking, road transport and state trading has also added greatly to the government's power over the rest of the economy. In this respect India is somewhat similar to China's command economy.

A greater reliance is now placed on financial incentives rather than physical controls but state planning and the public sector remain intact. However, it is important to note that the Indian public sector is confined mainly to industry and infrastructure while agriculture and domestic trade fall in the private sector. Recent attempts have been made not so much to replace the public sector as to make it efficient. The monopoly of the public sector in some domains (e.g. electricity) is also being relaxed by allowing the public and private sectors to coexist.

Liberalisation in India started as a response to evident weaknesses which had developed in the controlled economy. Industrial controls (there are no controls on Indian agriculture, which contrasts with the situation in China where government intervention in agriculture was the rule during the Mao period) and a protective regime led to inefficiencies and a high capital intensity of industrial growth. Restrictions on the expansion of productive capacity meant high costs of production in a large number of small firms unable to reap economies of scale. In the absence of international specialisation and with an assured and protected domestic market, Indian industry had little incentive to look for export markets.

When Rajiv Gandhi succeeded his mother as Prime Minister he gave the policy of economic liberalisation a great impetus. The initial emphasis in 1985 and 1986 was on deregulation and decontrol.[38] Although not abandoned, the import-substitution strategy was accompanied by import liberalisation and export promotion measures. Examples of liberalisation are: a reduction of industrial licensing coverage to 25 industries, delicensing of 82 pharmaceutical products and a lowering of the number of production items on the reserved list for small-scale production. However, despite an open-door policy the government continues to exercise import controls.

As regards foreign investment, the official guidelines divide industries into three groups: (i) where foreign investment may be allowed, (ii) where no foreign investment but only technical collaboration is permitted, and (iii) where no foreign collaboration is permitted. Foreign investment and collaboration are generally allowed only in the case of 'high tech' industries. In the case of medium and 'low tech' industries (e.g. food, textiles and paper) only technical collaboration (but no foreign investment) is allowed.

Thus, the Indian economy has not been liberalised as much as was initially expected. The public sector continues to be important (although there is less emphasis on it) and 'privatisation' of state-owned enterprises is not foreseen. The reasoning of the 1956 Industrial Policy Resolution and its underlying priority of indigenous development and autonomy of modern technology remains important.

It is too early to assess the impact of the above liberalisation measures. It may be tempting to suggest that an acceleration of industrial growth in the mid-1980s which coincided with some economic liberalisation was due to these policy shifts. However, as we shall discuss in Chapter 5, this growth may just as well have been due to the acceleration of agricultural growth after several years of stagnation.

The economic policies introduced by the V. P. Singh government in India in December 1989 gave much greater emphasis to equity than to growth. Some of the elements of the new policy were: much greater attention to agricultural development (more than 50 per cent of the planned resources are to be allocated to rural development), a greater thrust on the creation of employment and the removal of poverty especially among the poorest groups, a greater emphasis on female education, maternal and child health care and women's employment.

The technology policy of the Rajiv Gandhi government – a reckless import of foreign technology – was reversed since it was considered inconsistent with the objectives of equity and employment and control of conspicuous consumption. The V. P. Singh minority government pledged to slow down the import and use of capital-intensive labour-displacing technology and to limit approval of new manufacturing units that call for imported equipment. The document on Approach to the Eighth Five-Year Plan (1990–95) laid particular stress on building endogenous technological capacity and incorporation of a technological dimension in each of the sectoral plans and programmes. It proposed to promote district-level councils of science and technology to ensure adaptation of technology to local conditions.[39]

With the coming into power of the Congress minority government in May 1991, some of the above measures (viz. building endogenous technological capacity) seem to have been put in cold storage. In the interest of promoting international competitiveness of Indian industry, import of foreign technology and inflow of foreign investment have been liberalised. Limit for foreign equity in joint ventures with

Indian partners has been raised from 40 per cent to 51 per cent. To attract multinationals it is proposed to establish a special board 'to negotiate with a number of international firms and approve direct foreign investment in selected areas'.[40] In future it would be easier for the public and private firms to acquire foreign technology.

The new government has introduced drastic adjustment reform measures unprecedented in the history of independent India. In early July 1991, the rupee was devalued twice (to the tune of about 20 per cent). This adjustment of the exchange rate was necessitated by the trade imbalance and the serious balance of payments situation. The fiscal deficit of the central government was quite serious – about 8 per cent of GDP in 1990–91 compared to 6 per cent at the beginning of the 1980s and 4 per cent in the mid-1970s. This deficit has been met by borrowing, which has raised the debt burden to about 55 per cent of the GDP.[41]

The central government deficit has been caused by several factors: double-digit inflation, large subsidies on food and fertilisers, indiscriminate protection to industry, failure of the public sector to generate investible surplus, and poor export performance.

Industrial licensing is virtually abolished (with the exception of a few sensitive industries). In future, firms will not need special clearance to invest or expand their installed capacity. Measures are also introduced to improve the performance of the public sector. Up to 20 per cent of government equity shares will be sold and sick public sector enterprises will be rehabilitated or phased out. However, the minority government lacks the political muscle to privatise the public sector.

Fertiliser subsidy has been reduced and the price of fertiliser has been raised by 40 per cent (there has been no increase in fertiliser price since July 1981). It is proposed to compensate farmers through increases in food procurement prices. Sugar subsidy has also been reduced. In contrast, food subsidies for foodgrains (wheat and rice) have been raised, in order to mitigate hardship on the poor.

To control demand, the Indian budget (presented to the Parliament on 24 July 1991) raised corporate taxes, lowered depreciation allowances and raised duties on luxury goods.

From the foregoing, it is clear that the adjustment measures have not led to total deregulation or marketisation of the Indian economy. The public sector will not be privatised but its performance will be improved; all subsidies are not abolished – some are actually raised. While the government recognises the need 'to expand the scope and the area for the operation of market forces', it will continue to rely on direct measures/interventions to assist those who live outside the market economy, on the fringes of subsistence.

A drastic shift in policies towards liberalisation has been prompted by the need to obtain an IMF loan of several billion dollars. However, some of the adjustment reform measures, like reduction in fertiliser subsidy and industrial de-licensing, which hurts entrenched vested interests, are likely to be unpopular. For instance, the powerful lobby of the rich landowners may be quite disgruntled by the decision to reduce fertiliser subsidy. In fact, on this issue, rioting broke out in one of the Indian states. Subsequently, the proposal on fertiliser subsidy had to be modified so as to exempt small farmers from the burden of a higher price, through a system of dual pricing.

III CONCLUSION

We summarise the alternative development strategies adopted by both China and India over the 30 to 40 year period in Table 3.2. Such factors as administrative controls (centralised or decentralised), the role of the state and the choice of techniques show that both China and India followed broadly similar development strategies – heavy industrialisation and growth maximisation during the 1950s till the 1970s and market liberalisation in the 1980s.

Both China and India have decentralised decision-making since the mid-1960s. But the actual implementation of decentralisation seems to have fallen short of expectations. In China, state control weakened as a result of a limited introduction of market mechanism and the subsequent growth of a private economy. In the rural sector, a decline in central control is linked with the introduction of the agricultural responsibility system. Abolition of the commune system led to a weakening of the control of the party, the government and the collective institutions. The decline in the state procurement of foodgrains and the emergence of a private grains market further reduced the state role.[42]

However, despite the post-Mao economic reforms and subsequent growth of the private economy, public ownership of the means of production (including land) remains intact. The private enterprises and sideline activities still form only a small part of the total economy. Central control and planning have been reintroduced and the

Table 3.2 Strategies and policies over time (China vs. India)

Time period	China				India			
	Development strategy	Administrative control	State role	Choice of technique	Development strategy	Administrative control	State role	Choice of technique
1950s	Heavy industry	Centralised	Predominant state sector	Capital intensive	Heavy industry	Centralised	Public and private sector	Capital intensive
1960s – 1961–6	Agriculture	Centralised	Predominant state sector	Capital[1] & labour intensive	Heavy industry	Centralised	Public and private sector	Capital[1] & labour intensive
– 1966–9	Heavy industry	Decentralised	Some collective sector	Labour intensive	Agriculture	Decentralised	Public and private sector	Capital[1] & labour intensive
1970s	Agriculture & industry	Decentralised	State and collective sectors	Labour intensive	Agriculture & industry	Decentralised	Public and private sector	Capital[1] & labour intensive
1980s	Economic liberalisation	Decentralised	Increased role for collective and private sectors	Technology intensive – import of advanced technology	Economic liberalisation	Decentralised	Greater role for private sector	Technology intensive – import of advanced technology

Sources: The section for China is adapted from Suzanne Paine, 'Spatial Aspects of Chinese Development: Issues, Outcomes and Policies, 1949–79', Journal of Development Studies, January 1981; and Irma Adelman and David Sunding, 'Economic Policy and Income Distribution in China', Journal of Comparative Economics, September 1987.

[1] Case of technological dualism which was promoted in both countries as a planned strategy.

1990s may witness another phase of recentralisation in China's economic history. In India also, uncertainty prevails due to political instability that grew in 1990–91, with the fall of two minority governments in one year.

An issue related to state control is one of state planning and its consistency with market liberalisation. Compatibility between public ownership and the market economy is a real problem in the socialist economies at the best of times. It has preoccupied the Chinese leaders and planners since the late 1950s. The post-Mao reformers have faced a similar dilemma and a fear of losing central control seems to have dampened their enthusiasm for any further price reforms or 'marketisation' of the economy.

The dilemma of state control versus liberalisation also faces the Indian planners and policy-makers. Although a shift from planning to a free market system may lead to greater efficiency and higher growth, it tends to raise income inequalities and create social unrest. Under imperfect market functioning that prevails in the Indian economy some allocative inefficiencies would continue despite a shift away from planning and controls. Another factor restricting the scope for central action in India is the federal structure of government under which some crucial subjects like agriculture, education, health and other social services are state (provincial) responsibilities.

Both China and India have been marked by uneven agricultural and industrial growth throughout the period considered. To some extent this unevenness was planned. But to a certain degree it was also the result of exogenous factors (e.g. floods, famines and droughts) beyond the control of the policy-makers in the two countries. In China, notwithstanding the Maoist balanced development, excessive emphasis on capital accumulation and capital-intensive industrialisation led to a seriously unbalanced economy as it did in India during the first decades of planning. In the post-Mao period, a better balance was no doubt achieved between light and heavy industry. But a shift towards market-oriented development and priority to growth over equity, seem to have led to greater income inequalities (see Chapter 6).

Another striking similarity in the development performance of India and China is in respect of demand outstripping supply leading to inflationary pressures and balance of payments problems. In both cases liberalised imports of foreign technology due to an import-intensive production pattern (and shortfalls in foodgrains production leading to further imports) have contributed to fiscal imbalances.

It would therefore be interesting to examine the extent to which public actions and policies led to outcomes that were uneven and unbalanced in respect of growth and economic and social inequalities. This is done in Chapters 5 and 6. Were these outcomes the results particularly of the different political systems prevailing in the two countries? An answer to this question will be the concern of the last chapter.

Notes and References

1. Kuan Chen, Gary H. Jefferson, Thomas G. Rawski, Hongchang Wang and Yuxin Zheng, 'New Estimates of Fixed Investment and Capital Stock for Chinese State Industry', *China Quarterly*, June 1988.
2. Anupam Gupta, *Overall Rate of Growth and Sectoral Rates of Growth – A Study of Instability in Economic Development*, paper presented at the VIIIth World Economic Congress of the International Economic Association, New Delhi, 1–5 December 1986.
3. This and the above paragraph are based on private communication with Professor Thomas Rawski of the University of Pittsburgh, USA.
4. Carl Riskin, *China's Political Economy – The Quest for Development Since 1949*, New York, Oxford University Press, 1987, pp. 128–9.
5. Liang Wensen, 'Balanced Development of Industry and Agriculture', in Xu Dixin and others, *China's Search for Economic Growth – The Chinese Economy since 1949*, Beijing, New World Press, 1982.
6. I owe this point to Erik Baark.
7. Government of India, Planning Commission, *Second Five Year Plan, 1956–61*, New Delhi, 1956.
8. See Amit Bhaduri, *Alternative Development Strategies and the Poor*, 1989.
9. The Fourth Plan was delayed by three years due to the Indo-Pakistan war of 1965, two agricultural droughts of 1965 and 1966 and interruption of foreign aid.
10. Suzanne Paine, 'Balanced Development: Maoist Conception and Chinese Practice', *World Development*, April 1976.
11. Riskin, *China's Political Economy*, pp. 128–9.
12. Azizur Rehman Khan and Eddy Lee (eds), *Agrarian Policies and Institutions in China after Mao*, Bangkok, ILO, ARTEP, 1983; and Lardy, *Agriculture in China's Modern Economic Development*, 1983.
13. Yang Jianbai and Li Xuezeng, 'The Relation Between Agriculture, Light Industry and Heavy Industry in China', *Social Sciences in China*, June 1980.
14. Ibid, pp. 207–8.
15. Shujie Yao and David Colman, 'Chinese Agricultural Policies and Agricultural Reforms', *Oxford Agrarian Studies*, vol. 18, no. 1, 1990; and Bruce Stone, 'Relative Prices in the People's Republic of China: Rural

Taxation through Public Monopsony', in John W. Mellor and Raisuddin Ahmed (eds), *Agricultural Price Policy for Developing Countries*, Baltimore, Johns Hopkins University Press, 1988.

16. *Statistical Yearbook of China 1988* (Chinese edition), p. 763.
17. Suzanne Paine, 'Development with Growth: A Quarter Century of Socialist Transformation in China', *Economic and Political Weekly*, Special Number, August 1976.
18. Nicholas R. Lardy, 'Regional Growth and Income Distribution in China', in Robert F. Dernberger (ed.), *China's Development Experience in Comparative Perspective*, Cambridge, Harvard University Press, 1980.
19. Alexander Eckstein, *China's Economic Development – The Interplay of Scarcity and Ideology*, Ann Arbor, University of Michigan Press, 1975, p. 364.
20. For a general discussion of local foodgrains self-sufficiency, see Riskin, *China's Political Economy*; and Nicholas R. Lardy, *Agriculture in China's Modern Economic Development*, Cambridge, Cambridge University Press, 1983.
21. Benedict Stavis, *Making Green Revolution: The Politics of Agricultural Development in China*, Rural Development Monograph No. 1, Ithaca, New York, Cornell University Rural Development Committee, 1974.
22. I owe this point to Ajit Ghose of the ILO World Employment Programme.
23. Yao and Colman, *'Chinese Agricultural Policies. . .'*.
24. Paine, *Economic and Political Weekly*, 1976, p. 1371.
25. This is indeed reflected in Mao's following statement in Wan-sui: 'The importance we attach to agriculture is symbolised by the quantity of steel products which we are allocating to agriculture.' See 'Mao Tse-tung ssu-hsiang wansui' (Long Live Mao Tse-tung's Thought) translated by the US Joint Publications Research Service, and published under the title: 'Miscellany of Mao Tse-tung Thought'; cited in Suzanne Paine, 'Balanced Development: Maoist Conception and Chinese Practice', *World Development*, April 1976.
26. Michael Lipton, 'Transfer of Resources from Agriculture to Non-agricultural Activities: The Case of India', *IDS Communication Series No. 109*, 1972.
27. A. S. Kahlon and D. S. Tyagi, *Agricultural Price Policy in India*, New Delhi, Allied Publishers Private Ltd, 1983, and 'Intersectoral Terms of Trade', *Economic and Political Weekly*, 27 December 1980.
28. See Ravi Srivastva, *Planning and Regional Disparities in India*, paper presented at the Conference on 'The State and Development Planning in India', School of Oriental and African Studies, London, 21–24 April 1989.
29. Raj Krishna, 'The Centre and the Periphery – Interstate Disparities in Economic Development', in *Facets of India's Development – G. L. Mehta Memorial Lectures*, Bombay, Indian Institute of Technology, 1986.
30. Jagdish N. Bhagwati and Padma Desai, *INDIA – Planning for Industrialisation*, London, Oxford University Press, 1970.

31. Krishna Bharadwaj, 'Regional Differentiation in India – A Note', *Economic and Political Weekly*, Annual Number, 1982.
32. I. S. Gulhati and K. K. George, 'Interstate Distribution Through Budgetary Transfers', *Economic and Political Weekly*, vol. 13, no. 11, 1978.
33. See P. Aguigner, 'Regional Disparities since 1978', in S. Feuchtwang, A. Hussain and T. Pairault (eds), *Transforming China's Economy in the 1980s*, vol. 2, London, Zed Books Ltd 1988.
34. Rizwanul Islam, 'Growth of Rural Industries in Post-Reform China: Patterns, Determinants and Consequences', *Development and Change*, October 1991.
35. Daniel Southerland, 'Beijing Reinforces Central Planners' Role and Extends Austerity', *International Herald Tribune*, Zurich, 2–3 December 1989.
36. I owe these points to Chris shu-ki Tsang, Hong Kong Baptist College.
37. *International Herald Tribune*, Zurich, 14 August 1989.
38. For a discussion of the Indian liberal economic reforms, see T. N. Srinivasan, 'Economic Liberalisation in China and India: Issues and an Analytical Framework', *Journal of Comparative Economics*, September 1987; also reprinted in Bruce Reynolds (ed.), *Chinese Economic Reforms: How Far, How Fast?* New York, Academic Press, 1988.
39. Government of India, Planning Commission, *Approach to the Eighth Five Year Plan (1990–95)*, New Delhi, May 1990 (Draft), pp. 41–3.
40. Budget Speech by Dr Manmohan Singh, Minister of Finance, Government of India, Budget for 1991–92, *Times of India*, Bombay, 25 July 1991
41. Ibid.
42. Gordon White, 'Riding the Tiger: Grass Roots Rural Politics in the Wake of the Chinese Economic Reforms', in Ashwani Saith (ed.) *The Re-emergence of the Chinese Peasantry – Aspects of Rural Decollectivisation*, London, Croom Helm, 1987.

4 Linkages and Imbalances*

In Chapter 2 we examined Hirschman's concept of imbalances and high-linkage industrial growth without providing its empirical analogue. The main purpose of this chapter is to provide a measurement of these linkages. Both backward and forward output and employment linkages are estimated for China and India using input–output (I/O) tables (for China the latest table available is for 1981[1] and for India it is for 1984–5).[2] A comparison is also made with the Philippines, Indonesia, Malaysia, Bangladesh and Turkey.

Backward linkages depend on the intermediate inputs required for sectoral output whereas forward linkages depend on induced output growth. For example, growth in agricultural output generates demand for such activities as agricultural implements, fertilisers, water pumps, storage, processing, transportation, marketing and distribution, etc.

A high degree of sectoral balance and interdependence implies strong linkages which would generate growth impulses throughout different sectors. Conversely, limited interdependence would mean that linkages are concentrated only in a few sectors, resulting thereby in conditions of unbalanced development.

We wish to examine whether intra-industry and intersectoral linkages in China and India, as well as in other developing countries, are high or low, and whether high linkages are necessarily associated with high rates of growth. Have these countries followed a high-linkage strategy and, if so, what policy measures did they adopt to promote the growth of linkages?

Thus, this chapter also provides some empirical underpinnings to the strategies of heavy industrialisation and local self-reliance discussed in Chapter 3.

The I/O technique used here is subject to some important limitations. The effects of changes in final demand on the different 'industries' are expressed in increments of value added and not increments of investment because, given potential increases of value added or final demand, investment can be determined by the coefficients in a dynamic I/O model. However, the static I/O model used/cited in this chapter does not give any indication of the requirements of, or responses to, investments in new capital goods or inventories. Another limitation of the I/O model is that it abstracts from supply/

capacity and foreign exchange constraints so that any increase in final demand is easily met through domestic production. This assumption is quite unrealistic, as we shall note in Chapter 5. These limitations need to be borne in mind in interpreting the I/O coefficients analysed here.

I SECTORAL OUTPUT AND EMPLOYMENT LINKAGES

1.1 China

Using the 24 × 24 I/O table for China for 1981, we have estimated the backward and forward output and employment linkages for the Chinese economy (see Tables 4.1 and 4.2). (For the estimation methodology used, see Appendix 4.1.) For example, the direct backward output coefficient of the agricultural sector (sector no. 1 in the tables) is 0.26 ranked at 23rd place among the 24 sectors. Although the indirect linkage is 1.23 which is higher than the direct linkage, the rank of total backward linkage of agriculture is still very low (being 23, almost at the bottom of the list of sectors). The forward linkage of agriculture is relatively higher, being at the 16th rank. However, the total forward linkage index is 0.88, that is, below the national average level of forward linkage.

The variation based on rank correlation (see column 7 in Tables 4.1 and 4.2) is high for backward linkages and low for forward linkages. This implies that (i) the benefits from an additional unit of investment in agriculture are mostly concentrated within this sector, and (ii) benefits from an additional unit increase in output are shared more evenly with the other sectors. In general the output effects are more widely dispersed than the employment effects.

As noted in Chapter 2, high backward and forward output linkages tend to be associated more with heavy industry and intermediate goods than with agriculture and primary production. The results in Tables 4.1 and 4.2 support this view for output linkages but not for employment linkages. For example, the high backward and forward output linkages are associated with metallurgical and chemical industries which have relatively low direct as well as indirect employment linkages. On the other hand, agriculture and light industry show low output linkages.

The subsistence nature of Chinese agriculture seems to explain its low output linkages. Modern commercial and plantation agriculture

Table 4.1 Output linkages in China

(a) Backward linkage

Sector	(1) Dir. link.	(2) Rank	(3) Indir. link.	(4) Total link.	(5) Index	(6) Rank	(7) Var. of (4)	(8) Rank	(9) Dir./Total (%)
1. Agriculture	0.26	23	1.23	1.49	0.74	23	3.64	2	17.6
2. Forestry	0.11	24	1.05	1.15	0.58	24	4.53	1	9.2
3. Animal husbandry	0.39	18	1.21	1.60	0.80	20	3.29	5	24.5
4. Sideline production	0.45	15	1.49	1.94	0.97	14	2.61	17	23.0
5. Fisheries	0.33	20	1.29	1.62	0.81	19	3.07	9	20.4
6. Metallurgical industry	0.64	6	1.70	2.34	1.17	5	3.13	8	27.3
7. Electricity industry	0.30	21	1.25	1.54	0.77	22	3.20	7	19.2
8. Coal and coke industry	0.40	17	1.39	1.79	0.89	17	2.87	11	22.5
9. Petroleum industry	0.42	16	1.37	1.79	0.89	18	3.39	3	23.3
10. Heavy chemical industry	0.62	9	1.56	2.17	1.08	9	2.80	12	28.4
11. Light chemical industry	0.66	5	1.68	2.34	1.16	6	2.41	19	28.1
12. Heavy machinery industry	0.60	12	1.71	2.31	1.15	7	2.66	16	25.9
13. Light machinery industry	0.61	11	1.73	2.34	1.17	4	2.16	23	26.1
14. Building material industry	0.52	13	1.48	2.00	1.00	13	2.52	18	25.9
15. Heavy forest industry	0.46	14	1.41	1.87	0.93	15	2.88	10	24.6
16. Light forest industry	0.63	8	1.53	2.15	1.07	11	2.27	22	29.1
17. Food industry	0.73	3	1.44	2.16	1.08	10	2.72	15	33.6
18. Textile industry	0.69	4	1.85	2.54	1.27	2	3.35	4	27.3
19. Clothing & leather industry	0.74	1	2.01	2.75	1.37	1	2.39	20	27.0
20. Paper-making industry	0.63	7	1.67	2.29	1.14	8	2.78	13	27.3
21. Other industries	0.61	10	1.52	2.13	1.06	12	2.37	21	28.7
22. Construction	0.73	2	1.75	2.48	1.24	3	1.93	24	29.3
23. Transport, posts and telecommunications	0.29	22	1.26	1.55	0.77	21	3.23	6	18.5
24. Commerce, catering and service trades, supply and marketing of materials	0.38	19	1.41	1.79	0.89	16	2.78	14	21.2

(b) Forward output linkage

Sector	(1) Dir. link.	(2) Rank	(3) Indir. link.	(4) Total link.	(5) Index	(6) Rank	(7) Var. of (4)	(8) Rank	(9) Dir./Total (%)
1. Agriculture	0.50	16	1.39	1.89	0.88	16	2.92	10	26.5
2. Forestry	0.76	7	1.96	2.72	1.26	6	1.89	22	28.0
3. Animal husbandry	0.56	15	1.38	1.94	0.90	15	2.69	13	28.8
4. Sideline production	0.65	9	1.49	2.14	1.00	11	2.39	16	30.4
5. Fisheries	0.16	23	1.08	1.24	0.57	23	4.08	2	12.8
6. Metallurgical industry	1.01	2	2.13	3.15	1.46	4	2.46	15	32.2
7. Electricity industry	0.89	3	2.37	3.26	1.51	2	1.55	24	27.3
8. Coal and coke industry	0.79	6	2.36	3.15	1.46	3	1.67	23	25.1
9. Petroleum industry	0.75	8	2.02	2.78	1.29	5	2.15	19	27.1
10. Heavy chemical industry	1.02	1	2.24	3.26	1.51	1	1.98	21	31.2
11. Light chemical industry	0.57	13	1.57	2.14	0.99	12	2.63	14	26.7
12. Heavy machinery industry	0.42	18	1.37	1.79	0.83	17	3.39	7	23.4
13. Light machinery industry	0.27	20	1.15	1.42	0.66	20	3.45	6	19.0
14. Building material industry	0.87	4	1.24	2.12	0.98	13	2.89	11	41.2
15. Heavy forest industry	0.82	5	1.58	2.40	1.12	8	2.33	17	34.2
16. Light forest industry	0.43	17	1.33	1.76	0.82	18	2.81	12	24.3
17. Food industry	0.21	22	1.17	1.38	0.64	22	3.77	3	15.5
18. Textile industry	0.65	10	1.78	2.43	1.13	7	3.50	5	26.7
19. Clothing & leather industry	0.23	21	1.18	1.41	0.65	21	3.67	4	16.3
20. Paper-making industry	0.56	14	1.52	2.08	0.97	14	3.03	8	27.1
21. Other industries	0.63	12	1.57	2.19	1.02	10	2.32	18	28.6
22. Construction	0.00	24	1.00	1.00	0.46	24	4.90	1	0.0
23. Transport, posts and telecommunications	0.63	11	1.68	2.31	1.07	9	2.15	20	27.3
24. Commerce, catering and service trades, supply and marketing of materials	0.32	19	1.38	1.70	0.79	19	2.93	9	18.6

Source: Our estimates.

Table 4.2 Employment linkages in China

(a) Backward linkage

Sector	(1) Dir. link.	(2) Rank	(3) Indir. link.	(4) Total link.	(5) Index	(6) Rank	(7) Var. of (4)	(8) Rank	(9) Dir./Total (%)
1. Agriculture	1713.50	1	274.80	1988.30	3.09	1	4.71	1	86.2
2. Forestry	222.47	8	38.36	260.83	0.41	22	4.46	2	85.3
3. Animal husbandry	897.18	3	716.72	1613.90	2.51	2	3.38	7	55.6
4. Sideline production	134.79	14	362.84	497.63	0.77	12	2.50	14	27.1
5. Fisheries	900.69	2	289.51	1190.20	1.85	4	3.86	3	75.7
6. Metallurgical industry	119.99	15	263.81	383.80	0.60	19	2.36	18	31.3
7. Electricity industry	80.61	19	142.72	223.33	0.35	23	2.17	20	36.1
8. Coal and coke industry	446.21	4	171.70	617.91	0.96	8	3.75	6	72.2
9. Petroleum industry	37.42	23	141.49	178.91	0.28	24	1.62	24	20.9
10. Heavy chemical industry	92.98	18	277.34	370.32	0.58	21	1.94	22	25.1
11. Light chemical industry	79.12	20	414.91	494.03	0.77	13	2.40	16	16.0
12. Heavy machinery industry	169.01	11	261.24	430.25	0.67	16	2.45	15	39.3
13. Light machinery industry	159.67	13	269.13	428.80	0.67	17	1.95	21	37.2
14. Building material industry	160.21	12	228.71	388.92	0.60	18	2.20	19	41.2
15. Heavy forest industry	190.41	9	186.74	377.15	0.59	20	2.75	12	50.5
16. Light forest industry	232.03	7	246.18	478.21	0.74	14	2.39	17	48.5
17. Food industry	62.26	22	1272.34	1334.60	2.07	3	3.84	5	4.7
18. Textile industry	76.38	21	640.12	716.50	1.11	5	3.09	8	10.7
19. Clothing & leather industry	31.18	24	577.02	608.20	0.95	10	2.67	13	5.1
20. Paper-making industry	99.22	17	518.26	617.48	0.96	9	2.95	9	16.1
21. Other industries	103.47	16	518.66	622.13	0.97	7	2.94	10	16.6
22. Construction	174.70	10	328.22	502.92	0.78	11	1.82	23	34.7
23. Transport, posts and telecommunications	355.99	5	107.49	463.48	0.72	15	3.85	4	76.8
24. Commerce, catering and service trades, supply and marketing of materials	341.29	6	308.23	649.52	1.01	6	2.92	11	52.5

67

(b) Forward linkage

Sector	(1) Dir. link.	(2) Rank	(3) Indir. link.	(4) Total link.	(5) Index	(6) Rank	(7) Var. of (4)	(8) Rank	(9) Dir./Total (%)
1. Agriculture	1713.50	1	362.00	2075.50	3.43	1	4.51	3	82.6
2. Forestry	222.47	8	480.18	702.65	1.16	6	2.16	15	31.7
3. Animal husbandry	897.18	3	295.02	1192.20	1.97	3	3.84	4	75.3
4. Sideline production	134.79	14	302.26	437.05	0.72	14	2.02	19	30.8
5. Fisheries	900.69	2	79.47	980.16	1.62	4	4.65	2	91.9
6. Metallurgical industry	119.99	15	439.82	559.81	0.93	9	1.93	21	21.4
7. Electricity industry	80.61	19	600.41	681.02	1.13	8	1.99	20	11.8
8. Coal and coke industry	446.21	4	530.91	977.12	1.62	5	2.54	13	45.7
9. Petroleum industry	37.42	23	493.66	531.08	0.88	10	2.12	17	7.0
10. Heavy chemical industry	92.98	18	1234.92	1327.90	2.19	2	3.60	5	7.0
11. Light chemical industry	79.12	20	251.49	330.61	0.55	19	1.72	23	23.9
12. Heavy machinery industry	169.01	11	170.83	339.84	0.56	18	3.04	7	49.7
13. Light machinery industry	159.67	13	182.34	342.01	0.57	17	2.76	8	46.7
14. Building material industry	160.21	12	216.77	376.98	0.62	16	2.68	10	42.5
15. Heavy forest industry	190.41	9	320.67	511.08	0.84	12	2.12	18	37.3
16. Light forest industry	232.03	7	252.94	484.97	0.80	13	2.57	12	47.8
17. Food industry	62.26	22	115.33	177.59	0.29	22	2.34	14	35.1
18. Textile industry	76.38	21	178.52	254.90	0.42	21	2.59	11	30.0
19. Clothing & leather industry	31.18	24	77.28	108.46	0.18	24	1.70	24	28.7
20. Paper-making industry	99.22	17	214.26	313.48	0.52	20	2.15	16	31.7
21. Other industries	103.47	16	322.89	426.36	0.70	15	1.89	22	24.3
22. Construction	174.70	10	0.00	174.70	0.29	23	4.90	1	100.0
23. Transport, posts and telecommunications	355.99	5	332.55	688.54	1.14	7	2.69	9	51.7
24. Commerce, catering and service trades, supply and marketing of materials	341.29	6	185.11	526.40	0.87	11	3.31	6	64.8

Source: Our estimates.

is likely to show much higher output linkages than traditional agriculture (as is indeed shown below by the example of Malaysia). The low output linkages may also be due to the type of agricultural pricing policy that was followed particularly prior to 1979. The procurement prices of foodgrains are known to have been kept much lower than the market price at least before 1979. The low price means low producer incomes which may restrict the demand for products of input-supplying industries (e.g. farm equipment) in the manufacturing sector.

The employment linkages are high for agriculture, animal husbandry and fisheries. The direct linkages are dominant, being 86.2 per cent and 82.6 per cent of the total backward and forward linkages respectively.

The high forward linkages may be due to the additional employment generated in the storage, processing, transportation and distribution of agricultural output. These activities seem to have grown particularly rapidly since 1979. Nolan and Paine have noted rapid growth of rural truck ownership which reflects growth in rural trade and a resulting demand for transport facilities.[3] Related employment may also be generated through the construction of infrastructural facilities (feeder roads, silos, etc.) that would be needed for the storage and transport of agricultural output to the final consumer. Unfortunately the Chinese I/O table is not disaggregated enough to enable any quantification of the employment potential of these activities, in particular of the growing rural trade sector.

We rank below direct backward output linkages (Table 4.1, column 2) and indirect backward output linkages (Table 4.1, column 3). The paired rankings show a positive and high correlation between direct and indirect linkages in most cases, which suggests that one could consider either direct or indirect linkages without affecting the analysis very much (only animal husbandry and the machinery industry show low association).

Tables 4.1 and 4.2 also show that the indirect output as well as employment linkages for all the sectors are greater than the direct linkages. Inter-industry linkages would tend to grow with higher levels of economic development; so will the indirect effects of a given increase in output in one sector on other sectors of the economy.

Direct:	1	2	3	4	5	6	7	8	9	10	11	12	13	14	15
Indirect:	1	3	14	2	7	6	8	10	9	11	4	5	13	15	12
Direct:	16	17	18	19	20	21	22	23	24						
Indirect:	18	17	23	16	19	21	20	22	24						

Table 4.3   Backward and forward linkages: a summary analysis (China)

Sector	Employment linkages		Output linkages	
	Backward	*Forward*	*Backward*	*Forward*
1. Agriculture	+	+	−	−
2. Forestry	−	+	−	+
3. Animal husbandry	+	+	−	−
4. Sideline production	−	−	−	(+)
5. Fisheries	+	+	−	−
6. Metallurgical industry	−	−	+	+
7. Electricity industry	−	+	−	+
8. Coal and coke industry	−	+	−	+
9. Petroleum industry	−	+	+	+
10. Heavy chemical industry	−	+	+	+
11. Light chemical industry	−	−	+	−
12. Heavy machinery industry	−	−	+	−
13. Light machinery industry	−	−	+	−
14. Building material industry	−	−	(+)	−
15. Heavy forest industry	−	−	−	+
16. Light forest industry	−	−	+	−
17. Food industry	+	−	+	−
18. Textile industry	+	−	+	+
19. Clothing & leather industry	−	−	+	−
20. Paper-making industry	−	−	+	−
21. Other industries	−	−	+	+
22. Construction	−	−	+	−
23. Transport, posts and telecommunications	−	+	−	+
24. Commerce, catering and service trades, supply and marketing of materials	+	−	−	−

Notes: +   indicates the index is above average level (i.e. greater than unity).
 (+) indicates the index equals average level (or unity).
 −   indicates the index is below average level.

A summary analysis of linkages in China is presented in Table 4.3. A linkage index greater than unity means that a unit increase in investment (or output) in a particular sector will yield above–average backward or forward linkages with other sectors in the economy. On the other hand, if the index is below unity, the additional activity in a given sector will lead to only a limited effect on the rest of the economy.

Most of the sectors of the Chinese economy have low employment linkages. As the 1981 I/O table would seem to capture mainly the Mao period this situation may be partly explained by the heavy influence of the Soviet model of growth especially during the 1950s. One would expect some shift in the linkage coefficients resulting from the implementation of post-Mao economic reforms which have brought about changes in technology, product mix and institutions. It would therefore be interesting to repeat the exercise using the 1985 I/O table when it becomes possible.

1.2 India

For India, we have aggregated 89 sectors into 20 sectors to make them roughly comparable to the sector classification for China.

Tables 4.4 and 4.5 show output and employment linkages for India. The following broad conclusions can be drawn from these tables:

(1) Like China, the direct output linkages of Indian sectors are very low, suggesting the significance of indirect output linkages. However, this is not the case with employment linkages of many sectors. For example, direct backward employment linkages for agriculture, fisheries and transport, posts and telecommunications are quite high; so are the direct forward employment linkages for textiles, the food industry, agriculture, fisheries, construction and the machinery industry.

(2) The high backward output linkages are found in heavy industry sectors (e.g. metallurgical, petroleum and chemical industries) and light industry sectors (e.g. food and textile industries). While forward linkages are also high for heavy industry sectors, they are low for food and textile industries.

(3) High backward and low forward output and employment linkages occur in construction and food and textile industries.

(4) The sectors with high forward and backward employment linkages are agriculture, paper making and transport, posts and telecommunications.

(5) High forward and low backward employment linkages occur in petroleum and chemical industries, and the building materials industry.

Table 4.4 Output linkages in India

Sector name	Sector no.	Backward linkage (1) Dir. link.	(2) Rank	(3) Indir. link.	(4) Total link.	(5) Index	(6) Rank	(7) Var. of (4)	(8) Rank	(9) Dir./total (%)	Forward output linkage (1) Dir. link.	(2) Rank	(3) Indir. link.	(4) Total link.	(5) Index	(6) Rank	(7) Var. of (4)	(8) Rank	(9) Dir./total (%)
Agriculture	1	0.22	17	1.22	1.44	0.75	16	3.28	6	15.1	0.35	12	1.13	1.48	0.71	15	3.21	7	23.7
Forestry	2	0.13	20	1.12	1.25	0.65	19	3.55	2	10.5	0.52	8	1.36	1.88	0.91	11	2.45	13	27.6
Animal husbandry	3	0.54	11	1.28	1.82	0.95	13	2.61	10	29.7	0.16	19	1.08	1.24	0.60	18	3.62	4	12.7
Fisheries	4	0.14	19	1.09	1.22	0.64	20	3.64	1	11.2	0.16	18	1.06	1.22	0.59	19	3.67	3	13.1
Metallurgical industry	5	0.54	9	1.53	2.08	1.09	9	2.86	7	26.2	0.86	2	1.75	2.61	1.26	3	2.34	17	32.8
Electricity industry	6	0.36	15	1.40	1.76	0.92	14	2.55	11	20.4	0.42	11	1.52	1.94	0.93	9	2.28	18	21.6
Coal and coke industry	7	0.21	18	1.10	1.31	0.69	18	3.50	5	15.9	0.66	6	2.45	3.11	1.50	2	1.45	20	21.4
Petroleum industry	8	0.74	2	2.22	2.97	1.55	1	3.53	4	25.1	1.52	1	4.98	6.50	3.13	1	1.62	19	23.4
Chemical industry	9	0.60	5	1.61	2.20	1.15	4	2.72	8	27.1	0.82	4	1.72	2.55	1.23	4	2.39	14	32.3
Machinery industry	10	0.58	10	1.59	2.17	1.14	5	2.44	15	26.7	0.29	15	1.21	1.50	0.72	13	3.44	5	19.1
Building material industry	11	0.54	10	1.49	2.03	1.06	10	2.33	17	26.6	0.85	3	1.41	2.26	1.09	5	2.54	11	37.5
Wood products	12	0.46	13	1.37	1.83	0.96	12	2.47	13	24.9	0.76	5	1.38	2.14	1.03	6	2.37	16	35.5
Food industry	13	0.81	1	1.56	2.37	1.24	2	2.19	19	34.3	0.13	20	1.06	1.20	0.58	20	4.13	1	11.3
Textile industry	14	0.66	3	1.59	2.26	1.18	3	2.45	14	29.4	0.31	14	1.19	1.49	0.72	14	3.68	2	20.4
Clothing & leather industry	15	0.56	8	1.54	2.10	1.10	7	2.24	18	26.5	0.35	13	1.31	1.66	0.80	12	2.83	9	20.9
Paper-making industry	16	0.57	7	1.52	2.09	1.09	8	2.49	12	27.3	0.47	10	1.48	1.95	0.94	8	2.66	10	24.1
Other industries	17	0.38	14	1.34	1.72	0.90	15	2.63	9	22.1	0.24	16	1.23	1.47	0.71	16	3.13	8	16.6
Construction	18	0.65	4	1.50	2.16	1.13	6	2.17	20	30.3	0.20	17	1.19	1.39	0.67	17	3.24	6	14.5
Transport, posts and telecommunications	19	0.46	12	1.53	1.98	1.04	11	2.39	16	23.0	0.48	9	1.45	1.94	0.93	10	2.38	15	25.0
Commerce, storage & warehouse	20	0.25	16	1.18	1.43	0.75	17	3.54	3	17.3	0.53	7	1.44	1.97	0.95	7	2.53	12	27.1

Source: Our estimates.

Table 4.5 Employment linkages in India

	Backward linkage									Forward linkage								
Sector	(1) Dir. link.	(2) Rank	(3) Indir. link.	(4) Total link.	(5) Index	(6) Rank	(7) Var. of (4)	(8) Rank	(9) Dir./total (%)	(1) Dir. link.	(2) Rank	(3) Indir. link.	(4) Total link.	(5) Index	(6) Rank	(7) Var. of (4)	(8) Rank	(9) Dir./total (%)
Agriculture	2059.80	1	213.60	2273.40	2.90	1	4.30	1	90.6	2059.80	1	254.50	2314.30	2.49	2	4.22	1	89.0
Forestry	76.29	16	110.05	186.34	0.24	18	2.09	14	40.9	76.29	16	406.90	483.19	0.52	15	1.97	15	15.8
Animal husbandry	n.a.		n.a.	n.a.	n.a.					n.a.		n.a.	n.a.	n.a.				
Fisheries	378.22	8	78.32	456.54	0.58	14	3.70	2	82.8	378.22	8	87.49	465.71	0.50	17	3.63	4	81.2
Metallurgical industry	282.81	12	353.41	636.22	0.81	10	2.67	7	44.5	282.81	12	672.38	955.19	1.03	8	1.92	16	29.6
Electricity industry	324.05	11	240.43	564.48	0.72	12	2.60	9	57.4	324.05	11	425.77	749.82	0.81	11	1.99	14	43.2
Coal and coke industry	60.05	18	114.52	174.57	0.22	19	2.32	13	34.4	60.05	18	936.16	996.21	1.07	7	1.39	19	6.0
Petroleum industry	15.63	19	231.11	246.74	0.31	17	1.68	17	6.3	15.63	19	2840.47	2856.10	3.08	1	2.08	13	0.5
Chemical industry	168.93	13	462.67	631.60	0.80	11	1.85	16	26.7	168.93	13	1205.67	1374.60	1.48	3	2.76	9	12.3
Machinery industry	367.57	10	385.74	753.31	0.96	7	2.56	12	48.8	367.57	10	231.81	599.38	0.65	14	3.17	6	61.3
Building material industry	408.53	6	342.21	750.74	0.96	8	2.58	11	54.4	408.53	6	652.67	1061.20	1.14	5	2.46	10	38.5
Wood products	160.11	14	251.24	411.35	0.52	15	1.94	15	38.9	160.11	14	568.88	728.99	0.78	13	2.15	12	22.0
Food industry	381.52	7	1273.78	1655.30	2.11	2	2.83	6	23.0	381.52	7	85.13	466.65	0.50	16	4.04	2	81.8
Textile industry	594.54	3	877.66	1472.20	1.88	3	2.62	8	40.4	594.54	3	241.93	836.47	0.90	9	3.92	3	71.1
Clothing & leather industry	107.72	15	541.09	648.81	0.83	9	1.67	18	16.6	107.72	15	332.77	440.49	0.47	18	1.79	18	24.5
Paper-making industry	545.77	4	420.05	965.82	1.23	5	2.93	5	56.5	545.77	4	460.13	1005.90	1.08	6	2.82	8	54.3
Other industries	67.90	17	268.82	336.72	0.43	16	1.43	19	20.2	67.90	17	193.30	261.20	0.28	19	1.86	17	26.0
Construction	520.12	5	405.60	925.72	1.18	6	2.59	10	56.2	520.12	5	218.35	738.47	0.80	12	3.21	5	70.4
Transport, posts and telecommunications	757.92	2	265.48	1023.40	1.30	4	3.45	3	74.1	757.92	2	427.68	1185.60	1.28	4	2.97	7	63.9
Commerce, storage & warehouse	367.77	9	195.90	563.67	0.72	13	3.32	4	65.2	367.77	9	465.52	833.29	0.90	10	2.28	11	44.1

Source: Our estimates.
Note: n.a. = not available.

Table 4.6   Backward and forward linkages: a summary analysis (India)

Sector	Employment linkages		Output linkages	
	Backward	Forward	Backward	Forward
1. Agriculture	+	+	−	−
2. Forestry	−	−	−	
3. Animal husbandry	n.a.	n.a.	−	−
4. Fisheries	−	−	−	−
5. Metallurgical industry	−	(+)	+	+
6. Electricity industry	−	−	−	−
7. Coal and coke industry	−	(+)	−	+
8. Petroleum industry	−	+	+	+
9. Chemical industry	−	+	+	+
10. Machinery industry	−	−	+	−
11. Building materials industry	−	+	(+)	(+)
12. Wood products industry	−	−	−	(+)
13. Food industry	+	−	+	−
14. Textile industry	+	−	+	−
15. Clothing & leather industry	−	−	+	−
16. Paper-making industry	+	+	(+)	−
17. Other industries	−	−	−	−
18. Construction	+	−	+	−
19. Transport, posts & telecommunications	+	+	(+)	−
20. Trade, storage & warehousing	−	−	−	−

Notes: + indicates the index is above average level (i.e. unity).
(+) indicates the index equals average level (or unity).
− indicates the index is below average level.
n.a. = not available.

Table 4.6 provides a summary analysis of linkages in India. A comparison between this Table and Table 4.3 for China shows several similarities, e.g. high output linkages in petroleum, metallurgical and chemical industries, and high employment linkages in agriculture and low employment linkages in clothing, leather and machinery industry in both countries. There are also dissimilarities; for paper making industry employment linkages are high for India but low for China but the output linkages show similar signs; and for fisheries, employment linkages are low for India but high for China. One explanation for this divergence may be differences in the degree of capital intensity and scale of production in the industries concerned. For example, it is plausible that high employment linkages for paper making in India are explained by the existence of the small-scale sector in paper making. According to a 1984–85 survey, there were over 21,000 small-scale establishments (employing fewer than 10 persons) on paper, paper products and printing, or 4.5 per cent of the total number of small-scale industrial establishments not registered under the Factory Act of India (1948). They accounted for over 4 per cent of output of the small industrial establishments.[4] In contrast to India, the paper making industry in China consists mainly of large-scale state enterprises.

II   AN AGGREGATE ANALYSIS: CHINA AND INDIA

For purposes of China–India comparisons we also undertook a more aggregated analysis of the five sectors according to the International Standard Industrial Classification (ISIC), namely, agriculture (including fisheries, forestry and animal husbandry), industry (including mining and quarrying), construction, transport (including posts and telecommunications) and trade (including commerce and services). The sectoral distribution of output and employment linkages (backward and forward) is presented in Tables 4.7 and 4.8. In the case of China (Table 4.7), since the data on the intermediate demand for construction is missing, the direct forward linkage sector in the table is zero. We can nevertheless estimate this sector's indirect and total linkages which are given in the table.

The results for the two countries are very similar, except that in the case of China the backward employment linkages of the industrial sector are relatively more dispersed to the agricultural sector than is the case in India.

Since the Chinese development strategy/policy follows a three-tiered sectoral classification – agriculture, light industry and heavy industry – we also estimated linkages on the basis of the following five blocks – agriculture, rural non-farm activities, light industry, heavy industry and other sectors – to examine (a) intra-sectoral interdependence between farm and non-farm activities, and (b) inter-sectoral interdependence between agriculture, light industry and heavy industry. The results (which are presented in Statistical Appendix Table A.4.5) did not show any significant difference from those presented in Table 4.7.

All the sectors considered (with the exception of construction) seem to be quite self-reliant and vertically integrated. In other words, any benefits generated by an additional activity (i.e. increase in the final demand in the case of backward linkages and an increase in

Table 4.7 Sectoral distribution of total output and employment linkages
(China) (percentages)

Sector	Agriculture (1)	Industry (2)	Construction (3)	Transport (4)	Trade (5)
	A. *Output linkages* (Backward)				
1.	78.8	15.3	14.5	5.9	9.1
2.	19.3	81.2	41.5	27.3	32.0
3.	0.0	0.0	39.7	0.0	0.0
4.	0.8	1.6	2.5	63.8	1.4
5.	1.1	1.9	1.8	3.0	57.5
Σ	100.0	100.0	100.0	100.0	100.0
	(Forward)				(Σ)
1.	58.8	34.1	5.1	0.4	1.6	100.0
2.	6.6	83.1	6.7	0.9	2.6	100.0
3.	0.0	0.0	100.0	0.0	0.0	100.0
4.	5.8	36.7	8.8	46.3	2.4	100.0
5.	5.3	26.4	3.9	1.3	63.1	100.0
	B. *Employment linkages* (Backward)				
1.	97.2	65.0	58.2	21.9	32.6
2.	2.1	30.8	14.9	9.0	10.3
3.	0.0	0.0	22.2	0.0	0.0
4.	0.3	2.0	2.8	66.2	1.4
5.	0.4	2.2	1.9	2.9	55.7
Σ	100.0	100.0	100.0	100.0	100.0
	(Forward)				(Σ)
1.	93.2	4.8	1.1	0.2	0.7	100.0
2.	41.6	46.6	5.8	1.6	4.4	100.0
3.	0.0	0.0	100.0	0.0	0.0	100.0
4.	24.0	13.7	5.1	54.5	2.7	100.0
5.	20.5	9.2	2.1	1.5	66.6	100.0

Source: Our estimates.

output (GDP) in the case of forward linkages) goes back to each
sector itself rather than being shared by other sectors. This emerges
quite clearly from Tables 4.7 and 4.8 which show, for China and
India, the percentage allocation of output and employment effects
between a given sector and the rest of the economy.

Table 4.8   Sectoral distribution of total output and employment linkages
(India) (percentages)

Sector	Agriculture (1)	Industry (2)	Construction (3)	Transport (4)	Trade (5)
A. *Output linkages* (Backward)					
1.	78.5	9.1	4.7	4.3	3.0
2.	14.0	74.8	27.6	27.2	10.6
3.	1.3	2.4	46.7	2.1	1.7
4.	1.2	3.2	3.9	55.7	5.0
5.	4.9	10.4	17.2	10.7	79.8
Σ	100.0	100.0	100.0	100.0	100.0
(Forward)					(Σ)
1.	73.7	20.5	2.4	1.3	2.1	100.0
2.	6.2	79.8	6.7	3.9	3.5	100.0
3.	3.9	16.9	73.7	2.0	3.6	100.0
4.	3.7	23.6	6.6	54.8	11.3	100.0
5.	4.8	24.7	9.2	3.4	57.9	100.0
B. *Employment linkages* (Backward)					
1.	94.3	32.7	15.2	11.0	11.4
2.	3.2	50.5	16.8	13.2	7.6
3.	0.5	2.8	49.1	1.8	2.1
4.	0.7	5.4	6.0	67.7	9.0
5.	1.4	8.6	12.8	6.3	69.9
Σ	100.0	100.0	100.0	100.0	100.0
(Forward)					(Σ)
1.	92.8	4.9	1.0	0.8	0.6	100.0
2.	24.0	57.6	8.3	7.0	3.1	100.0
3.	11.9	9.7	73.0	2.9	2.5	100.0
4.	9.5	11.5	5.5	66.8	6.7	100.0
5.	17.7	17.0	10.9	5.8	48.6	100.0

Source: Our estimates.

The low sectoral interdependence in China noted above is the result of the Maoist strategy of local self-reliance, under which rural enterprises and factories were encouraged to use locally available raw materials and to introduce vertical integration by producing for themselves materials and intermediate goods needed for production.

Riskin has noted that having discarded markets and central planning to coordinate the economy, 'Mao sought to minimise the need for coordination by means of self-reliance.'[5] While this was true for the Cultural Revolution period, conflicts between markets and central planning remained during the intervening period, between the end of the Great Leap and the beginning of the Cultural Revolution. It also resurfaced during the post-Mao period.

India also followed a self-reliant strategy until the early 1980s which may partly explain its low sectoral linkages in Table 4.8.

III   COMPARISON WITH OTHER DEVELOPING COUNTRIES

We now compare the ranking of Chinese industries on the basis of output linkages (1981) with those of India (1984–85), the Philippines (1965), Indonesia (1969) and Malaysia (1965).[6] Similarly, ranking on the basis of backward employment linkages is compared between China (1981), India (1984–85), Bangladesh (1976–77),[7] and Turkey (1967).[8]

Since the classification of I/O tables varies from country to country we chose 19 common sectors for comparison. The Chinese and Indian linkages are estimated by combining the disaggregated I/O output tables into 19 common sectors. For China, 'light' and 'heavy' sectors for forestry, chemicals and machinery industries are aggregated by their light and heavy branches, and agriculture is combined with sideline production (which includes hunting, collecting fruit and village-run enterprises). For the remaining countries, we adopt the approximation procedure suggested by Panchmukhi (1975)[9] – taking the average of the linkage coefficients and then re-ordering them to form the common ranks for the 19 sectors.

3.1   Comparison of Output Linkages

Table 4.9 ranks sectors according to direct and total output (backward) linkages in China, India, the Philippines, Indonesia and Malaysia. While the periods for I/O tables for India and China are rather close, those for Malaysia, the Philippines and Indonesia date back to the 1960s. Since output per capita in these three countries was much closer to that in China and India in the 1980s, one might argue that, in principle, the ranking of industries among these countries should

Table 4.9 Comparative ranking of direct and total backward output linkages in five Asian countries

Sector	China[c] (1981) D	T	India (1984/5) D	T	Philippines[a] (1965) D	T	Indonesia (1969) D	T	Malaysia[a, b] (1965) D	T
Agriculture	17	16	17	16	17	17	14	15	10	8
Forestry and forest industry	16	17	15	15	11	12	8	9	12	4
Animal husbandry	13	14	11	12	14	15	15	14	10	8
Fisheries	15	15	19	19	16	16	12	13	16	15
Metallurgical industry	5	4	9	9	5	3	9	11	9	3
Electricity industry	18	19	14	13	12	11	16	16	13	6
Coal and coke industry	12	13	18	18	2	8	na	na	2	14
Petroleum industry	11	11	2	1	2	8	17	17	2	14
Chemical industry	6	7	6	4	3	7	5	6	4	1
Machinery industry	9	5	7	5	6	2	1	1	8	12
Building material industry	10	10	10	10	na	na	na	na	na	na
Food industry	3	8	1	2	10	9	3	8	3	5
Textile industry	4	2	5	6	4	6	4	5	1	10
Leather industry	1	1	3	3	1	1	2	3	5	9
Paper-making industry	7	6	8	8	8	5	7	4	11	11
Other industries	8	9	13	14	7	10	13	2	6	13
Construction	2	3	4	7	9	4	6	7	7	2
Transport, posts and telecommunications	19	18	12	11	15	13	11	10	14	7
Commerce, catering and services trades, supply and marketing of materials	14	12	16	17	13	14	10	12	15	16

Note: D, T, are ranks of direct and total backward linkages.
[a] Coal and Petroleum industry are combined.
[b] Agriculture and Animal Husbandry sectors are combined.
[c] Clothing and Leather industry are combined.

be closer to that in India and China than would be the case if the most recent tables were used. This premise is based on the assumption that the stage of development influences the composition of output and inter-industry linkages. Indeed, the direct and total backward output linkages for agriculture and agriculture-related sectors are almost identical for China, India and the Philippines.

Identical ranking is somewhat surprising since we would have expected that differences in the organisation of production and institutions in China and India would be reflected in differences in their I/O coefficients. In 1975, in analysing linkages in industrialis-ation and development strategies, K. N. Raj questioned early find-ings (based on input–output tables) about the similarities in linkage structures and patterns of sectoral interdependence.[10] Raj argued that these depended not only on the stage of development of a country and the growth rates achieved, but also on such institutional factors as the pattern of consumer demand and the resulting income distribution, scale of consumer preferences, motivations and the pattern of organisation of economic and social life in general. Does the similarity of the above results suggest that institutional factors – collective organisation of agriculture and agro-industrial complexes in Mao's China, consumption patterns and income distribution, etc. – do not exercise much influence?

For Malaysia and, to a lesser extent, Indonesia, the ranking of agriculture is much higher. This may be due partly to plantation agriculture in Malaysia (which is commercially and technologically more advanced) versus subsistence agriculture in India and China. This explanation is at variance with the general belief that plantation agriculture is an isolated enclave.

For consumer goods industries like leather, textiles and food, the rankings for China and India are also quite similar. However, the situation is different for heavy industry sectors like the metallurgical industry and the coal/coke industry for which the ranking in China is much higher than that in India; and the petroleum industry for which the ranking is much lower in China than in India. It is difficult to explain this divergence. One explanation may be the high investment rates in China made possible by a high domestic savings rate (nearly 30 per cent of national income),[11] whereas in India the rate of domestic savings has been somewhat lower which may have pre-vented Indian heavy industry from realising its full capacity. To quote Raj (1975), 'the rate of domestic saving has remained at a relatively low level, inadequate to sustain even moderately high rates of investment.

Though a core of capital goods industries had been built up, part of the capacity so created has therefore tended to remain unutilised for lack of demand'.[12]

3.2   Comparison of Employment Linkages

Table 4.10 ranks sectors according to direct and total backward employment linkages in China, India, Bangladesh and Turkey. It is interesting to note that industry ranking for China and India is very similar for the following sectors: agriculture, petroleum industry and chemicals industry. However, the ranking is very different in the case of fisheries, coke and coal industry, textiles, paper making and construction. For these industries, ranks are much higher in India, which suggests that these industries are much more employment generating there than in China. In the case of the machinery industry, the ranking is identical on the basis of direct linkages but much lower in China on the basis of total linkages. This would suggest that the indirect employment effects of the Indian machinery industry are much higher than those of the Chinese machinery industry. The comparison of China with Bangladesh and Turkey also shows some wide variations in industrial employment rankings. But these variations occur mainly in the non-agricultural sectors like textiles, and transport and communications.

The employment structures are more varied between countries than the output structures (this is suggested by the lower correlation coefficients for employment than for output). This is to be expected since output is more likely to be technologically determined than employment which depends more on local practices and institutional structures.

IV   LINKAGES, GROWTH AND IMBALANCE

Our estimates show that output linkages are low for agriculture in China, India and the other developing countries considered. If one followed the Hirschmanian strategy of development discussed in Chapter 2, a relative neglect of agriculture would be justified. In actual practice, however, in conditions of large surplus labour in countries like China and India, this strategy of unbalanced development may not contribute to human development and employment generation. First, although output linkages for agriculture are low,

Table 4.10 Comparative ranking of direct and total backward employment linkages in four countries

Sector	China[a] (1981) D	China[a] (1981) T	India[b] (1984/85) D	India[b] (1984/85) T	Bangladesh[c] (1976/77)	Bangladesh[c] (1976/77) D	Bangladesh[c] (1976/77) T	Turkey[d] (1967) D	Turkey[d] (1967) T
Agriculture	1	1	1	1	(i)	1	2	2	2
					(ii)	4	10		
Forestry	8	18	16	18		6	17	3	3
Animal husbandry	3	2	na	na		2	15	1	1
Fisheries	2	4	8	14		5	18	1	1
Metallurgical industry	12	17	12	10		17	16	8	11
Electricity industry	16	19	11	12		18	11	18	18
Coal/coke industry	4	8	18	19		na	na	5	8
Petroleum industry	19	20	19	17		20	14	19	19
Chemical industry	15	15	13	11		16	4	15	17
Machinery industry	10	14	10	7		14	12	14	16
Building materials industry	11	16	6	8		19	5	12	14
Wood products	7	12	14	15		8	13	10	13
Food	18	3	7	2		11	7	17	4
Textiles	17	5	3	3		9	1	11	5
Clothing and leather	20	10	15	9		13	3	16	9
Paper-making	14	9	4	5		15	8	13	15
Other industries	13	7	17	16		12	6	9	12
Construction	9	11	5	6		10	9	7	7
Transport & communications	5	13	2	4		7	19	4	6
Commerce, etc.	6	6	9	13		3	20	6	10

Notes: D, T, are the ranks of direct and total backward linkages.
[a] Wood products is light forest industry.
[b] Forestry and logging are combined.
[c] Agriculture is separated by (i) grain crops and (ii) cash crops and the correlation is based on grain crops sector.
[d] Animal husbandry and fisheries are combined.

employment linkages are quite high. Since labour is an abundant resource its fullest utilisation would merit high priority. Furthermore, the economic plans of both China and India have laid down objectives not only of growth but also of employment generation. This means that planners must give a high enough weight to growth as well as employment.

Furthermore, the inducement effect of investment discussed by Hirschman seems to have been limited in China and India, both of which followed a strategy of local self-reliance (during the 1960s and 1970s). Thus high linkages may not lead to high growth rates if conducive policies are not introduced and complementary inputs are not available.

China did not follow a policy of appreciably raising investment in agriculture. In principle, a higher investment share for agriculture should raise its backward output linkage because a more advanced agricultural sector will require greater industrial inputs like farm equipment and fertilisers.

4.1 Linkages and Growth

According to Hirschman's strategy, emphasis on non-key sectors like agriculture with low output linkages would tend to lower national growth rate than what would be possible if key sectors like heavy industry and infrastructure with high output linkages were favoured. This assertion does not seem to hold good in the case of either China or India.

A reallocation of resources from heavy industry to agriculture can raise agricultural output without sacrificing overall growth, as is shown by the recent experience in China. Rates of growth of agricultural, industrial and national output for different time periods, show that the overall growth rate did not decline in the post-Mao period when heavy industry was de-emphasised and greater emphasis was placed on 'light' industry to produce consumer goods (see Table 4.11).

Table 4.11   Annual growth rates of sectoral and national gross output in China

Sector / Period	Agriculture	Industry			National output
		Industry	Heavy	Light	
1953–62	–0.3	8.7	17.6	4.8	3.9
1963–70	5.9	14.8	14.9	14.6	12.0
1971–78	4.3	8.5	8.5	8.5	7.2
1978–84	9.5	8.9	6.6	11.7	9.3
1984–88	3.9	15.9	15.2	16.8	8.4

Source: *Statistical Yearbook of China* (1986 and 1990) (Chinese edition); *and China's Industry Economy Yearbook*, 1990.

In India, a slow agricultural growth is reported to have constrained industrial growth. Rangarajan[13] did a simulation exercise to examine the effects of a higher-than-expected agricultural growth rate on growth of industrial and national production. He found that a 1 per cent increase in agricultural growth led to a 0.5 per cent increase in the rate of growth of industrial output and a 0.7 per cent increase in the rate of growth of national income. Since the mid-1970s agricultural growth has been quite slow, lagging behind industrial growth. (From 1980–81 to 1983–84, the agricultural growth rate was only 3.5 per cent compared with 6.2 per cent per annum for industry.) From 1978 to 1984, the Chinese agricultural growth rate was even higher than the rate of industrial growth (see Table 4.11).

4.2 Intra–Rural and Rural–Urban Linkages

The growth of sectoral interdependence and a reduction of imbalances can also be promoted through a well-integrated development of rural–rural and rural–urban linkages. An example of the former is rural small industry which provides inputs for agriculture and processes its output. As a result of the Chinese rural reforms, the bulk of the increased private farm household savings is channelled into investments in rural industry and sideline activities. Furthermore, the increase in agricultural productivity has generated additional purchasing power in the rural areas which in turn has created demand for locally-produced consumer goods. Rural industrialisation in its turn provides a basis for agricultural mechanisation by providing investments into agriculture. During the first phase of rural reforms, the village and township enterprises contributed a substantial portion of their annual net profits as investments in agriculture for purchase of farm machinery, for example.[14] However, this portion may subsequently have declined because of the relatively greater and quicker profitability of rural industry than of agriculture.

With rapid growth of rural industries in China, many of them enjoy increasing linkages not so much with agriculture within the rural sector, but with modern large-scale urban industry through subcontracting. Under this mechanism, large-scale industry provides the necessary technology, markets and technical know-how to the rural industrial sector. (For example, in the textile industry, production of fabrics and garments can depend on small units of production for manufacturing components, or for weaving and cleaning of raw cotton or silk, as the case may be.) These rural–urban linkages are generally more advanced in developed regions and weak in industrially backward regions. There is also some empirical evidence to suggest that linkages through sub-contracting improve with the size of the enterprises.

Rural–urban linkages other than through sub-contracting have also been established in China: rural non-farm enterprises are now encouraged to establish joint ventures with urban industry for the processing and marketing of farm products. Another form of rural–urban linkage in China is through the financial budgets and allocation of resources at different levels of administration. For example, the county finance bureau collects a portion of the profits of the urban collective enterprises to finance rural investment and infrastructural projects.

In the case of India, opinions have varied on whether agricultural growth stimulated rural non-farm output and employment. In 1978, Vyas and Mathai argued that such linkages were weak on account of skewed income gains in agriculture and inadequate rural infrastructure.[15] Subsequent studies have shown the existence of more positive linkages.[16] A recent World Bank study[17] based on (i) cross-section data on Indian states and districts and (ii) a semi-input–output table for 1979–80, estimated a sizeable agricultural income multiplier (i.e. an increase in agricultural value added generating additional value added in the non-farm sector) in both rural and urban areas. It also noted that production and consumption linkages were stronger in the richer agricultural states than in the poorer ones.

However, the types of linkages for China noted above are much less developed in India. A relatively slower agricultural growth and a bi-modal rural development strategy may account for slower and less successful rural industrialisation in India than in China. In the latter, a uni-modal agricultural strategy combined with rapid agricultural growth in the post-Mao period, has led to growth of both farm and non-farm output and employment.

Generally, weaker linkages in India may also be due to protective measures in favour of small industry which include: exemption from excise duties and licensing, special access to imported materials and reservation of certain production items exclusively for small industry through government legislation, state purchase of products on a preferential basis, concessional loans from banks and credit institutions, and supply of raw materials on a priority basis. In addition to these concessions, under the Integrated Rural Development Programme (IRDP), very small rural enterprises run by landless workers or tribal people are offered subsidies and low-interest loans.[18] These policy measures may partly explain the lack of incentive on the part of Indian rural small industry to enter into sub-contracting arrangements with urban large industry.[19]

V   CONCLUSION

In this chapter we have considered three types of linkages: (i) output linkages, (ii) employment linkages, and (iii) induced investment linkages. With the data available, we were able to estimate only the first two which are shown to be in conflict in both China and India.

The Hirschmanian linkage approach which we tested, is rather static and examines high linkage activities at a point of time to determine key growth-inducing investments. The dynamic aspects of the linkages are missing from this approach. In some sense linkages are also the outcomes of past policies and measures. For example, the 1981 I/O table for China reflects the outcomes of Maoist policies like local self-reliance. Whether the shifts in policies introduced in 1979 would be reflected in the linkage coefficients can be determined only by estimating these coefficients on the basis of the I/O tables for recent years, e.g. 1985 and later (these tables were not available to us at the time of writing).

We have noted that for both China and India, the output linkages of agriculture are low. This may be due to the subsistence nature of agricultural production in the two countries. If past policies were directed more towards commercialisation of agriculture, the linkages might have been higher. In the case of China (and perhaps also India) these low linkages may also be explained by the type of agricultural price policy adopted before 1979.

Our estimates based on I/O tables for China and India suggest low linkages and sectoral interdependence in both the countries. (These estimates do not capture the effects of subsequent policies of economic liberalisation.) However, our discussion in Section IV suggests that *a priori*, one would expect that there is greater sectoral interdependence and smaller *imbalance* in China than in India. This may be partly because of a different pattern of demand, institutions and policies as was noted by Raj.

Having completed our analysis of the concepts and measurement of uneven development, we are now ready to turn to issues of outcomes in terms of growth (Chapter 5), equity (Chapter 6) and access (Chapters 7 to 9).

APPENDIX 4.1: METHODOLOGY USED FOR ESTIMATING BACKWARD AND FORWARD LINKAGES

The methodology used for estimating the output and employment linkages is well summarised by Bulmer-Thomas.[20] This appendix is mainly based on this summary.

Output Linkages

Backward Linkage

Let us assume that the supply–demand equation for production in a country's economy is: $X = M.1 + f$, where X is an $n \times 1$ gross output vector for n sectors whose elements are x_j ($j = 1, 2, \ldots, n$); M is an $n \times n$ intermediate demand matrix where its element m_{ij} is the value of the intermediate demand of the i-th sector for the j-th sector, f is an $n \times 1$ final demand vector, and $1 = (1,1,\ldots,1)$ is the unit vector.

Further, we assume fixed proportions and constant returns to scale in production, i.e. $m_{ij} = a_{ij} \cdot x_j$, where a_{ij} is constant. Since the a_{ij}s measure the direct stimulus to sector i from investment in sector j, the direct backward linkage can be defined as $\sum_i a_{ij}$ for sector j.

Now we have the input–output production model:

$$X = AX + f \tag{1}$$

where A is the matrix of coefficients a_{ij}, so that:

$$X = (I - A)^{-1} f = Rf \tag{2}$$

where the elements of the matrix R, r_{ij}, denote output generated directly and indirectly in the i-th sector when the final demand of the j-th sector increases by one unit. Therefore, the total backward output linkage for sector j can be defined as $\sum_i r_{ij}$. The *indirect* backward linkage will therefore be $\sum_i (r_{ij} - a_{ij})$.[21]

A normalisation procedure is often carried out by comparing the 'average' stimulus created by one sector with the overall average.[22] It is the total backward linkage index $\dfrac{\sum_i r_{ij}}{(1/n)\sum_i \sum_j r_{ij}}$, where the denominator indicates the average stimulus for the whole economy when all final demands increase by unity. It implies that if a sector's backward linkage index is greater than unity, investment in this sector will generate above-average linkage.

The above backward linkage does not, however, tell us how many sectors will share the benefits of a backward linkage effect of investment in a given sector. Whether the sharing of benefits among sectors is even or uneven can be determined by estimating the variation of the linkage as follows:

$$\frac{\left(1/(n-1)\sum_i (r_{ij} - 1/n\sum_i r_{ij})^2\right)^{1/2}}{(1/n)\sum_i r_{ij}} \tag{3}$$

A low variation in sector j means that the benefits of the stimuli provided by investment in this sector would be evenly shared. Instead, a high variation would imply uneven sharing of benefits.

The ratio of direct to total backward linkage gives the relative importance of the direct effects of the investment in the sector.

Forward Linkage

Jones[23] constructed forward linkage indices on the basis of the following allocation model:

$$X = M'1 + V \tag{4}$$

where V is the vector of value added. By assuming

$$m_{ij} = b_{ij} \cdot X_i \tag{5}$$

we have $X = B'X + V$ and

$$X = (I - B')^{-1}V = D'V \tag{6}$$

where d_{ij} denotes the gross output generated in sector j by using the increased output (which is created by unit increase in value added in sector i) in sector i distributed to sector j.

The total forward linkage is therefore defined as $\Sigma_j d_{ij}$ and the direct forward linkage is defined as $\Sigma_j b_{ij}$ and the indirect linkage is defined as $\sum_j (d_{ij} - b_{ij})$, for sector i.

Employment Linkages

Backward Linkage

If we assume that output is a linear function of employment in each sector, and that labour is homogeneous, we have:

$$n_i = \ell_i/x_i \tag{7}$$

where ℓ_i is employment in sector i, and n_i is a constant for sector i ($i = 1,2,\ldots,n$), which measures the employment created directly in sector i. Therefore, we can define n_i as direct backward employment linkage.

Now

$$\ell = \bar{n}\, X \tag{8}$$

where $\bar{n}$ is diagonal matrix of elements n_i $(n_{ii} = n_i \geq 0;\ n_{ij} = 0,\ i \neq j)$. Substituting X by equation (2) above, we obtain:

$$\ell = \bar{n}\, R\, f = Kf$$

where k_{ij} – the elements of K – measures the employment created directly and indirectly in the i-th sector when the j-th sector's final demand changes by unity. Therefore, the total backward employment linkage for sector j can be defined as $\sum_i k_{ij}$.

Indirect backward employment effects can be obtained by subtracting the direct effects from the total effects, i.e. $(\sum_i k_{ij}) - n_j$.

The ratio of $n_j / \sum_i k_{ij}$ will give the relative importance of the direct employment effects.

Forward Linkage

By substituting (6) into (8), we obtain:

$$\ell = \bar{n}(I - B')^{-1}\, V = Q'V$$

The total forward employment linkage will be defined as $\sum_j q_{ij}$ for sector i.

Since labour is assumed to be homogeneous, the direct forward employment effect is the same as the direct backward employment effect, n_i. Therefore, the indirect forward employment effects is $(\sum_j q_{ij}) - n_i$.

APPENDIX 4.2: ESTIMATION OF EMPLOYMENT FOR CHINA AND INDIA

China

The disaggregated employment data are not published by the State Statistical Bureau of China, and access to such unpublished data is extremely difficult (the author tried to obtain this information unsuccessfully in Beijing in September 1988).

The employment data for agriculture, animal husbandry and forestry was obtained from the World Bank's 'China – Economic Model and Projections' (1985).[24] The data for (i) construction, (ii) transport, posts and telecommunications, and (iii) commerce, catering and service trades, supply and marketing of materials, are obtained from the *Statistical Yearbook of China* (*SYC*).[25]

The employment data for the remaining sectors were estimated by the following methods and assumptions:

(a) To estimate employment in total sideline production, we assume that sideline production is a linear function of labour input (which is a basic assumption of the I/O model). From *SYC* (1984, p. 133) we obtain the output of sideline activities for 1981, which is 37.2 billion yuan; the output of the village-run industrial enterprises is 27.8 billion yuan which is produced by 3.8 million workers.[26] Under the linearity assumption, the total employment in sideline production would be:

$$3.8 = 37.2/27.8 = 5.1 \text{ million}.$$

(b) The number of state-owned employees in the fisheries sector in 1981 is estimated by averaging figures for 1980 (0.084 million) and 1982 (0.083 million) which gives an estimate of 0.0835 million. The number of non-state-owned employees is assumed to grow at a constant annual rate from 1981 to 1985. Since we have the data for 1983 and 1985, we can estimate backwards in time to obtain the number of employees in 1981, which is 3.85 million.[27] Thus, the total employment in the fisheries sector for 1981 is:

$$0.0835 + 3.85 = 3.93 \text{ million}$$

(c) For the industrial sectors, we assume that the proportion of the total labour force in each sector to the total labour force in the industries as a whole is the same as the proportion of the state-owned labour force in each sector to the total state-owned industrial labour force. That is:

$$\frac{(1) \text{ No. of employees in sector } i}{(2) \text{ Total no. of employees in industry}} = \frac{(3) \text{ No. of state-owned employees in sector } i}{(4) \text{ Total no. of state employees in industry}}$$

Since we have the data for (2), (3) and (4), we can estimate data for (1).

India

The employment data for India for 1984–85 are obtained on the basis of the following estimation procedure.

(a) We have the employment data for industries (only the factory sector) for 1983–84 from the *Annual Survey of Industries – Summary of Results for Factory Sectors* (1987, New Delhi).[28] We also have the aggregate employment data on the manufacturing sector from the Government of India (1981). Under the following assumption:

$$\frac{(1) \text{ No. of employees in sector } i \text{ (factories only)}}{(3) \text{ Total no. of employees in factories}} = \frac{(2) \text{ No. of employees in sector } i}{(4) \text{ Total number of employees in manufacturing sector}}$$

(b) The data for (i) agriculture, (ii) construction, (iii) commerce, trade, etc., and (iv) transport and communications, are obtained from *A Technical Note on the Sixth Plan of India (1980–85)*.[29]

(c) Since we have the employment data for agriculture for 1984–85, we assume that in 1984, the forestry, logging and fisheries sectors had the same employment ratio to total agricultural employment as in 1971. The ratios for 1971 are obtained from the *National Accounts Statistics, 1970–71 to 1975–76* (GOI, 1978, p. 126).[30]

Notes and References

*   This chapter was written in collaboration with Dr Yue Ma, Economics Department, University of Strathclyde, Glasgow (formerly University of Manchester), England. It draws heavily on my article (with Yue Ma) entitled: Sectoral Interdependence in the Chinese Economy in a Comparative Perspective, *Applied Economics* (Chapman and Hall, London), August 1990.
1. Economic Forecasting Centre of State Planning Committee, *National Input–Output Table – 1981*, Chinese Version, Beijing, Statistical Press, 1986.
2. Government of India, Planning Commission, *A Technical Note on the Sixth Plan of India (1980–85)*, New Delhi, 1981.
3. Nolan and Paine, in China 1975–1985, in Ashwani Saith (ed.), *The Re-emergence of the Chinese Peasantry*, London, Croom Helm, 1987. Towards an Appraisal of the Impact of Rural Reform.
4. Government of India, Central Statistical Organisation, *Directory of Manufacturing Establishments Survey, 1984–85*, New Delhi (draft, undated).
5. Riskin, *China's Political Economy*, 1987, p. 203.
6. V. R. Panchmukhi, 'Linkages in Industrialisation – A Study of Selected Developing Countries in Asia', *Journal of Development Planning*, no. 8, 1975, pp. 121–65.
7. Ahsanul Habib, Charles Stahl and Mohammed Alauddin, 'Inter-Industry Analysis of Employment Linkages in Bangladesh', *Economics of Planning*, vol. 19, no. 1, 1985, pp. 24–38.
8. Jack Diamond, 'Inter-Industry Indicators of Employment Potential', *Applied Economics*, vol. 7, 1975, pp. 265–73.
9. Panchmukhi, 'Linkages in Industrialisation'.
10. K. N. Raj, 'Linkages in Industrialisation and Development Strategy: Some Basic Issues', *Journal of Development Planning*, no. 8, 1975.
11. World Bank, *CHINA – Long-term Development Issues and Options*, Baltimore, Johns Hopkins University Press, 1985, p. 24.
12. Raj, 'Linkages in Industrialisation and Development Strategy'.
13. C. Rangarajan, *Agricultural Growth and Industrial Performance in India: A Study of Interdependence*, Research Report No. 33, International Food Policy Research Institute, Washington DC, 1982; and C. Rangarajan, 'Industrial Growth – Another Look', *Economic and Political Weekly*, Annual Number, April 1982.
14. Ajit Kumar Ghose, 'The People's Commune, Responsibility Systems and Rural Development in China, 1965–1984', in Ashwani Saith (ed.),

The Re-emergence of the Chinese Peasantry, London, Croom Helm, 1987, pp. 64, 78.

15. V. S. Vyas and George Mathai, 'Farm and Non-farm Employment in Rural Areas: A Perspective for Planning', *Economic and Political Weekly*, Annual Number, February 1978.
16. S. Deshpande and L. K. Deshpande, 'Census of 1981 and the Structure of Employment', *Economic and Political Weekly*, 1 June 1985.
17. Peter B. Hazell and Steven Haggblade, 'Rural–Urban Growth Linkages in India', Agriculture and Rural Development Department, *Working Papers, No. WPs 430, Washington DC, World Bank*, May 1990.
18. Amiya Kumar Bagchi, *Public Intervention and Industrial Restructuring in China, India and Republic of Korea*, New Delhi, ILO/ARTEP, 1987, pp. 130–31.
19. Ashok V. Desai, 'Technology Acquisition and Applications: Interpretations of the Indian Experience', in Robert E. B. Lucas and Gustav F. Papanek (eds), *The Indian Economy – Recent Developments and Future Prospects*, Delhi, Oxford University Press, 1988.
20. V. Bulmer-Thomas, *Input–Output Analysis in Developing Countries*, Chichester, John Wiley & Sons, 1982.
21. H. B. Chenery and T. Watanabe, 'International Comparisons of the Structure of Production', *Econometrica*, no. 4, 1958.
22. P. N. Rasmussen, *Studies in Intersectoral Relations*, Amsterdam, North Holland, 1957.
23. Leroy P. Jones, 'The Measurement of Hirschmanian Linkages', *Quarterly Journal of Economics*, May 1976.
24. World Bank, *China – Long-term Development Issues and Options*, Washington DC, 1985, Annex 4 on 'Economic Model and Projections'.
25. State Statistical Bureau, *Statistical Yearbook of China*, 1981, p. 106.
26. Samuel P. S. Ho, 'The Asian Experience in Rural Non-agricultural Development and its Relevance for China', *World Bank Staff Working Papers No. 757*, Washington DC, 1986.
27. *Agricultural Yearbook of China* (State Statistical Bureau), 1981 to 1985.
28. Government of India, Central Statistical Organisation, *Annual Survey of Industries – Summary of Results for Factory Sectors*, New Delhi, 1987, pp. 70–87.
29. Government of India, *A Technical Note on the Sixth Plan of India (1980–85)*, New Delhi, 1981.
30. Government of India, *National Accounts Statistics, 1970–71 to 1975–76*, New Delhi, 1978, p. 126.

Part II
Development Outcomes

5 Development Outcomes: Growth

This chapter analyses the development performance in China and India in the light of the strategies and policies discussed in Chapters 3 and linkages and imbalances examined in Chapter 4. The declared objectives of the strategies were both growth and equity. In this chapter, we examine whether rapid rates of growth were achieved in practice, and if so, whether they were due to the strategies that were adopted. To answer these questions, sectoral output and productivity growth rates as well as rates of sectoral investments during the different time periods are reviewed.

I OUTPUT GROWTH

1.1 India

India's growth rates fluctuated a great deal almost throughout the period from 1961 to 1982, indicating inherent instabilities in the economy. The use of three-year averages did not contribute much to a reduction of these fluctuations.

The overall growth rate has generally been below the plan targets (with the exception of a few short periods) suggesting internal imbalance and shortfalls in plan achievements. Consistency in plan targets and their achievement would imply that distortions preventing growth are avoided, that sluggish growth in one sector does not retard growth in other sectors. Below-target rates of long-run growth of about 3.5 per cent (instead of the targeted growth rate of 5 per cent) meant a very slow growth of per capita income particularly since the population growth rate has been quite high throughout the planning period.[1]

Apart from the below-target growth rate, Indian growth has also been much slower than that of the Chinese and most other countries.

Nevertheless, the strategy of heavy industrialisation adopted during the Second Plan (1956–61) achieved positive results in terms of a high rate of growth of net value added in the capital-goods sector compared to that in the consumer-goods sector. The share of capital

Table 5.1   Sectoral output shares (China and India) (percentages)

Sector \ Year	I. China (share of national income at 1970 prices)					
	1954	1958	1964	1971	1979	1985
Agriculture	63.8	50.7	52.1	39.4	32.3	32.2
Manufacturing	15.0	27.2	29.1	42.2	49.9	48.9
Construction	2.9	5.0	4.0	4.2	3.8	3.7
Transport	3.1	4.0	3.8	3.9	3.8	3.7
Trade	15.1	13.0	10.8	10.3	10.0	10.9
Total	100.0	100.0	100.0	100.0	100.0	100.0

	II. India (share of NDP at 1970 prices)				
	1951–52	1960–61	1970–71	1978–79	1982–83
Agriculture	70.4	64.7	58.5	52.9	51.1
Manufacturing	11.6	14.2	16.3	17.0	19.0
Construction	4.4	5.2	6.6	5.7	6.1
Transport	3.7	4.5	5.6	7.8	7.9
Trade	9.9	11.4	13.0	16.6	15.9
Total	100.0	100.0	100.0	100.0	100.0

Sources: Based on *Statistical Yearbook of China* (1986, pp. 40–1) for China, and *National Accounts Statistics* for India.

Notes: (1) National income and NDP are three-year moving averages.
(2) Figures may not add to 100 due to rounding.
(3) Manufacturing includes mining and quarrying (it covers sectors 6 to 21 of I/O tables noted in Chapter 4).
(4) For China, trade includes: commerce, catering, service trades and supply and marketing of materials. For India, it includes: trade, hotels and restaurants. Neither country's figures include the whole services sector since such aggregate data are not available for China.

goods in industrial output rose from 5 per cent in 1956 to 18 per cent in 1979–80.[2] A high rate of growth of output in the capital-goods sector however did not contribute to raising the overall growth rate because of the small initial share of industry in the GDP (see Table 5.1). In contrast, in China a high rate of industrial growth contributed to raising the overall growth rate because of the much higher initial weight of the industrial sector.

During the decade 1960–70, special exogenous factors, on which strategy had little control, accentuated sectoral imbalances in the Indian economy. First, conflicts with Pakistan and China during

1962–65 led to a shift of resources away from development pro-grammes. Secondly, severe drought in 1966 and 1967 resulted in an absolute decline in GDP. During the third decade, 1970–78 (Fourth Plan, 1969–74, and Fifth Plan, 1975–80), inter-sectoral imbalances got aggravated due partly to two exogenous factors – the Bangladesh crisis of 1971 and the oil price shocks of 1973.[3]

Having examined briefly the overall output growth we now turn to output trends for agriculture and industry separately.

Agricultural Growth. Fluctuations in the national rate of growth of output were accompanied by fluctuations in agricultural growth rates which were low despite the Green Revolution. From the 1950s to the 1980s, the agricultural growth rate (based on NDP at 1970–71 prices) was much lower than the industrial growth rate. The agricultural growth rate in India was well below the rate for China (also on the basis of GNP adjusted for purchasing power parity).

Agricultural output grew faster in the 1950s and again during 1978–83 than during the 1960s and early 1970s (see Table 5.2). Bardhan has explained output variability in terms of agriculture's increased dependence on inputs like fertilisers and the increased incidence of floods, deforestation and soil erosion.[4] Although wheat yields in the northwestern parts of India did increase, this rise in land productivity did not contribute to the overall growth of agricultural output. During the early 1980s, that is, during the Sixth Plan (1980–85), an acceleration of growth of agricultural output seems to have resulted primarily from an increased utilisation of available infrastructure, better irrigation facilities and an increase in yield per acre (or land productivity). This turned India from a net importer of foodgrains to an exporter.

To what extent was this outcome due to the nature of the agricul-tural strategy adopted and the agricultural price, distribution and investment policies that were followed? A policy package for the agricultural sector included PL 480 imports from the United States, fair price shops, internal government procurement of foodgrains and creation of food zones preventing inter-zonal free trade.[5]

A low agricultural growth rate in the 1960s and 1970s can partly be attributed to the policy decision in the Second Plan (1956–61) to allocate relatively lower public investment resources to agriculture than during the First Plan period (1951–56). A comparison between Table 5.2 on sectoral growth rates and Table 5.4 on sectoral invest-ment shares shows that agricultural growth performance is largely

Table 5.2   Annual sectoral growth of output (China and India)
(percentages)

Sector \ Year	I. China (Annual growth of national income at 1970 prices)				
	1954–58	1959–63	1964–71	1972–79	1979–85
Agriculture	1.8	−0.4	3.7	3.0	8.1
Manufacturing	25.0	−9.8	13.8	7.7	7.7
Construction	23.9	−14.1	8.5	4.8	10.0
Transport	15.4	−12.0	8.0	5.5	7.3
Trade	3.8	−7.3	7.2	5.7	9.5
National average	7.9	−5.4	7.9	5.6	8.1
Per capita annual growth rate	5.4	−6.1	5.1	4.0	6.7

	II. India (Annual NDP growth at 1970 prices)			
	1951–60	1960–70	1970–78	1978–83
Agriculture	2.9	1.9	2.1	3.2
Manufacturing	5.8	4.8	5.1	6.7
Construction	5.3	6.2	3.0	5.7
Transport	7.0	5.7	6.6	4.5
Trade	4.2	5.1	5.4	3.1
National average	3.7	3.1	3.5	4.1
Per capita annual growth rate	1.6	1.0	1.3	2.1

Sources: Based on *Statistical Yearbook of China* (1986, p. 41) for China, and
NAS for India.

Notes: (1) National income and NDP data are three-year moving averages.
(2) Figures may not add up to 100 due to rounding.

explained by trends in investment shares so that a fall in the agricultural growth rate corresponds to a decline in its investment share. Furthermore, the composition of industrial investment was also skewed in favour of heavy industry and against agricultural inputs. Thus lower priority was given to investment in fertiliser plants than to heavy engineering plants. This may have further impeded agricultural growth.[6]

However, from the Third Plan onwards there were policy shifts in development strategy. While the 1950s were characterised by industrial development and institutional changes in agriculture (e.g. land reforms), during the 1960s investment in irrigation, fertilisers and new technology of HYVs (high-yielding varieties) received priority. The agricultural policy also stressed price incentives to farmers and supplies of inputs to them at favourable prices.[7]

The effects of the above favourable measures on agricultural growth were slow to occur, perhaps partly due to the severe drought of the mid-1960s. Hence lowest agricultural growth rate during the 1960s (see Table 5.2) cannot be attributed entirely to policy: bad weather conditions were partly to blame.

Industrial Growth. During 1970–82, compared with other countries the average rate of industrial growth of middle-income countries – that is, 5.3 per cent – was one percentage point higher than that of India. The Indian rate during 1970–82 was only slightly above that of 23 low-income countries according to the World Bank classification.[8]

The rates of industrial growth have also been well below the industrial targets laid down in successive plans. (For example, the target growth rates for industry for the first three Five-Year plans were 7, 10.5 and 10.7 per cent per annum respectively whereas the achieved rates were 6, 7.2 and 8 per cent per annum.)[9]

Imbalances were observed in the divergent growth rates for output of consumer, intermediate and capital goods. During the 1965–66 to 1979–80 period, heavy machinery industry (both electrical and non-electrical) grew much faster than the consumer goods industries like food and textiles. From the mid-1960s onwards the growth of output of heavy industry decelerated whereas the growth of consumer goods industries continued without any acceleration.

There is considerable controversy regarding the causes of industrial stagnation in India. The explanations put forward by different authors include: slow growth of agricultural output and resulting low wage goods supply and low demand for industrial goods; a slow-down of the rate of growth of public investment especially in infrastructure like railways and power; and industrial regulations and controls (e.g. industrial licensing system and indiscriminate protection from foreign competition).[10]

The industrial licensing system was intended to ensure that the choice of industrial plants, their technology and location would lead to social instead of private profitability. No systematic criteria seem to have been used to measure such profitability, or to consider whether social profitability could be achieved through fiscal incentives instead of direct controls and government intervention.[11]

Other objectives of the licensing system were to promote balanced spatial development and to control monopolies. These objectives do not seem to have been achieved either. The policy of industrial location of plants was guided more by political considerations than those of economic efficiency. Moreover, a dispersal of industrial plants across different states was considered to raise competition by increasing the number of plants and to lower monopoly power. However, in the absence of any provisions to prevent large industrial houses from acquiring existing undertakings, the industrial licensing system remained ineffective in checking concentration of industrial ownership.

A sudden jump in industrial production has taken place since the mid-1980s. It may be argued that this may in part have been the result of a new liberalisation policy to foster competition, efficiency and technological progress. But such a causal relationship is not likely since the effect of liberalisation measures would be felt only after a time lag. It is more plausible that the accelerated industrial growth was due to the 'buoyant demand conditions led by the resurgence of agricultural growth as also the good supporting performance of key infrastructure sectors'.[12] As noted in Table 5.2, the annual agricultural growth rate increased from 2.1 per cent in the 1970s to 3.2 per cent in the late 1970s and early 1980s. Some increase in industrial output may also be explained simply by the 'wider coverage of industries and reallocation of weights rather than from technological progress, improvement in productivity or better utilisation of capacity'.[13]

It is also mainly the import-oriented consumer durables industry (which caters for a small upper-income class) which has expanded rapidly since 1984–85, perhaps as a result of the policy of industrial delicensing. A recent report of the Indian Economic Advisory Council (the Chakravarty Report) states: 'the growth of intermediate goods and consumer non-durables has averaged significantly lower than the growth of consumer durables. This may reflect an industrial production pattern skewed in favour of richer sections of society. It also reflects the rapid growth in the organised sector incomes in this period.'[14] It is therefore quite possible that the new liberalisation measures (e.g. financial incentives) will reinforce rather than reduce existing income gaps between the rich and the poor.

The structural imbalance in the Indian economy is reflected not only in the pattern of growth and production discussed above. It is also manifested in the fiscal system, balance of payments problem and inflationary pressures. The fiscal imbalance is reflected in the growing reliance on deficit spending, increase in defence spending and the increasing cost of central and state subsidies. Exports are becoming increasingly import-intensive; so is the production of consumer durables. Increasing imports have caused a foreign exchange constraint which has been further exacerbated by an increase in debt service payments, a levelling off of worker' remittances from abroad, and the drought of 1987–88 which led to heavy imports of food and other essential commodities.[15]

Thus the types of strategy and policies followed had no doubt an impact on growth performance, but a number of exogenous factors beyond the control of the planners and policy-makers also had a role to play.

1.2 China

Like India, China has also suffered from instability and imbalances in overall output growth as well as from wide gaps between agricultural and industrial growth rates (the latter particularly till the beginning of the post-Mao period).

In China, foreign trade and increasing imports in the 1980s may also partly explain economic imbalances. Although like India China's share of foreign trade is small, it has been increasing during the post-Mao period. Most of the exogenous shocks are likely to be limited particularly to export processing zones. However, foreign aid (China was much less dependent on aid than India at least until 1980) may account for fewer imbalances than in the case of India where fluctuations in the volume of foreign aid during different periods seem to have had a significant impact on the degree of deviation of sectoral growth rates from the average growth rates in the economy.

Agricultural Growth. While the overall output growth rates have been far higher than those in India, the rates of agricultural output growth during the Mao period were well below what could have been achieved through the pursuit of the right policies and incentives. (See Table 5.2.) For example, grain output increased only a little faster than the growth of population so that per capita grain consumption in the mid-1970s was the same as in the mid-1950s.[16] While historically the Chinese PRC agricultural growth was reasonable compared to that in the earlier periods, it was rather low by international standards. Neither was it much higher than that of Indian agriculture.

Lardy has argued that allocative inefficiencies in Chinese agriculture were caused by production planning. Had liberal market policies and price mechanism been introduced, higher agricultural output could have been achieved. However, this is not necessarily true since in both China and India the total factor productivity in agriculture had declined although India adopted a more open price mechanism than China (see below).

Wong has estimated that in both China and India the growth of agricultural output was able to keep pace with that of population thanks to an increase in inputs like fertilisers and machinery.[17] However, this increase was achieved at the cost of efficiency since technical change had only a limited impact.

Agricultural output can be raised either by raising the area under cultivation or by raising yields per acre. Since the area declined, the only feasible solution was to raise yields through mechanisation and increase in agricultural inputs. Despite the much higher yields in China than in India, the agricultural output of foodgrains declined in 1985 and subsequently (see below). This shortfall necessitated grain imports, thus creating balance of payments problems.

Between 1985 and 1988 – the second phase of economic reforms – output of foodgrains as well as of such cash crops as cotton, stagnated. Average grain output per capita dropped from 394 kg in 1984 to 326 kg in 1988, and cotton output per capita during the same period declined from 6.1 kg to 3.9 kg.[18]

The above discussion suggests that the rapid agricultural output growth during the first phase of rural economic reforms could not be sustained during the second phase, thus raising the degree of imbalance. This situation is consistent with the U-turn shown in the estimation of the Lardy index (see Chapter 3, Table 3.1).

Although during the first phase of reforms (1979–85) the agricultural and industrial growth rates were nearly in balance, during the period 1985 to 1988, the growth of agricultural output lagged far behind that of industrial output. This period witnessed an average rate of industrial growth of 17.8 per cent per annum as against that of 3.9 per cent for agriculture.[19] This performance seems to be inconsistent with the policies favouring rural economic reforms which should, in principle, have raised agricultural output growth. Does it mean that the rural reforms have run their course and reached saturation point?

The slowing down of growth of agricultural output (foodgrains) since the mid-1980s seems to have been due to a lack of adequate state investment in agriculture, below-market procurement price, lack of private investment in agriculture due to a shift of investible resources to quicker-yielding rural industry and urban sideline activity, poor weather conditions especially in the north and a national decline in crop area. Low private investment in agriculture may be explained by terms of trade which were not particularly favourable to agriculture since the first-stage reforms showed only a moderate adjustment in the trend. Furthermore, the Chinese policy of decollectivisation may also have had some negative impact. Since the abolition of communes, minor irrigation works have not been as well maintained as earlier, with the result that growth in agricultural output might have suffered. Finally, the government seems to have underestimated the importance of long-term state investment in infrastructure to sustain a significant and stable agricultural growth.

Industrial Growth. In contrast to industrial stagnation in India, China recorded impressive rates of industrial growth throughout the PRC since 1949, particularly during the Mao period (1954–58 and 1964–71) (see Table 5.2). High industrial growth rates have been accompanied by a high and constantly rising share of industrial investment (see Table 5.4). This rapid industrial growth was clearly policy-induced. It is most unlikely that China could have achieved very high industrial growth without a clear policy of primacy of capital accumulation, sacrifice of consumption and emphasis on heavy industry.

Emphasis on heavy industry and relative neglect of light industry has been noticeable since the early 1950s. After a temporary parity between growth rates of light and heavy industry intra-industrial imbalances grew rapidly. In 1950, the share of light industry in gross value of production was 70 per cent, whereas in 1979 it was only 39.5 per cent. In the post-Mao period, a significant readjustment between light and heavy industry has taken place. Heavy industry has become much less dominant than during the Mao period.[20]

Within the heavy industrial sector there has been structural disequilibrium, with the energy, transport and raw materials sectors lagging behind the rest, leading to increased imports of raw materials like rolled steel, copper and zinc. During the first three-quarters of

1988, the output of raw iron, cloth and processed steel rose by only 4.9, 6.1 and 8.4 per cent per annum respectively while the real growth of industrial production (as noted above) was over 17 per cent.[21]

The above imbalance seems to have induced the Chinese government to give greater attention to the infrastructural requirements of industry, e.g. electricity, transport and communications.

II GROWTH OF AGRICULTURAL AND INDUSTRIAL PRODUCTIVITY

We now turn to growth of productivity in agriculture and industry and examine whether the policy measures adopted had much to do with the productivity trends over time.

Labour productivity in agriculture and industry for China and India is estimated in Table 5.3 on the basis of GNP/GDP data expressed in 1980 international dollars adjusted for purchasing power parity. We have taken the census years for India for lack of reliable time series data for workers employed in agriculture and industry.

2.1 Agricultural Productivity

Between 1951 and 1981, the GDP per worker in agriculture in India increased only marginally and more slowly than the GDP per worker in industry. Thus the gap in relative productivity differential between agriculture and industry has been continuously rising. In the case of China on the other hand, although GNP per worker in agriculture was much lower than that in industry, it was much higher than in India. This gap had a tendency to decline after 1971 as is shown in Figure 5.1 which also demonstrates that GNP per worker in industry in China is much higher than that in India.

In China, agricultural GNP per worker more than doubled between 1951 and 1985, but it actually declined in 1961, the year following the Great Leap Forward period. This doubling of agricultural output per worker in China contrasts with its near constancy in India.

In interpreting data in Table 5.3 one needs to bear in mind that the output data for China and India are not strictly comparable. In China, prior to 1984, the output of village industry was included under agricultural output, whereas in India it is included under

Table 5.3   Ratio of GDP per worker in industry to GDP per worker in
agriculture (China vs. India)

Year	China GNP per worker in industry (at 1980 international dollars)	GNP per worker in agriculture	Ratio	India GDP per worker in industry (at 1980 international dollars)	GDP per worker in agriculture	Ratio
1951[1]	4,923	1,048	4.70	1,385	925	1.50
1961	5,980	844	7.08	1,987	1,017	1.95
1971	12,081	1,247	9.69	2,951	1,166	2.53
1981	13,536	2,064	6.56	3,475	1,159	3.00
1985	14,172	2,991	4.74	–	–	–

Sources: Data on GNP/GDP for China and India are taken from Robert Summers and Alan Heston, 'A New Set of International Comparisons of Real Product and Prices: Estimates for 130 Countries, 1950–1985', *Review of Income and Wealth*, March 1988. These data are adjusted for purchasing power parity.

The data for GDP in agriculture and industry were derived by using shares of GDP in these two sectors (taken from the *Statistical Yearbook of China* and *National Accounts Statistics of India*).

Note: The data for workers employed in agriculture and industry for India were taken from the Censuses of population, and for China they were taken from *Statistical Yearbook of China*. For India, data for 1961 and 1971 are taken from CSO: *National Accounts Statistics*, January 1978, Appendix 1 on 'Distribution of Workers'. As there were differences between the two censuses in respect of identification criteria of workers and non-workers, the Registrar-General conducted a resurvey of both the censuses of population on a sample basis (during December 1971 and July 1972). The estimates for India of the number of workers for 1961 amd 1971 are according to the 1971 concept.

[1] Data are for 1952 for China.

industrial output. After 1985 therefore this reclassification would have had the effect of lowering relative output per industrial worker.[22] Furthermore, data are in terms of GNP for China and GDP for India.

What explains the near constancy of agricultural labour productivity in India? Growth in agricultural labour productivity can be attributed to two factors: (a) a rapid growth of the industrial sector to absorb surplus labour in agriculture, and (b) technological change in agriculture through the Green Revolution and/or biotechnological breakthroughs. Neither of these two factors seems to have had any favourable effect on the growth of labour productivity in Indian agriculture. This may have been due to several years of bad weather and somewhat slow initial diffusion and adoption of the Green Revolution technology. A deceleration of industrial growth from the mid-1960s onwards did not allow a rapid absorption of agricultural surplus labour. Neither did the Green Revolution contribute to a reduction in this labour surplus. It may be that the level of labour productivity in agriculture in India was too low at the time of introduction of HYVs (high-yielding varieties) to enable the farm sector to make appreciable private investments in new technology.[23] Furthermore, growth of population added to an already sizeable workforce. These factors may partly explain why the share of the labour force in Indian agriculture has remained stable and high between 1951 and 1971.

The Chinese labour productivity in agriculture rose particularly rapidly since 1981 thanks to the agricultural responsibility system. However, the conditions for such labour and land agricultural productivity increases (e.g. agricultural mechanisation, organisational innovations and governmental measures for building up infrastructure through investments in water, soil conservation and chemical fertilisers) were in many ways laid during the earlier Mao period.[24] The organisation of communes also had a favourable effect on agriculture through mobilisation of rural surplus labour for capital construction in irrigation and drainage, although in other respects it may have contributed to inefficiencies.

But why, during the Mao period, did not agricultural output and productivity increase much (see Figure 5.1)? Wrong policies such as low public investment in agriculture and an absence of incentives may be two main explanatory factors. Riskin has argued that low grain procurement prices and local foodgrains self-sufficiency failed to provide adequate motivation for growth of agricultural output and productivity.[25] In addition peasants were reluctant to make private investments.

So far we have examined only a partial index of agricultural productivity. But a more appropriate index of the efficiency of resource use in agriculture would be total factor productivity or a combined effect of capital and labour inputs. Wong has computed total factor productivity in Chinese and Indian agriculture on a comparative basis.[26] His estimates relate to physical outputs and inputs and are based on statistically estimated production elasticities in the absence of detailed price information. They show that in both countries during 1960–83, while land and labour productivity in agriculture increased, the total factor productivity declined. This

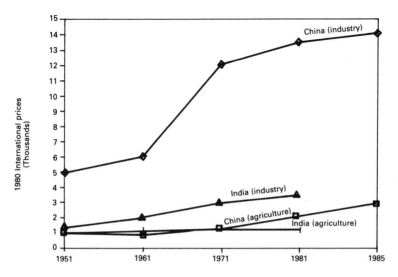

Figure 5.1   GNP per worker in agriculture and industry in China and India

Source: Based on data in Table 5.3.

inconsistency of trends between partial and total factor productivities is in contrast to the historical experience of the advanced countries where the two moved in the same direction. The similarity between China and India is peculiar considering that the two countries followed different agricultural policies with divergent political systems. A similar pattern of agricultural development would therefore suggest that the policy and institutional differences did not have much effect on the outcome.

2.2 Industrial Productivity

Significant gaps in agricultural/industrial productivity in China also explain serious output growth imbalances. As shown in Figure 5.1, China's industrial productivity is much higher than its agricultural productivity; it is also much higher than the industrial productivity in India. Several factors explain this phenomenon in China. First, a very high degree of capital intensity accounts for high industrial productivity. Second, control of rural to urban migration may tend to keep agricultural labour productivity low (especially if rural industry is not growing rapidly) and industrial labour productivity high. Third,

China is an exceptional developing country in which the share of GNP originating in industry was over 50 per cent in 1987 (compared to about 20 per cent in India). Lack of tertiary activities, which were considered non-productive in the socialist national accounting system, contributed to a relatively very high share of industrial GNP in China. On the other hand, in India and other developing countries, the shares of GNP originating in services and tertiary activities are sizeable.

In India, deceleration of industrial growth, in the mid-1960s and subsequently till the mid-1980s, may have been partly due to the low levels and slow growth of industrial productivity. In fact, efficiency in factor use in manufacturing actually declined. Estimates of total factor productivity growth per annum for the manufacturing sector for the period 1959–60 to 1979–80, ranged from −0.2 per cent to 0.3 per cent.[27] However, between 1975–76 and 1981–82 factor productivity growth improved, rising to 0.8 per cent per annum.[28]

Slow improvement in total factor productivity suggests that increase in industrial labour productivity was due to an increase mainly in capital intensity. An increase in industrial incremental capital–output ratios (ICORs) (see Table 5.5) seems to confirm this phenomenon. Several factors have accounted for low efficiency in factor use: underutilisation of capacity, fragmentation of production units into uneconomic sizes partly due to a policy of regional dispersal, and rising costs of materials and services provided by the public sector.

In the case of China, there are very divergent estimates of total factor productivity in industry. Many of these estimates show that long-term productivity growth was either constant or even negative.[29] Recent adjustments and revised estimates by Chen *et al.*, Jefferson and Rawski show an annual rate of increase of 1.3 per cent, which is higher than the Indian estimates noted above.[30] However, the approach followed by the above authors may have led to an overestimation of total factor productivity in China. They seem to have ignored depreciation of new investment and scrapping of capital each year which would tend to underestimate growth of capital assets.[31]

A recent study based on a sample survey of 400 state-owned manufacturing enterprises shows that total factor productivity recorded a positive growth rate between 1980 and 1985 reaching its peak in 1985. It started declining thereafter, particularly in 1986 and 1987 presumably due to the adverse effects of an overheated economy.[32] Was the higher total factor productivity in the post-Mao period due to the policies of economic liberalisation? There is no clear evidence of this causation particularly since liberalisation and industrial economic reforms have not been as rapid and extensive as was originally intended. Furthermore, policy shifts like reduction of compulsory procurement targets were introduced at the same time as such institutional reforms as decentralised decision-making in the agricultural and industrial sectors.[33] Thus it becomes rather complex to disentangle the factors that accounted for an accelerated growth in total factor productivity in the post-Mao period.

III SECTORAL INVESTMENT AND EFFICIENCY

The decline in total factor productivity or its very slow growth noted above suggests allocative inefficiencies and low rates of return on investments. In the absence of any direct estimates of marginal rates of return on sectoral investments, we resort to an indirect measure through sectoral investment shares and incremental capital–output ratios (ICORs).

The sectoral investment shares for China (collective and private investments are not included) and India (figures are for total investment including private investment) are given in Table 5.4. In China the gap between agriculture and industry was narrower during 1963–70 than during the two subsequent periods.

The investment share of Indian agriculture in the past two decades was more than twice or three times as high as that for China except during the last period (Table 5.4). The share of investment in Chinese agriculture during 1978–84 was lower than the share during 1953–62. Although during the Sixth Plan (1980–85) the planned share of agriculture was 11 to 14 per cent, the actual share during this period did not exceed 3 to 4 per cent.[34] The government lowered its share of investment in agriculture on the assumption that private investments would increase as a result of growth in agricultural household incomes in the wake of rural economic reforms. However, it appears that such private investment did not increase as expected. Indeed, farm household savings were channelled more into housing and consumer durables (e.g. washing machines and TV sets) than into agricultural fixed capital assets, irrigation and land improvement. Since 1978, the stocks of consumer durables have risen extremely rapidly – the number of TV sets possessed per 100 rural households rose from 0.1 in 1978 to 6.6 in 1988[35] and of radios from 5.1 to 21.1 during the same period. Furthermore, as noted in Chapter 4,

Table 5.4   Sectoral investment shares (China and India) (percentages)
(1970 prices)

Sector \ Year	I. China 1954–58	1959–63	1963–70	1971–78	1978–84
Agriculture	13.3	16.9	12.3	11.3	7.6
Manufacturing	44.4	57.7	57.6	65.6	72.2
Construction	6.8	2.0	3.3	1.7	1.6
Transport	28.7	20.4	22.7	18.0	13.7
Trade	6.8	3.0	4.1	3.2	4.9
Total of five sectors	100.0	100.0	100.0	100.0	100.0

	II. India 1950–59	1959–69	1969–77	1977–82
Agriculture	37.2	27.1	27.8	29.7
Manufacturing	30.9	41.0	40.2	41.0
Construction	3.4	4.7	2.8	3.3
Transport	19.1	21.6	16.9	15.4
Trade	9.4	5.5	12.2	10.5
Total of five sectors	100.0	100.0	100.0	100.0

Sources: Based on *Statistical Yearbook of China* (1986, p. 376) for China, and *National Accounts Statistics* for India.

Notes: (1) Figures do not always add up to 100 due to rounding.
(2) While for China, figures are for state investment, for India they are for total investment.
(3) In the case of China, the figures for manufacturing may be overstated since the capital stock data include residential construction and such other 'non-productive' investments which the state-owned industrial enterprises provide, e.g. housing, schools, health clinics and stores for workers.

investment in agriculture financed out of profits of rural industry seems to have stabilised or declined since the mid-1980s due to a fall in the rate of profit of such investment and growing investment opportunities in urban areas.

It is not clear why so little private investment in China has gone into land improvement. Wiens notes that this may be 'due to low crop prices and consequently low rates of return in crop cultivation'.[36] Another factor may be uncertainty and risk due to short land lease. Land in China continues to be state-owned – it is leased to peasants for an average of fifteen years which is not long enough to induce long-term household investments. However, land lease in some areas has been for as long as thirty years which suggests that this factor is not as important as low rates of return.

'Accumulation' by the communes also declined by 35 per cent during 1978–81. Although data are not available it would appear that collective labour accumulation (construction and maintenance of ditches, irrigation channels, etc.) declined with a switch in agricultural organisation from the communes to the households.

Notwithstanding the relatively low share of investment per hectare, applications of chemical fertiliser in China in 1977 were about three times the average level in India (see Chapter 7). From 1977 to 1980, fertiliser applications in China grew more than 70 per cent compared to less than 35 per cent in India. Furthermore, there was an appreciable growth in large and medium tractors and in the proportion of irrigated land area. Although India also expanded land area under irrigation and multiple cropping, its efforts seem to have been less successful due partly to organisational and institutional constraints, e.g. an absence of local community organisations to tackle water management problems at the farm level.[37]

In the subsistence agrarian economies like those of China and India, investment is not the only constraint to agricultural growth: many institutional and technological constraints like inadequate irrigation infrastructure and its poor maintenance can also account for slow agricultural growth. The high rates of growth of agricultural output in China in the early 1980s could in fact be explained partly by the organisational/institutional innovations during the Mao period. In the case of India, inadequate infrastructure and organisational bottlenecks in maintenance of irrigation facilities have been noted as some of the factors retarding agricultural growth.

The wide gaps between China and India in respect of agricultural investment are somewhat misleading. In the case of China, the investment figure of 10 per cent or so is an underestimate since collective farm investments and labour investment (which were substantial) are not included. Furthermore, the fact that price subsidies on the use of non-farm inputs in agriculture were as high as 30 to 50 per cent would further raise the share of investment in Chinese agriculture. Finally, investment in agricultural inputs (fertilisers, agricultural machinery, etc.) also needs to be taken into account.

Despite the much higher share of investment in agriculture in India throughout the 1950–82 period, agricultural output has not grown as

Table 5.5   Incremental capital–output ratios (China and India)
(1970 prices)

| Sector \\ Year | I. China | | | | |
	1954–58	1959–63	1964–71	1972–79	1979–85
Agriculture	1.33	−19.09	1.03	1.54	0.35
Manufacturing	0.98	−4.15	1.70	2.70	2.27
Construction	0.83	−0.63	1.38	1.32	0.48
Transport	5.79	−8.16	10.45	12.58	6.03
Trade	1.34	−0.72	0.76	0.83	0.59
Average for five sectors	1.36	−4.07	1.80	2.61	1.48

| | II. India | | | |
	1951–60	1960–70	1970–78	1978–83
Agriculture	2.12	3.74	4.40	4.57
Manufacturing	4.71	8.98	8.76	8.97
Construction	1.52	2.06	2.70	2.55
Transport	7.43	11.88	7.93	11.53
Trade	2.49	1.37	3.11	5.38
Average for five sectors	3.06	5.03	5.56	6.39

Sources: Based on Statistical Yearbook of China (1986, pp. 40–1, 376) and investment deflators from Chen et al., China Quarterly, June 1988, for China, and National Accounts Statistics for India.

fast as in China. Could it be due to greater capital efficiency in Chinese agriculture in which the ICORs for all the four time periods were much lower than those for India? (see Table 5.5). Part of the explanation for these low ratios may be the underpricing of investment goods (in relation to world prices) in China and their overpricing in India. There are some indications that capital in Chinese agriculture is used much more intensively than in India. The high ICORs in India on the other hand are explained partly by inefficiency in the utilisation and management of capital. The composition of agricultural investments in India also seems to be different from that in China. Much of the Indian investment is made into large hydroelectric or irrigation projects with very low capacity utilisation and poor water management systems.

The Chinese policy of forcing the rural population/labour to stay in the rural areas would also tend to explain under-capitalisation of agriculture, leading to a large gap in capital efficiency between agriculture and non-agriculture. In the post-Mao period, under-capitalisation of agriculture may also be explained by a relatively greater profitability and quick-yielding effects of investments in rural industry and other non-farm activities. Collective and private investments seem to have shifted from the farm to the non-farm sector.

In the industrial sector, most of the private investment resources have been channelled into quick-yielding and high-profitability sectors like consumer durables. In contrast, the share of public investment in the transportation, infrastructure and energy sectors has been declining. Investment imbalance is also recorded between light and heavy industry. Throughout the PRC period, heavy industry accounted for the highest share of total industrial investment. Clearly this resulted from the official policy of high rates of capital accumulation at times even at the expense of a rise in consumption.

The dispersion of sectoral ICORs around the national average, (through the Harrod-Domar accounting entity) imply differences in sectoral savings rates. In a mixed economy like that of India, a constraint to industrialisation may not simply be a limited capacity of the capital goods sector (as assumed in the Mahalanobis model) but a lack of incentive to save and invest which reflects a low demand for capital goods.[38] This factor would pose less of a constraint in a centrally planned economy like that of China.

IV CONCLUSION

This chapter has attempted to explore whether development outcome in terms of growth of output and productivity can be clearly attributed to the nature of strategies and policies adopted by China and India. The tentative conclusion that we reach is that in both countries some of the outcome was certainly policy-induced. But the evidence is not all that clearcut, particularly in India, where several exogenous factors (like bad harvests and wars) interacted with the role of policies in influencing agricultural growth in particular and overall output growth in general. However, in the case of China (particularly in the post-Mao period but also during the Mao period), the growth as well as stagnation of agricultural output and productivity is much more clearly linked with the types of agricultural policies adopted.

Notes and References

1. NCAER, *Focus on Some Major Imbalances in the Indian Economy*, paper for the Annual Day of the NCAER, New Delhi, 5 April 1986.
2. Isher Judge Ahluwalia, *Industrial Growth in India*, Delhi, Oxford University Press, 1985, Ch. 1.
3. P. N. Dhar, 'The Indian Economy – Past Performance and Current Issues', in Robert E. Lucas and Gustav F. Papanek, (eds), *The Indian Economy – Recent Developments and Future Prospects*, Delhi, Oxford University Press, 1988.
4. Pranab Bardhan, *The Political Economy of Development in India*, Oxford, Basil Blackwell, 1984, p. 16.
5. See Jagdish N. Bhagwati and Sukhamoy Chakravarty, 'Contributions to Indian Economic Analysis: A Survey', *American Economic Review*, Supplement, Part 2, September 1969.
6. Jagdish Bhagwati and Padma Desai, *INDIA: Planning for Industrialisation*, London, Oxford University Press, 1970, pp. 115–17.
7. See John W. Mellor, *The New Economics of Growth – A Strategy for India and the Developing World*, Ithaca, Cornell University Press, 1976, Chs. 2 and 3.
8. Ahluwalia, *Industrial Growth in India*.
9. Ibid., pp. 12–14.
10. See Bardhan, *The Political Economy . . .*; Ahluwalia, *Industrial Growth in India*; and B. B. Bhattacharya and C. H. Hanumantha Rao, *Agriculture–Industry Interrelations – Issues of Relative Prices and Growth in the Context of Public Investment*, paper presented at the VIIIth World Economic Congress of the International Economic Association, New Delhi, 1–5 Dec. 1986.
11. Bhagwati and Desai, *INDIA: Planning. . . .*
12. Government of India, Ministry of Finance (Economic Division), *Economic Survey, 1988–89*, New Delhi, 1989, p. 43.
13. C. T. Kurien, 'Indian Economy in the 1980s and on to the 1990s', *Economic and Political Weekly*, 15 April 1989.
14. Government of India, Ministry of Finance, *Report of the Economic Advisory Council on the Current Economic Situation and Priority Areas for Action* (Chakravarty Report), New Delhi, December 1989, p. 6.
15. Ibid.
16. Dwight Perkins and Shahid Yusuf, *Rural Development in China*, Baltimore, Johns Hopkins Press, 1984, p. 31.
17. Lung-fai Wong, *Agricultural Productivity in China and India: A Comparative Analysis*, paper presented at the Symposium on Feeding the People of China and India, American Association of the Advancement of Science Annual Meeting, Chicago, Illinois, 15 February 1987.
18. See 'Economic Structural Imbalance: Its Causes and Correctives', *Beijing Review*, 4–10 September 1989.
19. Ibid.
20. Nobuo Maruyama, 'The Mechanism of China's Industrial Development – Background to the Shift in Development Strategy', *Developing Econ-*

omies, December 1982; and Donald Hay and Shujie Yao, *A Review of Economic Reforms and Trends of Industrial Development in China, 1978–1988*, Institute of Economics & Statistics, Oxford, May 1990 (mimeo).

21. *Monthly Bulletin of Statistics*, China, cited in Tsang Shu-ki, *Problems of Monetary Control for a Socialist Developing Economy under Reform – The Case of China*, Working Paper Series, Hong Kong Baptist College, School of Business, June 1989, p. 26.

22. Y. Y. Kueh, 'The Maoist Legacy and China's New Industrialisation Strategy', *China Quarterly*, Sept. 1989.

23. Massoud Karshenas, 'Intersectoral Resource Flows and Development: Lessons of Past Experience', *ILO/WEP Research Working Paper Series No. WEP 10–6/WP.99*, Geneva, June 1989.

24. Riskin, and K. N. Raj, 'Agricultural Growth in China and India – Role of Price and Non-Price Factors', *Economic and Political Weekly*, 15 January 1983.

25. Carl Riskin, 'Feeding China – The Experience since 1979', *WIDER Working Paper No. 27*, Helsinki, November 1987.

26. Lung-fai Wong, *Agricultural Productivity*. . . .

27. Isher Judge Ahluwalia, *Industrial Growth in India – Stagnation Since the Mid-Sixties*, Delhi, Oxford University Press, 1985, p. 132.

28. I. J. Ahluwalia, A. D'Souza and V. Deepak, *Trends in Productivity Growth in Indian Manufacturing* (forthcoming), cited in Isher Judge Ahluwalia, 'Industrial Policy and Industrial Performance in India', in Lucas and Papanek, *The Indian Economy* . . . .

29. See, for example, Gene Tidrick, 'Productivity Growth and Technological Change in Chinese Industry', *World Bank Staff Working Papers, No. 761*, Washington D.C., 1986; World Bank, *China's Long-term Development Issues and Options*, Baltimore, Johns Hopkins University Press, 1985; and Nicholas R. Lardy, 'Technical Change and Economic Reform in China: A Tale of Two Sectors' (unpublished), June 1987.

30. Chen Kuan, Wang Hongchang and Zheng Yuxin, Gary Jefferson and Thomas G. Rawski, 'Productivity Change in Chinese Industry: 1953–1985', *Journal of Comparative Economics*, December 1988.

31. Hay and Yao, *A Review of Economic Reforms*.

32. D. Hay and S. J. Yao, *Determinants of Productive Efficiency in Chinese Manufacturing Enterprises, 1980–87*, paper submitted to International Conference on the Chinese Economy, Shenzhen, January 1990.

33. Shigeru Ishikawa, *Socialist Economy and the Experience of China – A Perspective on Economic Reform*, Alexander Eckstein Memorial Lecture, 18 March 1985.

34. Shujie Yao and David Colman, 'Chinese Agricultural Policies and Agricultural Reforms', *Oxford Agrarian Studies*, vol. 18, no. 1, 1990.

35. China, State Statistical Bureau, *Zhong Guo She Hui Tong Ji Zi Liao* (China Social Statistics) 1990, Section 4.

36. Thomas B. Wiens, 'Issues in Structural Reforms of Chinese Agriculture', in Bruce L. Reynolds (ed.), *Chinese Economic Reform – How Far, How Fast?*, New York, Academic Press, 1988, p. 92.

37. Bardhan, *The Political Economy.* . . .
38. Amit Bhaduri, 'Alternative Development Strategies and the Poor', paper presented at the ILO/SAREC Workshop on the Interrelationship between Macroeconomic Policies and Rural Development,: Geneva, 11–13 December 1989.

6 Development Outcomes: Inequalities

In Chapter 5, development outcomes were examined in terms of growth of output, productivity and investment efficiency. In this and the following chapters, 7, 8 and 9, we are interested in reviewing the outcomes of development policies in terms of inequalities of access to technology, health and education. This chapter discusses unequal outcomes with regard to such aspects as income, consumption and other inequalities. These are considered in the context of (i) rural–urban differences, (ii) inter-regional or provincial variations and (iii) class distinctions.

The rural–urban distinction is not very meaningful, particularly in the case of China. This dichotomy is usually considered in terms of spatial or geographical boundaries and such criteria as population density and administrative functions. Mere geographical concentration or dispersion of activities is of little interest for economic analysis. We are therefore more interested in the economic and social criteria underlying the dichotomy: income, productivity and technology differentials. However, the economic criteria may not necessarily coincide with the administrative criteria. In the case of China, a distinction between rural and urban areas is primarily administrative. For example, many Chinese areas that are designated as 'rural' especially 'along the Eastern rim and hinterland around large cities, resemble urban conurbations'.[1] In terms of density of population and range of socio-economic activities (e.g. manufacturing, transport and education), they are similar to towns and urban centres. It is therefore quite likely that the rural–urban comparisons made below suffer from a margin of error. This limitation needs to be borne in mind in interpreting rural–urban inequalities.

I RURAL–URBAN INEQUALITIES

Rural–urban disparities prevail in most developing countries. But the Mao period in China has long been cited as a model of equitable development of rural and urban areas. We discussed in Chapter 3 the Maoist strategy of egalitarian development which was aimed at reducing various types of economic and social disparities. In this section we examine whether the Maoist strategy was actually implemented and whether the Indian experience with reduction of inequalities is radically different from that of China.

1.1 Income Inequalities

We consider two measures of income inequality, namely, the Gini coefficients and income distribution by population deciles.

Gini Coefficients

Table 6.1 measures changes in income inequalities in China and India in terms of Gini coefficients. These estimates show that rural income inequality in China remained almost unchanged between 1952 and 1978 but increased between 1978 and 1983. The rural economic reforms during this period led to a decline in the income share of the poorest peasants and an increase in the share of the richest. Urban inequality also remained unchanged between 1952 and 1978 but declined between 1978 and 1983, presumably because of narrower differences between wage grades in the state-fixed wage system and a much slower pace of market-oriented urban reforms. Furthermore, the total income inequality (with or without accounting for subsidies) increased between 1952 and 1978 but declined since then. The inclusion of urban subsidies for 1978 and 1983 substantially increases the degree of urban–rural inequality. The Chinese urban population enjoys several types of subsidies to which the rural population is not entitled. To give a few examples: subsidies for grain and vegetable oils, for housing, and for health care and maternity. Furthermore there are retirement, disability and death benefits. All these tend to widen the urban–rural income differentials.

The post-Mao decline in overall income inequality is explained by the much faster growth of rural than urban incomes resulting from the rural institutional reforms (household responsibility system and decollectivisation).

For a China–India comparison, we rely on the NCAER estimates of income surveys for India (Table 6.1), since a number of other estimates are based on data collected from different, often noncomparable, sources. A problem in comparing the Chinese and Indian Gini coefficients is that the former are based on per capita income whereas the NCAER data are based on household incomes (except for 1975–76). Furthermore, an assessment of changes in income inequality over time within India is vitiated by differences in

Table 6.1   Changes in income inequality in China and India

Sector	Gini coefficients		
‾	*1952*	*1978*	*1983*
I. China			
Rural	0.23	0.22	0.26
Urban	0.16	0.16	0.14
Total (without urban subsidies)	0.25	0.32	0.28
Total (including urban subsidies)	0.25	0.44	0.41
II. India	*(1964–5)*	*(1967–8)*	*(1975–6)*
			(Household income) *(Per capita income)*
(Income inequality)			
Rural	0.35	0.46	0.39	0.33
Urban	0.46	0.45	0.41	0.41
Total	0.41	0.46	0.42	0.38
(Consumption inequality)[1]	*(1952–3)*	*(1960–1)*	*(1970–1)*	*(1977–8)*	*(1983)*
Rural	0.33[2]	0.32	0.28	0.33	0.30
Urban	–	0.34	0.33	0.35	0.32

Sources: For China – Irma Adelman and David Sunding, 'Economic Policy and Income Distribution in China', *Journal of Comparative Economics*, September 1987; also reprinted in Bruce L. Reynolds (ed.), *Chinese Economic Reform: How Far, How Fast?* Academic Press, Inc., New York, 1987.

For India – NCAER, *Household Income and Its Disposition*, New Delhi, 1980. Coefficients for 1964–5 are taken from Pranab K. Bardhan, 'The Pattern of Income Distribution in India – A Review', in T. N. Srinivasan and P. K. Bardhan (eds), *Poverty and Income Distribution in India*, Calcutta, Statistical Publishing Society, 1974, p. 105.

[1]Based on National Sample Survey (NSS) data and cited in A. N. Agarwal, H. O. Varma and R. C. Gupta, *INDIA – Economic Information Yearbook, 1988–89*, New Delhi, National Publishing House, 1988, p. 50.

[2]Taken from A. K. Ghose, 'Rural Poverty and Relative Prices in India', *Cambridge Journal of Economics*, vol. 13, 1989.

Note: While the Chinese coefficients are based on *per capita* income, the NCAER estimates of Indian coefficients are based on household incomes. The Chinese and Indian estimates are therefore not strictly comparable.

coverage and concepts and the lack of comparability of Gini coefficients for different years. For example, the NCAER 1967–68 survey uses the net income concept, whereas the 1975–76 survey uses gross income.

Difference between the Gini coefficients based on household and per capita income (as is shown for India for 1975–76) can arise on account of the varying sizes of households. If the household size among the poorer sections of the population is larger than among other sections, the Gini coefficient with per capita income will be higher than that based on household income. The opposite would be the case if the household size among the poorer sections of the population were smaller.

These differences suggest that in the rural areas the household size of the poorer sections of the population is smaller than that of the other sections. (An NCAER longitudinal study with panel households for 1970–71 and 1981–82 gives clear evidence of a relative decline in the household size among the poor sections. Differences in fertility rates among different income categories did not explain this decline.)[2] This is, however, not true in the case of urban areas where the household size across all sections of the population tends to be similar. The lower Gini coefficient with per capita income in the total population is, of course, due to the lower Gini for the rural population. The above phenomenon seems to be explicable in terms of economic as well as non-economic factors discussed below.

The per household contribution to the rural-to-urban migrants is proportionately larger among the poorer sections than among others, for two reasons. First, the push factor is stronger among the poorer households since they enjoy limited access to non-labour resources. Second, not subjected to caste-based rigidities in inter-occupational mobility, the poorer groups respond freely to a much wider range of demand for labour in urban areas than the richer segments of the rural population. The latter consist of upper castes or dominant castes who are subject to various rigidities due to social status, caste and religion. These rigidities greatly limit the range of labour demand to which the rich groups can respond. As it happens, there is a perennial excess of labour supply against this limited range of labour demand. This puts a barrier to successful migration and causes the household size of the richer sections of the rural population to rise relative to that for the poorer sections.[3]

An NCAER study argues that income concentration declined in India between 1967–68 and 1975–76.[4] It notes that during this period, minimum wage fixation was introduced in the agricultural sector in several Indian states. The decline in income inequality would imply that a relative rise in the wage of the poor was more than the increase in the incomes of the rich. Since the decline in the Gini coefficients is rather small, it may well be explained by the non-comparability of data and coverage discussed above.

Between 1964–65 and 1967–68, rural and total income inequality actually increased. If we assume that these estimates are comparable, one plausible reason for this change may be the short-run effects of the Green Revolution which occurred in the mid-1960s.

Income Shares by Deciles

Generally higher Gini coefficients in India than in China suggest greater income inequality in the former.

As a cross-check we look at the alternative measure of income inequality, namely, decile distribution of households and their respective income shares (on a per capita income basis). A comparison between 1964–65 and 1975–76 shows that the income share of the bottom 20 per cent of the households was only 7.5 per cent and 6.9 per cent respectively. The top 20 per cent of the households accounted for 47.5 per cent and 46.6 per cent respectively. In other words, income inequality remained almost unchanged during this period.[5]

In China, the bottom 40 per cent of the households in 1979 accounted for 18.4 per cent of income, whereas the top 20 per cent accounted for 22.5 per cent. The corresponding figures for India for 1975–76 (the latest year for which income data are available) were 15.7 per cent and 49.3 per cent respectively. In other words, there was less income inequality in China than in India. The rural income inequality in China was also lower: the bottom 40 per cent of rural households accounted for over 20 per cent of the income as against 16.9 per cent in India: the top 20 per cent got 39.4 per cent income in China and 46.6 in India. The urban income inequality was also lower in China: the bottom 40 per cent accounting for 30 per cent of income and the top 20 per cent accounting for 28 per cent (as against 15.6 per cent and 33.6 per cent respectively in India).[6]

But in post-Mao China, limited market mechanism, a gradual introduction of the ownership of private property, private enterprises and self-employment, are likely to raise income inequality. Growth in income and consumption inequalities is accepted and the government allows some people to 'grow rich quickly', allegedly in the interests of efficiency and growth. According to a 1987 survey by the State Administration for Industry and Commerce, a large majority of self-employed workers in industrial and commercial occupations receive an average annual income which is about two times the average earnings of workers in state-owned enterprises.[7] Even if one takes account of the subsidies to which the latter (but not the former) workers are entitled, the incomes of the self-employed are still higher.

In post-Mao China inequalities reflect imbalances not so much between urban and rural areas as between the rich and the poor. Today the number of families earning 10,000 yuan (who are considered rich) is increasing. The bulk of rich people are engaged in 'private' activities based on private ownership or use of resources, e.g. the self-employed, taxi drivers, writers and the staff of joint ventures with foreign firms. It is estimated that about '10 per cent of the nation's 12 million self-employed industrial and commercial workers earn over 10,000 yuan a year, and 1 per cent of these earn far more – up to hundreds of thousands of yuan'.[8] This rapid growth of 'rich' people seems to be a direct result of the policies that encourage self-employment and the private economy.

1.2 Consumption Inequalities

In view of the difficulties in comparing income data between China and India, it would be useful to examine trends in consumption inequalities. For India, while there are no long series on income data, the National Sample Survey (NSS) regularly collects consumption data which are also available for the early 1980s (this is not the case for income data). Since consumption expenditure tends to be more stable than income, it can be used as a proxy for 'permanent' income distribution.

Consumption inequalities tend to be lower than inequalities in income distribution as the Gini coefficients based on consumption expenditure are lower than those based on income (see Table 6.1). This may be explained partly by the fact that at lower deciles of population, household consumption may exceed income (dissaving) whereas a higher proportion of income is saved at higher deciles. Despite this factor Indian Gini coefficients based on consumption are higher than those for China based on income, suggesting greater inequality. The NSS data underestimate consumption of the rich – a factor which may underestimate an inter-temporal increase in inequality.

In India there seems to be no clear trend showing a decline in

Table 6.2   Consumption and family income per capita in China (1952–85)

Year	Consumption per capita (yuan at 1985 prices)			Family income (yuan at current prices)				
	Rural	Urban	Ratio	Rural			Urban	Ratio
	(R)	(U)	(U/R)	Per worker	Per resident	Per worker	Per resident	(U/R)
1952	97	249	2.6	–	–	–	–	–
1957	113	315	2.8	152	73	833	254	3.5
1962	100	282	2.8	–	–	–	–	–
1965	129	332	2.6	204*	98*	817**	243**	2.5
1975	164	453	2.7	–	–	–	–	–
1978	169	514	3.0	338	134	–	–	–
1979	191	535	2.8	381	160	–	–	–
1980	205	575	2.8	433	191	–	–	–
1981	225	584	2.6	486	223	888	500	2.2
1983	263	603	2.3	592	309	977	573	1.8
1985	324	754	2.3	690	398	1,426	821	2.0
1987***	393	997	2.5	–	–	–	–	–
1989***	518	1409	2.7	–	–	–	–	–

Annual growth rate (%):

1952–78		2.2	2.8	3.8	3.8	–0.25	–0.51	(1957–65)
1979–85		9.2	5.6	9.2	15.5	12.6	13.2	(1981–85)
1985–89		9.8	16.8	–	–	–	–	

Sources: (1) *Zhongguo tongji nianjian* (Statistical Yearbook of China), 1986 (Chinese version), pp. 624 and 646; and 1990, p. 290.
(2) *Statistical Yearbook of China*, 1981 (p. 441); 1983 (p. 499) and 1986 (pp. 576 and 582) (sample survey data).

Notes: * Estimated by assuming that expenditure–income ratio per resident and the worker–resident ratio per family is the same as in 1957.
** For 1964.
*** Data are in current prices.

overall consumption inequalities although there seems to be some decline in rural inequality. Consumption inequalities remain higher in urban than in rural areas. But in real terms the gap may perhaps be narrower since urban prices are generally higher than the rural and the price differentials may increase over decile groups.[9]

In China, the ratio of urban to rural consumption per capita was over 2:1 in 1989 but it declined since 1978 thanks to the rural reforms. Rural–urban income gaps have also narrowed over time (see Table 6.2).

A few points need to be borne in mind when interpreting consumption data in Table 6.2 for farm and non-farm population; these are converted into real terms by deflating the urban figures by the worker cost of living index and the rural figures, by the nationwide retail price index. This may tend to overstate the growth of rural consumption since rural consumers do not have easy access to goods sold at official retail prices.[10] Using the farm purchase-price index as a deflator for rural consumption raises real consumption for the period 1972–78, and to a lesser extent for the period 1979–85, thus lowering the rates of growth of rural consumption. Sample surveys of rural and urban incomes and consumption (covering 12,050 families in 82 cities and 31,435 peasant families in 600 counties throughout the country) show that between 1978 and 1984 both rural incomes and consumption rose more rapidly than urban income/consumption. The average annual growth of rural incomes per resident (15.5 per cent) during 1979–85 is unprecedented and is several times higher than the 3.8 per cent annual growth for the period between 1952 and 1978 (Table 6.2). The *per capita* urban income and consumption in Table 6.2 would tend to be underestimated since urban subsidies are not included.

Commodity Composition of Consumption

Ratios of average rural to average urban consumption per capita on different items (Table 6.3) in China and India show that (i) in India average rural–urban consumption disparities as well as those by each item of expenditure have widened; (ii) in China these disparities have on average narrowed, although in the case of expenditure on clothing they have widened – in 1988 rural consumption on clothing was only 27 per cent of urban consumption whereas in 1965 it was 41 per cent; (iii) the pattern of consumption remained largely unchanged in India whereas it showed substantial shifts in China. Changes in the pattern of rural consumption have been particularly noticeable since the introduction of rural reforms. A smaller proportion of the total family budget is now spent on food and clothing, and a greater proportion on housing.

A phenomenally high ratio of rural to urban spending on housing in China needs some explanation. In the wake of rural reforms, the Chinese peasants have been spending the bulk of their increments in incomes on the building of houses which are privately owned. How-

Table 6.3   Rural to urban consumption ratios by expenditure categories
(China vs. India)

Item of Expenditure	China			India		
	(1965)	*(1983)*	*(1988)*	*(1967–8)*	*(1983)*	*(1988)*
Food	0.50	0.49	0.45	0.86	0.76	0.73
Clothing	0.41	0.37	0.27	0.90	0.77	0.72
Fuel	0.84	1.53	1.43	0.73	0.69	0.79
Housing	0.47	3.60	9.08	–	–	–
Daily articles	0.52	0.59	0.41	–	–	–
Cultural activities	1.07	0.26	0.40	–	–	–
Total consumption	0.43	0.49	0.43	0.74	0.68	0.66

Sources: (1) China: *Statistical Yearbook of China, 1984*, pp. 463 and 473;
and 1989, p. 626 and p. 646.
(2) India: *National Sample Survey Report No. 319* (Provisional),
38th Round, 1983; and NSS 44th Round, 1988–89.

Note: Data for India on housing, daily articles and cultural activities are
included under other categories which are not comparable to the
Chinese classification.

ever, in urban areas so far there is virtually no private ownership of
houses or apartments. A new scheme of privatisation of housing is
not getting off the ground because urban housing is heavily subsidised
and urban people spend only a nominal amount on house rent. This
partly explains very low urban expenditure on housing.

Of course, the gap between rural and urban consumption per
capita noted in Table 6.3 may be somewhat narrower in practice
because of lower rural prices than urban prices. In the case of India,
it is estimated that the rural–urban price differential may range from
8 per cent to 15 per cent.[11] Secondly, under-reporting of domestically
produced food and other goods and services in rural areas may also
explain why the estimates exaggerate rural–urban gaps. In fact, in
China the rather low rural to urban consumption ratios for food seem
to be due to under-reporting of non-marketed food. (In 1983, home-
produced food accounted for nearly 60 per cent of the total.)[12]

The household income and consumption surveys considered above
tend to underestimate income gaps because they omit income from
capital and incomes in kind (e.g. rice ration) which are more important in towns than in rural areas. There are other problems also in
comparing average incomes and expenditures in rural and urban

areas, e.g. price differentials between the two sectors as noted above, valuation of farmers' self-consumption, differences in sources of income and in average size of families. Thus it may be more useful to examine gaps in output per worker, which we do below.

1.3 Disparities in Output Per Worker

As we noted in Chapter 5, the gaps between output per worker in agriculture and in industry are particularly wide in China. Since 1971, these gaps have been narrowing in China but widening in India (see Chapter 5, Table 5.5 and Figure 5.1).

The wide gaps in the ratios for the two countries seem to be explained by much higher investment in the Chinese industry and relatively greater output shifts from agriculture to industry without any corresponding shifts of manpower out of agriculture. In China rural to urban migration remains controlled and regulated. In India also the rate of migration is quite low. Thus, the proportion of manpower in agriculture has remained quite high.

In theory, labour flows from rural to urban areas should reduce income inequalities by keeping the urban wage down and by raising the average rural *per capita* incomes. Indeed, as we noted in Chapter 1, the Lewis and Fei-Ranis models of development postulate poverty alleviation through such labour transfers. However, in practice, in neither India nor China did this factor have any income equalising effect. Presumably the rigid migration control measures by the Chinese government make the Lewis–Fei-Ranis type models irrelevant. Although the Chinese economy resembles the Lewis model in the sense that it has a modern industrial system and a backward agricultural sector (as is indicated by the impressive ratio of GDP per worker between industry and agriculture in Chapter 5, Table 5.5), the assumption of perfect competition and free flow of labour movements from rural to urban areas does not hold. Although the post-Mao economic reforms allowed farmers to take up casual jobs in cities and towns, discrimination against the rural residents taking formal urban jobs still prevails.

The labour supply factor may also be relevant for explaining labour productivity differentials which determine income disparities. Rural wages could stay low if it were less burdensome to be unemployed in rural areas compared to the urban. Also if urban workers were more easily organised (a general phenomenon) then rural wages would be lower, other things being equal. Furthermore, self-employed activities in urban areas are in general demand-constrained (output must be sold) while peasant production is supply-constrained (output can be self-consumed). This implies that the peasants apply more labour to their non-labour assets thus reducing the average labour productivity.

Increasing sectoral labour productivity differential in India is further suggested by data on rural poverty and income distribution. In the Sixth Five-Year Plan (1980–85), the Indian planners concluded that nearly 50 per cent of the Indian population remained below the absolute poverty line. They also admitted that the number of unemployed and underemployed had increased over the past decade. According to the Planning Commission norms, roughly one-third of Punjab's rural population is still below the poverty line.[13] (It is important to note that Punjab is one of the fastest growing states in India.) Extremely uneven distribution of land and increasing population pressures seem to be the major reasons for the persistent rural poverty. The situation in other Indian states which are growing much less rapidly, is likely to be even worse. For example, in the case of Bihar, the already high incidence of rural poverty seems to be rising still further owing to an extremely small land base for the majority of rural households.[14]

This situation contrasts with that in China where drastic land reforms in the early 1950s eliminated one of the major causes of rural poverty (see below).

1.4 Financial Disparities

Rural–urban inequalities may also be reflected in financial disparities between rural and urban areas. In the 1950s and 1960s, in India net resource flows both on private capital account and on government account moved from non-agriculture into agriculture.[15] In the 1970s this trend was reversed: there was an increased outflow from the rural sector in the form of financial savings. It is estimated that the savings ratio of agricultural and non-agricultural households was about 10 per cent and 6 per cent respectively; or an average rural savings rate of around 8 per cent.[16] The expansion of financial institutions (e.g. cooperative credit societies and nationalised commercial banks) and a slowdown of investment in physical farm assets seem to account for these financial outflows from the rural sector.

In China, the importance of the mobilisation of rural surpluses seems to have gradually declined since the Chinese industrial sector ploughed back incremental output into investment for industrialisation.[17] It is estimated that agriculture's contribution was about 16 per cent of the state funds for urban development in the 1950s and only 6 per cent in the 1970s.[18]

In most developing countries rural capital and financial markets are far less developed than the urban. Credit policy tends to be urban-biased. This bias may be manifested in higher effective rates of interest and greater credit rationing in rural than in urban areas, relatively higher average credit/deposit ratio in urban areas relative to rural areas, and concentration of net deposit bank offices in rural areas and net credit bank offices in urban areas.[19]

A study by the National Institute of Bank Management in India concluded that 'the inter-state distribution of institutional finance in India showed a pronounced regressive bias against the low-income states which are predominantly rural'. This bias is noticeable in Table 6.4 on the distribution of deposits and advances (covering only commercial banks) by rural and urban population groups which shows that rural deposit-to-credit (DC) ratios are higher than the urban ratios. The higher DC ratios for Indian rural groups suggest that the credit policy may have drained the rural sector of credit.[20] However, too much reliance cannot be placed on DC ratios as an indicator of the adequacy of credit supply in relation to credit requirements. This ratio may be high or low depending on the absorptive capacity of bank credit, the level of development of the region in question, and the availability of own resources of borrowing, etc.

Since the early 1970s Indian policy has promoted the supply of agricultural credit to poor farmers through the creation of new institutions like regional rural banks and the National Bank for Agriculture and Rural Development, and the introduction of such measures as concessional interest rates on agricultural loans. There are some indications that improved agricultural credit, *inter alia*, has contributed to agricultural growth in India. The States with the highest yield per hectare (Punjab and Haryana) also show the largest availability of formal credit, and the States with low yields (Madhya Pradesh and Rajasthan) have low credit availability.

The relatively lower DC ratios for China (Table 6.4) suggest that credit availability is not scarce in rural areas. The credit policy, particularly in the post-Mao period, is intended to favour the rural sector through subsidised credit and low interest rates and charges.

Table 6.4   Deposit-to-credit ratios in China and India

Population group	Year				
	(1969)	(1978)		(1985)	
	India	China*	India	China	India
Rural	2.7	1.5	1.9	1.1	1.5
Semi-urban	2.5	–	2.1	–	1.9
Urban	1.7	0.3	1.6	0.5	1.6
Metropolitan	0.9	–	1.1	–	1.2
Total Average	1.2	0.5	1.4	0.6	1.4

Sources: (1) China: *Statistical Yearbook of China*, 1986, p. 530. Rural advances cover loans to state-owned agricultural units and loans to rural communes, production brigades and teams. Urban advances cover loans to industrial production enterprises, industrial supply and marketing enterprises and materials supply departments and individual industrial and commercial units in urban areas.
(2) India: Banking Statistics, *Basic Statistical Returns*, Reserve Bank of India (RBI). Data supplied to the author by the RBI.

Note: * for 1979.

Loans to agriculture (state farms, collectives and households) increased from 13 billion yuan in 1979 to 41 billion yuan in 1985 – an increase of over 317 per cent. The interest rate for credit to rural areas was lower (4.32 per cent) than that for urban loans to state-owned industrial and commercial enterprises and urban collective enterprises (5.04 per cent). Loans to households for farm equipment purchases and loans to credit cooperatives were charged a still lower rate of a little over 2 per cent per annum.[21]

The savings deposits of the Chinese rural households have increased substantially as a result of substantial increases in rural incomes. From 1978 to 1982 the marginal propensity to save of peasant families was estimated at about 23 per cent. The rural township enterprises are one of the main sources of rural savings and capital accumulation. Between 1979 and 1984, deposits by rural enterprises with the rural credit cooperatives increased nearly four-fold whereas loan advances to these enterprises rose by nearly ten-fold.[22]

1.5   Why Less Inequality in China?

What accounts for lower inequalities in China? Clearly the Maoist egalitarian policies discussed in Chapter 3 must have had a role to play. The drastic land reforms and the public ownership of property and land in the early 1950s considerably reduced rural inequalities. On the other hand, in the case of India, income and consumption disparities arise from unequal distribution of land and other assets and income from self-employment.

In the early 1950s China introduced drastic land reforms – by redistributing land from the rich landlords to the poor peasants – which eliminated one of the major causes of rural inequalities in most developing countries. Thus, the landless workers disappeared in China, whereas in India the number of these workers has grown. (However, in China, land reforms reduced only intra-village and not inter-village inequalities in land distribution.)

In India, land reforms did not involve much land redistribution, and ceilings on landholdings and other measures were often dodged by the rich landlords. It is well known that legislation on land ceilings was bypassed through fictitious land transfers to friends and relatives. It is estimated that by October 1986, for India as a whole the 'declared surplus' of land was only 7.4 million acres. Only 5.8 million acres were taken over and a little over 4 million acres were distributed,[23] which amounts to a little over 1 per cent of the total cultivated land. With the exception of Punjab, Haryana and Uttar Pradesh, the consolidation of land holdings was also limited. Till March 1986, the total area consolidated was 54.4 million hectares, or about 30 per cent of the estimated total land area that could be consolidated.

In China, greater rural equality is also due to the extensive network of public distribution of food and food rationing. Under this system, the government was able to procure foodgrains from the surplus areas and deliver them to the deficit areas, thus reducing regional disparities. Food rationing and subsidies ensured very low prices for food and other necessities like vegetables and cooking oil. The government spent enormous amounts of money on price subsidies to protect the urban consumers. Although there was no formal rationing in rural areas the food deficit areas were also supplied foodgrains at heavily subsidised prices.[24]

Furthermore, a minimum floor for rural consumption within the communes and the public welfare system of 'five guarantees' (food, clothing, housing, medical care and burial expenses) during the Mao period were intended to reduce inequalities.

Public distribution of food and rationing has also existed in India since the early 1950s. Sale of foodgrains through fair price shops has been in force off and on, to regulate inter-state movement of food-grains, to keep their prices stable and subsidised, and to provide distressed and food-short areas with adequate supplies of food. While the objectives of the Indian food distribution policy were similar to those in China, its implementation seems to have been more difficult. For instance, during the 1970s there was reluctance on the part of the surplus states (who tended to underestimate production) to share their surpluses with the deficit states.[25] Furthermore, the coverage of the system is limited largely to urban areas (except in the case of the state of Kerala where it also benefits rural population).[26] The ma-jority of the rural poor are known to have no access to the public distribution system.[27] Unless food subsidies are directed specifically to the low-income groups (by subsidising basic foods eaten by the poor), their benefits might well accrue to the upper-income groups. Implementation of food subsidies in India may also have been dif-ficult due to a combination of other factors, namely, administrative weaknesses, rapidly growing demand for food and food supply bot-tlenecks and growing budget deficits.

A reason for relatively greater urban income equality in China is the policy of wage controls. In China, wage differentials are much narrower than in India and most other developing countries. During the Mao period, narrow wage differentials – both intra-firm and inter-industry – were consistent with the policy of egalitarianism. These differentials played a much less important role in providing worker incentive than did the non-pecuniary and ideological factors. Wage controls and fixation of wages by the government also kept interprovincial variations rather low despite differences in the degree of industrialisation.

Although wage controls have been relaxed during the post-Mao period, the wage differentials between different skills continue to be much narrower in China than in most developing countries.

II REGIONAL INEQUALITIES

2.1 Regional Trends

The distribution of income and consumption discussed above would be related to regional distribution of output and incomes. It is therefore useful to examine regional trends also in economic and social inequalities.

Being large economies, both China and India inevitably suffer from wide inter-regional variations which are caused partly by the local peculiarities like soil fertility and climate in specific regions and partly by the macroeconomic policies like investment allocation which have favoured some regions more than others (see Chapter 3). In India, the coastal areas and big cities are more advanced industrially and commercially than the hinterland or interior of the country. This is partly the result of colonial powers bestowing favours on coastal areas for reasons of trade and commerce.

In the case of China also regional disparities continue despite redistributive measures adopted during the Mao period. In principle, in a socialist economy control of movements of capital and labour, foreign trade and investment should limit regional inequalities. But in actual practice, the persistence of these inequalities may be explained by the extreme initial unevenness at the time of the Revolution in 1949.[28] Secondly, some of Mao's policies – e.g. local self-reliance and promotion of rural industry in the hinterland – seem to have reinforced regional inequalities which the redistributive policies were actually designed to reduce. For example, the policy of local self-reliance led to a vertical integration of economic activities (see Chapter 4), discouraged specialisation and interprovincial trade and thus maintained if not aggravated regional imbalances. During the Mao period, interprovincial trade in both agricultural and industrial goods was quite restricted.[29] Restrictions in commodity flows, combined with restrictions in labour movements, must have discouraged not only sectoral interdependence (discussed in Chapter 4) but also provincial interdependence.

Therefore, our next task is to examine the extent of regional inequalities in China and India. This is accomplished through a quantitative measurement of these inequalities on the basis of three sets of variables:

(a) *Economic variables*, e.g. income and consumption per capita and share of output and employment in industry;

(b) *Social variables*, e.g. share of urban population, share of literates in total population, state expenditure per capita on education and health, enrolments, teacher–pupil ratios and number of schools per capita, doctors, hospitals and hospital beds per thousand population; and

(c) *Technological variables*, e.g. share of R and D expenditure in industry, number of scientists and engineers, area under HYVs, tractor-ploughed area, power-irrigated area and agricultural consumption of electricity.

2.2 Measurement of Regional Inequalities

To measure regional imbalance we use cross-sectional data for 29 Chinese provinces and for 16–20 Indian states (depending on data availability). The basic data are presented in the *Statistical Appendix*. The methodology used to measure the degree of imbalance is to estimate standard deviation (SD) and coefficient of variation (Co.V) across provinces. Our intention is to determine:

(i) change in the degree of unevenness over time within the two countries; and

(ii) relative degree of imbalance between the two countries at a point in time.

To estimate (SD) and (Co.V) we use population-weighted mean for each variable. Unweighted or arithmetic averages are less satisfactory since different provinces vary in respect of size, population, income and other related economic variables. Thus it is essential to adjust the variable quantities to obtain unbiased results.

If we estimate the population's deviation using the weighted mean, then the unbiased estimator of the variance is:

$$\hat{\sigma}_w^2 = \frac{1}{n - 2 + n \sum_{i=1}^{n} w_j^2} \sum_{i=1}^{n} (X_i - \bar{X}_w)^2$$

where $\{ X_i, \ldots X_n \}$ is the random sample;

w_j is weight and $\sum_{j=1}^{n} w_j = 1$;

X_w is weighted mean and $\bar{X}_w = \sum_{j=1}^{n} w_j X_j$

(For proof, see Appendix 6.1.)

Inequalities with respect to technological, health and education variables are examined in Chapters 7 to 9. The disparities in respect of economic and social variables are discussed below. The statistical results are presented in Table 6.5. In the case of China, between 1957 and 1971 when the policy of local self-reliance and food self-sufficiency was in force, regional disparities increased in terms of state per capita income, remained unchanged in terms of per capita consumption, declined in terms of the share of output originating in industry, but increased in terms of output share in agriculture. However, between 1981 and 1985, regional disparities declined in terms of per capita income and consumption and output share in industry but they increased slightly in terms of share of output in agriculture. This divergence between the Mao and post-Mao periods seems to be due to shifts in development strategy and policies. The abandonment of policies of local self-reliance and local food self-sufficiency may have contributed to reduced regional inequalities in incomes.

In the case of India, unevenness has increased in respect of state per capita incomes (the Co.V having risen from 0.42 in 1981 to 0.47 in 1986). But in the case of the industrialisation index (the share of output originating in industry) the disparity has declined, as is shown by the fall in the Co.V from 0.48 in 1981 to 0.44 in 1986.[30]

China shows less disparity in terms of degree of industrialisation as measured by the share of output originating in industry, than does India. However, if one looks at the share of workers employed in industry, regional variations in China are much higher (Co.V being 0.52 for China and only 0.38 for India). This suggests vast productivity differentials between provinces which would be lower if rural to urban and interprovincial migration were allowed. China also shows greater variation than India in respect of state per capita incomes and the degree of urbanisation.

In the case of agriculture also there are regional variations in both the countries. Though these variations have been declining in China they remain higher than those in India. Agricultural and industrial disparities are somewhat similar in China. In the case of India, agricultural disparities are relatively lower than the industrial (the Co.Vs for agriculture being much lower) (see Table 6.5). This was also the situation in China in the 1950s. For 1957 (the early Mao period) Lardy estimated coefficients of variation for agricultural and industrial per capita value added which showed that agricultural output was much more evenly distributed than industrial output (the

Table 6.5 Regional inequalities in China and India

Indicator	China			India		
	WM	SD	Co.V	WM	SD	Co.V
Per capita income						
(1957)	194.0	123.3	0.64	–	–	–
(1971)	352.8	271.2	0.77	637.4	169.5	0.27
(1981)	588.6	462.1	0.78	764.6	321.5	0.42
(1985)	841.5	622.9	0.74	847.5	402.1	0.47
Per capita consumption						
(1957)	118.4	50.9	0.43	–	–	–
(1971)	157.6	68.4	0.43	54.64	13.61	0.24(1972)
(1981)	289.9	90.5	0.31	62.09	15.56	0.25(1977)
(1985)	410.2	112.6	0.27	64.17	13.79	0.21(1983)
Agricultural output						
(1957)	55.7	18.5	0.33	–	–	–
(1971)	65.2	33.1	0.51	53.7	9.7	0.18(1970)
(1981)	45.7	11.5	0.25	46.2	9.0	0.19
(1985)	44.3	11.5	0.26	43.4	10.6	0.24
Industrial output						
(1957)	36.3	18.4	0.51	–	–	–
(1971)	51.0	19.5	0.38	18.1	7.5	0.41
(1981)	40.7	10.2	0.25	20.5	7.6	0.38
(1985)	40.0	7.4	0.18	21.2	8.1	0.40
Agricultural workers						
(1971)	–	–	–	26.0	7.3	0.28
(1981)	13.9	9.7	0.69	24.0	5.0	0.21
(1986)	11.3	7.7	0.68	–	–	–
Industrial Workers						
(1961)	–	–	–	4.8	1.4	0.30
(1971)	–	–	–	3.6	1.3	0.36
(1981)	45.8	9.7	0.21	11.2	4.3	0.38
(1986)	21.6	11.3	0.52	–	–	–
Urban population						
(1961)	–	–	–	20.3	8.8	0.43
(1971)	–	–	–	22.1	8.8	0.40
(1981)	20.8	14.6	0.70	25.0	8.6	0.34
(1986)	45.9	15.4	0.33	–	–	–
Illiterates/semi-literates						
(1971)	–	–	–	32.3	9.6	0.30
(1981)	–	–	–	39.0	10.1	0.26
(1985)	25.2	8.5	0.34	–	–	–

Source: Based on Appendix Tables A6.1 to A6.16. *notes overleaf*

Notes: (1) WM = population-weighted mean; SD = standard deviation; Co. V = coefficient of variation.
(2) Chinese data for the Mao period are in current prices whereas data for the post-Mao period are in 1981 constant prices. Hence the two may not be comparable.
(3) The agricultural workers for China cover only state employees and collective workers. Hence the low figures.
(4) In the case of urbanisation in China, the definition of urban population was changed after 1984, which makes it impossible to compare the situation in 1981 and 1986.
(5) The Indian consumption *per capita* is per month; hence the very low WMs.

coefficient being 0.92 for industry and 0.19 for agriculture).[31]

In the case of India, the Bhalla and Tyagi study shows a highly uneven pattern of agricultural growth across districts and provinces. It analyses growth performance of Indian agriculture to examine spatial disparities at the state and district levels for the triennia, 1962–65, 1970–73 and 1980–83.[32] These disparities are explained largely by the introduction of high-yielding varieties during the mid-1960s only in selected areas in the north. The new technology contributed to a rapid growth in land productivity in those provinces and districts which had good irrigation facilities. The arid areas in the eastern part of India were unable to avail of the new technology for lack of adequate irrigation infrastructure. This is reflected in an increase in Co.V. from 0.45 in 1962–65 to 0.49 during 1970–73. During 1980–83, the coefficient remained at the level for 1970–73. Although land productivity disparities have not increased during the latter two periods, disparities in male worker productivity (which is the main determinant of wage rates) have, which suggests an increase in disparities of rural living conditions both between provinces and between districts within provinces.

For the 1950s, Williamson compared inter-regional income inequality between China and India among other countries and found it to be much higher in China than in India (the population-weighted coefficient for India being 0.28 compared to 0.39 for China).[33] It is perhaps these serious inequalities (as a legacy of the pre-1949 era) that prompted the Mao regime to pursue a policy of regional balance even at the expense of economic growth.

Social inequalities in terms of urbanisation rates have declined in both China and India; and in terms of literacy rates regional inequalities have declined in India. However, a comparison between China and India of regional inequalities in terms of literacy is not very meaningful. First, there are no time series data for China for comparable years. Secondly, the semi-literates who are included under 'illiterates' also cover drop-outs from primary schools. Thus the Chinese definition of literacy is different from the Indian.

To conclude, it is clear from Table 6.5 that regional inequalities are high in both China and India in respect of some indicators but not others. While income and consumption inequalities are lower in China than in India, regional disparities seem to be higher.

Chinese Coastal vs. Non-Coastal Areas

To verify whether the coastal areas are actually more advanced we divided the Chinese provinces into two groups, namely, coastal regions (11) and backward regions (18). The coastal regions include: Beijing, Tianjin, Zhejiang, Hebei, Jiangsu, Fujian, Guangdong, Guangxi, Liaoning, Shandong and Shanghai. The non-coastal regions cover: Shanxi, Inner Mongolia, Jilin, Heilongjiang, Anhui, Jianxi, Henan, Hubei, Hunan, Sichuan, Guizhou, Yunnan, Tibet, Shaanxi, Gansu and Qinghai, Ningxia and Xinjiang. We estimated the SDs and Co.Vs separately for different development indicators. The results are presented in Table 6.6. The coastal areas/provinces do not indicate less disparity in respect of all the variables considered. For example, there are greater variations in per capita income and consumption in the coastal provinces than in the non-coastal provinces, perhaps due partly to the predominant economic position of Beijing, Shanghai and Tianjin within the coastal areas.

Agricultural output disparities have been consistently higher in the coastal provinces than those in the non-coastal provinces.

During the Mao period, the Chinese government developed those traditional areas which were mostly flat lands and near big rivers, e.g. Heilongjiang and Jilin, which may partly explain lower disparities in the non-coastal areas during this period. But the value of Co.V for 1971 compared to other years was particularly high (0.45) for non-coastal areas, which suggests that calculations for single years are subject to random shocks caused by such factors as droughts and bad weather.

Over time regional disparities in respect of agricultural output declined in the coastal provinces but somewhat increased in the

Table 6.6   Regional inequalities between Chinese coastal and non-coastal areas

Indicator	Coastal provinces			Non-coastal provinces		
	WM	*SD*	*Co.V*	*WM*	*SD*	*Co.V*
Per capita income						
(1957)	254.8	180.0	0.71	136.8	48.5	0.35
(1971)	507.5	410.2	0.81	212.9	59.8	0.28
(1981)	829.2	663.3	0.80	349.8	84.0	0.24
(1985)	1133.5	909.0	0.80	508.6	119.3	0.23
Per capita consumption						
(1957)	133.5	64.8	0.49	104.8	35.7	0.34
(1971)	173.2	95.2	0.55	145.9	41.5	0.28
(1981)	347.5	176.9	0.51	256.9	59.1	0.23
(1985)	432.1	141.2	0.33	383.6	76.4	0.20
Agricultural output						
(1957)	51.3	25.8	0.50	58.6	9.3	0.16
(1971)	41.3	21.6	0.52	76.0	34.5	0.45
(1981)	42.5	15.1	0.35	48.3	8.9	0.18
(1985)	41.7	14.7	0.35	46.4	9.6	0.20
Industrial output						
(1957)	44.5	19.7	0.44	21.9	8.3	0.38
(1971)	59.5	22.7	0.38	39.8	12.2	0.31
(1981)	51.9	17.5	0.33	38.8	8.7	0.22
(1985)	40.9	7.7	0.19	39.1	7.3	0.18
Urban population						
(1981)	26.0	20.5	0.79	16.4	7.4	0.45
(1986)	52.2	8.1	0.15	39.9	10.4	0.26
Agricultural workers						
(1981)	8.6	4.7	0.54	17.0	11.6	0.68
(1986)	7.1	3.8	0.54	13.8	9.1	0.66
Industrial workers						
(1981)	48.3	6.8	0.14	43.4	10.2	0.23
(1986)	26.2	7.8	0.30	16.4	5.1	0.31
Illiterates/ semi-literates per 1,000 pop.						
(1985)	232.8	40.6	0.17	263.2	67.1	0.25
Per capita investment						
(1985)	334.2	165.3	0.49	155.8	71.9	0.46
Foreign capital used per capita						
(1985)	9.0	3.4	0.38	0.4	0.2	0.50

Source: Based on Appendix Tables A6.1 to A6.16.

Notes: (1) The data for *per capita* income, *per capita* consumption, share of income in agriculture and industry, for 1957 and 1971 are for current prices, and for 1981 and 1985, constant prices. The data for *per capita* state investment and foreign capital used *per capita* are at current prices.
(2) Also see footnotes to Table 6.5.

---

non-coastal provinces (see Table 6.6). What explains this phenomenon? Could it be due to a differential impact of the rural responsibility system or to the result of 1970 administrative decentralisation which might have aggravated inequalities by reducing the capacity of the central government to transfer investment and inputs to poorer non-coastal areas?

Regional disparities in industrial output were greater in the coastal than the non-coastal provinces. But in this case the disparities declined over time in both the categories. Does the policy of rural industrialisation and growth of collective and private industrial enterprises explain this situation? In the post-Mao period, the growth of the collective as well as private sectors has been particularly rapid. If the policy of promotion of rural industry had a particularly positive impact on the growth of industry-poor regions, one could argue *a priori* that regional industrial imbalances would decline. In other words, to explain a decline in inter-provincial industrial inequalities, one would have to assume that, other things being equal, rural industry grew faster in the non-coastal than the coastal areas. But in actual practice, the reverse was true – by and large the rural industry growth rates of output were higher for the coastal provinces. The coastal growth rates were also generally above the national average growth rates for rural industry.[34] During the post-Mao period, the share of coastal provinces in the national output of rural industry also showed an increase, suggesting an increase in concentration of rural industry in these provinces.

A recent study has shown that regional inequalities in the distribution of rural industry (covering village and township enterprises only) had increased between 1979 and 1985.[35] The conclusion is however reversed (for 1984 and 1985, the only two years considered) if private industrial enterprises are also included. Can one conclude from this that the observed decline in regional industrial inequalities is due to the growth of private enterprises? The available empirical evidence does not seem to be conclusive.

III CLASS INEQUALITIES

Economic inequalities and imbalances also have their origin in class and social structure. But conventional economic analysis rarely proceeds in terms of class or occupational categories when discussing rural–urban income and consumption differences.

In capitalist societies, private ownership of the means of production particularly land (apart from such determinant factors as religion, caste and gender), is directly related to the class and social hierarchical structures. In socialist economies like the Chinese, although land reforms eliminated private land ownership in the early 1950s, class conflict did not disappear. Classes based on asset ownership – capitalists and workers – were replaced by bureaucrats and party cadres representing government and the political power structure on the one hand, and workers and peasants on the other.

Kraus[36] has identified two models of social class stratification in China: the first, pertains to the social classes based on property relations, namely, workers, peasants and professionals which continued even after the Revolution; the second model refers to class distinctions along occupational lines, e.g. government bureaucrats, party cadres and the professional intelligentsia.

The awards and privileges of the party cadres and bureaucrats in the upper echelons of the Chinese political hierarchy give these classes incomes and fringe benefits (apart from political influence) which are well above those that are at the lower rungs of the occupational ladder. One finds mention of privileges like special access to cars, foods and other scarce goods, special rooms in hospitals, favours in admissions to educational institutions, recruitment and allocation of housing.[37] But these privileges seem to have been offered only to a limited number of élite cadres.[38] Also these privileges and perks appear miniscule compared to those enjoyed by Indian party members, politicians and top civil servants. They also seem much less glaring than those in most other market-oriented developing countries.

In India there are several rural classes with conflicting group interests – agricultural labourers, small landholders, independent cultivators (the so-called 'bullock' capitalists) and large landowners. These categories are distinguished by the size of landholdings, the use of family or hired wage labour and the nature of technology. Private ownership of property (land and assets) and income from self-employment create inequalities between social classes which are directly related to ownership of the means of production. In the rural sector, rich farmers who own the bulk of land form the most dominant class, and landless workers, the most dispossesed class. It is estimated that the average income per capita of the large farmer (Rs. 2,024) is just over four times that of the small farmer (Rs. 500). Average income and consumption per capita are the lowest for the small farmer and the landless worker. In the urban sector, the class of marginal self-employed workers is the poorest with income and expenditure per capita being lower than that of the medium farmers.[39]

The Green Revolution is noted to have accentuated these class inequalities and is alleged to have led to rural proletarianisation. The rich peasantry has become more dominant thanks to its control of the bulk of marketed surplus.[40] Sheila Bhalla and Das Gupta[41] show that in Punjab and Haryana in the wake of the Green Revolution the distribution of operated land has shifted to the new capitalist farmers. As a result the class of landless workers has grown with rural artisans and the dispossessed peasants joining its ranks. While there is no doubt that the large farmers have benefited more from the Green Revolution than the small farmers, the latter have also adopted and benefited from the HYVs. Therefore, polarisation of the rural sector may have been exaggerated.[42] The Green Revolution has led to growth of independent cultivators who are larger and politically more significant than the larger landholders whose proportion has been declining.[43]

Agricultural price policy is another factor whose influence tends to vary among different classes of rural producers and consumers partly because of the uneven distribution of the marketed agricultural surpluses between large and small farmers.[44]

Worsening terms of trade and lower agricultural prices would hurt producers whose welfare loss is transferred to consumers of foodgrains (particularly the rural landless workers and the urban poor) via lower prices. On the basis of a general equilibrium model de Janvry and Subbarao[45] show how output increase in agriculture resulting from lower food prices would benefit small farmers and urban marginal workers. They argue that the clash of interest is between buyers and sellers of food rather than between sectoral classes. While this may well be true, the issue of equity and social welfare is quite complex. For example, the landless agricultural workers may benefit in terms of income effect but not in terms of employment effect. In conditions of lower prices, the large farmers may prefer to withhold their marketable surpluses in the expectation of a future rise in prices and may lower their demand for landless workers. The small farmers with smaller agricultural surpluses can much less afford to hoard; neither can they influence prices through their actions. The situation of deficit farmers (who often have to work on others' farms for a money wage) would be even worse – they would lose in terms of both income effect and employment effect.

In the case of the industrial sector, the capitalists and the big business and commercial houses and traders, and civil servants make up a dominant social class. Jha[46] argues that a new intermediate class, consisting of peasant proprietors, small industrialists, traders and other self-employed groups, has emerged as a powerful political force in India. He believes that government economic policies like protection of small-scale industry, have benefited the self-employed classes. So has inflation benefited large farmers and traders through higher food prices and through black marketing. But the professional and salaried classes have suffered on account of a fall in real wages. The traders and other self-employed, as well as the bureaucrats, have exploited economic shortages to their advantage thus leading to further inflation.

Jha's analysis of classes is oversimplified. Class inequalities in India seem to be much more complicated. For instance, the so-called intermediate self-employed class is a heterogeneous mass of several interest groups without a common cause.

Family inheritance is another basis for class distinctions in both China and India, and in developing countries in general. Those from rich and well-to-do families tend to enjoy better access to jobs, education and privileges than people with ordinary family backgrounds. However, in China a poor family background was less of a stigma in the Mao period than in the post-Mao period when inequality and differences between social and economic classes began to resurface. One of the main reasons for growing class inequalities during the post-Mao period is the re-emergence of some form of private ownership of property and increasing income from self-employment. Although in the rural areas, land is still collectively owned, its use and benefits are acquired by private households. Similarly, in the case of the urban sector, private commerce, sideline activities, services, and most recently the emerging private ownership of houses, apartments and cars, account for new class-based social and economic inequalities.

As we shall examine in Chapters 8 and 9, access of children from worker and peasant backgrounds to higher education and social services like health is more restricted than in the Mao period. The post-Mao urban economic reforms seem to favour the Liptonian urban class in several ways. For example, the urban industrial worker can take early retirement with one child taking over his or her place in the factory. Furthermore, urban youth do not have to go to the rural areas, whereas the rural people are still restricted from moving to the urban areas. There are subsidies for urban food and housing but no such subsidies are offered to rural areas.

IV CONCLUSION

In this chapter we have described three sets of inequalities: rural–urban inequalities, regional inequalities and class inequalities. China shows lower income/consumption and class inequalities than India but not regional inequalities. Yet as we noted in Chapter 3, while both countries have followed very similar development strategies, their outcomes have turned out to be quite different. Does this mean that strategies have little impact on the outcome? We maintain that this is not plausible. A growth maximisation strategy (which was followed by both countries) can *a priori* lead to greater income and consumption inequalities but need not do so if appropriate redistributive measures can be adopted and implemented to redistribute the fruits of growth.

In China during the Mao period, notwithstanding the existence of rural–urban disparities, poverty and extreme inequalities were reduced more successfully than in India. This better performance has clearly been policy induced. Redistributive measures kept the prevailing inequalities from getting worse, and in many cases actually reduced income inequalities.

APPENDIX 6.1: MATHEMATICAL PROOF OF UNBIASED ESTIMATION OF VARIANCE[47]

Assume μ and σ^2 are the unknown population mean and variance, n is the

number of observations, X_i , X_j are independent sample of observations, w_i, w_j are weights and $\sum\limits_{i=1}^{n} w_i = 1$, the weighted mean is: $\overline{X}_w = \sum\limits_{i=1}^{n} w_i X_i$.
Then,

$$E(\hat{\sigma}_w^2) = \frac{1}{n - 2 + n \sum\limits_{j=1}^{n} w_j^2} \sum\limits_{i=1}^{n} E \left(X_i - \sum\limits_{j=1}^{n} w_j X_j \right)^2$$

$$= \frac{1}{n - 2 + n \sum\limits_{j=1}^{n} w_j^2} \sum\limits_{i=1}^{n} E \left[(X_i - \mu) - \sum\limits_{j=1}^{n} w_j (X_j - \mu) \right]^2$$

$$= \frac{1}{n - 2 + n \sum\limits_{j=1}^{n} w_j^2} \sum\limits_{i=1}^{n} E \left[\sigma^2 - 2 w_i \sigma^2 + \sum\limits_{j=1}^{n} w_j^2 \sigma^2 \right]$$

$$= \sigma^2$$

$$\text{(since } E(X_i - \mu)(X_j - \mu) = 0, i \neq j)$$

Hence,

$$\hat{\sigma}_w^2 = \frac{1}{n - 2 + n \sum\limits_{j=1}^{n} w_j^2} \sum\limits_{i=1}^{n} (X_i - \overline{X}_w)^2$$

is unbiased estimator for the population variance.

Notes and References

1. Ehtisham Ahmad and Athar Hussain, *Public Action for Social Security in China*, paper prepared for a workshop on Social Security in Developing Countries, London School of Economics, July 1988.
2. See National Council of Applied Economic Research (NCAER), *Changes in Household Income, Inter-class Mobility and Income Distribution in Rural India*, A Longitudinal Study, 1970–71 – 1981–82, (mimeo), New Delhi, 1986.
3. This point is due to Idrak Bhatty and his staff, NCAER, New Delhi.
4. NCAER, *Household Income and its Disposition*, New Delhi, 1980, p. 123.

5. Ibid.
6. Nicholas R. Lardy, 'Consumption and Living Standards in China, 1978–83', *China Quarterly*, December 1984.
7. Cited in Dai Yannian, 'Dealing with Unfair Income Gaps', *Beijing Review*, 15–21 August 1988.
8. Ibid.
9. P. K. Bardhan, 'The Pattern of Income Distribution in India: A Review', in P. K. Bardhan and T. N. Srinivasan (eds), *Poverty and Income Distribution in India*, Calcutta, Statistical Publishing Society, 1974.
10. Dwight Heald Perkins, 'Reforming China's Economic System', *Journal of Economic Literature*, June 1988.
11. See G. K. Kadekodi, 'The Cost of a Balanced Diet', in R. Sinha *et al.*, *Poverty, Income Distribution and Employment – A Case Study of India*, Glasgow, Delhi, Oxford Project Report, 1978, Part II (mimeo); and G. S. Chatterjee and N. Bhattacharya, 'On Disparities in Per Capita Household Consumption', in Bardhan and Srinivasan, *Poverty and Income Distribution*, p. 195.
12. *Statistical Yearbook of China*, 1986, p. 584.
13. Sudipto Mundle, 'Land, Labour and the Level of Living in Rural Punjab', in A. R. Khan and Eddy Lee (eds), *Poverty in Rural Asia*, Bangkok, ILO/ARTEP, 1983.
14. Sudipto Mundle, 'Land, Labour and the Level of Living in Rural Bihar', in Khan and Lee, ibid.
15. Ashoka Mody, 'Resource Flows Between Agriculture and Non-agriculture', *Economic and Political Weekly*, Annual Number, March 1981.
16. A. Mody, 'Rural Resources Generation and Mobilisation', *Economic and Political Weekly*, March 1983.
17. Dwight Perkins and Shahid Yusuf, *Rural Development in China*, Baltimore, Johns Hopkins Press, 1984.
18. Ibid, p. 19.
19. Anand G. Chandavarkar, 'The Financial Pull of Urban Areas in LDCs – The Phenomenon of Urban Bias in its Financial Aspects and Some Possible Correctives', *Finance and Development*, June 1984.
20. N. J. Bhatia, 'Trends in Credit-Deposit and Investment-Credit–Deposit Ratios of Scheduled Commercial Banks, 1969–1985', *Reserve Bank of India Bulletin*, May 1987.
21. Gregory C. Chow, *The Chinese Economy*, Harper & Row Publishers, 1985, p. 233; and *Almanac of China's Economy*, 1981, pp. 662–63.
22. On-Kit Tam, 'Rural Finance in China', *China Quarterly*, March 1988.
23. P. Radhakrishnan, 'Land Reforms: Rhetoric and Reality', *Economic and Political Weekly*, 24 November 1990.
24. Ehtisham Ahmad and Athar Hussain, *Public Action for Social Security in China*.
25. See A. S. Kahlon and D. S. Tyagi, *Agricultural Price Policy in India*, New Delhi, Allied Publishers Private Ltd, 1983, pp. 448–51.
26. Amartya Sen and Jean Drèze, *Hunger and Public Action*, Oxford, Clarendon Press, 1989, p. 209.
27. Alain de Janvry and K. Subbarao, *Agricultural Price Policy and Income*

Distribution in India, Delhi, Oxford University Press, 1986.
28. See Suzanne Paine, 'Spatial Aspects of Chinese Development Issues, Outcomes and Policies, 1949–79', *Journal of Development Studies*, January 1981.
29. Thomas P. Lyons, 'Interprovincial Trade and Development in China, 1957–1979', *Economic Development and Cultural Change*, January 1987.
30. This result is consistent with that of a recent study which concludes that 'all the secondary activities taken together show much less regional disparity than the registered (large) manufacturing sector'. See Ravindra H. Dholakia, 'Regional Aspects of Industrialisation in India', *Economic and Political Weekly*, 18 November 1989.
31. Nicholas R. Lardy, *Economic Growth and Distribution in China*, Cambridge, Cambridge University Press, 1978.
32. G. S. Bhalla and D. S. Tyagi, *Patterns in Indian Agricultural Development – A District Level Study*, New Delhi, Institute for Studies in Industrial Development, 1989.
33. Jeffrey G. Williamson, 'Regional Inequality and the Process of National Development – A Description of the Patterns', *Economic Development and Cultural Change*, Part II, July 1965.
34. Rizwanul Islam, 'The Growth of Rural Industry in Post-Reform China: Patterns, Determinants and Consequences', *Development and Change*, October 1991.
35. Tuoyu Wang, 'Regional Imbalances', in William A. Byrd and Lin Qingsong, (eds), *China's Rural Industry: Structure, Development and Reform*, Oxford, Oxford University Press, 1990.
36. Richard Curt Kraus, *Class Conflict in Chinese Socialism*, New York, Columbia University Press, 1981.
37. Graham Young, 'Control and Style: Discipline and Inspection Commissions since the 11th Congress', *China Quarterly*, March 1984; and William L. Parish, 'Egalitarianism in Chinese Society', *Problems of Communism*, January-February 1981.
38. Parish, ibid.
39. de Janvry and Subbarao, *Agricultural Price Policy* . . . 1986.
40. T. J. Byres, 'The New Technology, Class Formation and Class Action in the Indian Countryside', *Journal of Peasant Studies*, July 1981.
41. Sheila Bhalla, 'Agricultural Growth: Role of Institutional and Infrastructural Factors', *Economic and Political Weekly*, 5 and 12 November 1977; and Biplab Das Gupta, *Agrarian Change and the New Technology in India*, Geneva, UNRISD, 1977.
42. Lloyd I. Rudolph and Susanne Hoeber Rudolph, *In Pursuit of Lakshmi – The Political Economy of the Indian State*, New Delhi, Orient Longman, 1988, p. 2.
43. Michael Lipton with Richard Longhurst, *New Seeds and Poor People*, London, Unwin Hyman, 1989.
44. In India, in 1960–61, about 18 per cent of the medium and large farmers (which accounted for over 61 per cent of the total farm land) delivered more than two-thirds of the marketed surplus. See Utsa Patnaik, 'Output and Marketable Surplus of Agricultural Products: Contributions by Cultivating Groups, 1960–61, *Economic and Political Weekly (Review of*

Agriculture), December 1975.
45. de Janvry and Subbarao, *Agricultural Price Policy* . . ..
46. Prem Shankar Jha, *INDIA – A Political Economy of Stagnation*, Delhi, Oxford University Press, 1980.
47. I am grateful to Dr Yue Ma of Economics Department, University of Strathclyde, for this mathematical proof.

7 Classes, Technology and Access

The economic/spatial inequalities and imbalances will be influenced by the unequal access of different income and social classes to assets, technology, information and other inputs.

There is a link between technology and income distribution in all economies. Technology and technical change are not neutral with respect to resource base and social classes.[1] Their impact may be biased in favour of certain factor owners and socioeconomic groups and against others. Some social groups (e.g. large farmers and landlords) enjoy political power which they may exercise for manipulating government policies (e.g. agricultural price policy and terms of trade) to their advantage. Institutional and economic policy environment, within which technological change occurs, is hardly neutral as among different social and other interest groups. For example, in India the Green Revolution was concentrated on 'regions that were already well-endowed, on crops already profitable and on farmers already rich'.[2]

In this chapter we shall discuss these biases, particularly (a) commodity bias or greater priority to some crops and commodities over others and (b) regional/locational bias in favour of large landowners and in favour of some regions more than others.

The above biases are likely to prevail in both planned and market economies although in planned socialist economies the State may exercise direct control or ownership of resources and keep biases in check.

Our main purpose in this chapter is not to review technology policies *per se* but instead to study how they influence access. Therefore in Section I we examine issues of differential access to technology in China and India against the backdrop of their broad technology approaches and policies. Section II is devoted to issues of access to technology and inputs in the agricultural and industrial sectors. The contrast between large and small farmers is considered in terms of access to technology, credit and irrigation. In Section III we deal with class and commodity bias in agricultural research, and in Section IV with regional/inter-provincial inequalities of access to inputs and technology.

148

I TECHNOLOGY POLICIES AND APPROACHES

Our concern here is to study access of rural and urban producers to technology and inputs produced domestically or imported and to consider the influence of technology imports on inequality and uneven domestic development. A comparison in this respect between India and China is meaningful despite their different approaches to technology imports, indigenous technology development and self-reliance. As noted in Chapter 3, both countries have been guided by similar objectives – growth, poverty alleviation and fulfilment of basic needs.

In both China and India, the goal of technological self-reliance was motivated by a desire to build domestic capabilities. Technology can be viewed as an instrument to raise productivity and output, earn foreign exchange, and generate employment, etc. In China during the Mao period, technology's role in generating employment was not considered all that important since full employment was at any rate guaranteed. The policy of walking on two legs – a mixture of traditional and advanced technologies – was instead guided by other considerations like defence and the need to utilise local resources. In the case of India, the need to protect 'traditional technologies' and promote 'appropriate technologies' was clearly influenced by employment considerations.

1.1 China

During the Mao period the existence of a 'mass science' movement was a unique experiment which finds no parallel in any other developing country. This movement, together with the development of local technology systems at the commune level, were a peculiarly Chinese innovation to promote the growth of local rural industry in a spirit of self-reliance.[3] The characteristics of the local technology systems, namely, participation of the local population and direct links of science and technology to production and rapid diffusion of innovations, were said to be favourable to ensuring maximum access of the rural poor to scientific and technological inputs.

However, opinions differ about the true impact of the science movement and the local technology systems. Their achievements may have fallen short of expectations partly owing to the shortage of qualified science and technology personnel at the local level and poor links between state and commune production units.[4] But the four-level research network which combined state R and D and extension system with the commune system linking production and research, must have contributed to an increase in grain output and productivity during the Mao period (see Table 7.1), although the expansion of grain output was achieved at the expense of cash crops.

In the post-Mao period, a shift from collective to household farming led to the disappearance of local technology delivery system. But the need for such a system to alleviate rural poverty and destitution was indeed recognised. Thus in 1982, the government introduced a ten-year plan to establish 'agro-technical centres' to consolidate hitherto dispersed local agricultural services like seed production, soil analysis and fertiliser distribution.[5] More recently, in 1985, under the auspices of the State Science and Technology Commission (SSTC), a new programme on the transfer of technology to rural areas – known as the SPARK Programme – was started to bring about the technological transformation of the rural economy.

The SPARK Programme is different from the earlier mass science movement. While the latter encouraged self-reliant initiatives at the local commune level, the new programme follows more of a top-down approach. SSTC has introduced a centrally administered scheme to upgrade the technological levels in rural areas (in agriculture, animal husbandry, rural industry and housing, etc.).

It is too early to assess the success of the SPARK Programme, but it seems to have generated enthusiasm to revitalise the rural economy. A progress report for this Programme for 1988 notes that since 1986 over 14,500 projects accounting for 8.75 million yuan of investment have been implemented.[6] This is a very modest investment in relation to China's technology budget or to total agricultural investment. It cannot therefore compensate for the overall neglect of agricultural investment.

However, the success of the rural responsibility system in generating additional incomes should create additional demand for improved technologies. In the final analysis, the success of the SPARK Programme will depend largely upon the closeness of collaboration between central institutions like the SSTC and the municipal and local bodies.

More recently, a special programme, *Jishu fupin* (Technology for the poor), has been introduced to disseminate technology to the backward rural areas. Whether this programme is particularly helpful to the target beneficiaries and is as successful as the earlier four-level network, remains to be seen.

In the post-Mao period, especially during the first phase of economic reforms, China introduced an open-door policy under which imports of foreign investments and technology were encouraged. The Ten-Year Plan announced in 1978 laid down ambitious development targets which could not be achieved without the import of advanced technology and know-how. The Plan reiterated priority to the programme of 'Four Modernisations' (agriculture, industry, defence and science and technology). Computerisation of industry and other sectors also received much attention.[7] Export processing zones were introduced to attract foreign capital and technology, as were joint ventures, cooperative production and compensatory trade.

The above import liberalisation (the so-called 'foreign leap forward') led to a drain on balance of payments and foreign exchange reserves. It may have also inhibited the development of indigenous technology, a priority in Mao's policy of self-reliance. Furthermore, liberal technology imports seem to have benefited mainly the advanced regions like Guangdong and Jiangsu rather than the rural areas in the hinterland.

1.2 India

In India also there had been similar technology policy initiatives and measures ever since independence. The 'appropriate technology' movement ante-dated independence and received its inspiration from the Gandhian ideals of self-reliance. Unlike the Chinese mass science movement which rested on a national network of communes, in India the appropriate rural technology projects were isolated and *ad hoc* in nature. There was also an ambivalence towards this technology among government scientific and technological bodies as well as academic and scientific institutions.

In 1985–86, India liberalised its economic policies and encouraged the import of foreign investments and technology in an apparent reversal of earlier policies of technological self-reliance. Yet its technology import policy does not seem to be as flexible as that of China. It is more cautious and largely inward-looking with permission of imports granted only on a selective basis.[8]

Foreign collaboration agreements are used as a major channel for technology transfer. But inadequate efforts have been made to absorb and assimilate imported technology. Lack of R and D resources and domestic research effort linked to productive activity seem to explain this situation. R and D in private industry remains rather limited and public R and D tends to be isolated from concrete production problems.[9] Pilot plant facilities remain inadequate and domestic design capacity poor.[10] Efforts to match design capacity with manufacturing capacity (particularly in such sectors as chemicals and fertilisers) have been quite limited. These factors at least partly account for the relative technological backwardness of Indian industry.

II ACCESS TO TECHNOLOGY AND INPUTS

The demand for industrial technology in China (as in India) should increase under conditions of market socialism and freedom of the enterprises to take managerial and technological decisions. A rapid increase in rural incomes as a result of economic reforms has raised demand for improved technology also in agriculture and rural non-farm production. We examine these twin aspects below.

2.1 Agricultural Sector

There are two basic types of agricultural innovations: mechanical innovations characterised by tractorisation and other machinery inputs, and biological innovations such as high-yielding varieties of seeds (HYVs). Empirical observations show that in countries with abundant land resources technological change in agriculture tends towards mechanical innovations, whereas in land-scarce countries, agricultural research is biased towards biological types of innovations. Both China and India are land-scarce countries. It would therefore be interesting to examine the sources of growth of agricultural yields and land productivity in the two countries with a view to determining the relative importance of biological and mechanical innovations.

In China, the sown area has been declining since the early 1950s, but foodgrain production from declining land area has been higher than in India. As noted in Table 7.1, grain yields per unit of land were more than twice that of India between 1949 and 1982 and three times that of India since 1982. In the case of rice, land productivity in China was more than twice that of India in 1949 but it rose to four times in the early 1980s. In the case of wheat, in 1949 per unit land yields were about the same for China and India but in China they rose much faster than in India.

Table 7.1   Land productivity and agricultural yields by crops
(China and India) (kg per ha)

Year	China			India		
	Grains	*Rice*	*Wheat*	*Grains*	*Rice*	*Wheat*
1949	1028	1890	645	553	771	655
1952	1320	2408	735	580	764	763
1957	1463	2693	855	587	790	682
1965	1628	2940	1020	629	862	827
1978	2528	3975	1845	1022	1328	1568
1979	2783	4245	2138	876	1074	1436
1980	2738	4133	1890	1023	1336	1630
1981	2828	4320	2108	1032	1308	1691
1982	3124	4886	2449	1035	1231	1816
1983	3396	5096	2802	1162	1457	1843
1984	3615	5370	2970	1149	1417	1870
1985	3480	5250	2940	1175	1552	2046
1986	3525	5340	3045	1142	1482	1998
1987	3630	5415	3045*	1166**	1473**	1995**
1988	3630	5355	2985	–	–	–
1989	3690	5595	3150	–	–	–
Period growth rates (%)						
1978–82	24.0	22.9	32.7	1.3	–7.3	15.8
1982–87	16.0	10.8	24.3	12.6	19.6	9.8
1978–87	43.6	36.2	65.0	14.1	10.9	27.2
1952–78	91.5	65.0	151.0	76.2	73.8	105.5
1978–89	46.0	40.8	70.1	–	–	–

Sources: (1) China: *Statistical Yearbook of China*, 1987, p. 148; and *Agricultural Statistics, 1988–89*, Ministry of Agriculture, Beijing.
(2) India: *Agricultural Statistics at a Glance*, 1988, pp. 7, 9, 11; and *Economic Survey 1988–89, p. S–17*.

Notes: (1) In China, grains include rice, wheat, maize and tuber crops (5kg of tuber = 1 kg of wheat). Tubers include mainly sweet potatoes. In the urban areas, potato is treated as 'vegetable', whereas in the rural areas, it is regarded as grain. In India grains include: rice, wheat, maize, pulses, barley and millets.
(2) Data for India are for fiscal years – from 1949–50 to 1987–8.
* *SYC* 1988 (Chinese version), p. 253.
** Provisional.

Although period growth rates (see Table 7.1) are sensitive to the base period used, they show that the increase in grain yields was much higher during the first phase of the post-Mao reforms (1978–82) than during the second. This is because the grain output during the latter phase failed to grow rapidly due to a lack of adequate price incentive and low state investment in agriculture. Nevertheless, the growth in grain yields was higher in the post-Mao period than during the earlier period.

What accounts for the above differences between China and India? Our next task is to answer this question.

Biological Innovations

The much higher land productivity in China of grain crops (particularly of rice) and its regular increase are due mainly to successful biological innovations in HYVs, heavy inputs of fertilisers, multiple cropping and power irrigation. During the Sixth Five-Year Plan (1981–86) more than 80 new cultivars of wheat were sown on three million hectares of land. The Chinese Research Institute of Agricultural Economics has estimated that progress in science and technology was responsible for 27 per cent of the increase in gross agricultural output during 1972–80, 35 per cent during 1978–83 and 30–40 per cent during 1981–86.[11] These figures refer to the combined effects of biological and mechanical innovations and thus do not indicate the relative importance of biological innovations alone. Nevertheless, a useful indication is obtained from unofficial estimates by Wong, which show that between 1960 and 1980, fertilisers accounted for a 20 per cent increase in land productivity whereas machinery contributed to only a 12.6 per cent rise.[12]

Evidence on recent cellular engineering breakthroughs (merging of cells extracted from two different varieties) in China shows that crop yields have further increased. The use of bio-fertilisers has led to an average increase in wheat yields. The per hectare yields of grains could be further raised by another 10 to 30 per cent by using biopesticides.[13]

In India, HYVs have raised yields of wheat, and to a lesser extent, rice. The area under wheat HYVs increased from 35.5 per cent in 1970–71 to 83.4 per cent in 1986–87. In the case of rice, HYVs accounted for 15 per cent of rice area in 1970–71 and 57.6 per cent in 1986–87.

High-yielding innovations in agriculture call for adequate complementary inputs of fertiliser, irrigation water, power and other infrastructure. Most of these inputs were observed to be much higher per unit of cultivated area in China compared to India (see Table 7.2). For example, a comparison between India and China (see Table

7.3) shows that the Chinese input of fertiliser per hectare of arable land and per capita was much higher than that in India throughout the 1970s and 1980s. At present, it is three times higher, while the power irrigated area is twice as high as in India. Also, the growth of fertiliser consumption in China during the 1970s and 1980s was much faster than in India and most other developing countries. This may be due to a lower price of fertiliser in China than in India relative to the output price. Although fertiliser prices are allowed to float in China, the State continues to exercise some control on supply channels and thereby on price. Price reduction may have increased market demand for fertilisers and therefore given a boost to their production. The greater application of fertilisers in China may tend to reduce the cost of production; it may also free labour from manual work (e.g. for obtaining organic fertilisers). Thus, whether the use of fertiliser would reduce costs depends on the opportunity cost of labour and the farmers' estimation of the value of leisure vs. work.

More intensive fertiliser inputs combined with HYVs thus seem to explain the higher agricultural yields in China than in India. This is illustrated in Figure 7.1. The vertical axis measures land productivity whereas the horizontal axis measures the inputs of fertilisers and irrigation. V_1 and V_2 are the two HYVs representing different technological levels. P_2 is the highest productivity that can be achieved with V_1 applying F_1 inputs of fertiliser and irrigation. Beyond this point, any extra inputs would not raise productivity any higher. It would appear that given the much higher input applications, China has been able to achieve this level whereas India has not. The Indian level of productivity is shown by P_1. This lower level is due to the lower amounts of complementary inputs.

A comparison of China and India shows that although China has lower land area under HYVs of rice than India (Table 7.2) the gap between India and China may be somewhat exaggerated, especially as the Chinese varieties are one generation more advanced than those in India. It is worth noting that HYVs of rice and wheat were introduced in Chinese agriculture in the 1950s much earlier than in India (the mid-1960s). It is noted that they also matured much earlier and were resistant to cold weather which enabled multiple cropping.[14] This situation is shown in Figure 7.1 by V_2 indicating much higher yields in China.

If the Chinese HYVs are one generation more advanced than those in India (i.e. V_2 instead of V_1 in Figure 7.1) China could achieve much higher land productivity P_3 by raising its fertiliser and irrigation

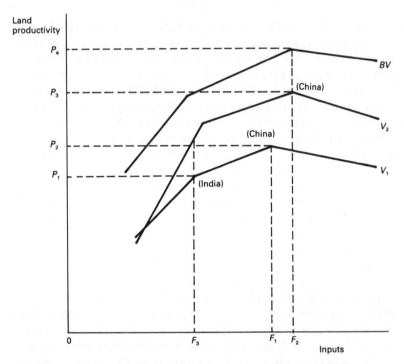

Figure 7.1   Land productivity differences between China and India

inputs. However, India could not progress beyond P_2 without developing higher generation varieties and/or by switching to genetically engineered varieties (exploiting the potential of the bio-revolution). This latter possibility is shown by the development of biotechnology variety *BV* which enables higher land productivity from given inputs. To the extent that biotechnological breakthroughs involve saving of such inputs as fertilisers, this option may be preferred to the development of more advanced HYVs under existing technology.

However, in his study of sources of agricultural growth in China and India, Wong has shown that in both countries there was little net gain from technical change. The growth of agricultural productivity has been achieved largely through increased use of factor inputs.[15] This suggests that appropriate policies to raise efficiency in resources use can raise agricultural output further.

As Figure 7.1 shows, HYVs need complementary inputs like fertilisers and irrigation to maximise productivity. Thus the issue of

Table 7.2 Indicators of technological level in agriculture
(China vs. India)

Item	China		India	
Total net sown area (million ha)	144	(1985)	141	(1984–5)
Net irrigated area (million ha) Of which:	44	(1985)	41	(1982–3)
Power irrigated area (million ha)	25	(1985)	11	(1982–3)
(%)	56	(1985)	27	(1982–3)
Fertiliser input (kg per ha)	176	(1986)	57	(1986)
Area under HYVs (%) Wheat	–		83	(1986–7)
Rice	28	(1986)	57	(1986–7)
Agricultural consumption of electricity as % of total consumption	–		19	(1985–6)
Number of tractors (per 1,000 ha)	6	(1984)	0.6	(1984–5)
Tractor-ploughed area (mill. ha)	36	(1986)	–	

Sources: (1) China: *Statistical Yearbook of China, 1986* and *China Agriculture Yearbook, 1986*. (2) India: *Indian Agriculture in Brief*, (Ministry of Agriculture, New Delhi), pp. 256–7, and *Agricultural Statistics at a Glance*, p. 76.
– = not available.

access to biological technology really boils down to that of access to these complementary inputs and credit supplies once a new HYV is innovated.

Small vs. Large Farmers

The Chinese data on agricultural inputs and technology are not disaggregated by the type of farms or by types of three-tier agrarian structure which prevailed during the Mao period. Unlike India, in China a distinction between small and large farms is not as important as that between collective farms and state farms. The latter are mainly very large farms with much more assured supplies of inputs and technology.

Development Outcomes

Table 7.3   Fertiliser consumption in China and India (1971–86) (kg)

Year	Per ha of arable land		Per capita	
	China	*India*	*China*	*India*
1971	44.7	14.5	5.4	4.2
1976	63.8	20.1	6.8	5.3
1981	150.2	34.0	15.0	8.2
1986	176.2	57.1	16.1	12.5
Rate of Growth (per cent per annum)				
1971–76	7.4	6.6	4.7	4.7
1976–81	18.6	11.0	17.0	9.1
1981–86	3.2	10.9	1.4	8.7

Source: FAO, *Fertiliser Yearbook*, Rome, 1987, vol. 37, p. 18.

Access of small farms and state farms to inputs and technology can be measured by three indicators: (a) application of fertilisers, other chemicals and electricity per hectare, (b) percentage of farm land irrigated and ploughed by machinery and (c) farm machinery inputs in terms of horsepower. The *China Agricultural Yearbook* contains some of these data on the basis of which Table 7.4 below is estimated. In the *Yearbook* the tables referring to state farms are specific to the state farms only, whereas the tables referring to 'agriculture' as such refer to small farms. Below, we examine the experience of State vs. collective farms in China and small vs. large farms in India. The input of chemical fertiliser per unit of land sown is almost identical for state and collective farms. However, the input of chemical fertilisers per unit of output is much higher in the former. The state farms are much more mechanised/tractorised than the collective farms. The land–man ratio for state farms is also much higher than that for collective farms. While the state farms are cultivated very extensively, the collective farms are much more intensive in the use of such inputs as chemicals, irrigation water and labour.

The rural economic reforms in the post-Mao period have led to the emergence of private marketing and distribution agencies which (like any others in a market economy) tend to make quick profits by creating artificial scarcities. Furthermore, one would expect that the richer households have better access to supply of agricultural inputs

Table 7.4 Access to technology and inputs in China
(state vs. collective farms) (1985)

Indicator	State farms	Collective farms
Agricultural machinery input (hp per 1,000 ha)	2,600	2,000
Large/medium tractors (no. per 1,000 ha)	14.9	5.9
Small tractors (no. per 1,000 ha)	13.9	26.6
Chemical fertilisers		
(i) kg per 1,000 ha	122.5	123.6
(ii) tons per 1,000 tons of grain	69.7	46.8
(iii) tons per 1,000 tons of cotton	117.4	42.8
(iv) tons per 1,000 tons of oil crops	1752	889

Source: *China Agriculture Yearbook*, 1986.

and technology than the poorer ones. Conroy reports that the distribution of agricultural inputs was inequitable partly due to supply and distribution problems and partly due to 'appropriation through the use of political and administrative power and personal relationships'.[16] Cases of corruption in the distribution of chemical fertilisers to the farmers are frequently reported in the Chinese press. Although fertiliser prices have been declining relative to other prices, speculation by officials or private profiteers has destabilised these prices. Decentralised decision-making may have further encouraged hoarding of fertiliser by the marketing and distribution agencies.

In India the issue of access to technology has been debated extensively, particularly in the context of the impact of the Green Revolution (GR) on equity and growth in agriculture. The Indian experience of the GR shows that both large and small farmers adopted HYVs, particularly in Punjab where technology diffusion was quite rapid, but also in areas with moderate adoption rates. However, the smaller farmers were somewhat slower in adopting the new technology due in part to risk aversion and limited investible resources.

Notwithstanding the widespread adoption of the new agricultural technology, studies have shown that the GR benefited the large farmers (who have better access to resources and greater political clout) much more than the small farmers, thus leading to greater rural inequality in income distribution.[17] The small farmers have been disadvantaged in respect of irrigation water, credit supply and supplies of fertilisers. In the case of fertiliser use however, there is no conclusive evidence to support the hypothesis that the small farmers were particularly discriminated against. In 1977, the share of small and marginal farms in total fertiliser use was estimated at about 32 per cent which is not so insignificant. According to an NCAER survey undertaken from 1968–69 to 1970–71, 'the proportion of gross cropped area fertilised per holding increased with farm size, but the intensity of fertiliser use per hectare of cropped area was greatest on small holdings'.[18]

As noted above, irrigation water and fertilisers are two important input requirements for the efficient use of HYVs. Since small farmers have lower incomes, they are less likely to be able to afford these inputs out of their own meagre savings and are therefore forced to resort to borrowing from both formal and informal channels. Access to credit therefore becomes a dominant factor in ensuring effective access to necessary inputs.

As noted in Chapter 6, in China there does not seem to be any lack of credit availability in the rural areas. There is a general trend towards supplying capital to the countryside on the basis of low-interest loans rather than budgetary allocations. In India, on the other hand, there are indications that formal credit institutions have been biased against small farmers who often have to resort to private money lenders (generally large farmers) charging exorbitant interest rates. These money lenders are estimated to have provided two-thirds of the total amount borrowed by small and marginal farmers. Furthermore, it is reported that 'of the 54 million ownership holdings less than 2 ha in size, only 8 million had access to cooperative credit'.[19]

Access to irrigation facilities also seems to have been biased against small farmers for much of the planning period. The factors explaining differential access are not only economic but also political and institutional. The distribution of surface water tends to be biased in favour of large farmers because of their political influence and greater access to institutional credit, presumably on grounds of economies of large scale.

Lately, equity considerations have led to a shift in policy emphasis in favour of increased access to technology by small farmers through private tubewells, credit, etc.

Table 7.5 Use of mechanical technology in agriculture
(China vs. India) (000)

	China			India	
Year	Large/medium tractors	Small tractors	Year	Tractors	Power tillers
			1970–71	33.40	1.45
1965	72	4	1972–73	21.81	1.31
1978	557	1373	1978–79	54.80	2.33
1979	667	1671	1979–80	62.75	2.53
1980	745	1874	1980–81	70.00	2.12
1981	792	2037	1981–82	84.10	2.35
1982	812	2287	1982–83	63.05	2.25
1983	841	2750	1983–84	76.17	2.75
1984	854	3298	1984–85	85.00	4.22
1985	852	3824			
1986	866	4526			
1988	870	5958			
1989	848	6539			
Growth rate:					
1978–86			1978–79 to		
	5.6	10.9	1984–85	7.6	3.0
1978–89	3.9	15.2	–	–	–

Source: (1) China: *Statistical Yearbook of China*, several years; and *Agricultural Statistics*, 1988–89.
(2) India: *Indian Agriculture in Brief*, Ministry of Agriculture, 1986, pp. 74–5.

Mechanical Innovations

The above discussion may give the impression that mechanical innovations in agriculture were much less important than the biological innovations in explaining productivity growth. While this may well be true, mechanical innovations have also played their part.

Table 7.5 shows that in China the use of small walking tractors doubled between 1982 and 1986 whereas that of large and medium tractors remained more or less stable. The growth of large tractors between 1978 and 1986 was much slower than that of small tractors. Furthermore, the degree of tractorisation, which is more economical at larger scale of production (e.g. that of the former communes), has declined with a shift from collective to family farming. Under the agricultural responsibility system, land holdings per household or production team are much smaller, which makes the use of large tractors uneconomical. This suggests that large machinery is likely to be much less important in future than the use of fertilisers and high-yielding varieties.[20]

In the case of India, the absolute number of tractors is much smaller than that in China, but their growth is slightly higher due to its smaller base. The number of tractors per 1,000 ha is also much lower in India – 0.6 as against 6 in China (see Table 7.2). This suggests the higher level of farm mechanisation in China, and may also partly explain the higher land productivity in China noted above. Since the Chinese level of mechanisation is already much higher, China seems to put 'more emphasis on fertiliser whereas the Indians put more emphasis on machinery'.[21]

Impact on Equity and Welfare

The combined impact of both the biological and mechanical innovations discussed above is likely to be beneficial for both small and large producers by generating higher incomes through higher productivity. However, this favourable effect has not been equitably distributed.

A beneficial impact could occur through an increase in labour input per unit of land which would offer greater employment and higher labour incomes.

Improvements in agricultural innovations also have welfare and equity implications via their impact on consumers. By reducing unit costs of production, say of food, technological change enables a lowering of consumer prices thus raising the real incomes and welfare of the consumers in general and of the poor consumers in particular. However, this assumes free functioning of markets in price determination which is not true in China where food prices are state controlled.

In India the above indirect contribution of HYV technology to equity through food security and a decline in relative price of food-grains has been more significant than the direct positive impact on employment in agriculture.[22]

2.2   Industrial Sector

Liberal imports and joint ventures with foreign firms are likely mainly to favour large-scale state-owned industries with their control of resources and more advanced technologies in providing access to technology and required inputs. This seems also to be true of the domestic transfers of technology from the state sector, namely the Chinese Academy of Sciences, to the productive sectors. However, the diffusion of this technology has been at a rather slow rate. Further, from 1979 to 1985, the major beneficiaries were the large and medium enterprises. Only about 10 per cent of the technology from the Academy went to the collective village and township enterprises.[23]

The poor diffusion of technology is explained by several factors. First is the failure of the potential technology users to recognise its importance in raising productivity, sales and profits. Secondly, it may be due to the cost and other problems in seeking access to relevant technology which, until 1979, was supplied free only to the state enterprises. Thirdly, in China R and D has been oriented more towards pure than to applied research, partly because the latter requires more funding.

There is another factor which impeded technology diffusion. Rigid state controls and vertical hierarchy as well as the industrial structure prevented a horizontal exchange of technology among a large number of industrial enterprises. On the other hand, complete state ownership and control of science and technology meant that the state could in principle ensure free technology exchange by any enterprises. This situation changed considerably in the 1980s. The introduction of market socialism and limited price reforms, the contract system of research, decentralisation of decision-making to the enterprises, the growth of joint ventures with foreign firms, and the introduction of new patent laws were all factors leading to a change of attitude towards sharing of technology among enterprises. Gradual privatisation implying competition has led to growing secrecy on the part of enterprises about technology and know-how.

In India, as we noted in Chapter 3, the industrial policy of controls and restrictions has meant limited imports of foreign technology through foreign investment. In general, outright purchase of technology through royalty payments is preferred to foreign investment as a means of technology transfer. The objective of technological autonomy continues to be pursued in India, perhaps much more rigorously than in China.

A recent survey of selected state-owned and private industrial establishments in India showed that with the exception of technical assistance through sub-contracting, there is relatively little inter-firm technology transfer. Whatever transfer does take place, involves discarded technologies.[24] It is not clear whether recent economic liberalisation and relaxation of restrictions on technology imports has improved the access of industrial enterprises to such technology.

Contract Research

In China a selective introduction of market principles has led to the emergence of a contract research system under which the productive sector pays for the technology to the suppliers, be it the Academy or national and provincial research institutes. There seem to be two main reasons for introducing the contract research system. First, contractual agreements between producers and users of technology indicate the existence of effective demand by the users who are likely to ensure a maximum utilisation of the technology. The second reason for the introduction of the contract system is to enable the research institutes to be partly self-financed so as to reduce the burden on the state budget which financed almost all research during the Mao period. The problem here is that under pressure to become self-financing, given the temptation to maximise profits, the behaviour of research and academic institutions has sometimes turned out to be socially sub-optimal. Many of these institutions are engaged in unrelated commercial pursuits (e.g. running hostels and printing firms).

Such reforms as higher profit retention rates, tax holidays, decentralised decision-making, etc. should encourage the enterprises to invest more in technological improvements, but the actual record is disappointing. The effects of the profit retention system are partly nullified by an increase in a number of taxes – income tax on profits, product and business taxes, etc. For instance, Baark has noted that 'in Tianjan the enterprises of the First Light Industry Bureau had to hand over 330 million of the 400 million yuan earned in 1985 to the State. . . . and frequently enterprises were able to spend only a couple of thousand yuan on technology or product development'.[25]

Contract research is at present rather limited although an increasing number of contracts are being signed between research institutes and productive enterprises. Whether or not in future, these lead to significant technological advance would depend on managerial factors internal to the enterprise and the degree of competition among firms.

Access of Rural Industrial Enterprises

China. In the past, rural industrial enterprises depended mainly on technologies that were locally available. The import of modern technology mainly from the Soviet Union was suited only to the large-scale state enterprises. The collective enterprises at the commune level were also supposed to rely mainly on indigenous raw materials and local technology consistent with a strategy of self-reliance. This inequitable access to technology and inputs resulted directly from the dualistic technology policy of walking on two legs, and could even be justified as imported technology had limited application to small industrial enterprises.

In the post-Mao period, favourable incentives for the promotion of township and village enterprises have led to their proliferation. The SPARK Programme described earlier in this chapter may have been an important factor in ensuring access of these enterprises to raw materials, technologies and credit, etc. The rising capital–labour ratio in many of these enterprises may in fact be evidence of an increased access.

But deregulation also set in motion speculation, hoarding and scarcities. Corruption and malpractices have been noticed, for example, in the distribution of iron and steel, coal and silk cocoons. But the major factor explaining this situation is the 'dual' pricing system which was introduced in 1985 for producer goods and intermediate products. Under this system, quotas 'within plan' are priced at below equilibrium levels, and items 'outside plan' are priced at much higher free market levels. (The distinction between these two price levels is quite arbitrary.) This dual pricing system was intended to be a compromise between controls and total price liberalisation. The Chinese government felt that a total liberalisation of prices of scarce raw materials and producer goods might lead to price spiralling, given the strong production linkages between them, examined in Chapter 4.

In the absence of any suitable mechanism for a macroeconomic management of the economy the policy of price deregulation seems to have backfired. Deregulation has encouraged speculators to step into the market to make quick profits. Thus shortages of raw materials and intermediate goods are not so much due to inadequate production as to hoarding, speculation and distribution bottlenecks.

Another reason for the above shortages is competition between the village and township enterprises and the larger state factories for the raw material supplies. The growth of the former in the wake of rural diversification resulting from rural reforms has caused a problem of differential access to raw material supplies. A study of silk cocoon production in Suzhou (Zhejiang) by the Institute of Rural Development of the Chinese Academy of Social Sciences noted severe competition between rural producers and the urban silk industry.[26] Although the local government had stipulated that farmers must sell their output to the state factories they continued to sell cocoons privately to rural households for home-based silk reeling and to village and township enterprises at a much higher price.

The above example suggests that the market mechanism does not really function in China. The state-sector producers cannot offer higher prices and pass on the costs to consumers. The small rural industrial enterprises produce goods (often of lower quality) which can even be sold at higher prices. This is a common paradox of socialist economies.

India. In the case of India, market functioning has been restricted through government intervention. India is one of the few developing countries protecting small industry in both product and factor markets (see Chapter 4). The rationale of protection for small industry lies in equity and the need to preserve the means of livelihood of those who are unlikely to find alternative sources of employment. But it may also have had the effect of slowing down industrial growth. The Indian protection policy has some parallel to the recent SPARK Programme in China. Under both these schemes, small enterprises are assured access to inputs and technology. However, in the past the Indian policy was known to be more protective than developmental, with the result that the technological levels of rural industrial enterprises remained quite stagnant. In China, on the other hand, the emphasis seems to be much more on a technological modernisation of these enterprises.

The position of rural industrial enterprises (and agriculture) in respect of access to technology is different from that of the large industrial sector. First, agricultural and rural industrial products are not patented, which means that technology is likely to be available more freely. Secondly, the State continues to play a major role in the provision of inputs and technology through agricultural and industrial research institutes.

III   CLASS AND COMMODITY BIAS IN AGRICULTURAL RESEARCH

As noted above, access to agricultural technology is not class neutral. The large farmers with greater political clout and better resources exploited and extracted privileged access to inputs and commodity markets.

The issue of commodity bias in research is relevant to the problem of technology access in several ways. First, as Ruttan has argued, equitable treatment of small farmers may necessitate preferential or at least favourable treatment at the research stage rather than at the stage of the application of technology.[27] Thus small-farm bias can be introduced through the selection for research of those commodities that are produced mainly by small farmers and/or regions character- ised by small farms. According to Ruttan, it is much more difficult to design technologies that are especially biased in favour of small farmers. Examples are given of research on beans in Latin America and dairy production in India to demonstrate a strategy of technology research based on considerations of equity.

Secondly, the technology may be both location specific and crop specific, which means that it will have to be tailored to the particular target beneficiaries. Thirdly, lack of research on basic small-farmer crops will tend to keep the output and productivity of these crops low, which means low incomes for the producers and their limited access to more advanced technology and inputs. This is a vicious circle of poverty and underdevelopment in agriculture.

In actual practice, agricultural research is generally biased against those crops which have little industrial use but are important for subsistence (e.g. cassava and sweet potatoes), which are mainly cultivated and eaten by poor farmers, and for which there is very little urban demand.[28] The allocation of research resources to differ- ent crops and disciplines is influenced by political factors and the preferences of powerful social groups. Furthermore, in developing countries, the cultivators of these crops are invariably small producers and poor farmers with little influence on research and extension programmes.

In India, agricultural research has been noted to be biased against major food crops like rice which is the staple diet of most poor people. In contrast, fruits and vegetables (the diet of relatively better-off people) receive much higher priority, disproportionate to their share in national agricultural output. This is shown in Table 7.6 which gives data on the allocation of research grants for 1981–82 by the Indian Council of Agricultural Research (ICAR). Furthermore, during 1979–82, no significant relationship existed between the share of expenditure on agricultural research in different states and their percentage contribution to national agricultural output.[29]

Table 7.6   Bias in agricultural research in India (1981–82)

Crop	Percentage of total exp. as research grant	Share of crop in total agri. output (%)
Rice	7.37	33.94
Wheat & other cereals	14.07	26.07
Millet & pulses	16.94	8.07
Fruits, veg. & other crops	61.61	31.88
Total	100.0	100.0

Source: Sudhir K. Mukhopadhyay, 'Factors Influencing Agricultural Research and Technology: A Case Study of India', in Iftikhar Ahmed and Vernon Ruttan (eds), *Generation and Diffusion of Agricultural Innovations: The Role of Institutional Factors*, Aldershot, Gower, 1988, p. 154.

In China also, in the past, research on some crops like soybeans, which were important in Chinese diet, remained rather neglected. Research concentrated mainly on problems related to production and processing.[30] In the post-Mao period, most of the funds are allocated for crop research and the range of crops has widened. But very large proportions of the funds are taken up by the day-to-day running expenses of the agricultural R and D institutes (see Table 7.7). This may partly explain why the contribution of agricultural research to an increase in land and labour productivity between 1960 and 1980 has been rather low.[31] Another explanation may be a relative decline in the resources allocated for R and D. (Chinese agricultural research expenditure as percentage of the value of agricultural output is estimated to have declined from 0.68 per cent in 1970 to 0.56 per cent in 1980.) Research intensity (defined as scientist man-years per US $10 million worth of agricultural output at 1980 constant prices) also declined between 1970 and 1980.[32]

Unlike India, agricultural research in China seems to have been concentrated mainly on basic crops like rice and wheat. In the case of rice China has done some pioneering work in biological innovations. The results of agricultural research are also widely and quickly disseminated to the farmers, thanks to China's interlinked agricultural research and extension network.[33]

Table 7.7 Allocation of funds for agricultural R and D institutions in China (million yuan)

Item	Year		
	1985	*1986*	*1987*
National total	488.9	466.1	466.7
Funds by level of government:			
Ministry of Agriculture	133.8	85.6	95.8
Provincial governments	229.7	227.9	370.9[a]
Prefecture governments	125.4	132.8	–
Funds by Outlets			
Institutional expenses[b]	283.6	333.2	314.5
Natural science funds	2.2	1.0	2.2
Scientific projects	106.7	110.2	146.8
Equipment purchase[c]	13.9	–	–
Other projects[d]	82.5	–	–
Science development funds	–	1.7	3.2
Funds by sector			
Crops	289.3	290.4	332.0
Animal husbandry	63.9	56.7	59.8
Fisheries	59.5	51.5	45.2
Agri. machinery/chemicals	52.9	22.1	20.7
Military farms[e]	23.3	25.4	19.0

Source: Data supplied by the Ministry of Agriculture, Beijing.

Notes: [a] Starting from 1987, the sources of funds are classified as either central government allocation or local government allocation.
[b] Institutional expenses refer to the expenses incurred for the daily operation of the agricultural R and D institutions.
[cd] In computing the data for these two items the Ministry of Agriculture also included funds diverted for construction of office buildings and laboratories. Therefore, the 1985 figures need to be treated with caution. Since 1986, funds for capital construction have been recorded under a separate entry which has been omitted from this table.
[e] Strictly speaking, military farms do not belong to the Ministry of Agriculture. For the sake of statistical convenience, the figures are included. Military farms were established in the early 1950s to reclaim the barren waste lands in the northwestern, northeastern and southern parts of China.

IV REGIONAL DISPARITIES

In Chapter 6 we have already examined spatial (regional) disparities in China and India in terms of broad economic and social indicators. Here we discuss these disparities in terms of technological factors, namely, allocation of R and D funds (for industry in the case of India and for all economic activities in the case of China), the share of power irrigated area, consumption of fertiliser per hectare, consumption of electricity for agricultural purposes and the share of tractor-ploughed area. However, strictly comparable data for all these indicators were not available. Nevertheless, estimates of weighted means, standard deviations and coefficients of variation reported in Table 7.8 give some broad indication of whether disparities are more marked in China or India. Regional disparities in China are quite high in respect of power irrigated area and fertiliser consumption, and for 1985 they are much lower there than in India in the case of the latter. Lower regional inequalities in respect of fertiliser consumption in China may be because local self-sufficiency might have encouraged a widespread diffusion of agricultural technology. On the other hand, in India the effects of the Green Revolution have been localised in the northern States. However, the coefficient of variation (Co. V) for 1988 has risen again. Could it simply be due to differences in coverage? Or are there any other explanations? It is difficult to determine this on the basis of patchy data.

In China, the differences in respect of allocation of R and D expenditure and scientific and engineering manpower are extremely high as is suggested by the very high coefficients of variation. This seems to be explained by overconcentration of industry in a few key provinces and in the autonomous municipalities of Beijing, Shanghai and Tianjin. Secondly, differences in data coverage (Chinese data cover both agriculture and industry whereas Indian data are for industry only) may account for some differences. Thirdly, in China agricultural research is much more decentralised to the local commune level than in India. The richer communes are likely to spend much more on R and D than the poorer communes – this may have accentuated regional variations. In India, although the regional differences regarding R and D expenditures are also high, they are much lower than those in China. The regional research laboratories under the Indian Council of Scientific and Industrial Research (CSIR), though perhaps similar to the Chinese in their organisational

Table 7.8   Spatial technological disparities in China and India

Indicator	China			India		
	WM	SD	Co.V	WM	SD	Co.V
Power-irrigated area						
(1982)	71.1	36.1	0.51	71.6	37.5	0.52
(1985)	71.6	37.4	0.52	–	–	–
(1988)	67.5	34.2	0.51	–	–	–
Fertiliser consumption per hectare						
(1981)	187.0	116.2	0.62	–	–	–
(1985)	587.2	259.7	0.44	103.5	63.7	0.61
(1988)	950.5	597.9	0.63	–	–	–
Tractor ploughed area						
(1981)	47.6	25.2	0.53	–	–	–
(1985)	37.5	21.9	0.58	–	–	–
(1988)	52.3	26.4	0.50	–	–	–
Agri. consumption of electricity						
(1981)	–	–	–	23.4	16.0	0.68
(1985)	–	–	–	25.5	16.2	0.63
Expenditure on R and D						
(1986)	83.5	80.1	0.96	14.8	10.4	0.70
Scientists/engineers per 1,000 population						
(1981)	0.8	0.6	0.78	–	–	–
(1986)	2.5	2.4	0.96	–	–	–

Source: Based on Appendix Tables A7.1 to A7.4.

Notes: WM = population-weighted mean, SD = standard deviation, Co.V = coefficient of variation.
 – = not available.

structure, are supplemented by R and D by private industry which seems to be quite dispersed. In China on the other hand, little in-house research is done by state-owned industry.

In China, in general the advanced cities and provinces in the coastal regions are known to have much higher indicators of agricultural modernisation than the backward regions in the hinterland. The

Development Outcomes

Table 7.9   Technological disparities between Chinese coastal and
non-coastal areas

Indicator	Coastal areas			Non-coastal areas		
	WM	*SD*	*Co.V*	*WM*	*SD*	*Co.V*
Power-irrigated area						
(1982)	81.9	19.0	0.23	58.3	23.5	0.40
(1985)	83.5	19.4	0.23	55.9	23.2	0.41
(1988)	76.6	31.4	0.41	61.1	32.5	0.53
Fertiliser consumption per hectare						
(1981)	234.3	110.1	0.47	139.2	78.4	0.56
(1985)	707.6	96.7	0.13	475.7	157.8	0.33
(1988)	1,182.6	568.2	0.48	722.9	428.2	0.59
Tractor ploughed area						
(1981)	54.1	21.1	0.39	42.4	22.9	0.54
(1985)	36.3	9.5	0.26	38.4	19.3	0.50
(1988)	62.1	22.7	0.37	43.3	22.2	0.51
Per capita R and D expenditure						
(1986)	130.9	68.5	0.52	11.9	4.1	0.35
Scientists and engineers per 1,000 population						
(1981)	1.1	1.0	0.89	0.6	0.2	0.33
(1986)	4.0	2.1	0.52	0.4	0.1	0.36

Source: Based on Appendix Tables A7.1 and A7.3.

policy of technology import and the retention of foreign exchange
from export proceeds is said to have favoured the coastal areas more
than the hinterland. During the post-Mao period, the ability of firms
to import technology from abroad is tied to their foreign exchange
earnings through the so-called 'foreign exchange retention system'.
This policy is not conducive to a balanced and even spread of foreign
technology throughout China. Restricted access of many areas to
foreign technology continues to maintain wide interregional economic and technological differentials.

To verify whether the coastal areas are more advanced technologically, the standard deviation and coefficients of variation are esti-

mated separately for four of the technological indicators noted in Table 7.8. The results are presented in Table 7.9.

As expected, variations within the non-coastal provinces are greater than those within the coastal provinces. One can conclude that a greater technological homogeneity and access for producers exists in the more advanced coastal provinces. There are two exceptions, however. With regard to per capita R and D expenditures and scientists and engineers, the variations are much greater within the coastal areas. This is explained by an overconcentration of industry in the autonomous municipalities.

V CONCLUSION

This chapter has examined issues of technology access in agricultural and industrial sectors in terms of small versus large producers. It shows that generally smaller producers in both China and India enjoy less access to technology and factor inputs. But contrary to expectations, large state farms in China do not use more fertilisers per unit of sown area than the smaller collective farms. But the former are more mechanised.

Both China and India suffer from differential access due to the technological factor. In both countries, there is a commodity bias in favour of certain crops. Both suffer from spatial technological disparities although they are somewhat more acute in China with a heavy concentration of industry in a few coastal areas and provinces.

Notes and References

1. See Frances Stewart, *Technology and Underdevelopment*, London, Macmillan Press, 1977; and Frances Stewart, 'Macropolicies for Appropriate Technology: An Introductory Classification', in Jeffrey James and Susumu Watanabe (eds), *Technology, Institutions and Government Policies*, London, Macmillan Press, 1985.
2. Ashok Rudra, 'Technology Choice in Agriculture in India over the Past Three Decades', in Frances Stewart (ed.), *Macro-Policies for Appropriate Technology in Developing Countries*, Boulder, Westview Press, 1987.
3. Shigeru Ishikawa, 'Technology Import and Indigenous Technology Capacity in China', *ILO/WEP Research Working Paper Series, WEP 2-22/WP. 185*. Geneva, January 1988.

4. Richard Conroy, 'The Disintegration and Reconstruction of the Rural Science and Technology System: Evaluation and Implications', in A. Saith (ed.), *The Re-emergence of the Chinese Peasantry*. London, Croom Helm, 1987.

5. Athar Hussain, 'Science and Technology in the Chinese Countryside', in Denis Fred Simon and Merle Goldman (eds), *Science and Technology in Post-Mao China*, Cambridge, Mass., Harvard University Press, 1989.

6. Progress Report on the SPARKS Programme for 1988 (in Chinese), SSTC, Beijing, 1989.

7. A. S. Bhalla, 'Computerisation in Chinese Industry', *Science and Public Policy*, August 1990.

8. K. K. Subramanian, 'Chinese Technology Policy in the 1980s', *Working Paper No. 206*, Centre for Development Studies, Trivandrum, Kerala, June 1985.

9. Amiya Kumar Bagchi, *Public Intervention and Industrial Restructuring in China, India and Republic of Korea*, New Delhi, ILO/ARTEP, 1987.

10. M. R. Bhagavan, 'Capital Goods Sector in India', *Economic and Political Weekly*, 9 March 1985; and Sukhamoy Chakravarty, *Development Planning: The Indian Experience*, Oxford, Clarendon Press 1987, Chapter 5.

11. UN Asian and Pacific Centre for Transfer of Technology, *Technology Policies and Planning – People's Republic of China*, Country Study Series, Bangalore, India, 1986, p. 81.

12. Lung-fai Wong, *Agricultural Productivity in the Socialist Countries*, Boulder, Westview Press, 1986, p. 97.

13. See Ma Yuanling, *Modern Plant Biotechnology and Structure of Rural Employment in China*, paper prepared for the ILO Technology and Employment Branch, Geneva, ILO, 1989 (draft).

14. Ben Stavis, 'Agricultural Performance and Policy: Contrasts with India', *Social Scientist*, May-June 1977.

15. Lung-fai Wong, *Agricultural Productivity in China and India: A Comparative Analysis*, paper presented at the Symposium on Feeding the People of China and India, American Association for the Advancement of Science Annual Meeting, Chicago, 15 February 1987 (March 1987, mimeo).

16. Richard Conroy, 'Laissez faire Socialism? Prosperous Peasants and China's Current Rural Development Strategy', *Australian Journal of Chinese Affairs*, no. 12, 1984.

17. Biplab Das Gupta, *Agrarian Change and the New Technology in India*, Geneva, UNRISD, 1977; and 1989. Michael Lipton with Richard Longhurst, *New Seeds and Poor People*, London, Unwin Hyman, 1989.

18. Cited in J. S. Sarma, *Agricultural Policy in India: Growth with Equity*, Ottawa, IDRC, 1982, p. 39.

19. Ibid., p. 39.

20. Wong, *Agricultural Productivity in China and India*.

21. Hussain, 'Science and Technology in The Chinese Countryside'.

22. See C. H. Hanumantha Rao, *Technological Change in Indian Agriculture – Emerging Trends and Perspectives*, Presidential Address, The

Golden Jubilee Conference of the Indian Society of Agricultural Economics, Bombay, 4–7 December 1989, p. 10.
23. Erik Baark, *High Technology Innovation at the Chinese Academy of Sciences*, Institute of Economics and Planning, Roskilde University Centre, Denmark, Sept. 1987, p. 10.
24. See Anil B. Deolalikar and Anant K. Sundaram, 'Technology Choice, Adaptation and Diffusion in Private and State-Owned Enterprises in India', in Jeffrey James (ed.), *The Technological Behaviour of Public Enterprises in Developing Countries*, London, Routledge, 1989.
25. Erik Baark, *Knowhow as a Commodity: Contracts and Markets in the Diffusion of Technology in China*, Research Policy Institute, University of Lund, 1986, pp. 44–5.
26. Private interview with Chen Jiyuan, Director, Institute of Rural Development of the Chinese Academy of Social Sciences (CASS), Beijing, September 1988.
27. Vernon W. Ruttan, *Agricultural Research Policy*, Minneapolis, University of Minnesota Press, 1982, p. 140.
28. Iftikhar Ahmed and Vernon Ruttan, 'Introduction', in Iftikhar Ahmed and Vernon Ruttan (eds), *Generation and Diffusion of Agricultural Innovations: The Role of Institutional Factors*, Aldershot, Gower, 1988.
29. Sudhir K. Mukhopadhyay, 'Factors Influencing Agricultural Research and Technology: A Case Study of India', in Ahmed and Ruttan, ibid.
30. Hussain, 'Science and Technology . . .'.
31. During this period, agricultural research accounted for 16 per cent of growth in labour productivity and 11 per cent of growth in land productivity. The corresponding contributions of other factors were: technical inputs, 81 per cent and 54 per cent; fertiliser, 50 per cent and 33 per cent; machinery, 31 per cent and 21 per cent respectively. See Wong, *Agricultural Productivity in the Socialist Countries*, pp. 93 and 97.
32. M. Ann Judd, James K. Boyce and Robert E. Evenson, 'Investing in Agricultural Supply: The Determinants of Agricultural Research and Extension Investment', *Economic Development and Cultural Change*, October 1986.
33. World Bank, *CHINA: Socialist Economic Development, Vol. II*, Washington DC, 1983, pp. 75–7; and Hussain, 1989, 'Science and Technology . . .'.

8 Access to Health Services

It is generally believed that countries at a higher stage of development are more likely to allocate adequate resources to health than those which are much poorer. Also such health status indicators as mortality rates are much lower in advanced countries than in the developing countries. For example, an analysis of 42 countries showed a positive correlation between low per capita income and poor health standards. In the sample which covered countries with infant mortality rates of over 100 per 1,000 births, 26 countries had per capita incomes below US $400, nine had per capita incomes between US $400 and 670 and a very small number had incomes per capita above US $800.[1] Notwithstanding this correlation, income *per capita* is only one of the explanatory factors for the state of health in developing countries – necessary but not sufficient to explain poor health conditions. Indeed, the China–India comparison which is our concern here, is a case of two countries with similar levels of average per capita incomes but with differences in the health status of their populations. The differences in the availability and distribution of health services in these two countries are, therefore, to be explained by other factors such as the nature of government policies and the effectiveness in their implementation, income distribution, and organisational/institutional endowments.

A comparison between India and China is interesting since these two countries account for a sizeable proportion of the Third World's population. It is particularly worthwhile to explore the impact, if any, of different policies and organisational structures on the provision and delivery of health services particularly to rural areas. For example, in China's state-controlled economy the government had a major obligation to provide health services everywhere particularly during the Mao period. Private health services were non-existent. Did these factors lead to greater access to health facilities?

Section I discusses the role of health organisation, and financing, including insurance, in the two countries to determine whether they explain the inequality of access to health services. Section II examines health status, access and utilisation indicators for China and India over time in the backdrop of the general health situation in the two countries over the past 30 to 40 years. Sections III and IV examine spatial disparities in terms of rural–urban and regional differences respectively. Section V investigates the nature of the urban and class bias in each of the two countries. Finally, the concluding section makes some general observations about access to health in China and India as an outcome of different policies and their implementation.

I HEALTH ORGANISATION, POLICIES AND FINANCING

1.1 China

The Mao Period

The Maoist focus on rural areas led to a decentralised organisation of health delivery services within the framework of communes. With limited financial and technical manpower resources it would have been impossible to provide modern services to the entire rural population. It was, therefore, logical to organise and finance the rural health care system on a decentralised collective basis.

The organisation of rural primary health care services (comprising the rural health centre, the brigade cooperative medical centre and the county general hospital) was based on the three-tiered structure of the rural economy (communes, brigades and production teams). The county hospital supervised technical work in commune and brigade hospitals, and undertook teaching and research in addition to providing medical services to rural areas. The district clinics undertook control and prevention of infectious diseases, maternity and child care, and family planning. They also provided professional guidance to medical workers and trained them for primary health care centres. Cooperative medical stations (or production brigade clinics) accounted for the treatment of about 60–70 per cent of out-patients. These stations were staffed largely by part-time medical aides and midwives who worked along with barefoot doctors. The latter were selected by the brigades from junior middle-school graduates and were given six months' training in medical sciences and traditional Chinese and Western medicine. To overcome the serious shortage of qualified medical manpower, lower skills were substituted for higher skills. The barefoot doctor scheme is but one manifestation of this pragmatism and of a commitment to provide rural medical care for the masses. The barefoot doctors contributed to the national economy through 'labour savings' – reduction of work days lost and savings in traveling and waiting time. The monetary value of these savings is estimated at about 1353 million yuan, which, for 1974, amounted to about 0.5 per cent of GDP and about 2 per cent of the total value of agricultural output.[2] Even though one may question the methodology used for such estimation the data highlight the significant economic contribution of the system of barefoot doctors.

A number of measures were adopted to redistribute health services from urban to rural areas in order to reduce inequality. First, urban medical personnel were transferred to rural areas either permanently or in mobile teams. Second, hospitals in big cities like Beijing and Shanghai charged lower room rates (about 50 per cent less) for poor peasants coming from rural areas. Third, rural health facilities were improved by integrating Western and traditional Chinese approaches to medicine. Fourth, the curriculum of medical colleges was reduced from six years to three years to overcome the shortage of medical personnel. The trade-off between quantity and quality of medical care was justified on the grounds of social equity. Fifth, the central government allocated additional resources for relatively poor rural areas to ensure a basic minimum level of health care.[3]

The political commitment to public health and collective agrarian structure was a major factor in the drive to ensure adequate access of the rural people to public health facilities. Motivation of the Chinese masses under collective organisations, community involvement and participation in preventive health programmes had a very favourable effect on the health status of the Chinese rural population. In the early 1950s massive national health campaigns were organised to eliminate the 'four pests' (rats, flies, mosquitoes and bed bugs) and to control malaria and schistosomiasis. This approach to mass mobilisation of labour sets China apart from India and is perhaps unique in developing world.

Decollectivisation in rural areas and the virtual autonomy of individual households in the post-Mao period has undoubtedly reduced the scope for mass mobilisation, a factor which may explain the resurgence of some infectious diseases in the early 1980s.

Health Financing.   Health resource allocation from GNP, at over 3 per cent for China in 1981 and only a little over 2 per cent for India provides a significant contrast.

Further, a well-developed health insurance scheme for the rural and urban areas (see below) enables a better performance in China. India has no rural health insurance scheme and the urban-based scheme covers only state employees and industrial workers.

During the Mao period, there were three major types of health care insurance in China: the compulsory public expenses medical insurance (*gong-fei yi-liao*) which covered state cadres and students; the compulsory labour medical insurance (*lao-bao yi-liao*) which covered workers and staff members in state-owned factories; and rural voluntary cooperative medical insurance (*hezhuo yi-liao*), organised at the level of the county (*xian*).

The Maoist policy of self-reliance and mass mobilisation of manpower for preventive health measures also implied local financing of health services through mobilisation of money and manpower. The major financial burden of preventive health measures was borne by the direct beneficiaries in the rural areas. The state budget financed county level health services, training of all health personnel, nonrecurrent grants for physical facilities, and vaccines and contraceptives. The commune health centres (now called district centres) were financed mainly out of contributions from collective welfare funds which depended very much on agricultural revenues. Thus, fluctuations in agricultural output also affected funds for rural health services. In the bad harvest years this meant low allocations for rural health services precisely when poor diet and illness increased the need for medical treatment.[4]

Between 1957 and 1971, the total social welfare expenditure on health, education and welfare was doubled. While, before the Cultural Revolution, the total health expenditure allocated to urban areas accounted for over two-thirds of the total, by the mid-1970s this ratio was reduced to 40 per cent.[5]

The Post-Mao Period

In the post-Mao period, there has been a partial privatisation of health services as part of an overall policy of economic liberalisation. Township and county hospitals enjoy greater autonomy and financial independence. The allocation of central funds to these institutions has been reduced on the assumption that they will become partially self-financing by charging fees for services rendered. The new policy has led to an increase in the number of rural private medical practitioners and some private hospitals in both urban and rural areas.

Hospitals and medical practitioners are allowed to retain profits from consultation and registration fees, sale of drugs and other charges which are the main sources of their incomes. The profit retention system has in some cases encouraged corruption through overprescription of drugs and injections.

In the past, inappropriate pricing policy – fixing of prices of health products at below cost – led to financial instability of health institutions and to shortages of some drugs and surpluses of others. Below-cost pricing has tended to discourage drug manufacturers from expanding production of some drugs. Although some general price reforms have been introduced, it appears that prices of drugs and other health products still continue to be fixed by the government.[6]

A private health sector now coexists with the state sector. The assumption of health policy is that a complementary pattern of private and public services will generate additional health services and facilities (in the form of manpower and hospitals) in response to growing demand[7] and will thus reduce the financial burden on the State.

In China, the private demand for health services has increased with a rapid increase in household incomes in the 1980s. The richer rural households are known to seek better-quality treatment at county hospitals. They often bypass the township hospitals whose facilities have declined as a result of decline in their resources from the State and a fall in the number of barefoot doctors. This seems to have led to a growing pressure on urban health facilities and underutilisation of rural public health services.

It has been argued that the rural reforms and a general shift towards privatisation of agriculture and health services have tended to weaken the Chinese rural health care system.[8] Three arguments are presented in defence of this view: the decline or collapse of rural health insurance, a fall in the number of barefoot doctors and a decline in the number of township and county health facilities resulting from a squeeze in financial grants from the central government.

We examine below the state of the system of barefoot doctors and of rural health insurance in the post-Mao period to determine if sufficient evidence exists to conclude that the rural health care system has actually weakened.

Barefoot Doctors. In the post-Mao period, the number of barefoot doctors in rural areas has no doubt declined considerably – from 1.03 million in 1980 to 905.8 thousand in 1985. This may be due to the fact that many barefoot doctors, who are paid low salaries, seem to have shifted to the much more profitable pursuit of farming. Apart from low salaries, the return to the cities of the urban youth (many of whom were rusticated to rural areas during the Cultural Revolution and were the source of supply of barefoot doctors) may also account for some of the decline in the number of these doctors.

However, this decline has been accompanied and at least partially offset by an increase in the number of private health practitioners which has grown in both urban and rural areas. It is estimated that there were, in 1984, 1.3 million rural private doctors and 1.2 million health workers. However, there is no clear evidence to determine whether private practice has fully made up for the shortfall caused by a decline in the number of barefoot doctors.

Another compensating factor is a qualitative improvement in the availability of health services, as private doctors are more qualified than the barefoot doctors whom they have replaced. Since these doctors usually live within the local community, they continue to provide health services to the rural people at a reasonable cost. Although the opportunity cost of private and barefoot doctors has risen, it does not appear to be significant.

There is some indication that private health facilities, drugs and consultations have become more expensive, which would imply that, with the growing rural income inequalities, the poor people are deprived of easy access to health manpower and institutions.

However, the composition of growth of private health services, the quality of services provided and the remuneration of those attracted into private practice are all matters on which information remains rather limited.

Rural Health Insurance. The coverage of rural health insurance has declined in the post-Mao period. This is due to a number of factors. First, dismantling of the communes has reduced funds available for collective activities including health care facilities. Secondly, it is now up to private households to pay for their medical treatment and expenses. Although the richer households may prefer a fees-for-services system of private quality medical care, the poorer households face the risk of ill health and disease without health insurance. Also there is no rural counterpart to the occupational health insurance which covers only formal employment generally in the urban areas; the self-employed, of which farmers are by far the most important, are, by definition, excluded from this coverage. Some of the differences in the rural and urban health services in China are due to this partial coverage of occupational health insurance.

Lastly, there is a decline in the proportion of insured persons due to an increase in private health care and in the number of temporary contract workers.

Has the decline in rural cooperative health insurance meant a decline in the access of the rural population to primary health care services? To answer this question, one needs to know whether (a) alternative forms of health insurance have developed, and if so, whether they have compensated for the decline in cooperative insurance, and (b) cooperative insurance was more effective than the private medical care which has emerged in the post-Mao period. As regards (a) different experiments have been underway to substitute for the decline in cooperative insurance in rural areas, e.g. peasant health insurance, children's insurance and insurance for workers of township enterprises. These experiences are very recent. It is therefore difficult to ascertain whether they are more effective and have successfully made up for the collapse of rural cooperative health insurance.

One thing is clear however. Even under the erstwhile cooperative insurance only certain modest health expenses were reimbursed. Peasants had to pay at least 50 per cent for simple treatment and more than 80 per cent for serious treatment in big urban or county hospitals. The fact that rural incomes have risen appreciably and rapidly would suggest a greater capacity of these people to pay for public and private health facilities. But there are wide spatial differences in per capita incomes which would suggest an inequitable distribution of health services across regions, localities and income groups despite rising *per capita* incomes.

That income inequalities lead to uneven distribution of health services is suggested by a study done in 1986 by the School of Public Health of the Shanghai Medical University.[9] This study covered three Chinese counties representing high, medium and low income per capita. It found that the high-income county maintained cooperative health insurance and a high percentage of working days were spent on primary health services. This was not true of the poorer counties which shifted to private medical care and where time spent on medical care declined considerably. In the latter, health personnel spent an increasing amount of their time on farming and other more lucrative activities.

Turning to (b), is private medical care more effective than cooperative health services? Data are not adequate enough to provide a clearcut answer but a study by Zhu *et al.*, in 1987[10] covering 104 villages, indicated that the rate and speed of contacts of out-patients with doctors were more frequent under the cooperative structure than under the private health care system. A much larger percentage of patients under the private system than under the cooperative stated that owing to the high cost of doctors' services, they had no contact with them during the two-week reference period. Thus the private group does not seem to enjoy as much access to health services as the cooperative group.

Any definitive comparative assessment of the cooperative health insurance and the new system of fees for services will have to await availability of more detailed information on private health expenditures, income elasticity of demand for private *vis-à-vis* public health services, consumers' preferences for different types of health services and so on.

1.2 India

The organisational and administrative structure of the Indian health services resembles that of China. The central government relies mainly on the state governments for implementation. Urban health services are provided at the state level through state or municipal hospitals and dispensaries. The rural health system has a three-tier structure (district, block and village), and health care is provided through primary health centres and sub-centres. The latter cover about 10,000 people each and are staffed by multi-purpose workers, whereas the former serve a population of 100,000. In addition to these centres, there are rural hospitals and dispensaries. In 1977, a centrally-sponsored scheme of Community Health Workers (CHWs) was introduced. The scheme trained CHWs for three months in the basics of first aid, hygiene and treatment of infectious diseases. The CHWs, somewhat similar to the Chinese barefoot doctors, were expected to provide basic health care facilities to a village or community with a population of 1,000. In addition, traditional midwives (*dais*) perform services outside the framework of government-sponsored health services.

Notwithstanding similarities in the organisation of the rural health institutions in India and China, their performance has been different, due partly to differences in politico-administrative organisation and motivation. The limitations of India's rural health centres have been recognised by the Sixth Plan (1980–85) which admits that 'the infrastructure of sub-centres, primary health centres and rural hospitals built up in the rural areas touches only a fraction of the rural population'.[11] The plan also concedes that the involvement of the people in solving their health problems has been almost non-existent.[12] Medical and health personnel have been noted for 'the high rates of absenteeism, diversion into private practice and low work output'.[13]

This situation is in contrast with that of China with its mass health campaigns involving popular participation and the commune health centres.

Health Financing. Information on financing of health services in India is much harder to find. The situation is even worse with respect to rural–urban distribution of resources allocated to the health sector.

Data on *per capita* public expenditure on health show wide geographical variations across the Indian states (Table 8.5). Although the variation coefficient declined from 0.81 in 1981 to 0.71 in 1986, it is still extremely high.

The share of the health sector in the total development budget has declined from 3.3 per cent in the First Plan (1951–56) to 1.9 per cent in the Sixth Plan (1980–85). Within the health sector, outlays are allocated to several programmes like control of communicable diseases, a minimum needs programme, primary health centres, family planning, research, education and training etc. In the absence of separate allocations for rural and urban programmes, we arbitrarily choose (i) minimum needs programmes and (ii) primary health centres as those which are particularly addressed to rural target groups as against more universal programmes like control of diseases which would have a more general incidence on all the different population groups. The shares of these two items in the total health budget would, therefore, indicate the level of priority assigned to them. The proportion of the total plan outlay on health going to primary health centres and dispensaries has considerably declined since the Second Five-Year Plan (1956–61). On the other hand, the Minimum Needs Programmes first introduced in the Fifth Plan (1974–79) account for a phenomenal increase in their share, from 5.7 per cent in the Fifth Plan to 15.7 per cent in the Sixth (1980–85) and 32 per cent in the Seventh (1985–90).[14] However, these are only plan outlays and not actual expenditures. It is difficult to forecast whether actual implementation of the plans will meet the targets or not.

So far we have considered only public expenditures on health. Health care in India is also financed by private resources through payments of doctors' fees, and purchases of medicines, etc. Unlike China, private and public health services in India have coexisted for a long time. Surveys of selected villages in Punjab showed that far more was spent on Westernised medical practitioners than on traditional ones, and only a small amount was spent on government services. In 1973–74, private out-of-pocket expenditures were about six times government expenditure on primary health care in Punjab.[15] This phenomenon may be explained by the increased incomes in Punjab in the wake of the Green Revolution, and by the preference for better-quality private medical services. This Punjab experience is similar to the increased demand in China for better-quality medical services following growth of rural incomes.

Unlike China, India has no rural health insurance scheme. The government labour insurance scheme is confined mainly to urban areas. This is also true of the Central Government Health Scheme (CGHS) which covers central government employees, members of parliament, and pensioners. In 1980–81, the CGHS benefited over 559,000 families at a total cost of Rs.145 million which amounts to about Rs.272 per family. The average contribution per family amounted to Rs.27 or 10 per cent of the total cost per family.[16] The Employees' State Insurance Scheme for industrial labour is jointly financed by contributions from the central government, employers and employees. By the end of 1987, the scheme had benefited over 27 million insured persons including families of workers.

II HEALTH STATUS, ACCESS AND UTILISATION

Having examined policies, programmes and resource allocation for the health sector, it is necessary to explore the extent to which they have led to the desired outcomes in terms of a better health status of the populations in China and India.

2.1 Measuring Health Status, Access and Utilisation

But first we define health status, access and utilisation in the developing country context and the indicators used to measure them.

Commonly cited indicators of health status include: (i) mortality rates (infant and overall); (ii) death rates attributable to specific diseases; (iii) life expectancy at birth; and (iv) anthropometric status which is a composite measure reflecting the influence of disease, nutrition and health care. The greater the mortality rate, the more likely it is that access to health services is limited, with poor conditions of delivery, untrained medical attendants and a low rate of immunisation; infant mortality rates are likely to be affected by weight at birth, nutritional status after weaning and the quality of infant care. Since nutritional standards affect health the anthropometric status of, say, children at different ages, can also be used to trace the impact of nutritional deprivation.[17] These status indicators give an indirect measure of the public health environment of which access to health services is one aspect.

Access to health services can be defined in terms of (a) access of rural and urban areas and social classes to available health facilities, and (b) their actual utilisation which would determine the level of satisfaction of health needs.[18] The factors determining access and utilisation are diverse. Income is only one factor, but other equally important ones include the nature of government policies and their effectiveness, income distribution and institutional and non-economic considerations (such as cultural and social constraints).

Physical distance from health facilities is another factor which can affect access. It is estimated that, in India, 15 per cent of the villages and 16 per cent of the rural population are more than 10 km away from any medical facility.[19] This suggests that for a large proportion of the population, access is difficult, particularly when transport and communication facilities are poor. While transportation bottlenecks also exist in China, there is likely to be a greater physical proximity of health services to clients thanks to the commune and brigade structure during the Mao period and rural townships during the post-Mao period.

Health access is generally measured in terms of delivery systems (e.g. doctors and beds per 1,000 population) and population characteristics (e.g. family income, insurance coverage).[20] The most frequently used indicators of access to health services are doctors, hospitals and hospital beds per 1,000 population. These indicators tell us about the availability of health facilities though not necessarily about their utilisation which would depend on physical access and demand for these services. Neither do they throw any light on the distribution of health services among different socio-economic groups.

Let us take the doctor/population ratio which is frequently used to measure adequacy of health services. Without an income dimension it cannot indicate access. Information on the share of the total population actually treated by doctors and hospitals is therefore needed to draw any inferences with regard to satisfaction of the basic need for health. Further, interregional variations in disease prevalence, not to mention class differences, are important. However, as this chapter shows, this is not the case, particularly in India, but also in China.

The usual health utilisation indicators are of three main types: those relating to (i) the types of services used, e.g. hospital, physician or home care, (ii) the purpose of the service received, e.g. preventive or curative, and (iii) the location of the service rendered, e.g. home, clinic or in-patient hospital.[21]

2.2 A China–India Comparison

We now compare China and India in terms of their health status, starting first with some aggregate indicators which were almost identical in 1960 for both countries but diverged markedly later. For example, life expectancy at birth was the same in 1960, but increased by 1981 to 67 years in China and to only 52 years in India. Similarly, infant mortality rates per 1000 live births (identical in 1960) declined by 1981 to 49 in China and 121 in India. Crude death rates per 1000 declined from 22 to 13 in India and from 24 to 8 in China in 1981.[22] Looking at population-to-doctor ratio, it is 2458 people per fully qualified Western doctor in China compared with 9900 in other low-income countries, and about 4,310 in middle-income countries.[23] If one includes doctors and nurses of indigenous medicine, the ratio for China becomes even lower – 892 (excluding barefoot doctors) as compared with 8790 in other low-income countries and 1860 in middle-income countries. In the case of India, in 1984 there were 2520 people per doctor and 1700 people per nursing person. Comparable data for China in the same year were: 1,000 and 1,710 respectively.[24]

It is not clear how reliable or accurate the above estimates are, considering that for India the ratio of population to nursing person was reported to be 4,670 in 1981[25] and only 1,700 in 1984. It is most unlikely that such a drastic decline in the ratio could take place during a short period of only three years.

In both China and India the health sector is notorious for inadequate and incomplete data. Whatever data are available are often not reliable due to inaccuracies and under-reporting, and at times, even wilful manipulation. As we examine below in Section III, official estimates of infant mortality rates in China were underestimated. In India, the data on stock of doctors are incomplete. As health is a state subject, registration of doctors is done only at state level. At present, there is no centralised registration system, which means that the Ministry of Health and Family Welfare (which issues an annual yearbook of health statistics) does not know when doctors in a particular state retire, die or go abroad. The central ministry has also no way of remedying shortfalls in data reported by states on health manpower. To overcome this problem, we resorted to the Indian population censuses for 1961, 1971 and 1981 which give complete all-India statistics on doctors and nurses. The discussion of spatial differences below therefore needs to be qualified by the above data limitations.

III   RURAL–URBAN INEQUALITIES

In sections III and IV, we examine spatial differences in health status, access and utilisation in terms of rural–urban and regional inequalities. Rural inequalities are analysed in respect of status indicators: infant and overall mortality rates; access indicators – doctors and hospital beds per 1,000 population: and utilisation indicators – percentage of total population treated in hospitals, number of babies delivered in clinics and ratio of hospital treatment to deaths.

3.1   Status

To measure health status in China and India, we first examine infant mortality rates (IMRs) (see Table 8.1). The IMRs are generally under-reported in most developing countries but particularly so in China. Judith Banister notes that mortality is especially acute in China in the case of infants who die in the first week of life.[26] Her estimates, which have been adjusted for under-reporting, are higher than the official Chinese estimates (Table 8.1). They have also started rising since 1981 – a peculiar phenomenon which may have something to do with a rise in births and the recent decline in rural health services noted above.

Even if one considers the higher estimates of IMRs by Banister and the World Bank, they are still much lower than those for India. China has also succeeded in lowering IMRs in both urban and rural areas. This outcome must have been a result of the provision of maternal

Table 8.1   Infant mortality rates in China and India (per 1,000 live births)

Year	China					India		
	Urban	Rural	National			Urban	Rural	National
			Official estimates	World Bank estimates	Banister estimates			
Pre-1949	120 (approx.)	–	200 (approx.)			–	–	–
1954[a]	–	–	138.5			–	–	–
1958[b]	50.8	89.1	80.8	214	146.3	–	–	146 (1951–61)
1973				91	56.2	82	138	129 (1971)
1974	28.0[c]	52.0[c]	47.0[c]	87	52.4	–	–	–
1975				84	48.6	–	–	–
1976	–	–	–	75	44.9	80	139	129
1981[d]	21.0	38.0	34.7	48	43.7	62	119	110
1982	–	–	20.3	45	45.9	65	114	105
1983	13.6[e]	26.5[f]	24.0	38	48.0	66	114	105
1984	13.4	24.4	–	36	50.1	57	105	104
1985	14.0[g]	25.1[h]	23.0	35	–	–	–	95
1986	14.3[i]	27.3[j]	–	–	–	–	–	–
1987[k]	18.3	30.3	28.0	–	–	–	–	–
1988[l]	13.9	23.6	21.0	31	–	–	–	97

Sources: CHINA: Data supplied by the Ministry of Public Health, Beijing; *Zhong Guo Ren Kou Zi Liao Shou Ce* (A Handbook of China Data), 1988; State Statistical Bureau, *Zhong Guo She Hui Tong Ji Zi Liao* (China Social Statistics), 1990; Judith Banister, *China's Changing Population*, Stanford, Stanford University Press, 1987; official estimates have been adjusted for under-reporting; D. Jamison *et al.*, *CHINA – The Health Sector*, Washington, D.C. World Bank, 1984; and World Bank, *World Development Reports*. INDIA: Government of India, Ministry of Health and Family Welfare, *Health Information of India*, New Delhi, 1987.

Notes: (a) Based on survey of over 50,000 people in 14 provinces; (b) Based on survey of Beijing and most of the counties and municipalities in 19 provinces; (c) Based on National Cancer Survey; (d) Based on Third National Census; (e) Based on survey of Beijing and 28 municipalities; (f) Based on data from 58 counties in Shanghai, Jiangsu and 12 provinces; (g) Based on data from Beijing and 36 cities; (h) Based on data from 72 counties in Shanghai, Jiangsu and 15 provinces; (i) Based on data from Beijing and 36 cities; (j) Based on data from 81 counties in Shanghai, Jiangsu and 14 provinces; (k) Based on data from Beijing and 36 cities, 72 counties in Shanghai, Jiangsu and 15 provinces; (l) Based on data from Beijing and 41 municipalities, and 84 counties in Shanghai, Jiangsu and 15 provinces.

and child health care services, and preventive measures such as immunisation of children, re-training of midwives, improved sanitation and safe drinking water supply. The nutritional factor can also explain rural–urban differences in IMRs. For China, between 1983 and 1986, the rural IMRs were nearly double the urban IMRs, whereas in 1958 they were much less than double, suggesting a widening of the gap. Malnutrition is known to be more serious in Chinese rural areas than in the urban in terms of both height and weight criteria. This may be partially explained by relatively low rural meat consumption, inter-provincial differences in food availability and lower rural food expenditure per capita. In 1979, a survey of 16 provinces and central municipalities found 'that a national average of 2.6 per cent of urban and 12.7 per cent of rural 7-year-old boys were stunted'.[27] The rural figure here may be underestimated since rural areas also include suburban areas near major cities.

In India also, high rural IMRs are likely to be due to malnutrition, low food availability and a lack of maternal and child health care facilities. Furthermore, female IMRs are higher than male IMRs because of a sex bias against nutrition of female children.[28] However, the state of Kerala is unique with the lowest IMRs among all the states. Kerala suffers from low per capita income and food availability yet accounts for very low IMRs which suggests that purely economic factors alone cannot explain health status. Non-economic factors such as high literacy (particularly female literacy), better hygiene and sanitation and successful policies to distribute health facilities equitably between rural and urban areas seem to have been far more important.

We now consider overall rural–urban mortality rates for males and females. Figures 8.1 and 8.2 plot these age-specific rates for China and India. It is interesting to note that the Indian situation in 1983 was similar to what prevailed in China in 1957, i.e. a higher death rate for females below 40 years. It is likely that maternal child health care in China was quite poor in 1957 when many more women of child-bearing age probably died at child birth. Secondly, it is also plausible that women enjoyed lower access than men to available health facilities.

In 1984 in China, death rates became higher for males than for females (Figure 8.2). Tremendous improvements in maternal health care since the 1950s may be an important factor in explaining this reversal of mortality trends.[29] In the case of India, on the other hand, female mortality rate remains higher than the male rate. The excess

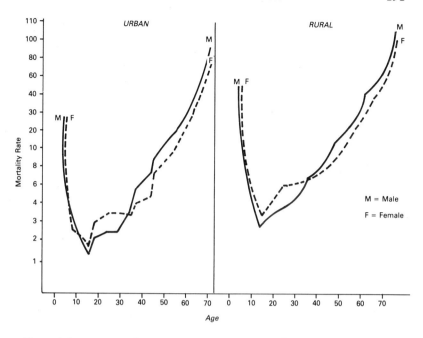

Figure 8.1   Age-specific mortality rates for males and females by rural and urban areas (India) (1983)

Source: Based on data in Government of India, *Health Information of India*, 1987, table 2.9, p. 49.

female mortality seems to be explained by discrimination against females within the household in respect of food allocation, health care and medical treatment.[30] Very poor maternal health care facilities in the Indian rural areas may be an additional factor accounting for relatively higher female mortality rates up to the age of 35 (Figure 8.1).

In India, there are also wide inter-regional variations in the female mortality rates. The excess female mortality rate is found mostly in the northwestern States like Punjab, Haryana and Rajasthan. Several factors of relevance need to be mentioned. In the paddy-growing eastern States the economic value of females is higher than in the northwestern States, as Bardhan notes.[31] Other factors which explain access of females to resources (which Bardhan did not consider) are cultural and kinship relations which vary across the North and South of India. Both these factors and the resulting greater autonomy of

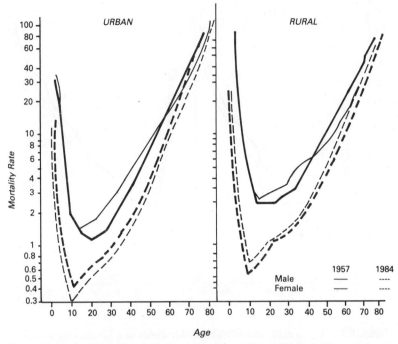

Figure 8.2   Age-specific mortality rates for males and females by rural and urban areas (China) (1957 and 1984)

Source: Rao Keqin, 'Health of the Chinese People', in *Public Health in the People's Republic of China* (General Editor, Cui Yueli), People's Medical Publishing House, Beijing, 1986, p. 83.

women as well as their higher literacy and political consciousness emphasise greater sexual equality in Kerala.[32]

The above facts for China are consistent with Preston's inference from data for 140 countries, that excess female mortality and sex discrimination decline with higher life expectancy and rapid industrialisation.[33] But Preston's analysis does not fit well with the Indian data. Despite higher life expectancy and urbanisation excess female mortality continues up to the ages of 35 to 40 years in both urban and rural areas (see Figure 8.1).

In China the overall death rate and infant mortality rate have started rising since 1979. It is estimated that during 1979 and 1986 the death rate increased by about 7 per cent, or from 6.21 per 1,000 in 1979 to 6.69 per 1,000 in 1986. Hussain and Stern explain this phenomenon in terms of an increase in the birth rate and a rise in the share of the aged (over 64 years of age).[34] Although the rise in the death rate does not fully coincide with the impact of the rural economic reforms, which started being felt mainly in 1982–83, the decline in the rural health services may partly explain this peculiar phenomenon.

3.2 Access

Medical personnel, hospitals and hospital beds per 1,000 population for urban and rural areas in China and India are given in Table 8.2. In China, from 1957 to 1984, the number of hospital beds in urban areas rose by over four times, whereas in rural areas it rose by over seventeen times. The number of medical personnel rose nine-fold in urban areas and three-fold in rural areas; of these the number of doctors increased five-fold in urban areas and a little over one and a half times in rural areas.

In India, between 1957 and 1965, the number of hospital beds doubled in rural areas and quadrupled in urban areas. In the 1980s, the increase in the number of beds slowed down. Between 1957 and 1965, the number of hospitals nearly doubled in urban areas but increased insignificantly in rural areas (Table 8.2).

For China, from 1965 onwards, the ratio of beds per 1,000 population has been much higher than that for India, whether one considers it for total or for urban or rural population. While the Indian rural ratio has remained almost constant, the Chinese ratio has risen consistently from 0.51 in 1965 to 1.41 in 1978 and 1.43 in 1988. Considering that the ratio for urban areas has been declining since 1978, the rural–urban disparity should also have declined.

In the case of the doctor–population ratio, China does better than India in the rural as well as urban areas. This may be partly due to the prevalence of the barefoot doctors' scheme in the former. However, for medical personnel the data are not strictly comparable since the barefoot doctors in China work part-time, whereas the Indian paramedical personnel work full-time. Even if we assume that one paramedic in India is equivalent to two barefoot doctors, the Chinese ratio would still be much higher.[35] It is worth noting, however, that no account has been taken of the differences in the quality of personnel between the two countries and over time.

Development Outcomes

Table 8.2   Health access indicators for China and India

Item/year	China			India		
	Total	Rural	Urban	Total	Rural	Urban
A. Institutions						
Hospital beds per 1,000 population						
1949	0.15	0.05	0.63	–	–	–
1957	0.46	0.14	2.08	–	–	–
1965	1.06	0.51	3.78	0.58	0.14	2.48
1978	1.94	1.41	4.85	0.70	0.12	2.39
1984	2.10	1.48	4.77	0.70	0.12	2.52
1986	2.18	–	–	0.72	0.13	2.69
1988	2.28	1.43	5.60	0.74	0.15	2.72
1989	2.33	–	–	0.73	0.15	2.69
Hospitals per 1,000 population						
1957	0.065	–	–	–	–	–
1965	0.060	–	–	0.008	0.003	0.028
1978	0.066	–	–	0.009	0.003	0.028
1984	0.065	–	–	0.009	0.003	0.030
1986	0.060	–	–	0.010	0.003	0.034
1988	0.056	–	–	0.013	0.005	0.038
1989	–	–	–	0.012	0.005	0.037
B. Manpower						
Doctors per 1,000 population						
1949	0.67	0.66	0.70	–	–	–
1957	0.84	0.76	1.30	0.55	0.33	1.54
1965	1.05	0.82	2.22	0.77	0.47	1.95
1978	1.08	0.73	2.99	0.86	0.49	2.07
1984	1.34	0.82	3.60	–	–	–
1986	1.37	–	–	–	–	–
1988	1.49	0.93	2.95	–	–	–
1989	1.56	–	–	–	–	–
Nurses per 1,000 population						
1949	0.06	0.02	0.25	–	–	–
1957	0.20	0.05	0.94	0.73	0.39	2.28
1965	0.32	0.10	1.45	0.68	0.38	1.88
1978	0.42	0.19	1.74	0.80	0.47	1.86
1984	0.59	–	–	–	–	–
1988	0.76	0.37	1.78	–	–	–

Sources: China: *Statistical Yearbook of China*, several years; and *Zhong guo wei sheng lian jian* (*China Health Statistical Yearbook*), Beijing 1989, p. 568.
India: Government of India, Directorate-General of Health Services, *Health Information of India*, several years, and Censuses of Population for 1961, 1971 and 1981.

Note: Coefficients for India for doctors and nurses are based on population census data for 1961, 1971 and 1981.

3.3 Utilisation

Information on the utilisation of health facilities is very hard to find for either China or India. In the case of India, the National Sample Survey (NSS) data are out-of-date, and it appears that recent NSS rounds have not attempted the updating of information. Data under the Sample Registration System (SRS) provide more recent information (for 1976–78) which we use in Table 8.3. In 1965 the percentage of the total population treated in hospitals varied widely across states. With the exception of Kerala and Tamil Nadu, the share of states for which data were available fell below 50 per cent. In 1986, Himachal Pradesh, Kerala, Orissa and Punjab exceeded the 50 per cent level but the percentage for Kerala declined from 80 per cent in 1965 to about 64 per cent in 1986. This situation may be explained by the gradual improvement in the economic status of the population there as a result of remittances from the Middle East. The private health and medical facilities have also considerably improved in the past few years. This may have led to a shift towards an increase in demand for private medical services.

The situation in Assam and Orissa, two rather backward states, where the utilisation ratio has increased over time, contrasts with that of Kerala where it declined. This may be explained by the fact that the poor people in Assam and Orissa cannot afford private facilities and thus have to rely on government facilities. But the same reasoning would not apply to an increase in the ratio for Punjab which is one of the richest states in India.

Another index of utilisation of medical facilities is the number of births in hospitals or health centres, and by trained medical personnel if they are delivered at home. There are wide inter-regional variations in these ratios also. It is somewhat surprising that the two states with the highest per capita incomes – Punjab and Haryana – show the lowest ratios for rural deliveries in hospitals or health centres: the ratios for urban deliveries are also extremely low. This may be due to the seclusion of women and the very high ratios of babies delivered at home by trained medical personnel, which indicates utilisation of health personnel but not health facilities. With the exception of Kerala, the rural–urban disparity is quite marked in most states including the economically prosperous states of Haryana, Gujarat and Punjab.

Social customs rather than purely economic factors seem also to explain the low rates of deliveries in hospitals in Punjab and

Table 8.3   Health utilisation ratios (India)

State	Percentage of[1] total population treated in government hospitals		Percentage of[2] total deliveries in government hospitals or health centres (1976–78)		Percentage of[2] total deliveries at home attended by a doctor or trained nurse (1976–78)	
	(1965)	(1986)	(Rural)	(Urban)	(Rural)	(Urban)
Andhra Pradesh	–	–	5.8	45.6	11.0	21.1
Assam	7.8	22.5	5.3	33.4	5.3	16.3
Bihar	–	–	–	–	–	–
Gujarat	–	–	5.6	45.8	5.1	16.8
Haryana	–	40.8	1.2	10.7	20.1	48.8
Himachal Pradesh	–	63.6	2.3	37.9	18.7	50.0
Jammu & Kashmir	–	–	1.7	10.0	5.1	40.4
Karnataka	–	13.3	8.3	50.6	13.8	10.6
Kerala	80.2	63.7	37.4	63.8	18.4	20.6
Madhya Pradesh	8.2	5.0	0.9	39.8	5.4	6.0
Maharashtra	–	4.7	8.6	66.3	6.7	5.7
Orissa	47.0	86.4	2.1	16.5	10.0	25.4
Punjab	46.4	65.3	1.7	5.9	27.6	70.3
Rajasthan	45.0	–	0.7	12.9	3.7	16.6
Tamil Nadu	53.7	–	21.3	59.0	14.4	22.0
Uttar Pradesh	–	8.2	0.4	13.2	5.0	45.6
West Bengal	23.8	–	–	–	–	–
All India	–	–	7.1	43.1	9.4	23.1

Sources: [1] UN, *Poverty, Unemployment and Development Policy – A case study of selected issues with reference to Kerala*, New York, 1975, p. 139. Data relates to 1965. Data for 1986 were supplied by the Directorate General of Health Services, Ministry of Health and Family Welfare, New Delhi.
[2] Office of the Registrar General, *Sample Registration System*, 1976–78, New Delhi, 1983; cited in Leela Visaria, 'Infant Mortality in India – Levels, Trends and Determinants', *Economic and Political Weekly*, 17 August 1985, p. 1400.
– = not available.

Haryana. Traditionally Hindu and Muslim women have been unwilling to be treated by male doctors. Such reluctance is not the case among the Christian population of Kerala, which may explain the relatively low ratios of home deliveries and high ones in the hospitals. The lower rates of deliveries in hospitals in Punjab and Haryana are thus due to social and religious factors which in turn are perpetuated by lower levels of literacy.

In the case of China, the proportion of hospital births was much higher: 73.6 per cent for urban areas and 36.4 per cent for rural areas with an average for China as a whole being 43.7 per cent in 1985.[36]

The widespread rural–urban disparity in the utilisation of health services is also confirmed by the indicator of hospital visits. A West Bengal survey of 1964–65 estimated that only one in eight in rural, as opposed to one in four in urban areas, managed one visit per quarter.[37] The number of patients admitted to hospitals and dispensaries shows that people in Kerala state utilise health facilities more than those in West Bengal.[38] The better utilisation of health services in Kerala may be due to the easier access of the rural population to available health services – health centres and sub-centres are more evenly distributed between rural and urban areas. The average catchment area covered by a hospital is generally quite low (less than 50 square kilometres) which suggests a wide spread of medical facilities and their greater accessibility and utilisation. This factor is important since direct and indirect costs are involved by the users of medical services; and the greater the distance of medical facilities the higher these costs particularly for those working on daily wages.[39] This spatial factor seems to be as important as the higher levels of education in explaining the greater utilisation of health services in Kerala.

Combining seriousness of illness with medical attention is a variant of the share of population receiving treatment, similar to the ratio of hospital treatment to deaths (used by Sen and Kynch).[40] This index for two Bombay hospitals showed that the male ratio for both adults and boys was much higher than the female ratio. However, one needs to be cautious in inferring sex or regional bias. Social, cultural and religious factors limiting recourse to doctors, uneven regional distribution of diseases, and age-structure and associated medical requirements, all contribute to lower female rates. Unless there is an adequate number of female doctors in hospitals, the female hospital admission rate is bound to be low. Further, women are likely to visit a hospital (and be admitted) only in case of serious illness, unlike men, who are outdoors more often, and are more exposed to injuries, accidents and occupational hazards.

In China, data on the utilisation of health services are scarce. But the rate of occupancy of hospital beds (for which some information is available) is quite high and the rate has been nearly constant (varying between 82 to 84 per cent) between 1975 and 1987.[41] Also a China–US collaborative study of the use of health services in Shanghai County, and a special health interview survey carried out there in May 1981, noted high occupancy rates for the county and commune hospitals, with the former showing higher rates of utilisation in terms of bed occupancy, average length of stay in hospital and admission rates per 100 out-patient visits.[42] A number of factors may account for this situation – differences in seriousness of illness, larger service areas of county hospitals and preference of peasants for higher-quality medical services at the county hospitals.

There is, of course, the possibility that differences in utilisation are simply a reflection of differences in the basic need for health services, in availability of facilities and in per capita incomes. To provide a partial assessment of the relative need for health services, the US–China study adopted the number of visits for 100 days of disability (measure of seriousness of illness) to measure the extent to which the need for health care was satisfied. It showed that this index varied a great deal depending on the type of medical insurance. It ranged, in terms of visits per 100 disability days, from a low of 37 for those covered by labour and welfare insurance, to 47 for those in 'low cost' co-operative insurance systems and, finally, to a high of 80 visits for those in 'high cost' co-operative systems.[43]

IV REGIONAL INEQUALITIES

Inter-provincial variations were estimated for China and India by estimating standard deviation and coefficients of variation. These are presented in Table 8.4. The results show that unevenness is somewhat less marked in China than in India in respect of hospitals and hospital beds. In the case of per capita health expenditure, the variations are quite high and similar in both countries.

Unevenness within the Chinese coastal and non-coastal areas/ provinces is shown separately in Table 8.5. Contrary to expectations, the coastal provinces show greater unevenness in respect of doctors and health care personnel than the non-coastal provinces. This paradox may perhaps be explained by the overconcentration of medical personnel in the three capital cities, Shanghai, Beijing and Tianjin. This suggests that China is no different from most market economy developing countries. There is a clear city or urban bias in the location of public goods and services. However, in the case of *per capita* public health expenditure the coefficients of variation between

Table 8.4   Regional inequalities in access to health services in China and India

Indicator	China			India		
	WM	SD	Co. V	WM	SD	Co. V
A. *Manpower*						
Doctors per						
1,000 population						
(1981)	1.45	0.83	0.57	0.31	0.16	0.53
(1986)	1.51*	0.87*	0.57*	0.35	0.19	0.55
(1989)	1.82	0.98	0.54	–	–	–
Health care personnel						
per 1,000 population						
(1981)	3.45	1.77	0.51	0.83	0.58	0.70
(1986)	3.66*	1.79*	0.49*	0.07	0.03	0.46
(1988)	3.93	1.97	0.50	–	–	–
B. *Institutions*						
Hospitals per 1,000						
population						
(1981)	0.08	0.05	0.62	0.01	0.009	0.67
(1986)	0.06	0.03	0.51	0.01	0.009	0.60
(1988)	0.07	0.04	0.58	0.03	0.026	0.70
Hospital beds per						
1,000 population						
(1981)	2.18	0.73	0.33	0.83	0.38	0.46
(1986)	2.37	0.85	0.36	0.91	0.42	0.46
(1988)	2.50	0.92	0.37	1.18	0.62	0.53
C. *Expenditure*						
Per capita public health						
expenditure						
(1977)	–	–	–	16.56	5.02	0.30
(1981)	4.32	3.43	0.79	30.80	25.02	0.81
(1986)	–	–	–	50.37	35.79	0.71

Source: Based on Appendix Tables A8.1 to A8.7.

Notes: WM = population – weighted mean, SD = standard deviation, Co. V = coefficient of variation.
 * for 1984.
 – = not available.

two sets of provinces are not that different, suggesting that the government does not favour the coastal areas in allocating resources. In the case of hospitals the coefficient of variation in the coastal provinces is much lower, indicating greater evenness in their spatial distribution within this group.

Data on regional disparities during the Mao period are inadequate

Table 8.5   Regional Inequalities between Chinese coastal and non-coastal areas

Indicator	Coastal areas			Non-coastal areas		
	WM	*SD*	*Co. V*	*WM*	*SD*	*Co. V*
A. *Manpower*						
Doctors per						
1,000 population						
(1981)	1.66	1.25	0.75	1.29	0.40	0.31
(1984)	1.72	1.35	0.78	1.37	0.36	0.26
(1989)	2.13	1.46	0.69	1.58	0.45	0.28
Health Care						
personnel per						
1,000 population						
(1981)	3.89	2.63	0.67	3.12	0.85	0.27
(1984)	4.11	2.66	0.65	3.33	0.87	0.26
(1988)	4.45	2.91	0.65	3.52	0.93	0.26
B. *Institutions*						
Hospitals per						
1,000 population						
(1981)	0.06	0.02	0.36	0.09	0.05	0.61
(1986)	0.04	0.008	0.17	0.07	0.03	0.38
(1988)	0.05	0.014	0.30	0.07	0.04	0.58
Hospital beds per						
1,000 population						
(1981)	2.17	0.93	0.43	2.18	0.60	0.27
(1986)	2.46	0.64	0.26	2.31	0.52	0.22
(1988)	2.66	1.21	0.46	2.40	0.69	0.30
C. *Expenditure*						
Per capita public health						
expenditure						
(1981)	4.88	3.30	0.68	3.87	3.60	0.93

Source: Based on Appendix Tables A8.1, A8.4 and A8.6.

which makes it difficult to compare Mao and post-Mao periods. Yet there are indications that during the 1950s and 1960s substantial inter-provincial inequalities prevailed. There were also differences in 'efficiency' in providing curative health services.[44] The proportions of production brigades with cooperative health programmes in 1972 and 1973 also varied a great deal. Lampton concludes that substantial interprovincial and rural–urban variations remained 'even though the absolute level of service climbed everywhere'.[45]

In India also regional inequalities were quite serious during the 1960s and 1970s in respect of nutritional intake and utilisation of health services.

V CLASS AND URBAN BIAS

In section III we noted wide rural–urban differentials in access to health services in both China and India, although they are less glaring in the former. In discussing shortcomings of policy as regards health, one must keep in mind that rural–urban inequalities in income distribution inevitably constrained outcomes.

It seems odd that there would be an urban bias in China given Mao's egalitarian policies. There was also opposition to his rural-oriented health policies and programmes. The rural cooperative medical system, for instance, did not start until 1968. In the early 1950s, a disproportionate share of the limited resources was allocated to urban health services patterned on the urban-based Soviet system. In addition, pre-existing hospitals were located mainly in urban areas and party leaders and trade unions lobbied for medical care for the urban industrial workers. Lampton states:

> Leaders of large urban areas (e.g. P'eng Chen) have been in a relatively strong position to influence health policy. They have been able to inhibit the Center from exerting pressure on the Weishengpu (Ministry of Public Health) to transfer substantial curative services to distant rural areas. Their strength derives from several sources, the most important of which is the fact that big medical facilities are already in the cities. Reinforcing this, the insured cadres and workers (by the millions) are concentrated in urban areas. In the political tugging and hauling, prevailing interests, efficiency, and strategic location predispose the Weishengpu to be relatively more responsive to urban problems.[46]

Cases of class bias in the provision of health services have also been noted. Lampton points out that specific categories such as contract, part-time and temporary workers were denied benefits extended to regular cadres. Further, workers in heavy industry became quite militant in pressing for service and, upon occasion, even occupied medical facilities.[47] The number of contract and casual workers has continued to increase during the post-Mao period but this category of workers remains uncovered by occupational insurance.

A number of senior Party cadres were entitled to 'free medical services' which led to the creation of vested interests for maintaining high-quality urban-based health services. Parish speaks of senior cadres having 'special rooms, and sometimes whole wings reserved for them in hospitals'.[48]

In India, the basic conditions were similar as regards inequality of access to health services. The reliance was basically on economic growth and corresponding private demand and budgetary expenditures. However, at no time in its history did India introduce the cooperative rural health insurance that prevailed in China. Unequal income distribution, élitist biases, existence of such pressure groups as factory workers and trade unions, were conditions somewhat similar to those in China. Also in India there was liberal rural to urban migration, in contrast to controls on labour movement in China. Thirdly, there was no explicit Mao-type rural revolution to provide an overall favourable framework for rural health services. Although an equivalent of the Chinese barefoot doctor scheme (the community health workers) was tried out, it did not function well due to opposition to the scheme from the élitist medical profession. The Indian Medical Association had opposed it on the grounds that the community health workers did not provide a basic minimum quality of service.

The Indian Planning Commission acknowledged in 1978 that the health delivery system was concentrated mostly in urban areas. Further the beneficiaries were largely the affluent classes.[49]

An author from the medical profession notes that this failure to deliver health care to the rural poor has been due to a lack of professional and political will to share the benefits of development with the underprivileged.[50] He also describes how modest attempts to deliver health services in rural areas have failed. He cites, as an example, the Mandwa self-help project which covered 30 villages across from the harbour of Bombay. This project was intended to explore whether the villagers themselves could be taught the simple medical skills and make use of the equally simple available tools to look after their own health problems.[51]

The project faced a number of problems, the most significant of which were the difficulty of finding teachers to train local villagers in basic health care, and of convincing doctors that villagers could be so trained. Furthermore, the local leadership and power structure dominated by the rural élites showed open hostility to the project, which has now been terminated.

Another pilot project in Madhya Pradesh (Project Poshak) that lasted from 1971 to 1975, was concerned with the provision of rural health services and nutrition for very young children.[52] The project used existing rural health centres and other infrastructure. During its implementation, the project encountered several problems including that of low morale of the rural health workers, who were already overworked and on whom depended the success of the project. The State Government made no financial commitment to the project, which was eventually discontinued.

The above experiments suggest government indifference to rural projects and an urban/élitist bias in favour of the privileged classes which tends to be perpetuated by inegalitarian income and asset distribution.

In contrast, the success of the Chinese in providing adequate health care at the grass roots level during the Mao period was due, in part, to the generally egalitarian economic and social policies, and in part to the group motivation and commitment nurtured in the collective organisation in the rural areas. In the post-Mao period, the private health services have supplemented the public ones. Although the former involve higher costs of medical care (e.g. doctors' fees, hospital charges and costs of drugs) they are of better quality than the public services. A revealed preference of peasants for private health care, noted above, suggests that at least the better-off rural people can afford these services. But the poorer households are unlikely to be able to do so.

VI CONCLUSION

In this chapter we have shown that differences existed between China and India in respect of health status, access and utilisation of health services. China has much lower mortality rate and much longer life expectancy than India. Further, even though rural–urban inequality prevails in China, there is a better balance between rural and urban health services. Hospital beds and medical personnel per 1,000 in the Chinese rural areas have been consistently rising over time, in contrast to their virtual constancy in India. Given the higher density of rural health services in China, the poor enjoy a better access to these services there than in India and many other developing countries. What explains this superiority of China?

First, more favourable policies and programmes certainly had an important role to play. China spends a far greater proportion of GNP on health services than India. Secondly, rural cooperative health insurance and system of barefoot doctors in China until recently accounted for a reasonable provision of health services to the rural population. Although it is claimed that under the post-Mao reforms, decline in rural health insurance and in the number of barefoot doctors, have led to a deterioration of health services, the evidence is rather mixed. The introduction of private health services and allowing of private practice has enabled the provision of more and better-quality services which may have, at least partially, compensated for any negative effects of the post-Mao reforms. Thirdly, particularly during the Mao period, non-pecuniary incentives, mass motivation under collective organisations and community participation in preventive health programmes have had a very positive effect on the health status of the Chinese rural population. In contrast, the Indian experience shows that popular participation and community involvement are virtually absent. Finally, a political commitment on the part of the Chinese leaders to provide health services to the rural areas should also be noted as an important factor.

Access to health services in a mixed economy framework (which now prevails in both China and India) cannot be attributed entirely to the favourable public policies and programmes and their effective implementation. Private demand for health services and functioning of market for health services and products, the nature of income distribution, spatial distribution of health facilities and the efficiency with which these facilities are organised at the local level, and absence of delivery systems to reach the very poor, are some of the factors which may also explain inequity of access.

Notes and References

*   This chapter draws heavily on my article 'Access to Health Services', *Journal of International Development*, vol. 3, no. 4 (July) 1991.
 1. World Bank, *World Development Report*, 1985, Washington DC and New York, Oxford University Press, 1985, tables 1 and 23.
 2. Tei-Wei Hu, 'Health Care Services in China's Economic Development', in Robert F. Dernberger (ed.), *China's Development Experience in Comparative Perspective*, Cambridge, Mass. Harvard University Press, 1980; and P. G. K. Panikar, 'Financing Health Care in China: Implications of Some Recent Developments', *Economic and Political Weekly*, 19 April 1986.
 3. Tei-Wei Hu, 'Health Care Services in China's Economic Development'.
 4. David M. Lampton, 'Health, Conflict and the Chinese Political System', *Michigan Papers in Chinese Studies, No. 18*, Ann Arbor, Michigan University, 1974.

5. Nicholas R. Lardy, *Economic Growth and Distribution in China*, Cambridge, Cambridge University Press, 1978, p. 178.
6. William C. Hsiao, *The Incomplete Revolution: China's Health Care System Under Market Socialism*, paper prepared for the Conference on the Social Consequences of the Chinese Economic Reforms, Fairbank Centre for East Asian Research, Harvard University, 13–15 May 1988.
7. Ibid.
8. See World Bank, *Financing Health Services in Developing Countries – An Agenda for Reform*, Washington DC, 1987; and Amartya Sen and Jean Drèze, *Hunger and Public Action*, Oxford, Clarendon Press, 1989.
9. Hsiao, *The Incomplete Revolution*.
10. See Yinong Shao, *The Chinese Health System*, London, Office of Health Economics, UK, 1988.
11. Cited in Ashish Bose, 'Evolution of Health Policy in India', in Ashish Bose and P. B. Desai, (eds), *Studies in Social Dynamics of Primary Health Care*, New Delhi, Hindustan Publishing Corporation, 1983, p. 39.
12. Ibid, p. 40.
13. Lincoln Chen, 'Coping with Economic Crisis: Policy Development in China and India', *Health Policy and Planning*, vol. 2, no. 2, 1987, p. 141.
14. Government of India, Directorate General of Health Services, *Health Information of India*, New Delhi, several years.
15. Robert L. Parker, 'Health Care Expenditure in a Rural Indian Community', *Social Sciences and Medicine*, vol. 22, no. 1, 1986.
16. Debabar Banerji, *Health and Family Planning Services in India*, New Delhi, Lok Paksh, 1985, pp. 295–6.
17. WHO, 'Methodology of Nutritional Surveillance', *Technical Report Series, No. 593*, Geneva, 1976.
18. Philip Musgrave, 'Measurement of Equity in Health', *World Health Statistics Quarterly*, vol. 39, no. 4, 1986, pp. 325–35.
19. Government of India, Office of the Registrar General, *Survey on Infant Mortality and Child Mortality*, New Delhi, 1979, p. 11.
20. Ronald Anderson, 'Health Status Indices and Access to Medical Care', *American Journal of Public Health*, vol. 68, no. 5, 1978.
21. Ibid.
22. These data are taken from World Bank, *World Development Report, 1983*, New York, Oxford University Press, 1983; and UNICEF, *State of the World's Children, 1982–83*, New York, 1983.
23. World Bank, *CHINA: Socialist Economic Development, Vol. III*, Washington DC, 1983, p. 7.
24. World Bank, *World Development Report, 1990*, New York, Oxford University Press, 1990, table 28, p. 232.
25. World Bank, *World Development Report, 1988*, New York, Oxford University Press, 1988, table 29, p. 278.
26. Judith Banister, *China's Changing Population*, Stanford, Stanford University Press, 1987.
27. Carl Riskin, 'Feeding China: The Experience since 1979', *WIDER Working Paper No. 27*, Helsinki, November 1987.
28. Amartya Sen and Sunil Sen Gupta, 'Malnutrition of Rural Children and the

Sex Bias', *Economic and Political Weekly*, Annual Number, vol. XVIII, nos 19–21, May 1983; and Jocelyn Kynch and Amartya Sen, 'Indian Women: Well-being and Survival', *Cambridge Journal of Economics*, vol. 7, nos 3–4, September/December 1983.

29. Mary E. Young and Andre Prost, 'Child Health in China', *World Bank Staff Working Papers, No. 767*, Washington DC, 1985.
30. Leela Visaria, 'Infant Mortality in India – Level, Trends and Determinants', *Economic and Political Weekly*, 24 August 1985; and Amartya K. Sen, 'Family and Food: Sex Bias in Poverty', in T. N. Srinivasan and Pranab K. Bardhan (eds), *Rural Poverty in South Asia*, New York, Columbia University Press, 1988.
31. Pranab K. Bardhan. 'Sex Disparity in Child Survival in Rural India', in Srinivasan and Bardhan (eds), ibid.
32. Gopalakrishna Kumar, 'Gender, Differential Mortality and Development: The Experience of Kerala', *Cambridge Journal of Economics*, December 1989.
33. Ibid; and S. H. Preston, *Mortality Patterns in National Populations*, New York, Academic Press, 1976.
34. Athar Hussain and Nicholas Stern, *On the Recent Increase in Death Rates in China*, London School of Economics, July 1988 (mimeo).
35. See Rushikesh M. Maru, 'Health Manpower Strategies for Rural Health Services, India and China, 1949–1975', *Economic and Political Weekly*, Special Number, August 1976.
36. *Yearbook of Chinese Public Health for 1986*, Beijing, People's Health Press, 1986, p. 475 (in Chinese).
37. Taras Maitra, Banamali Dey and Nikhilesh Bhattacharva, 'An Enquiry on the Distribution of Public Education and Health Services in West Bengal', *Sankhya*, Series C (Quantitative Economics), vol. 36, parts 2 and 4, June 1974, p. 543.
38. Moni Nag, 'Impact of Social and Economic Development on Mortality: A Comparative Study of Kerala and West Bengal', *Economic and Political Weekly*, Annual Number, May 1983.
39. UN, *Poverty, Unemployment and Development Policy – A Case Study of Selected Issues with Special reference to Kerala*, New York, 1975, pp. 138–40.
40. Kynch and Sen, 'Indian Women . . .'.
41. *Statistical Yearbook of China, 1988* (Chinese version), p. 000.
42. Robert L. Parker and Alan R. Hinman, 'Use of Health Services', *American Journal of Public Health*, vol. 72, Supplement, 1982.
43. Ibid.
44. David L. Lampton, 'Performance and the Chinese Political System: A Preliminary Assessment of Education and Health Policies', *China Quarterly*, September 1978.
45. Ibid.
46. Lampton, 'Health, Conflict . . .
47. Ibid.
48. W. Parish, 'Egalitarianism in Chinese Society', *Problems of Communism*, January–February 1981.
49. Bose, 'Evolution of Health Policy . . .', p. 35.

50. N. H. Antia, 'An Alternative Strategy for Health Care: The Mandwa Project', *Economic and Political Weekly*, 21–28 December 1985; and N. H. Antia, 'The Mandwa Project – An Experiment in Community Participation', *International Journal of Health Services*, vol. 18, no. 1, 1988.
51. Antia, 'An Alternative Strategy for Health Care'.
52. David F. Pyle, 'From Pilot Project to Operational Program in India: The Problems of Transition', in Merilee S. Grindle (ed.), *Politics and Policy Implementation in the Third World*, Princeton, Princeton University Press, 1980.

9 Access to Education

Access to education or equality of educational opportunities can be defined in several ways. It may mean equality of access to schooling of children of different social and economic classes; or equal opportunity, after schooling, in terms of outcome or results, i.e. children from different social classes would acquire similar income, occupational status and political power.[1] In the real world, even if children start with equal educational opportunities, they may end up with different outcomes with respect to status and earnings, depending on job opportunities available, natural ability and family background, etc. Another aspect of access to education is the effective utilisation of this opportunity which would depend on several factors like affordability, opportunity cost of schooling, motivation, etc.

Differences in educational opportunity can also be defined in terms of inequalities in the school system, e.g. in respect of educational opportunity; quality of schooling; magnitudes of the impact of education on earnings; and investment in education. These in turn would affect access to the labour market. However, in the labour market, differential returns on education may also arise due to discrimination against certain social and economic classes – lack of social and occupational mobility, discrimination in employment and wage payments – so that equal levels of education attained would not yield equal returns.[2]

Inequalities may occur between:

(a) *Economic classes* (low-income, middle-income and high-income groups of the population);
(b) *Geographical locations* (differences between access of rural and urban populations). This case may be somewhat similar to (a) above if income differentials coincided with locational differences; and
(c) *Social classes* (e.g. minorities in China, and backward and scheduled castes in India and classes in the form of gender groups).

Situations (a), (b) and (c) may all be interrelated. For example, proponents of the 'human capital' thesis argue that education increases human skills and labour productivity so that expansion of educational facilities should reduce income inequality. Bowles introduced class aspects into the economics of education by arguing that in capitalist market-oriented economies, because of labour market imperfections, the rewards from higher education would accrue mainly to the élite groups, whereas those from primary education, mainly to the masses.[3]

Rural or urban location of educational facilities also accounts for differential access and quality of education. A concentration of schools in urban areas means that the urban population has better access to information, inputs and supply of teachers, etc. In rural areas, on the other hand, schools are scattered over long distances which limits children's access to them.

However, even if physical facilities were more easily available, access of the rural poor to education would be limited by their extremely low ability to pay for it. This low capacity to pay cannot be easily overcome through borrowing in conditions of imperfect capital markets and high interest rates on loans. Thus the lower the levels of income of the parents of school-going children, the higher would be the cost of education and the lower the returns.

To put the problems of educational access in broader perspective, Section I is devoted to a brief overview of educational policies in China and India. We then discuss the problem of educational access in respect of economic inequalities in Section II, spatial differences in Section III and class access or access of the minorities in Section IV.

I EDUCATIONAL POLICIES

Educational policies in China suffered from political vicissitudes much more than they did in India. At the time of the Revolution in 1949, the objectives of economic development guided the shape of Chinese policy measures towards primary, secondary and higher education. But this orientation changed with the Great Leap Forward and Cultural Revolution, periods during which political and ideological factors came to the fore. In Chapter 3 we noted a narrowing of gaps between professional and manual workers as one of the components of Mao's egalitarian strategy. To achieve this goal a number of educational reforms were introduced: abolition of a formal examination system; inclusion of physical labour on farms and in factories; political education as part of the school curriculum; introduction of informal means of education (part-time schools and spare-time educational schemes) to impart practical skills linked more directly to farming and rural non-farm activities; and appointment of workers and peasant as teachers to give practical orientation to education and to disgrace intellectuals.[4]

Considerations of quality were secondary to raising the numbers of literate people in the rural, and to a lesser extent, the urban areas. The Party felt that earlier educational policies based on quality considerations had promoted élitism and urban bias. To correct this bias, the rural educational policy provided for such programmes as literacy, vocational education and training in practical scientific and research activities linked to agriculture. (See Chapter 7 for discussion of mass science movement and four-level research network in rural areas.) This policy was pursued often at the expense of higher education which suffered during the Cultural Revolution for lack of funds and, in cases, led to the closure of institutions.

Anti-intellectual campaigns led to a decline in the prestige of higher education, whose quality also suffered as a result of such measures as a reduction in the length of courses, the participation of students in political and revolutionary activities, and the despatch of teachers to rural areas for political and ideological activities.

In the post-Mao period, a new educational policy gave highest priority to the expansion and improvement of higher education. The policy-makers recognised that the programme of Four Modernisations could not be implemented without an adequate supply of highly qualified manpower. In 1985, in China, the enrolment ratio for higher education was as low as 5 per cent, much lower than that in India and many other developing countries (see Figure 9.1).

To achieve the objective of a rapid expansion in higher education, policy reforms were introduced at both secondary school and university levels. In the former case, as we shall discuss below, high-quality Key Schools were reintroduced to prepare entrants to university and other higher educational institutions. Efforts were made to improve the quality of education by reintroducing the examination system, reforming the curriculum, upgrading and standardising teaching materials, offering higher salaries and better living conditions to university teachers, and paying bonus and supplementary rewards for extra teaching loads and research.[5]

As part of a policy of 'marketisation' of the economy, in many cases student subsidies have been reduced and even replaced by charging fees. This is also intended to reduce the state burden for the financing of higher education and raise overall expenditure devoted to it.

As long as expenditures on higher education remain low (see

below), the objective of rapid expansion of higher education is unlikely to be achieved, at least in the short run. Also the reappearance of competitive examinations and Key Schools suggests that some élitism may be creeping back into the educational system. As we discuss below, the new system favours urban-based students (who enjoy better educational facilities, in Key Schools, for example, which are based generally in the urban areas) and those who are academically gifted.

In contrast to China, in India there have been no initiatives (at least until recently) for promoting work-oriented rural education at the primary and secondary levels. In general, Indian educational policies have continued to neglect rural primary education, earmarking relatively low amounts of allocations to it. The bulk of such expenditures is taken up by payment of teachers' salaries with little allocation for capital investments. The Seventh Five-Year Plan of India (1985–90) notes:

> Although the Indian education scene since independence has been characterised by massive quantitative expansion at all levels, it is still to undergo the kind of transformation envisaged in the National Policy. It is faced with a staggering backlog; the level of illiteracy is as high as 63 per cent; to achieve universal elementary education . . . there will be need to enrol fifty million more children; vocationalisation of secondary education has yet to make headway; there is very significant pressure on the higher educational system and a decline in the standards of quality. [6]

It is the above lacunae that led to the design of a new educational policy for India in May 1986 which aims at: promotion of universal literacy through such schemes as non-formal and adult education; equality of education for women, scheduled castes and scheduled tribes; greater vocationalisation of education at the secondary level and restructuring of courses to include teaching of high technology; improvements in standards of teaching through training of teachers at higher levels of education; quantitative and qualitative improvements in higher education through distance learning and increased flexibility in combination of courses.[7]

In the *National Policy on Education* 1986, a special section was devoted to 'Education for Equality' to alleviate inequalities in the access of women, scheduled castes and tribes and the handicapped at different levels of education. Rural–urban and regional inequalities as well those among different social groups have continued to persist. Therefore, special measures are proposed to favour the education of scheduled castes through, for example, scholarships, recruitment of teachers from among the scheduled castes and provision of better facilities for students. Particular attention is also paid to the provision of educational facilities in the tribal areas where it is proposed to open more primary schools and non-formal and adult education centres.

Adult education including literacy (particularly among the 15–35 age group) is regarded as an important element in the promotion of educational equality. Programmes of distance learning, workers' education by employers and trade unions, use of TV and other learning media and the establishment of rural educational centres are the means of providing adult education.

It is planned to raise the quality of higher education through improvements in curricula and teaching methods, use of audio-visual aids and electronic equipment and development of scientific and technological materials.

The seriousness of the 1986 educational policy to remove inequalities in education remains in doubt, however. For example, one of the proposals laid down in the Seventh Five-Year Plan (1985–90) sought to establish during the plan period 500 modern model (*Navodaya*) schools, one in each district, at the cost of Rs.500 crores (Rs.5,000 million) each. These schools seem to be somewhat similar to the Key Schools in China. They are modelled on the public school system, and are therefore likely to perpetuate existing inequalities (and the élitist system) rather than removing them.[8] By the end of 1990, there were 261 *Navodaya* schools in 29 states of India.

The cost of new model schools is very high, particularly in contrast to the very limited resources at the disposal of existing secondary schools. At higher educational levels also, costs per student continue to rise substantially. Thus the goal of raising the quality of higher education may be thwarted by a lack of adequate resources, especially in the face of rapidly growing population and increasing demand for education. As we note below in the section on the financing of education, the share of Indian plan outlays devoted to education has fallen consistently in successive plans. Unless this trend is corrected, the policy objective of higher quality of education is unlikely to be fully achieved.

A Review Committee (appointed to review the National Policy on Education 1986), whose report was published in early 1991 reviewed, *inter alia*, the performance of *Navodaya* schools. It found that the *Navodaya* scheme is very costly in terms of high capital expenditure and high student expenditure *per capita*, and its performance fell well below expectations. The Committee therefore recommended that no new *Navodaya* schools should be established.[9]

II ECONOMIC INEQUALITIES

Economic inequalities in respect of education may arise from (a) a differential capacity of individuals and households to pay for education; (b) uneven allocation of investment resources at different levels (primary, secondary and higher) and types (rural and urban) of education. Below we examine whether a positive correlation exists between per capita incomes and education in China and India, and whether differential educational investments between urban and rural areas have something to do with educational inequalities.

2.1 Income and Education

The ability of an individual or household to pay for education largely determines access to it in most market-oriented developing countries. The poorer the rural population, the less it can afford to 'buy' education especially if it is costly. Since rural incomes are very low, access of the rural population is likely to be relatively more limited than that of the urban. An international cross-section analysis shows a positive correlation between average per capita income and literacy rate because incomes provide the resources with which private expenditure on education is likely to be financed.[10] But does this hypothesis also hold in a socialist economy like that of China where such basic needs as education may be financed/subsidised heavily by the state for social and political reasons? *A priori* in China where most schools are state-owned and education heavily subsidised, the cost of education to individuals should be low or negligible. We used Chinese provincial data on population by educational attainment, i.e. percentages of the population who are (i) illiterate or semi-illiterate; (ii) primary school leavers; (iii) junior secondary school leavers; (iv) senior secondary school leavers, and (v) college graduates. The relationship between per capita income (Y) and population by educational attainment (P) was determined by using the following equation: $P = a + b Y$. The regression results for the above five categories shown in Table 9.1 are statistically significant only for secondary

Table 9.1 Relationship between income and education in China
(Regression results) (1982)

Dependent variable		a (constant)	b (income per capita)	Adjusted R^2	t-Statistic of b	F-Statistic of b
1. *Illiteracy*						
Linear	=	28.5	−0.0086 (+0.003)	0.19	−2.7	7.5
Log	=	5.7	−0.4 (0.09)	0.41	−4.5	20.4
2. *Primary*						
Linear	=	34.8	−0.003 (0.002)	0.032	−1.4	1.9
Log	=	3.8	0.05 (0.07)	−0.018	−0.7	0.5
3. *Junior Secondary*						
Linear	=	13.4	0.008 (0.002)	0.43	4.7	22.0
Log	=	0.19	0.43 (0.12)	0.30	3.6	12.8
4. *Senior Secondary*						
Linear	=	3.2	0.008 (0.0008)	0.75	9.4	88.0
Log	=	−2.5	0.7 (0.14)	0.47	5.1	26.0
5. *College*						
Linear	=	−0.05	0.0013 (0.0002)	0.63	7.0	48.0
Log	=	−7	1.02 (0.14)	0.66	7.4	55.0

Source: Based on Appendix Table A9.1.

Note: Standard errors are given in brackets.

school leavers and college graduates. The population with primary school education shows almost no correlation with income per capita. Can one therefore conclude that in a socialist economy universal primary education is a social and political goal and that there is therefore no *a priori* reason for expecting a positive correlation between income and education?

In the case of India, we undertook a similar test using 1981 Census data by educational attainment (see Table 9.2). Only the equation for higher secondary education was statistically significant at a 5 per cent level of confidence.

Table 9.2 Relationship between income and education in India (Regression results) (1981)

Dependent variable	a (constant)	b (income per capita)	Adjusted R^2	t-Statistic of b	F-Statistic of b
Primary					
Linear	92.3	(0.027)	0.008	0.38	0.14
		(0.071)			
Log	1.86	0.43	0.009	1.08	1.17
		(0.40)			
Middle (includes junior and higher secondary)					
Linear	59.6	−0.0061	0.002	0.19	0.038
		(0.032)			
Log	4.20	−0.040	0.0006	0.10	0.011
		(0.38)			
*Higher Secondary**					
Linear	7.53	0.037	0.34	3.19	10.18
		(0.012)			
Log	−1.52	0.76	0.29	2.92	8.52
		(0.26)			
Higher education					
Linear	4.02	0.0029	0.0081	1.07	1.15
		(0.0027)			
Log	−0.33	0.32	0.018	1.16	1.34
		(0.28)			
Illiteracy					
Linear	775.7	−0.13	0.047	0.92	0.84
		(0.14)			
Log	7.26	−0.11	0.033	0.76	0.58
		(0.15)			

Source: Based on Appendix Table A9.2.

Note: Standard errors are given in brackets.
* b coefficients for both equations are significant at 5 per cent level.

Of course, causation between income and education is difficult to determine through a simple regression analysis. Causation works in two ways. On the one hand, a rise in per capita incomes should lead to a greater demand for education. On the other hand, a higher level of educational attainment should enable an increase in income through higher earnings. In market-oriented countries like India, large earnings differentials are partly explained by educational/skill differentials. In socialist countries like China such earnings differentials are quite small even if one takes account of fringe benefits (housing, cost-of-living subsidies, etc.) which are far greater than earnings.

2.2 Financing of Education

China

It is generally believed that, compared to other developing countries, China has under-invested in education. China's investment in education as a proportion of GNP was nearly 3 per cent in 1986 – compared to 3.4 per cent for India,[11] a figure which is below the average for developing countries (4–5 per cent) and the advanced countries (over 6 per cent).[12]

There are several sources of investment expenditure in education: the central and local governments, local (rural townships) and private households. In the case of primary education, the State bears most of the expenses of the urban schools; this is not the case, however, for primary rural schools. The expenses of rural primary education are borne jointly by the State and rural townships (formerly communes). Under this two-tier system of educational investment the State finances state schools and subsidises *minban* (people-run) schools in rural areas. The State subsidy to *minban* rural school teachers varied between provinces, prefectures and counties, but on an average it was about one-third to one-half of teachers' salaries.[13]

The remaining expenses in the form of teachers' salaries and recurrent expenditures on repairs of school buildings and furniture, etc. were borne by the communes or local townships. For example, in Shandong province, between 1979 and 1982, 75 per cent of the educational expenditures in the countryside was raised by communes, brigades and the individual households.[14] Thus, the rural areas bear a disproportionate burden of investment in primary schools, whereas the State bears the burden of urban school investments. For this reason, in many poorer provinces and counties, the quality of primary school education is quite low, with old and dilapidated buildings, broken furniture, and inadequate teaching materials and aids. Furthermore, fluctuations in agricultural incomes cause certain instability in the financing of rural education by the local authorities. Unless the State raises its share of investment in rural education, the gaps between urban and rural educational facilities and their quality are likely to widen. (see section III).

Even in the prosperous rural areas, collective funds for primary and secondary education tend to be inadequate. This seems to have been the case since the introduction of the rural economic reforms which led to tremendous growth of investment opportunities in both farm and non-farm activities. If the rate of return on investment in agriculture and rural industry is higher and quicker-yielding than that in education, rural households and enterprises tend to divert resources away from education which yields returns after much longer gestation lags. There is one caveat however. Private and social demand for education is not determined by purely economic criteria like rates of return. To the extent that cultural factors have a role to play, the above purely economic argument regarding investment allocation between production and education may not hold good. For example, education in both China and India seems to raise social status and promotion prospects more than income and earnings. And in India higher education is generally associated with higher castes.

India

Tilak has estimated that rates of return on investment in primary education in India are much higher than those on higher educational investments. This finding is also confirmed by cross-sectional studies, particularly by the World Bank.[15] It is therefore surprising that the allocation of public resources to primary education in India has considerably declined over time (from 56 per cent of the total educational expenditure during the First Five-Year Plan, 1951–56, to 29 per cent during the Seventh Plan, 1985–90). The share of plan outlay on education fell from 7.8 per cent during the First Plan to 2.6 per cent in the Sixth Plan (1980–85), but has risen slightly to 3.5 per cent in the Seventh Plan. This decline refers only to the plan expenditure which forms only a part of the total educational expenditure in India.

Household expenditure on education as a proportion of GNP

declined from 2.5 per cent in 1970–71 to 2.1 per cent in 1982–83; per capita expenditure in real terms declined from Rs.16 to Rs.12.[16] Expenditures on education over time indicate a declining trend in rural–urban inequalities during the 1950s and 1960s. But regional inequalities between states in respect of educational expenditures continued to be quite wide. This is indicated by an increase in the coefficient of variation for per capita public expenditure on education from 0.59 in 1981 to 0.70 in 1985 (see Table 9.8).

Expenditure on middle schools and higher education has expanded a great deal. To some extent the greater investment in higher education relative to primary education is inevitable since the unit costs of higher education are much higher. But even if one takes account of this factor, university enrolments in India are overexpanded especially considering the persistence of graduate unemployment, i.e. excess of supply of educated people over demand. One explanation for this may be the greater political clout of the beneficiaries of higher education and another is the cultural demand for education among the higher economic and social classes noted above.

In India, the (rural) poor are reluctant to spend much on their children's education even when educational facilities are available. First, the backward castes and other disadvantaged poverty groups may not attach a high premium on children's education in the belief that formal schooling does not necessarily lead to better economic well-being when their opportunity cost (in terms of income forgone) is positive and at times quite high. Secondly, formal education in rural areas does not impart any work-oriented skills. If anything, it develops attitudes of rural children against rural life, farming and manual work in general. Thirdly, social inhibitions also stand in the way of female education in conditions of shortage of female teachers. Finally, the perception of the poor may be that education is unlikely to offer much upward social mobility.

We now turn to spatial access to education.

III   RURAL–URBAN INEQUALITIES

Spatial access to education may be measured by rural–urban differences. Two quantitative indicators of these differences are: (a) the geographical location of educational facilities, and (b) enrolment rates at different educational levels by rural and urban areas. Ideally, attendance rates would be a better index (since enrolment does not guarantee attendance) but in the absence of such data we have no choice but to use enrolment rates (i.e. enrolments as a proportion of school-age population). To add a qualitative dimension to the problem of educational access, we also examine wastage (i.e. retention rates and drop-outs) and pupil–teacher ratios.

Unequal distribution of schools and institutions of higher learning can explain inequality of access. A World Bank report has noted 'physical inaccessibility' as a constraint 'to universalisation of basic education'.[17] In China, physical accessibility to schools is likely to be higher in the densely populated areas than in the remote backward areas where distances between home and school are much longer and public transport is either negligible or totally absent. With the closure of low-quality primary and secondary schools since 1979 (it is estimated that about 58,000 primary and 47,000 secondary schools have been closed), the problem of physical accessibility may have been aggravated. The situation is somewhat similar in India where nearly 4 per cent of Indian villages and 4.4 per cent of the population were at a distance of two to five kilometres from a primary school. Nearly 32 per cent of villages and 33 per cent of the population are two to five kilometres from a secondary school. Nearly 15 per cent of villages and population are over ten kilometres away from a secondary school.[18]

Some indication of physical accessibility in China may be obtained from the number of primary and secondary schools per 10,000 population in rural and urban areas (Table 9.3). The data show wide gaps between rural and urban areas, particularly in the case of senior secondary schools whose number per capita was much higher in urban than in rural areas during the post-Mao period. The reverse is the case for junior secondary schools, which may suggest that rural children have relatively much less accessibility to senior secondary schools.[19] During the Mao period, the rural-urban gaps at the secondary level were much narrower.

3.1 Key Schools (Zhongdian)

The reintroduction of Key Schools in the post-Mao period is likely to exacerbate inequalities of access to education. These are high-quality élitist secondary schools (and to a lesser extent, primary schools) which in theory are open to any student (rural or urban) who qualifies for the entrance examination. But in practice, there seems to be a bias in favour of urban areas since there are fewer Key Schools in

Table 9.3 Physical availability of schools per capita in Chinese rural and urban areas (1962–85)

Year	Secondary schools				Primary schools	
	Senior secondary		Junior secondary			
	Urban* (per 10,000 of urban pop.)	Rural (per 10,000 of rural pop.)	Urban (per 10,000 of urban pop.)	Rural (per 10,000 of rural pop.)	Urban (per 10,000 of urban pop.)	Rural (per 10,000 of rural pop.)
Mao period						
1962	0.33	0.009	0.43	0.18	2.65	11.44
1965	0.27	0.01	0.41	0.14	4.37	27.31
1971	0.16	0.16	0.57	1.02	2.58	13.20
1974	0.68	0.28	0.24	0.86	2.37	13.50
1976	0.78	0.61	0.34	1.67	2.20	13.02
Post-Mao period						
1977	0.84	0.65	0.30	1.67	1.98	12.12
1979	0.72	0.34	0.30	1.24	1.84	11.26
1981	0.59	0.15	0.33	0.94	1.80	10.70
1983	0.45	0.10	0.35	0.88	1.60	10.40
1984	0.33	0.09	0.33	0.92	1.70	11.30
1985	0.29	0.08	0.32	0.96	1.70	11.50

Source: China, Ministry of Education, Statistics, 1949–1983, Beijing, 1984; Achievement of Education in China, Statistics, 1980–85, Beijing, 1986.

* Urban includes county seats and town schools.

Note: Figures for 1984 and 1985 may not be comparable with the rest since the definition of 'town' was changed in 1984.

rural areas. Gardner notes that this élitism was 'presented in terms of these institutions serving as models for emulation by demonstrating what could be achieved'.[20] These schools account for 50 per cent of the state educational budget although they constitute only 1 per cent of primary and 4 per cent of secondary schools.[21] Disproportionately large resources for Key Schools implies lower resources for ordinary schools.

Unequal access at the secondary level is further aggravated by restricted access to higher levels of education. The main entrants to the universities are increasingly from the Key Schools and not from the ordinary secondary schools at which the poor and rural children are enrolled. In Guangdong province in 1980 only 3.8 per cent of the graduates of higher secondary schools entered university, compared with 72 per cent from the Key School in Guangzhou city.[22]

The privileged position of Key Schools contrasts sharply with rural *minban* schools which generally prepare rural pupils for agricultural work rather than advanced study.

Parallel to the urban-based Key Schools are the Key Universities and colleges which are given priority in respect of higher financial allocations, more qualified teaching and research staff and better students. The very strict entrance and qualifying examinations for these universities tends to restrict the access of rural secondary students.

In the case of India, the élitist urban-based public schools designed on the British model, have existed for a long time, and their number has been growing rapidly in the past. Access to those schools is invariably confined to children of the wealthy and politically powerful. An emerging dualistic structure of education in India is reflected in 'the government and municipal schools for the children of the poor and the public schools for the children of the rich'.[23]

3.2 Enrolments

Gross enrolment rates in primary and secondary schools in India rose substantially over the period 1950–51 to 1983–84. Enrolment trends show that (a) in general, the rates are lower for scheduled castes/tribes than for other categories, (b) urban rates are higher than the rural rates at all educational levels, and (c) overall annual enrolment rates have been higher for girls than for boys (however, this is not true for the scheduled castes and tribes group).[24] In the case of China, sufficiently long time-series for these rates are not available. However, between 1982 and 1985 the rural enrolment rates declined

Table 9.4   Rural–urban enrolment inequalities in China (1982–85)

Year	Enrolment rate				Equality coefficient	
	Primary School		Secondary school (Lower level)			
	Rural	Urban	Rural	Urban	Primary	Secondary
1982	87.3	98.5	82.7	92.1	0.89	0.90
1983	82.9	94.1	77.0	91.2	0.88	0.84
1984	80.0	n.a.	75.0	97.7	n.a.	0.77
1985	74.8	n.a.	74.0	n.a.	n.a.	n.a.

Sources and Explanations:
(1) The enrolment rate for 1983 is calculated from *Zhongguo Nongcun Tongji Nian Jian*, 1986 (Agricultural Statistical Yearbook), Beijing, 1987, p. 277.
(2) The number of students in school is taken from *Achievements of Education in China 1980–85*, pp. 71 and 82. The urban students include county students also.
(3) The population of school-age children in 1983 is computed by dividing the number of students in 1983 by the 1983 enrolment rate.
(4) Under the assumption that the annual growth rates of the population of school-age children are 1.022% for rural areas and 1.027% for urban areas (which are approximately the average annual growth rates of population from 1964 to 1977 in the rural and urban areas – see *Statistical Yearbook of China*, 1986, p. 71), we estimate the population of school-age children in 1982, 1984 and 1985 on the basis of the estimated population for 1983.
Note: n.a. = not available.

for both primary and lower secondary schools. In the case of urban areas they declined at the primary school level but somewhat increased at the lower secondary level (Table 9.4). These results are particularly paradoxical since the rural economic reforms have raised rural incomes substantially and the growth of rural incomes is much faster than the growth of urban incomes, thus narrowing income inequalities. If educational access was income elastic there should, in principle, have been a much greater demand for rural education in the wake of spectacular increases in peasants' incomes. Could this decline be explained by a demographic factor? The birth control campaigns might have reduced the primary school-age population. Greater emphasis on quality rather than quantity and the lengthening of period of schooling may also have led to some decline in enrolment.[25]

The rural responsibility system under which employment opportunities in farming and non-farm activities have expanded significantly, may partly explain a decline in enrolment rates in the Chinese
rural areas. Immediate income-earning opportunities have tempted
parents to keep young children away from school. In other words, the
opportunity cost of schooling has gone up in relation to its short-term
benefits. The opportunity cost of labour will be high or low for a
household depending on its size in terms of number of children and
other adult members, its assets in terms of cultivable land, and its
income levels. A survey in Anhui Province showed that school
attendance declined in localities which had large arable land, low
population density and for families whose main source of labour
supply was school-age children.[26]

The opportunity cost of schooling is also influenced by the season-
ality of agricultural operations. In peak agricultural season and
periods of harvesting, the opportunity cost would be much higher
than during slack periods. If the school vacations were synchronised
with agricultural peaks, the adverse effects on enrolments and drop-
outs could be minimised. Such synchronisation does not seem to have
been planned in China with the exception of some areas (e.g. Quan-
jiao County in Anhui Province).[27] Regional variations in enrolment
rates may depend partly on the economic prosperity of the area so
that school attendance in richer areas like Jiangsu may be much less
affected than the poorer areas.[28]

Demand for education in the rural areas may also be explained by
the qualification requirements for jobs and access to those jobs. It is
reported that in China, at least, junior secondary education is necessary for a job in a local township enterprise. However, in the poorer
areas, such job opportunities are likely to be rare, suggesting a low
return on education, and greater pressure for children to work on the
farm or help with household chores. While the probability of finding
rural jobs is low, higher returns to education could, in principle,
accrue through mobility to the urban sector where jobs call for higher
educational requirements as is indeed the case in India. Yet in China,
this mobility has been restricted by decree. Although regulation of
labour flows from rural to urban areas has recently been relaxed, it is
still quite difficult for rural people to change residence and move to
urban areas on a permanent basis.

The Chinese enrolment for higher education is extremely low
compared to that in other developing countries including India (see

Higher Education Enrolment Ratio (%)

Figure 9.1   Higher education enrolment in China and other selected countries

Source: World Bank: *China Management and Finance of Higher Education*,
Washington DC, November 1986, p. 9.

Figure 9.1). University education suffered a great deal during the Cultural Revolution. The very low enrolment ratio indicates a very limited access for everybody. But the access of poorer students from rural areas is likely to be even more restricted. It is estimated that in 1985 less than 5 per cent of the Chinese youth went beyond secondary schooling. This is much lower than the higher education enrolment ratio for India. Figure 9.1 indicates three alternative enrolment projections for China by the year 2000: low (ratio of 10 per cent), medium (ratio of 12.5 per cent) and high (ratio of 15 per cent). All these alternatives involve an average annual rate of increase of over 10 per cent which is significant.

Rural–Urban Differentials

Differential access of rural and urban children to schooling is reflected in variations in enrolment rates. To measure relative access, we estimate what may be called an 'equality coefficient', which is the ratio of rural enrolment rate (E_r) to urban enrolment rate (E_u), so that E-Coefficient $= (E_r)/(E_u) = 1, < 1$ or > 1.

There would be equality between urban and rural areas when the coefficient is unity; urban bias when it is less than unity and rural bias when it is greater than unity. The lower the coefficient, the wider the rural–urban gaps; the higher the coefficient, the narrower these disparities.

In China for both primary and secondary education these coefficients are very high, although the coefficient for secondary education has declined from 0.90 in 1982 to 0.77 in 1984 (Table 9.4). These coefficients suggest a high degree of rural–urban equality.

It is interesting to compare the equality coefficients for China and India. Such a comparison is particularly relevant for the post-Mao period when emphasis on efficiency and quality instead of mass education is likely to encourage inequalities of the type prevalent in capitalistic economies. Differential quality of schooling (apart from enrolment rates) is another aspect of rural–urban differentials. In terms of academic standards, teaching facilities, materials and teachers, the quality of urban schools is generally much higher than that of rural schools.

The Indian coefficients, with the exception of those for the states of Kerala, Punjab and Tamil Nadu, are much lower than those for China (Table 9.5) which suggests that notwithstanding the post-Mao changes in educational policies the egalitarian policies of the Mao period are still reflected in the narrow rural–urban inequalities in enrolment rates. (During the Cultural Revolution, it is mainly the higher education that suffered; not the primary and secondary education.)

A third aspect of rural–urban differentials in access to education is the achievement in China of universal primary education in urban areas but not in rural areas. As noted in Section I on educational policies, one of the strategies for overcoming poor primary education in India is to offer free universal education as is done in China and in other developing countries. However, so far, the goal of universal primary education has not yet been achieved in either urban or rural areas.

Table 9.5   Rural–urban enrolment inequalities in India (1981)

| States | Equality coefficient | | | | | |
| | Age group (5–9 yrs) | | | Age group (10–14 yrs) | | |
	All	Males	Females	All	Males	Females
India[a]	0.56	0.64	0.46	0.62	0.75	0.44
Bihar	0.44	0.53	0.32	0.55	0.70	0.32
Madhya Pradesh	0.44	0.55	0.30	0.46	0.62	0.24
Uttar Pradesh	0.50	0.63	0.33	0.67	0.86	0.35
Rajasthan	0.44	0.59	0.22	0.52	0.70	0.20
Kerala	0.94	0.93	0.94	0.96	0.98	0.94
Gujarat	0.69	0.75	0.60	0.71	0.82	0.58
Maharashtra	0.68	0.75	0.60	0.67	0.79	0.53
Andhra Pradesh	0.58	0.66	0.49	0.49	0.60	0.35
Haryana	0.52	0.63	0.38	0.65	0.86	0.39
Karnataka	0.63	0.71	0.54	0.59	0.71	0.45
Orissa	0.68	0.77	0.59	0.61	0.74	0.46
Punjab	0.73	0.77	0.69	0.78	0.88	0.67
Tamil Nadu	0.77	0.83	0.70	0.66	0.77	0.52
West Bengal	0.56	0.62	0.52	0.64	0.72	0.55

Source: These coefficients are calculated on the basis of data in Census of Population, 1981, Series 1, *India – Paper 2 of 1983 Key Population Statistics Based on 5 Per Cent Sample Data*, New Delhi, 1983, p. 25.

Note: [a] Excludes Assam.

Gender Bias

The Indian data show much higher equality coefficients for males than for females. We were unable to estimate separate coefficients for Chinese male and female children in rural and urban areas. But male bias also prevails in China. In 1984 only 40 per cent of the Chinese general secondary school students and about 29 per cent of university students were girls.[29] Although the number of girls enrolled for higher education doubled between 1975 and 1984, that of boys tripled. These are of course average figures; the accessibility of rural girls to education is likely to be much less than that of urban girls.

In both China and India, social and economic factors seem to account for lower enrolment rates for girls than for boys. The traditional preference for boys over girls tends to leave girls at home to do household chores and help in rearing children. This is particularly likely in the case of low-income households which are unable to afford any domestic help. Girls would tend to have a higher opportunity cost of going to school than boys, thus discouraging investment in their education. In terms of opportunities in the labour market, the possibility of girls finding jobs, given the same education and ability as boys, is likely to be lower, which also suggests a lower return on investment in girls. Employers are reluctant to hire girls for fear that once married, long maternity leave would keep them away from work. (In China, the prevailing welfare system requires that women with children be supported by their employers.)

An additional disincentive to investment in girls' education is that, unlike boys, the parents would forgo return from investment in girls' education as soon as they are married and move out of the parents' household. The boys may continue to send remittances to parents even after they have moved away: this is not true for girls who are integrated into the families of their husbands.

Apart from these economic reasons, social inhibitions may explain relatively low female enrolments. Social attitudes prevent Indian parents from sending girls to secondary schools where there are no female teachers. Also girls are generally discouraged from attending co-educational schools.

The caste factor in India also influences parents' attitudes towards educating their daughters. It has been noted that the share of parents unwilling to educate daughters rises from 6 per cent in the high caste group to 36 per cent in the lowest caste group.[30]

Wastage in Education

The benefits from enrolments occur mainly through retention of pupils at school. Inequality in education is also reflected in different retention and drop-out rates for different social groups. Table 9.6 gives retention rates for China and India over a period of time. For India, the data are by castes; for China, they are for rural and urban areas (a similar breakdown for India is not available).

The retention rates for the two countries present some interesting contrasts.

Table 9.6 Retention rates in schools (China vs. India) (percentages)

India

Period	Primary school		
	Scheduled caste	Scheduled tribes	Others
1968–72	27.8	20.3	35.3
1969–73	28.8	21.3	36.9
1970–74	30.3	22.9	38.0
1971–75	31.4	22.3	38.6
1972–76	32.2	21.9	39.1
1973–77	33.5	20.5	38.8
1974–78	35.6	23.3	40.5

China

Period	Primary school		Period	Junior secondary school	
	Rural	Urban		Rural	Urban
1971–76	67.4	–	1972–75	83.0	86.6
1972–77	67.4	–	1973–76	–	93.3
1973–78	64.8	95.8	1974–77	–	80.6
1974–79	61.1	93.0	1975–78	96.7	82.8
1975–80	57.3	96.5	1976–79	67.5	82.8
1976–81	61.5	–	1977–80	33.7	73.9
1977–82	61.8	–	1978–81	50.2	93.8
1978–83	55.8	88.3	1979–82	52.2	94.2
1979–84	58.8	–	1980–83	53.4	93.3
			1981–84	56.7	–

Sources: (1) India: Data supplied by the Ministry of Education, Government of India, New Delhi.
(2) China: Retention rates are estimated on the basis of data on enrolments and graduates contained in *Achievement of Education in China – Statistics*, 1949–1983, and *Statistics*, 1980–85, Ministry of Education, Beijing. Retention rates are estimated as follows:

$$\text{Retention rate for period } t \text{ to } t + k = \frac{\text{Graduates at year } t + k}{\text{Entrants at year } t}$$

For primary schooling $k = 5$, whereas for junior secondary schools, $k = 3$.

First, while the retention rates for scheduled castes in India have improved over time (those for scheduled tribes remain more or less unchanged), these rates for rural areas in China have declined. One can roughly assume that scheduled castes/tribes are more likely to be rural-based than urban-based. A restricted sample survey of re-peaters and drop-outs in primary education, undertaken in early 1977, showed that wastage in rural areas was much higher than in the urban areas, and among girls rather than boys.[31] Secondly, the overall retention rates for China are much higher than those for India, implying that wastage through drop-outs and repeaters is lower. Thirdly, the urban retention rates in China are higher than the rural rates.

In 1982–83, an interview survey of 49 drop-outs from fifth grade in Jiangsu province indicated the main reasons for leaving school. These were: the need to contribute to family manpower; inability to pay school fees; and repetition of grade.[32]

In India, the reasons for drop-outs were similar. In the case of male pupils in primary schools, poverty and the need to help in the family business were reported to be the major reasons, whereas for female pupils, domestic work was paramount.[33]

3.3 Pupil–Teacher Ratios

Differential quality or efficiency of education is often measured by the pupil–teacher ratio, so that the lower the ratio, the higher in principle should be the quality of education. For China, these ratios for both urban and rural areas are quite low; and much lower than the average in other developing countries.[34] The major reason for low ratios, however, is 'low teaching loads rather than small classes'.[35] School teachers work part-time performing other duties like farming, and a policy of one subject per teacher also accounts for their underemployment.

During 1980–85, the share of rural primary and secondary teachers declined whereas that of urban teachers increased, implying a rela-tive increase in the rural pupil–teacher ratios and a decline in the quality of rural teaching. This phenomenon has been attributed to the post-Mao rural reforms under which rural teachers are entitled to private plots of land. The teachers' salaries are known to be quite low and land assets offer them a major source of supplementary income. In a study of 850 schools in Guangdong, teachers cultivating plots were said to neglect their teaching duties.[36] Although many teachers may have given up teaching for farming, this does not seem to be the whole story. The teachers are very poorly qualified: many of them may either have been dismissed, or put through teacher training schools to improve their skills and thereby the quality of education.

To overcome the problem of a decline in the quality of rural teaching, some provinces (e.g. Heilongjiang, Guizhou, Heibei, Jiangxi and Anhui) have introduced special incentives for those teachers who are willing to work in rural counties or border areas. According to a State Council directive of 1983, primary and secondary school teachers are offered bonuses according to seniority.[37]

In the case of India, the quality of education at the primary and secondary levels of education is known to be quite low. This low quality is reflected in high pupil–teacher ratios (and high drop-out rates). In India, pupil–teacher ratios tend to be higher than those in China (see Appendix Tables A.9.8 and A.9.9). Indeed, these ratios rose during the 1970–71 to 1985–86 period, suggesting some decline in quality of education.

IV   REGIONAL INEQUALITIES

Inter-provincial variations in access to education can be reflected in the number of primary and secondary schools per 1,000 population, allocation of state expenditure for education in different provinces, differences in the pupil–teacher ratios and in the enrolment ratios. To determine the extent of such variations, we have estimated standard deviation (SD) and coefficients of variations (Co.V) for these indicators over time. The results are presented in Table 9.7.

In India, regional disparities in primary and secondary enrolment rates have declined as is indicated by a decline in the Co.Vs between 1970 and 1985. Comparable data on enrolment rates in China are not available but partial indicators suggest that inter-provincial differentials in primary enrolments declined in the 1950s and 1960s. However, this did not occur at the general secondary school level.[38]

Inter-provincial variations in the pupil–teacher ratios for primary and secondary schools increased in both China and India although there was no clear trend over time.

In China, in 1985 the primary and junior secondary schools showed lower disparities in rural areas than in urban areas; the reverse was the situation in the case of senior secondary schools.

Table 9.7   Regional inequalities in educational access (China and India)

Indicator	China			India		
	WM	*SD*	*Co. V*	*WM*	*SD*	*Co. V*
Per capita education expenditure						
(1977)	–	–	–	35.10	10.98	0.31
(1981)	–	–	–	62.4	37.1	0.59
(1985)	–	–	–	109.6	77.0	0.70
Primary enrolments						
(1970)	–	–	–	80.3	25.8	0.32
(1985)	–	–	–	96.4	18.5	0.19
Junior secondary enrolments						
(1970)	–	–	–	36.8	12.1	0.33
(1985)	–	–	–	56.0	16.0	0.28
Primary schools per 1,000 population						
(1961)	0.8	0.3	0.35			
(1971)	1.3	0.5	0.36	0.8	0.6	0.70 (1970)
(1978)	1.1	0.5	0.42	0.8	0.6	0.78 (1977)
(1985)	0.9	0.4	0.41	–	–	–
Rural	1.1	0.4	0.37	0.8	0.6	0.70 (1985)
Urban	0.5	0.3	0.65	–	–	–
(1988)	0.8	0.3	0.41	0.8	0.4	0.52
General secondary schools per 1,000 population						
(1961)	0.03	0.01	0.39	–	–	–
(1971)	0.19	0.12	0.63	–	–	–
(1978)	0.26	0.15	0.58	–	–	–
(1985)	0.10	0.03	0.34	–	–	–
(1988)	0.09	0.03	0.31	0.028	0.017	0.61
Junior secondary schools per 1,000 population						
(1971)	–	–	–	0.23	1.13	0.59 (1970)
(1978)	–	–	–	0.24	0.10	0.45 (1977)
(1985)	0.08	0.03	0.39	0.8	0.6	0.48 (1985)
Rural	0.10	0.04	0.39			
Urban	0.13	0.06	0.44			
Senior secondary schools per 1,000 population						
(1961)	–	–	–	–	–	–
(1971)	–	–	–	0.7	0.03	0.37 (1970)
(1978)	–	–	–	0.7	0.04	0.49 (1977)

continued on page 232

Table 9.7 continued

Indicator	China			India		
	WM	SD	Co. V	WM	SD	Co. V
(1985)	0.02	0.01	0.56	0.8	0.05	0.55
Rural	0.01	0.007	0.73	–	–	–
Urban	0.06	0.03	0.49	–	–	–
Pupil/teacher ratio						
in primary schools						
(1960)	35.03	3.17	0.09			
(1970)	29.26	2.40	0.08	39.3	7.7	0.19
(1978)	28.25	3.64	0.13	39.6	9.6	0.24
(1985)	25.25	4.28	0.17	42.4	10.4	0.24
Rural	26.25	4.36	0.16	–	–	–
Urban	21.40	2.76	0.13	–	–	–
(1988)	23.10	3.60	0.15	–	–	–
Pupil/teacher ratio						
in junior secondary schools						
(1960)	25.0	2.2	0.09	–	–	–
(1970)	22.9	5.0	0.22	30.9	7.7	0.25
(1978)	20.8	2.7	0.13	31.4	9.5	0.30
(1985)	18.6	2.9	0.15	34.8	11.1	0.32
Pupil/teacher ratio in						
senior secondary schools						
(1960)	21.3	2.8	0.13	–	–	–
(1970)	23.6	3.9	0.16	25.6	4.4	0.17
(1978)	21.0	7.1	0.34	25.1	3.7	0.15
(1985)	15.2	2.1	0.14	28.8	8.1	0.28

Source: Based on Appendix Tables A9.1 to A9.8.

Note: For China, data for 1960 do not include Tibet and Tianjin; data for 1970 do not include Tibet, Guangxi and Zhejiang; data for 1978 do not include Tibet.
  – = not available.

Separate estimates of Co.Vs for coastal and non-coastal provinces do not show any clearcut differences or trends. In respect of allocation of educational resources to primary schools and teachers, inequalities in both groups of provinces are quite small. However, secondary schools are much more evenly distributed in the coastal areas than in the non-coastal areas (Table 9.8).

Low regional inequality in the distribution of educational facilities may to some extent be due to special government efforts in the 1980s to reduce spatial differences. In 1982, a 'designated' enrolment and

Table 9.8   Inequalities in educational access between Chinese coastal and non-coastal provinces

Indicator	Coastal provinces			Non-coastal provinces		
	WM	SD	Co. V	WM	SD	Co. V.
Primary schools per 1,000 population						
(1961)	0.83	0.23	0.28	0.86	0.33	0.38
(1971)	1.03	0.42	0.41	1.39	0.38	0.27
(1978)	0.90	0.37	0.41	1.27	0.44	0.35
(1981)	0.75	0.17	0.23	1.02	0.28	0.27
(1985)	0.75	0.30	0.40	1.02	0.36	0.35
(1988)	0.67	0.26	0.39	0.81	0.34	0.36
General secondary schools per 1,000 population						
(1961)	0.03	0.01	0.38	0.02	0.01	0.34
(1971)	0.19	0.11	0.58	0.19	0.12	0.64
(1978)	0.21	0.11	0.53	0.28	0.16	0.57
(1985)	0.09	0.01	0.14	0.10	0.03	0.28
(1988)	0.08	0.02	0.23	0.09	0.03	0.34
Pupil–teacher ratio in primary schools						
(1960)	34.7	3.09	0.09	35.3	3.18	0.09
(1970)	29.0	2.55	0.09	29.5	2.41	0.08
(1978)	28.19	5.10	0.18	28.3	2.46	0.09
(1985)	24.48	2.33	0.09	25.69	3.43	0.13
(1988)	23.30	3.70	0.16	23.10	3.60	0.15
Pupil–teacher ratio in junior secondary schools						
(1960)	25.2	2.4	0.09	24.8	2.1	0.08
(1970)	22.1	3.8	0.17	23.7	5.9	0.25
(1978)	20.4	2.3	0.11	21.1	2.9	0.13
(1985)	18.4	3.9	0.21	18.8	2.0	0.11
Pupil–teacher ratio: senior secondary schools						
(1960)	21.7	2.0	0.09	20.8	3.3	0.16
(1970)	23.1	3.8	0.16	24.7	4.2	0.17
(1978)	21.0	1.2	0.06	21.2	9.0	0.42
(1985)	15.0	2.4	0.16	15.3	1.9	0.12

Source: Based on Appendix Tables A9.5 and A9.7.

Note: For 1961, data do not include Tibet and Tianjin; for 1971, data do not include Tibet, and Guangxi and Zhejiang; for 1978, data do not include Tibet.

training system was introduced to overcome shortages of technical manpower in rural areas and the border provinces in the hinterland. According to this system, an entrance quota for agricultural, medical and teacher training colleges was reserved for students selected from among candidates recommended by the local counties.

As we noticed in Chapter 7, there is a considerable imbalance between coastal and non-coastal areas in respect of the ratio of scientists and engineers *per capita* (see Chapter 7, Table 7.9). This imbalance arises from the fact that very few educated people like to work in rural or remote areas. Furthermore, even students from the hinterland who go to coastal areas for higher studies tend not to return to their areas of origin.

The Chinese government took specific measures to attract qualified manpower to remote areas for two to five years. It required the universities to lower entrance requirements for students from remote areas. These students were required to enter into a contract with their local governments to give an undertaking that they would return to their county or province after graduation.

V   CLASS OR MINORITY ACCESS

5.1   China

In China, classes are based more on political lines than on social and economic ones. One political class dichotomy is cadres vs. non-cadres. The cadres represent the party and state officials; they may also encompass the bureaucrats and professionals whose access to education is generally more privileged than that of the peasants and workers who constitute the non-cadre class. In ethnic terms, there are the *Hans* – a majority *vis-à-vis* the national minorities – consisting of nearly 56 ethnic groups like the Tibetans, Kazaks, Mongols and Muslims who account for about 6 per cent of the total population and generally live in marginal and sparsely populated regions.

Cadres vs. Non-Cadres.   The cadres are known to enjoy privileged access to higher education in socialist economies. The professional and technical élite passing out of the institutions of higher education represent a 'new class' whose origins may be traced to unequal access to seats of learning. For example, the reintroduction of the Key Schools discussed above represents an élitist track which prepares school-age children from privileged backgrounds for scarce jobs in the higher echelons of administration and the professions. Data to determine differential access of cadres to education in China are hard to find. But such scattered information as exists points to inequalities based on economic status and political influence. For example, in 1979, of the entering class of 2,000 students at Beijing University, 39 per cent 'came from families of cadres and army officers, although these groups make up less than 5 per cent of the overall population'.[39] Another 11 per cent of the first-year class were children of the intellectual élite. In Zhejiang University in 1980, 25 per cent of the students had peasant backgrounds; 23 per cent were children of officials and employees and 28 per cent, children of intellectuals; and only 15 per cent were sons and daughters of workers. Similarly, at the Shanghai Teachers' Institute (which has students from eleven urban districts and ten small counties), over 45 per cent of students of science and liberal arts came from families of 'revolutionary cadres, army officers, staff and teachers', compared to only 15 per cent students from the countryside.[40]

This concentration is further encouraged by the system of entrance examinations reintroduced in the post-Mao period. Heavy emphasis is placed on such subjects as foreign languages, mathematics and biology which are not taught in the rural secondary schools. Thus, the criterion of academic achievement creates a bias in favour of urban and town-based students.[41]

For the Mao period, White gives data on class origins of enrollees – the share of 'workers'–peasants' ' children declined from 61 per cent in 1960 to 40 per cent in 1962; of 'workers and poor peasants', from 41 per cent in 1960 to 18 per cent in 1963. In contrast the share of children of 'landlords, rich peasants and capitalists' nearly tripled, rising from 8 per cent in 1960 to 23 per cent in 1962.[42] The situation seems to have been similar in the 1950s: it is noted that in 1957–58, 'just over one-third of the students at the tertiary level were from proletarian families',[43] implying that the remaining were children of the intellectuals and party cadres. The Cultural Revolution period may have been marked by some increase in the representation of workers'–peasants' children in higher educational institutions, but the evidence is not unequivocal. White concludes that the Cultural Revolution reforms had 'some limited redistributive impact but less than intended and this was more significant between urban strata than between city and countryside'. There are reports that rural and urban cadres continued to exercise influence and use personal contacts in securing places for their children in schools and universities.[44]

Minorities.   Access of national minorities to education needs to be examined in the context of the Maoist policy of 'proletarianisation of education'. Mao's educational strategy was intended to be egalitarian rather than élitist. Measures undertaken to favour minorities' education (e.g. spare-time tent and roving schools for nomadic populations and nationalities' institutes) were seen to improve their access to educational facilities. In 1971, the nationalities' institutes were reported to start enrolling 'students directly from the ranks of poor and lower-middle peasants and herdsmen'.[45] The problem of shortage of teachers in these special programmes was overcome through the introduction of crash teacher training courses especially designed for training minorities with poorer social backgrounds.

To the extent that the minorities are also the economically underprivileged and poorer groups living mainly in backward areas, the class interpretation of the Cultural Revolution period would be consistent with the economic interpretation and approach in the later period. As a result of the post-Mao reforms, educational access and opportunity is now geared towards human resources and economic development. The role of non-formal educational schools and nationalities' institutes has been de-emphasised. While the minorities continue to be supported through a 'policy of granting special funds for minority areas to assist in their economic and cultural development' (these areas receive about 8 per cent more capital construction funds than *Han* areas),[46] a major emphasis is now placed on expanding the enrolment of minorities through formal primary and secondary schooling instead of non-formal education. The share of students and teachers has been steadily increasing (since 1975) at different levels of education. But the 1982 Census data show that the level of illiteracy among the minority nationalities (43 per cent) is still much higher than that among the *Han* majority (31 per cent).[47]

To reduce this inequality of access, the Chinese Ministry of Education has introduced a special programme for minorities at colleges and universities. A lower minimum examination score, special tutoring and admission quotas for minorities are some of the redressment measures adopted in the post-Mao period. It is reported that in Inner Mongolia a university admissions quota of 20 per cent is recommended. Similar quotas apply to the provinces and main cities. The quota levels depend mainly on the average levels of education prevailing in the provinces and areas concerned. The quota system also requires that after graduation the students should return to their province of origin.

5.2 India

The special admissions quota for the Chinese minorities is somewhat similar to quotas for Indian scheduled or backward classes which constitute about 16 per cent of the total population according to the 1981 census. To promote equality of access to education, special seats are reserved for members of the underprivileged castes and classes at higher educational institutions like medical colleges and universities.

A study by Tilak, based on a sample survey of households in a district in Andhra Pradesh (India) undertaken in 1977, shows a considerable gender and caste bias in access to education: for all educational levels, access to education for men and for higher castes was higher than for women and for backward castes. As one moves from a low level of educational attainment to a higher level, the access to education of backward castes and of women becomes increasingly restricted. These survey results are confirmed by the all-India official estimates of growth of student enrolments, which show that despite an impressive increase in enrolment rates between 1950–51 and 1983–84, the poor, the disadvantaged and the backward classes have not benefited much. The gross enrolment rates for scheduled castes and tribes and for women remain much lower despite preferential access of these groups to jobs. A fixed quota for scheduled castes for certain jobs implies that a share of the labour market is regulated by the government in their favour. Even when equal access to sexes is offered, few women or backward class students choose to continue with higher education. This voluntary decision on the part of their families is based more on social considerations and their perceptions of job prospects.

In 1975–76, Bannerjee and Knight[48] undertook a survey in Delhi to assess caste discrimination in the job market. They found little discrimination among occupations requiring educational attainment, but some against production workers and unskilled labourers. The reason for this anomalous situation may be the different recruitment procedures for the two types of workers. Those educated in occupational skills are hired through vacancy announcements which are easier to monitor than the hiring of unskilled workers which is generally done through informal contacts.

Tilak's estimates show that rates of return on investment in education are higher for the scheduled castes/tribes (the underprivileged classes) than for the higher castes. This rather unusual result is perhaps due to the lower costs or investment in the education of backward castes, which, incidentally, also reflects the poor quality of their education. Another factor is the preferential access to jobs guaranteed by legislation. The Tilak study also shows that the relative advantage is higher at lower levels of education, implying that the benefits of higher education accrue mainly to the élites.[49]

However, one cannot place too much reliance on Tilak's estimates of private and social rates of return for different social classes. First, these results are not representative (they relate to only one district of one state) to enable any generalisations for the country as a whole. Secondly, the estimates do not take account of locational and qualitative differences in education which are quite significant in India. Part of the differences attributed to castes may well be due to quality differences (in respect of teachers and schools) between rural and urban areas.[50] In the rural areas, poor quality of education affects adversely both backward and high castes.

VI CONCLUSION

The above analysis suggests that inequalities in access to education in both China and India may be induced by the wide income inequalities between the rich and the poor, between the rural and the urban people and, in the case of China, between the cadres and the non-cadres. Widespread educational inequalities exist in both China and India; these are due to differences in the economic and social backgrounds of the school-going population. For example, in the case of China, reintroduction of university entrance examinations since 1978 gives an 'equal' opportunity for every candidate in the sense that anyone who passes the minimum standard will be admitted to college or university. The minimum standard is exactly the same for the children of different socio-economic backgrounds except for the children from minority regions for whom there is a lower minimum requirement for entering higher education. But in practice, this can only be a 'quasi-equality' situation, considering that the children of poorer households and social backgrounds are known to be less prepared for being able to attain the minimum standard.

Thus, inequality in education is a reflection of income inequalities between economic and social classes and between rural and urban people. These two types of inequalities are interdependent and cannot be discussed in isolation.

Notes and References

1. See Joseph P. Farrell, 'Educational Expansion and the Drive for Social Equality', in P. Altbach, R. Arnove and G. Kelly (eds), *Comparative Education*, London, Macmillan Press, 1982, p. 43.
2. For an empirical analysis of India along these lines, see Jandhyala B. G. Tilak, *The Economics of Inequality in Education*, New Delhi, Sage Publications, 1987. See, in particular, pp. 22–4.
3. Samuel Bowles, 'Class Power and Mass Education', Harvard University, October 1971 (mimeo); and S. Bowles, 'Education, Class Conflict and Uneven Development', in J. Simmons (ed.), *The Education Dilemma*, Oxford, Pergamon Press, 1980. For a critique of Bowles's arguments, see Jagdish Bhagwati, 'Education, Class Structure and Income Equality', *World Development*, vol. 1, no. 5, May 1973.
4. See Dwight Perkins and Shahid Yusuf, *Rural Development in China*, Baltimore, Johns Hopkins Press, 1984; and Nirmal Kumar Chandra, 'Education in China: From the Cultural Revolution to Four Modernisations', *Economic and Political Weekly*, Annual Number, May 1987.
5. World Bank, *CHINA – Management and Finance of Higher Education*, Washington DC, November 1986, p. 85.
6. Government of India, Planning Commission, *The Seventh Five Year Plan (1985–90)*, vol. I, New Delhi, October 1985, p. 252.
7. Government of India, Ministry of Human Resources Development, Department of Education, *National Policy on Education*, New Delhi, May 1986.
8. K. Subbarao, *Some Aspects of Access to Education in India*, paper prepared for a workshop on Poverty in India, held at Queen Elizabeth House, Oxford, October 1987.
9. Government of India, *Towards an Enlightened and Humane Society* (Report of the Committee for Review of National Policy on Education 1986), Government of India Press, Faridabad, 1991.
10. Frances Stewart, *Planning to Meet Basic Needs*, London, Macmillan Press, 1985, chapter 1.
11. UNDP, *Human Development Report – 1990*, New York, Oxford University Press, 1990, Table 14, p. 154.
12. World Bank, *CHINA – Issues and Prospects in Education*, Annex I to China:' Long-term Development Issues and Options', p. 45.
13. Han Zongli, 'An Inquiry into Investment in Universalising Primary Education', *Chinese Education*, vol. XVII, no. 3, Fall 1984, p. 62.
14. Ibid, pp. 68–9.
15. G. Psacharopoulos, 'Estimating Shadow Rates of Return to Investment in Education', *Journal of Human Resources*, vol. 5/1 (Winter) 1970; and Returns to Education – An Updated International Comparison', in T. King (ed.), 'Education and Income', *World Bank Staff Working Paper, No. 402*, Washington DC, 1980.
16. Jandhyala B. G. Tilak, 'Educational Finances in India', *Indian Journal of Public Administration*, July-September 1986, Special No. on 'Educational Policy and Implementation'.
17. World Bank, *CHINA: Issues and Prospects in Education*, p. 13.

18. Government of India, Office of the Registrar General, *Survey on Infant and Child Mortality*, New Delhi, 1979, p. 11.
19. We have obtained per capita figures for urban areas by dividing the number of schools by total urban population and rural schools by total rural population. It would be more appropriate to use the school-age population as the denominator if such data were available.
20. John Gardner, 'New Directions in Educational Policy', in Jack Gray and Gordon White (eds), *China's New Development Strategy*, London, Academic Press, 1982.
21. M. Engelborghes-Bestels, 'The New Man or a Lost Generation?: Education in the Four Modernisations Programme of the PRC', *Issues and Studies*, September 1985.
22. Chandra, 'Education in China . . .'.
23. Subbarao, *Some Aspects of Access* . . ..
24. Ibid.
25. Gardner, 'New Directions . . .'.
26. Hubert O. Brown, 'Primary Schooling and the Rural Responsibility System in the People's Republic of China', *Comparative Education Review*, vol. 30, no. 3, August 1986.
27. Wei Lining and Li Yongzeng, 'Education in China: The Past Four Years', *Beijing Review*, vol. 26, no. 4, 24 January 1983.
28. World Bank, *CHINA: Long-Term Development Issues and Options*, p. 125.
29. Stig Thogersen, 'China's Senior Middle Schools in a Social Perspective: A Survey of Yantai District', *China Quarterly*, March 1987, p. 90.
30. A. P. Barnabas, *Social Change in a North Indian Village*, Indian Institute of Public Administration, New Delhi, 1969.
31. K. N. Hiriyanniah and K. Ramachandran, 'India', in UNESCO, *The Dropout Problem in Primary Education – Some Case Studies*, Bangkok, 1984.
32. Cited in Brown, 'Primary Schooling . . .'. It was found that 'of more than 15,000 fifth graders, nearly half repeated at least one grade . . . the rate of repetition for all primary grades was over three times that of the urban schools and has been increasing steadily since 1970'.
33. B. N. Sarkar, 'Interstate Disparities in Education', in Jandhyala B. G. Tilak (ed.) *Education and Regional Development*, New Delhi, Yatan Publications, 1986, pp. 236–7.
34. World Bank, *CHINA: Socialist Economic Development*, vol. III, Washington DC, 1983, p. 150.
35. Ibid, p. 154.
36. *Jiaoyu Yanjiu*, March 1983. Cited in Brown, 'Primary Schooling . . .'.
37. Marianne Bastid, 'Chinese Educational Policies in the 1980s and Economic Development', *China Quarterly*, June 1984.
38. David M. Lampton, 'Performance and the Chinese Political System – A Preliminary Assessment of Education and Health Policies', *China Quarterly*, September, 1978.
39. This is based on information of the New China News Agency (NCNA). Cited in Fox Butterfield, *China Alive in the Bitter Sea*, New York Times Books, 1982, p. 199.

40. Mark Sidel, 'University Enrolment in the People's Republic of China, 1977–1981: The Examination Model Returns', *Comparative Education*, vol. 18, no. 3, 1982, p. 265.
41. Ibid.
42. G. White, 'Higher Education and Social Redistribution in a Socialist Society: The Chinese Case', *World Development*, vol. 9, no. 2, 1981, p. 156.
43. John Gardner, 'Educated Youth and Urban–Rural Inequalities, 1958–1966', in John W. Lewis (ed.), *The City in Communist China*, Stanford, Stanford University Press, 1971, p. 243.
44. Susan L. Shirk, 'Educational Reform and Political Backlash: Recent Changes in Chinese Educational Policy', *Comparative Education Review*, vol. 23, no. 2, June 1979.
45. See J. N. Hawkins, Educational Policy and National Minorities in the People's Republic of China: The Politics of Inter-Group Relations', in J. N. Hawkins (ed.), *Education and Social Change in PRC*, New York, Praeger Publishers, 1983, pp. 188–9.
46. Ibid, p. 195.
47. Jacques Lamontagne, 'Educational Development in the PRC: Regional and Ethnic Disparities', *Issues and Studies*, vol. 22, no. 9, September 1986, p. 83.
48. B. Bannerjee and J. B. Knight, 'Caste Discrimination in the Indian Labour Market', *Journal of Development Economics*, vol. 17, no. 3, April 1985.
49. See Tilak, *The Economics of Inequality . . .*, pp. 114–22.
50. Subbarao, *Some Aspects of Access . . ..*

10 Political Economy of Development

In this final chapter, we briefly review the major findings of the earlier chapters. In the light of those conclusions we wish to explore the political economy factors that may account for similarities as well as differences in development strategies and their outcomes.

Political economy considerations are not our major concern in this book. Yet one cannot really study the economies of China and India (and other developing countries for that matter) without touching on the socio-political contexts in which development strategies and policies are formulated and implemented. Therefore, this chapter simply speculates about the influence of non-economic forces on development outcomes in China and India.

I DEVELOPMENT OUTCOMES: CHINA AND INDIA

In Chapter 1, Table 1.1, we described alternative scenarios and combinations of strategies and their outcomes. Having examined the development performances of China and India in actual practice, we now summarise the relative outcomes in the two countries. This is done in Table 10.1.

From the 1950s to the 1970s both China and India followed somewhat similar development strategies – import substitution and self-reliance with a view to rapid industrialisation and technological independence. In the 1980s, both shifted away from state interventionism to market liberalisation. Thus faster growth in China cannot be attributed to differences in the growth strategies that were adopted, but rather to differences in their implementation.

In the case of China, it would seem that asset and land redistribution in the 1950s enabled a shift from conspicuous consumption to savings which made possible a consistently high rate of investment. But in India a failure to implement land reforms meant that the rich proprietary classes expropriated these resources in the form of agricultural subsidies. This may partly account for the decline in public investment in India and the adverse effect on growth.[1]

Furthermore, in India political power is perhaps too diffused

242

Table 10.1   Development outcomes in China and India

Item	China	India
I. Growth	High	Low
II. Inequality		
– Intraregional	Low	High
– Interregional	High	High
– Rural–urban	Low	High

among the many conflicting interest groups to generate a significant pressure for implementation of a growth-oriented strategy. In contrast, in China the absence of political parties and proprietary classes means that there is no more than a passive resistance to rapid growth policies.[2]

Higher growth in China was also more equitable at least during the Mao period (see Table 10.1). What explains this unusual compatibility between growth and equity? Could it be explained by what Streeten and Stewart called the 'steady tripod', i.e. a combination of asset reforms, appropriate technology and 'right' prices?[3] During the Mao period, the third leg of the tripod, i.e. right prices, do not appear to have been present however. Egalitarian development during this period required, above all, political commitment to the socialist ideology and non-market instruments of public action, which are more difficult to implement in democratic and liberal economies like that of India. One can argue that democratic institutions and a multi-party system have made the implementation of strategies, policies and programmes slower than in China.

Greater rural equality in China was due to a set of direct redistributive measures: a system of public distribution of food through rationing, low relative prices of food and other necessities and an equitable distribution of public services like health and education. These measures are either not as effective or are virtually absent in India and most other developing countries. The policy of state relief, the establishment of minimum standards of food consumption, state subsidy to accounting units whose output was too low, and the public welfare systems of 'five guarantees' for households without able-bodied earning members must have also contributed to reducing poverty and inequalities. There have never been similar consumption and welfare guarantees in India.

Although public distribution of food and rationing exist in India its coverage is limited largely to urban areas and the majority of the rural poor have no access to the public distribution system.

The Chinese experience with the public support schemes during the Mao period shows that the strategy of uneven development, with its concentration on growth maximisation, need not necessarily lead to increased inequalities if parallel redistributive measures can be effectively introduced and implemented. Indeed, higher growth enables an increase in resources for distribution.

In post-Mao China, although growth has accelerated, as a result of economic incentives, institutional innovations and technological research, there are indications that inequalities are also growing. Could the rapid growth strategy of this period be one of the causes of these inequalities and uneven development? Rapid growth has been officially endorsed and growing inequalities accepted as an inevitable price to be paid for it. The political will to implement Maoist redistributive policies has weakened, as is suggested by the official propaganda often 'lionising the newly rich and exaggerating their wealth'.[4]

In recent years in India also, despite reasonable growth rates, rural–urban disparities have not narrowed. Where they have, their impact on the standards of living of the poor has been negligible.

Neither China nor India seems to have succeeded in achieving the equity objective. The outcome of the 'uneven development' strategies adopted by them is testified by the continuation of a number of economic and social imbalances, e.g. vast regional and class inequalities of income and consumption and lack of access of the rural poor to education and health services. In China, an explicit policy of balanced development during the Mao period was not as effective as expected in reducing income gaps between town and country and between agriculture and industry. In India, both absolute and relative poverty remain acute despite more than forty years of planned development with declared goals of growth and equity.

China has undoubtedly achieved better results than India in providing the rural population with access to food and basic necessities and such social services as health and education. True enough, inequalities between urban and rural populations and areas continue to exist in China but the rural–urban gaps have narrowed over time. The agrarian reforms and success in labour mobilisation seem to have partly accounted for these better results. Similar measures were not introduced or implemented in India. In terms of growth of agricultural and industrial output also China has performed better than India although a comparison of the respective growth rates is not without measurement problems.

However, the situation regarding inter-regional inequalities is similar in China and India. Despite Mao's balanced development strategy, regional inequalities continue to prevail. In India too, the policy of balanced regional development, based on political expediency, was not very successful.

What accounts for the divergence as well as similarities in the achievement of economic and social objectives in the two countries? Below we attempt an answer to this question.

II POLITICAL FACTORS AND UNEVEN OUTCOMES

Political economy factors in development have been defined in different ways. We define them in terms of the role of state intervention, political commitment, ideology and vested interests of different socio-economic groups.

The role of the state in designing development strategies and policies and subsequently implementing them seems to have been important in both China and India. In China, during the Mao period, state control over the economy was paramount – a command economy was in place with full ownership and control of resources and means of production. In India also the public sector is dominant particularly in heavy industry and infrastructure. This means that its own performance largely determines the economic efficiency of the industrial sector as a whole and even the rest of the economy. India's relatively poor industrial performance may be due, in large part, to the inefficiency of the public sector enterprises which are known for their large excess capacity, poor management and huge losses. Until the early 1980s, tariffs, quota controls and indiscriminate protection of industry under an import substitution regime symbolised central state control. The economic liberalisation policies introduced in 1985 and 1986 have not reduced the importance of the public sector. The new measures are intended mainly to relax industrial licensing and state controls, but not to privatise state-owned enterprises.

Below we take two examples of the role of the state, namely, design of strategies and their implementation, to illustrate how political economy factors may have accounted for uneven development in China and India. The choice and design of a strategy and its implementation are likely to be the products of a mixture of political and economic factors. By affecting the relative rates of growth of incomes of different socio-economic groups, the alternative strategies and policies are likely to influence the structure of political power. The design of a strategy also influences the scope for exercise of political power through control of resource allocation.[5]

2.1 Design of Strategy

During the Mao period in China, the state played a significant role in formulating and implementing redistributive measures while also pressing for high growth through rapid capital accumulation. In the absence of such a two-pronged strategy inequalities in China might have been far greater.

But there have been lapses in the form of a poor and contradictory design of the development strategy and of the policies and programmes to implement them. For example, the strategies of local self-reliance and of balanced regional development turned out to be in conflict. Mao's failure to achieve greater equality in China (despite a balanced growth strategy) has been attributed to his ambivalence towards striking a good balance between state planning and market socialism.[6] Unable to reconcile the two for coordinating the economy, Mao decided to introduce local self-reliance as a means of reducing the need for coordination. The strategy of self-reliance and self-sufficiency seems to have reinforced regional inequalities and may in practice have neutralised the egalitarian effects of redistributive measures. The promotion of rural industry, within the framework of a local self-reliant strategy, seems to have widened regional inequalities. The agriculturally more advanced regions like Jiangsu became more successful in promoting rural industry than many agriculturally backward regions. Thus the poor regions remained poor whereas the richer regions became more rich.

In the post-Mao period, the reintroduction of Key Schools as part of a new educational strategy represented problems of contradictory design and implementation. For example, the objective of introducing these schools was two-fold: (i) development and improvement of ordinary schools through cooperation with them, and (ii) raising of quality standards.[7] However, in actual practice, the Key Schools and ordinary schools have competed rather than cooperating. An overwhelming endorsement of rapid modernisation by the top leadership meant an exclusive attention to raising rates of promotion to universities rather than on popularisation of education. The swing towards quality standards and élitism seems to have gone too far – it has been noted that 'significantly some of the most vocal champions for a strengthening of basic education for the masses are well-known intellectuals, not Maoist radicals'.[8]

Faulty design can also be illustrated with the case of industrial development strategy. The dual price system introduced during the reform period was based on a misconception that it would gradually lead to a free market system. The policy-makers failed to anticipate that such a system could encourage corruption as it actually did. Neither did they realise that a reform of the price system would not be effective without a structural change in the nature of the strictly controlled planned economy. During the first phase of the reforms (1978–85), the basic feature of the Chinese economy – tight controls by a multi-layered bureaucratic system – remained intact.

Further, strategy of overexpansionary development during the second phase of reforms was based on extensive borrowing from abroad as well as from domestic sources. Persuasion and coercion were used to issue State investment bonds to the Chinese wage earners. This led to unexpectedly high inflation and social hardships in the late 1980s. Such adverse consequences could have been minimised if the strategy was more carefully designed.

The development strategy and its design were not all that clearcut in China. More often a set of selective policies were introduced without a clear macroeconomic strategy. For example, alleviation of poverty which is concentrated in certain pockets (instead of being widespread) was often temporarily ensured through such measures as subsidies and increase in procurement prices for foodgrains.

In India also the design of the development strategy has not always been consistent with the declared goal of poverty alleviation. Among the several planning objectives, the growth of GDP per capita in practice turned out to be far more important than reduction of inequalities. For example, it was not until the end of the Third Plan (1966) that adequate emphasis was placed on agricultural development and on improvements in the rural standards of living. Even after this reorientation of strategy, the objective of equity was not achieved. This seems to have been due largely to the nature of the strategy and its implementation.

The agricultural strategy in India was based on the premise that resources should be concentrated on those regions and crops that yielded maximum returns. This meant support mainly for the 'progressive' farmers who invariably were already rich. Thus the strategy aimed at 'maximising short-run growth of commodity production rather than at reducing disparity between the richer and the poorer farmers, and that between advanced regions and backward regions'.[9]

Of course, the planners and policy-makers recognised the need to raise the standards of living of the poor farmers. To achieve this objective, during the Fourth and Fifth Plans, special relief schemes (e.g. Small Farmers' Development Agency, Marginal Farmers and Agricultural Labour and Drought Prone Areas Programme) were introduced. These schemes were not integrated into the main agricultural strategy, and opinions differ about their achievements.

In the case of industrial and technology policies also, some inconsistencies can be cited. A policy of import-substitution across-the-board conflicted with the objective of strengthening technological capability through absorption and innovation. A recent survey of 24 cases of technology imports into India shows how trade policy (import restrictions) encouraged product diversification but discouraged specialisation. Large and old firms are known to have brought political pressures to bear on the government to relax obstructionist policies. It is suggested that the government yielded to such pressures by 'giving up its attempt to force firms to buy technology from its laboratories in 1975, and in the early 1980s it relaxed its definition of "new" technology to permit modernisation'.[10]

Similar political pressures on the Chinese government are unlikely. Yet inadequacies of the design of R and D and science and technology (S and T) policies in China are worth noting. Despite the formulation of a new S and T Plan in 1978, not enough attention was paid by the government to a 'reform of the basic structure and design of the domestic science and technology system itself'.[11] Furthermore the S and T policy was unbalanced since science was allowed to advance far ahead of technology – the S and T applications are quite limited due perhaps to the reluctance of the industrial producers to profit from product and process innovations which in turn may be attributed to weak or inadequate incentives.

2.2 Implementation

Political economy factors also explain many lapses in the implementation of strategies, policies and programmes. In the case of China, there seems to have been a passive resistance to Mao's balanced strategy which may partly account for implementation delays and failures. Political factors like the fear of foreign intervention and pressures from Mao's rural constituency may partly explain the introduction of foodgrain self-sufficiency and the resulting inefficiencies in resource allocation. Other examples of bottlenecks in implementation may be cited, such as a tendency of the communes to exaggerate figures of foodgrains output, inadequate support for Mao's policy of 'agricultural priority', and delays in the implementation of Mao's rural health policy.

Mao's call for a reduction in the length of medical training met with political opposition as well as opposition from the medical bureaucracy. Lampton notes that 'although medical education was declared reduced to three years in 1968, it took until 1971 to implement this directive'.[12] Though passive, this opposition tended to weaken effective leadership and policy implementation since the process of compromise, coalitions or even purges was very time-consuming.

There is another aspect of the problem of implementation of policies and programmes. The outcomes of such policies may be partly those that were intended and others that were unintended and undesirable. The latter may be attributed to a poor design of strategy or policy or to its faulty implementation and poor indicators of performance. To take one example, the agricultural responsibility system in China has been highly successful in terms of the intended outcomes in the form of increases in agricultural output and incomes. But its unintended and undesirable outcomes need also to be noted – a decline in school enrolments, an incentive to have more than one child conflicting with the population control policy, a weakening of collective accumulation and ability to finance old-age security and cooperative health insurance, and a deterioration in the maintenance of minor irrigation works in the wake of decollectivisation.[13]

In the case of India also there have been implementation failures due to political factors. While China was quite successful in implementing agrarian reforms the Indian performance in this regard has been far from satisfactory. Unlike China, the Indian policy of land reforms did not involve much land redistribution. Instead, it consisted mainly of redistributing agricultural incomes through tenancy reforms, protection of tenants against eviction and ceilings on land holdings.[14] With the exception of some states like Kerala, the tenancy reform legislation has not been implemented. The implementation of Indian land reforms was hampered by the lack of systematic land records, corrupt local bureaucracy responsible for implementation and weak revenue administration. The legal provisions of the reforms were meant to be implemented by the local administration with the support of the village community. The village community consisted of powerful landlords whose vested interests were threatened by the provisions of the reform law which involved the abolition of the land proprietary rights.

Limited progress with agrarian reforms in India meant that the cleavage between the landowners and peasants continued. The rich landowners acquired political clout which they successfully exploited to extract political favours in terms of higher procurement prices and lower input prices. In China on the other hand, the elimination of private property and ownership of land and other assets did away with such vested interests and replaced them by communal and collective incentives, both material and non-material.

The new Indian policy on education and the scheme for the establishment of 500 modern schools along the lines of existing public schools, bears some resemblance to the Chinese policy of introducing Key Schools in the post-Mao period. During the Seventh Plan (1985–90) it is proposed to provide facilities 'for education of high quality and excellence in every district of the country' by establishing the above-mentioned schools.[15] In both China and India the inspiration for these schemes resulted from their leaders' quest for rapid modernisation and leap into the twenty-first century. But in neither case are the already existing educational facilities at primary and secondary levels of adequate quantity or quality. It is feared that given the scarcity of financial resources, the new schools are likely to contribute to widening the gaps in quality of education.[16]

The contrasting effects of political economy factors in China and India can also be illustrated with the example of famines and nutrition. Sen has argued that while famines occurred in China, they were rare or non-existent in India.[17] This is explained by the presence in India of strong press, democratic institutions and opposition parties which force the government to act quickly to modify ongoing policies and take preventive action. These political pressures do not exist in planned socialist countries like China. However, it is worth noting that these very factors that are invoked to explain preventive action to avoid famines, tend to slow down implementation of regular programmes like nutrition in a democratic society. Although the Chinese state was unable to avert the famine of 1959–61 it was much more successful than India in controlling malnutrition even without the sort of pressures and political consciousness that prevented famines in India. In a socialist economy like that of China production and distribution of food are much better integrated than in a market-oriented economy. This factor may have facilitated nutritional improvement. But it is unlikely that malnutrition in China could have been checked without Mao's egalitarian strategy and political commitment.

Another aspect of the great famine in China is the distribution of hardships across classes, income groups and regions that tends to be overshadowed by the enthusiasm to study the benefits of development rather than its costs. Apart from the reasons mentioned above, the famines could have been avoided or their costs minimised by China through links abroad. Isolation (apart from the absence of democratic institutions) might in fact have raised the costs of famine there.[18]

III POLITICAL ECONOMY OF URBAN BIAS

The political economy of urban bias is premised on the existence of an urban class whose interests and political clout are stronger than the rural interest groups. The strong political influence of urban groups can be explained by three main factors. First, urban population is better organised than the rural and exercises a more direct expression of its interests in the form of strikes and demonstrations. Secondly, the greater the urban population, the more strategic it is for the balance of power. Thirdly, central political power is usually identified with large urban agglomerations. Even the rural representatives in Parliament, since they are located in urban areas, may tend to be urban centred. The result is that the development strategy favours urban industry, and manipulates terms of trade in favour of the urban sector. Its outcome is noticed in continued rural–urban inequalities and in better services and cheaper food for urban people.

In both China and India some examples can be found which suggest the existence of an urban bias – e.g. under-allocation of investment in agriculture, vast rural–urban income and productivity differentials, disproportionately large investment allocation to urban-based industry and adverse rural terms of trade during prolonged periods. In the case of China still other elements of urban bias can be cited. For example, as noted in Chapters 8 and 9, access of children from worker and peasant backgrounds to higher education and to social services like health is more restricted in the post-Mao period. Under the post-Mao reforms favours continue to be given to the urban people in two ways: (i) urban industrial workers can take early retirement with one child taking over his or her place, (ii) subsidies are available for housing and health care as well as price hikes. In addition to these, urban youth do not have to go to the rural areas, whereas the rural people, especially well-educated youth, continue to be restricted from moving to the urban areas to seek formal employment opportunities. Furthermore, grain rationing in urban areas (which prevailed also during the Mao period) assures to urban people access to stable supplies of cheap grain. But it may contribute to widening fluctuations in per capita supplies of food-grains in rural areas.[19]

Pro-rural measures and programmes by both China and India can also be cited – e.g. rural reforms in post-Mao China and favourable rural terms of trade apart from rural health insurance schemes during Mao's China, price subsidies to agriculture and special rural employment guarantee schemes in the case of India.

In an aggregate sense, the net effect of conflicting urban and rural biases is difficult to determine. To form a judgement about the political influence of the urban class as an interest group, it is important to show that those who introduce such bias – the ruling political party and the government – are urban-based. Lipton argued that as a social class urban groups tend to dominate since they enjoy political clout which the rural groups lack. This may be true in many developing countries but the situation is much more complicated in China and India.

The backgrounds of political leaders and legislators in China and India (in terms of origins, occupations, etc.) were not necessarily urban-based. In the case of China, during the Mao period, a large proportion of party cadres came from the rural areas; so did the members of the armed forces. Indeed the People's Revolution had a rural origin. It is noted that 'the vast majority of the 4.5 million party members in 1949 were of peasant origin and many of them became officials in the post-revolutionary state machine'.[20] The policies of mass mobilisation during the Great Leap and Cultural Revolution periods also seem to have promoted the interests of the rural masses. Furthermore, under the collective agrarian structure, the Chinese rural people were organised: at times they even protested against rural–urban disparities through strikes and go-slow movements. But the dissolution of the communes has weakened this rural pressure.

Over time, the class composition of the Chinese Communist Party seems to have changed in favour of greater urban representation. It is reported that in the 1950s a special effort was made to recruit bureaucrats and industrial workers into the Party. By 1957, '13.7 per cent of the Party members were workers, 14.8 per cent intellectuals and 66.8 per cent peasants'.[21] This composition seems to have been further weighted in favour of the urban-based members with the pensioning-off of the old party cadres.

In the case of India, the class composition of the party seems to have moved in favour of members of rural origin and backgrounds. While in the early 1950s rural representation in the Indian Parliament was quite low, it gradually improved over time. The rich farmers have acquired increasing political power over the years particularly since the Green Revolution in the mid-1960s. The occupational backgrounds of the members of the Lok Sabha (the popularly elected lower house of Parliament) shows that (i) the share of full-time 'social and political workers' declined from nearly 25 per cent in the first Lok Sabha (May 1952 to 1954–55) to 11.5 per cent in the fifth Lok Sabha (1971–72 to 1975–76), (ii) the share of businessmen declined from 11 per cent to 7.5 per cent, and (iii) the share of agriculturists increased from 15 per cent to 34 per cent.[22] Thus it is clear that the class interests of the Indian politicians became increasingly rural.

The above class representations show opposing interest groups whose pressures may simply neutralise rather than reinforce urban-biased or rural-biased policies.

Therefore, a bias in favour of urban-oriented industrialisation and social policies like health and education has to be explained by other factors.

In India, two factors favour urban bias. First, the central government has a lion's share of investment resources but agriculture, education, health, etc. are state subjects. Therefore, the centre deliberately focuses its attention on the urban industrial sector. Thus the real issue is whether the political structure is centralised or decentralised. Political pressures tend to vary, especially when the centre and states are ruled by different political parties. Secondly, the urban middle class – organised sector workers and trade unions – can exert political pressure through strikes. Trade unions tend to be less organised in the rural sector. (The political pressure of trade unions seems to be less marked in China.)

In the case of China three factors seem to be relevant. First is the ideological factor: the Dengist philosophy of modernisation (even Westernisation) as against Maoist egalitarianism can be traced to ideological differences and approaches to development. Notwithstanding this, the fact remains that it was Deng who introduced rural economic reforms (household responsibility system), recognising that the modernisation of industry depended on the growth of agriculture and rural purchasing power.

The second factor is the open-door policy and the resulting external influences. In the history of post-revolutionary China, two periods are associated with such a policy. First, in the 1950s, opening to the Soviet Union resulted in economic, institutional and financial dependence. The Soviet model of heavy industrialisation and an urban-oriented health system are but two examples of such an influence. In the post-Mao period, the open-door policy meant opening to the West mainly for the import of technology but also for consumer and producer goods. Such a policy tends to reinforce urban influences as urban and industrial institutions and people normally have better links with the outside world.

Thirdly, as a corollary to the above, the international demonstration effect in consumption is felt more pervasively in the urban than in the rural areas. The symbols of Westernisation (Kentucky Fried Chicken, Maxims, night clubs, etc.) are all found in capital cities like Beijing and Shanghai where the influence of tourism is also stronger. Improved telecommunications, tourism and a liberal political ideology since 1979 have resulted in a widening of the gap between rural and urban areas.

To conclude, as Nolan and White have noted, 'urban-oriented policies need not reflect urban-dominated politics' and the 'political divide between city and country is less important than that between state and society, and . . . one ought to consider the degree to which state action transcends the sectional interests of both urban and rural population'.[23]

The spatial divide, or inter-regional variations, has also been motivated by political, economic and equity considerations. In the days of Mao, local self-sufficiency was guided more by political and equity considerations than by the economic concerns. On the other hand, the post-Mao policy of fostering coastal regions can be traced both to political ideology and the economic imperatives of earning foreign exchange through specialisation in exports in which the coastal regions have a comparative advantage over the hinterland.

In the case of India, the promotion of a regional balance was guided more by political considerations than by economic logic. In a democratic political process, the states are much more likely to receive economic rewards (in the form of steel plants, electronics factories and other industrial units) in exchange for votes and political support for the Party and central government in power. This has actually happened. In total disregard for economic efficiency and economies of large scale, sub-optimal industrial units are known to have been set up in several states purely for political reasons.

IV   THE CLASS DIVIDE

The political economy of the urban classes considered above is just one special case of the political interests of social classes and their influence on economic policies. While Lipton's urban class is based largely on sectoral interests, conventional class analysis is expressed in terms of classes (of capitalists and workers) based on ownership of the means of production.

During the Mao period, improvements in social relations between different classes (or a reduction of class antagonism), for example, between workers and peasants, and party workers and bureaucrats, was given high priority. The objective was not simply political but also economic. It was felt that mass campaigns by workers and peasants based on ideological motivation would contribute to economic development through investment by workers' initiative (the so-called u-factor of Kalecki).[24]

Did social relations or the class struggle have primacy over 'productive forces' during the Mao period? The answer to this question cannot be unequivocal. While it is true that social relations were given importance, harmonious relations between party cadres and the masses and peasants were expected to lead to higher production and marketed foodgrains.

In post-Mao China, class conflicts are not based so much on political or ideological factors as on economic factors. For example, the conflict is no longer between party cadres and the masses although the divergence of interests of these groups persists on account of corruption amongst the cadres. This clash of interests is manifested more in terms of income gaps between these two classes. Thus, the new class divide essentially boils down to the gaps between the rich and the poor in terms of income differences and to their differential access to goods and services and to corridors of power. The Chinese seem to have recognised the existence of the 100 million 'extremely poor' people in the country. Bettelheim cites examples of poor peasants attacking their rich neighbours out of resentment and frustration with growing income inequalities.[25]

A new class of rural élite is also emerging in the wake of increased commercialisation of the rural economy. The weakening of the power of the rural Party cadres is accompanied by the strengthening of economic power of the specialised households and private marketing agents.[26]

In the case of India, a number of authors like Mitra, Lipton and Bardhan have noted the importance of class relations and their influence on the political and economic gains of certain classes and group interests against others. For example, Mitra talks of a political alliance in the 1960s between the rural élite and the urban bourgeoisie. The former succeeded (according to Mitra) in extracting higher prices of agricultural products and lower prices for required inputs in exchange for sizeable rural vote banks in favour of the ruling political party.[27] Bardhan talks of the conflict of interests among the 'dominant proprietary classes', namely, the industrial capitalist class, rich farmers and the commercial class. The big industrialists acted as the backbone of the political party in power. Such industrial policies as import-substitution, industrial protection through trade restrictions and the development of a financial infrastructure to provide loans to private industry are explained in terms of the political influence of the proprietary classes. Bardhan argues that even the industrial licensing system, which on the surface appears to be inimical to the interests of this capitalist class, was exploited in their favour thanks to their great political clout and better access to decision-makers.[28] The three proprietary classes described by Bardhan have diffused interests which may partly explain why they did not generate a coherent development strategy in India.

The Marxian class conflict between capital and labour seems to be much less dominant in India than the sectoral interests of agriculture and industry. As noted above, the state wields a dominant influence on capital and labour which seems to explain why sectoral interests have been more successful than class-based groups in influencing political action and in the determination of economic policies and their outcomes.[29]

V   CONCLUDING REMARKS

In this book we have examined uneven development in the Third World in terms of development strategies and their outcomes. It has been shown that the design of development strategies is often deliberately geared towards imbalance. The outcomes of such strategies may be even or uneven. In the case of China and India, the outcomes in terms of growth, inequalities and access to technology, health and educational services have been uneven even though the intentions of the planners and policy-makers to implement uneven strategies were to achieve rapid development as well as equity. There is no easy way to explain the unintended or undesirable outcomes of development strategies. To some extent the blame may be laid on the poor design of strategies. Weaknesses in implementation tend to be another culprit. Both these factors are influenced by the political forces that condition the nature, design and implementation of strategies, policies and programmes. In both China and India, the political factors seem to have been quite important in explaining the development outcomes.

What kinds of political forces will mingle with the economic ones to shape the future development paths in the two countries is anybody's guess. But growing political instability in both the countries – though for different reasons – suggests that in future economic disequilibrium may be much more at the mercy of political forces than has recently been the case.

Notes and References

1. Pranab K. Bardhan, 'India', in Hollis Chenery *et al.*, *Redistribution with Growth*, London, Oxford University Press, 1974.
2. Ibid.
3. Frances Stewart and Paul Streeten, 'New Strategies for Development: Poverty, Income Distribution, and Growth', *Oxford Economic Papers*, November 1976.
4. Gordon White, 'Riding the Tiger: Grass Roots Rural Politics in the Wake of the Chinese Economic Reforms', in Ashwani Saith (ed.), *The Re-emergence of the Chinese Peasantry*, London, Croom Helm 1987.
5. See Warren F. Ilchman and Norman T. Uphoff, *The Political Economy of Change*, Berkeley, California University Press, 1969, pp. 242–3; and John W. Mellor, *The New Economics of Growth – A Strategy for India and the Developing World*, Ithaca, Cornell University Press, 1976, chapter XI on 'Planning and the Strategy for Growth'.
6. Carl Riskin, *China's Political Economy – The Quest for Development Since 1949*, New York, Oxford University Press, 1987.
7. Stanley Rosen, 'Restoring Key Secondary Schools in Post-Mao China: The Politics of Competition and Educational Quality', in David M. Lampton, *Policy Implementation in Post-Mao China*, Berkeley, California University Press, 1987.
8. Ibid, p. 351.
9. Ashok Rudra, 'Organisation of Agriculture for Rural Development: The Indian Case', in Dharam Ghai *et al.* (eds), *Agrarian Systems and Rural Development*, London, Macmillan Press, 1979.

10. Ashok V. Desai, 'Recent Technology Imports into India: Results of a Survey', *Development and Change*, October 1990.
11. Denis Fred Simon, 'Implementing China's Science and Technology Modernisation Program', in Lampton, *Policy Implementation* . . ..
12. David M. Lampton, 'Health Conflict and the Chinese Political System', *Michigan Papers in Chinese Studies no. 18*, Ann Arbor, Michigan University 1987.
13. David Zweig, 'Context and Content in Policy Implementation: Household Contracts and Decollectivisation, 1977–1983', in David M. Lampton, *Policy Implementation in Post-Mao China*, 1974, p. 34.
14. V. M. Dandekar and Nilakanth Rath, *Poverty in India*, Bombay, Indian School of Political Economy, 1971.
15. Government of India, Planning Commission, *The Seventh Five Year Plan (1985–90)*, vol. I, New Delhi, October 1985, p. 255.
16. K. Subbarao, *Some Aspects of Access to Education in India* – paper prepared for a Workshop on Poverty in India held at Queen Elizabeth House, Oxford, October 1987.
17. Amartya Sen, 'Development: Which Way Now?', *Economic Journal*, December 1983.
18. I owe this point to John Enos of Magdalen College, Oxford.
19. Carl Riskin, 'Feeding China: The Experience Since 1949', *WIDER Working Papers, WP. 27*, Helsinki, November 1987, p. 49.
20. John W. Lewis, *Leadership in Communist China*, Ithaca, Cornell University Press, 1963, p. 108.
21. Peter Nolan and Gordon White, 'Urban Bias, Rural Bias, or State Bias? Urban–Rural Relations in Post-revolutionary China', *Journal of Development Studies*, April 1984.
22. S. L. Chopra and O. N. S. Chauhan, 'Emerging Patterns of Political Leadership in India', *Journal of Constitutional and Parliamentary Studies*, vol. IV, no. 1, 1970, p. 126; and *Journal of Parliamentary Information*, vol. XVIII, no. 2, 1972, p. 372.
23. Nolan and White, 'Urban Bias, Rural Bias or State Bias?'.
24. Bruce McFarlane, 'Political Economy of Class Struggle and Economic Growth in China, 1950–1982', *World Development*, August 1983.
25. Charles Bettelheim, 'Economic Reform in China', *Journal of Development Studies*, July 1988.
26. G. W. Skinner, 'Rural Marketing in China: Repression and Revival', *China Quarterly*, September 1985; and Gordon White, 'Riding the Tiger: Grass Roots Rural Politics in the Wake of the Chinese Economic Reforms', in Ashwani Saith (ed.), *The Re-emergence of the Chinese Peasantry*, London, Croom Helm, 1987.
27. Ashok Mitra, *Terms of Trade and Class Relations*, London, Frank Cass, 1977.
28. Pranab, Bardhan, *The Political Economy of Development in India*, Oxford, Basil Blackwell, 1984.
29. Lloyd I. Rudolph and Susanne Hoeber Rudolph, *In Pursuit of Lakshmi – The Political Economy of the Indian State*, New Delhi, Orient Longman, 1987.

Statistical Appendix

Table A3.1   National income by sector (China)
(Three-year moving average)
(100 million yuan at 1970 prices)

Year \ Sector	Agri-culture	Manu-facturing	Const-ruction	Trans-port	Trade	Total
1954	589.22	139.10	26.84	28.46	139.50	923.12
1958	633.90	340.20	63.25	50.55	162.11	1,250.01
1959	565.94	429.60	72.80	65.49	168.10	1,301.93
1963	556.63	283.98	39.65	39.27	124.25	1,043.78
1964	621.00	347.00	48.00	46.00	128.00	1,190.00
1971	802.00	860.00	85.00	79.00	209.00	2,035.00
1972	830.00	941.00	87.00	84.00	217.00	2,159.00
1979	1,024.00	1,584.00	121.00	122.00	320.00	3,171.00
1985	1,634.00	2,480.00	215.00	186.00	552.00	5,067.00

Source: China Statistical Press (ed.), *Guomin Shouru Tongji Ziliao Huibian* (Compendium of National Income Statistics), 1949–85, Beijing, 1987.

Table A3.2   Net domestic product by sector (India)
(Three-year moving average)
(10 million Rs at 1970 prices)

Year \ Sector	Agri-culture	Manu-facturing	Const-ruction	Trans-port	Trade	Total
1951–2	10,450.0	1,722.0	659.0	543.5	1,477.0	14,851.5
1960–1	13,347.0	2,931.0	1,073.0	935.0	2,350.0	20,636.0
1970–1	16,532.0	4,611.0	1,855.0	1,572.0	3,687.0	28,257.0
1978–9	17,663.0	5,687.0	1,920.0	2,595.0	5,551.0	33,416.0
1982–3	20,070.0	7,381.0	2,399.0	3,092.0	6,274.0	39,216.0

Source: Government of India, Central Statistical Organisation (CSO), *National Accounts Statistics* (NAS), New Delhi, various years.

Table A3.3   Cumulative investment over 1954–85 period (China)
(100 million yuan at 1970 prices)

Year Sector	1954–58	1959–63	1964–71	1972–79	1979–85
Agriculture	59.4	177.78	187.0	300.0	214.00
Manufacturing	198.0	605.77	875.0	1,735.0	2,033.0
Construction	30.4	20.85	51.0	45.0	45.0
Transport	128.0	213.92	345.0	478.0	386.0
Trade	30.4	31.60	62.0	86.0	137.0
Total	446.2	1,049.92	1,520.0	2,644.0	2,815.0

Source: As Table A3.1.

Table A3.4   Cumulative investment over 1950–82 period (India)
(Rs 10 million at 1970 prices)

Year Sector	1950–59	1959–69	1969–77	1977–82
Agriculture	5,655.0	9,103.0	11,633.0	11,005.0
Manufacturing	4,696.0	13,781.0	16,766.0	15,202.0
Construction	511.0	1,585.0	1,175.0	1,222.0
Transport	2,911.0	7,241.0	7,071.0	5,730.0
Trade	1,432.0	1,841.0	5,098.5	3,895.0
Total	15,205.0	33,551.0	41,744.0	37,054.0

Source: Based on gross fixed capital formation, *National Accounts Statistics* (NAS) various years.

Table A4.1   Employment–output coefficients (China)

Sector no.	(1) Inter. demand	(2) Final demand	(3) Gross output	(4) Employ- ment	(5) Emp. per inter. demand (4)/(1)	(6) Emp. per final demand (4)/(2)	(7) Emp. per gross output (4)/(3)
	(100 million yuan)			(100 thousand)		(labour/million yuan)	
1	771.2	766.2	1,537.3	2,634.3	3,415.9	3,438.2	1,713.5
2	75.2	23.7	98.9	22.0	292.7	927.0	222.5
3	224.9	177.3	402.2	360.8	1,604.3	2,035.6	897.2
4	246.0	132.3	378.3	51.0	207.3	385.4	134.8
5	6.9	36.8	43.7	39.4	5,683.4	1,070.3	900.7
6	458.7	−6.1	452.6	54.3	118.4	−8,949.6	120.0
7	171.9	21.5	193.3	15.6	90.7	726.0	80.6
8	121.2	31.8	153.0	68.3	563.5	2,143.6	446.2
9	194.7	64.0	258.7	9.7	49.7	151.3	37.4
10	385.2	−6.6	378.6	35.2	91.4	−5,336.3	93.0
11	123.2	92.3	215.5	17.1	138.4	184.8	79.1
12	311.3	431.8	743.1	125.6	403.4	290.9	169.0
13	79.6	215.4	295.0	47.1	591.6	218.7	159.7
14	178.0	26.0	204.0	32.7	183.6	1,257.8	160.2
15	57.9	12.5	70.4	13.4	231.3	1,076.2	190.4
16	16.6	22.3	38.9	9.0	543.1	405.1	232.0
17	149.8	549.9	699.8	43.6	290.8	79.2	62.3
18	562.1	304.4	866.5	66.2	117.7	217.4	76.4
19	45.3	151.7	197.0	6.1	135.6	40.5	31.2
20	104.5	80.9	185.4	18.4	176.0	227.4	99.2
21	105.4	62.8	168.2	17.4	165.1	277.3	103.5
22	0.0	729.2	729.2	127.4	n.a.	174.7	174.7
23	147.4	86.6	234.0	83.3	565.1	962.1	356.0
24	159.4	345.1	504.5	172.2	1,080.0	499.0	341.3

Source: Our estimates.

Table A4.2 Employment–output coefficients (India)

		Employment (million)	Gross output (Rs. thous. mill.)	Employment/ gross output (per thous. Rs.)
1	Agriculture	94.708	459.786	0.206
2	Forestry	0.111	14.55	0.00762
3	Animal husbandry	n.a.	108.192	n.a.
4	Fisheries	0.432	11.422	0.0378
5	Metallurgical	3.438	121.567	0.0283
6	Electricity	0.927	28.607	0.0324
7	Coal/Coke	0.115	19.152	0.006
8	Petroleum	0.086	55.009	0.00156
9	Chemicals	2.751	162.852	0.0169
10	Machinery	5.358	145.768	0.03675
11	Building Materials	1.805	44.183	0.0409
12	Wood Products	0.344	21.485	0.016
13	Food	6.16	161.460	0.0382
14	Textiles	6.59	110.842	0.0595
15	Clothing & Leather	0.487	45.211	0.0108
16	Paper	1.261	23.105	0.0546
17	Others	0.287	42.27	0.00679
18	Construction	11.321	217.66	0.052
19	Transport & Communications	11.298	149.065	0.0758
20	Commerce etc.	16.64	452.459	0.03677

Source: Our estimates.
Note: n.a. = not available.

Table A4.3   Correlation matrices of output and employment
linkages (China)

	DBR	TBR	VTBR	MDFR	MTFR
Output					
TBR	0.92783				
VTBR	−0.60783	−0.63304			
MDFR	−0.24348	−0.25913	0.42261		
MTFR	−0.26783	−0.28087	0.52087	0.94000	
VTFR	0.50348	0.55043	−0.39826	−0.81217	−0.86435
Employment					
TBR	0.29652				
VTBR	0.47304	0.62348			
MDFR	1.00000	0.29652	0.47304		
TMFR	0.59739	−0.08348	0.597739		
VTFR	0.62609	0.32609	0.14552	0.62609	0.32261

Source: Our estimates.

Notes: DBR: direct backward linkage rank
TBR: total backward linkage rank
VTBR: the rank of the variation of total backward linkage
MDFR: modified direct forward linkage rank
MTFR: modified total forward linkage rank
VTFR: the rank of the variation of modified total forward linkage

Table A4.4   Correlation matrices of output and employment linkages (India)

	DBR	TBR	VTBR	MDFR	MTFR
Output					
TBR	0.98346	1.00000			
VTBR	−0.60752	−0.59098	1.00000		
MDFR	−0.01053	0.07820	0.27519	0.95789	
VTFR	0.25714	0.16391	−0.33383	−0.83910	−0.87820
Employment					
TBR	0.88571	1.00000			
VTBR	0.82707	0.62105	1.00000		
MDFR	1.00000	0.88571	0.82707	1.00000	
MTFR	0.07519	0.02406	0.07970	0.07519	
VTFR	0.79098	0.73383	0.64812	0.79098	0.07068

Source: Our estimates.

Notes: DBR: direct backward linkage rank
TBR: total backward linkage rank
VTBR: the rank of the variation of total backward linkage
MDFR: modified direct forward linkage rank
MTFR: modified total forward linkage rank
VTFR: the rank of the variation of modified total forward linkage

Table A4.5   Forward and backward output linkages (China)
(Sectoral Classification I)
(coefficients)

Agriculture	Non-farm	Light industry	Heavy industry	Others	Σ
1	2	3	4	5	
I. *Forward linkages*					
Direct forward linkages					
1 0.09	0.10	0.29	0.00	0.02	0.50
2 0.05	0.05	0.26	0.09	0.15	0.60
3 0.01	0.03	0.28	0.04	0.07	0.43
4 0.07	0.02	0.11	0.40	0.17	0.77
5 0.01	0.01	0.05	0.10	0.07	0.25
Indirect forward linkages					
1 1.03	0.04	0.22	0.08	0.08	1.45
2 0.04	1.04	0.22	0.15	0.11	1.55
3 0.02	0.02	1.17	0.09	0.07	1.38
4 0.08	0.05	0.26	1.36	0.20	1.95
5 0.02	0.01	0.08	0.10	1.06	1.29

Table A4.5 *continued*

	Agriculture 1	Non-farm 2	Light industry 3	Heavy industry 4	Others 5	Σ
	Total forward linkages					
1	1.12	0.14	0.51	0.08	0.11	1.95
2	0.09	1.09	0.48	0.23	0.26	2.15
3	0.03	0.05	1.45	0.13	0.15	1.81
4	0.15	0.07	0.37	1.76	0.37	2.72
5	0.03	0.03	0.14	0.21	1.13	1.54
II.	*Backward linkages*					
	Direct backward linkages					
1	0.09	0.17	0.18	0.00	0.02	
2	0.03	0.05	0.10	0.03	0.08	
3	0.02	0.08	0.28	0.04	0.11	
4	0.11	0.05	0.11	0.40	0.26	
5	0.01	0.03	0.03	0.07	0.07	
Σ	0.26	0.38	0.69	0.54	0.54	
	Indirect backward linkages					
1	1.03	0.06	0.14	0.05	0.08	
2	0.02	1.04	0.08	0.06	0.06	
3	0.04	0.07	1.17	0.09	0.11	
4	0.13	0.13	0.26	1.36	0.30	
5	0.02	0.03	0.05	0.07	1.06	
Σ	1.24	1.33	1.70	1.63	1.61	
	Total backward linkages					
1	1.12	0.23	0.31	0.05	0.10	
2	0.05	1.09	0.18	0.09	0.14	
3	0.06	0.15	1.45	0.13	0.23	
4	0.24	0.18	0.36	1.76	0.55	
5	0.04	0.05	0.09	0.14	1.13	
Σ	1.50	1.71	2.39	2.17	2.15	

Source: Our estimates.

Table A4.6   Forward and backward output linkages (China)
(coefficients)
(Sectoral Classification II)

	Agriculture 1	Industry 2	Construction 3	Transport 4	Trade 5	Σ
I. Forward linkages						
Direct forward linkages						
1	0.16	0.33	0.04	0.00	0.01	0.54
2	0.07	0.42	0.08	0.01	0.03	0.61
3	0.00	0.00	0.00	0.00	0.00	0.00
4	0.05	0.41	0.12	0.02	0.03	0.63
5	0.04	0.21	0.02	0.02	0.03	0.32
Indirect forward linkages						
1	1.09	0.39	0.07	0.01	0.02	1.58
2	0.08	1.42	0.07	0.01	0.03	1.61
3	0.00	0.00	1.00	0.00	0.00	1.00
4	0.08	0.41	0.07	1.01	0.03	1.59
5	0.05	0.23	0.04	0.01	1.02	1.33
Total forward linkages						
1	1.25	0.72	0.11	0.01	0.03	2.12
2	0.15	1.84	0.15	0.02	0.06	2.21
3	0.00	0.00	1.00	0.00	0.00	1.00
4	0.13	0.82	0.19	1.03	0.05	2.22
5	0.09	0.44	0.06	0.02	1.04	1.65
II. Backward linkages						
Direct backward linkages						
1	0.16	0.16	0.14	0.01	0.05	
2	0.14	0.42	0.53	0.22	0.30	
3	0.00	0.00	0.00	0.00	0.00	
4	0.00	0.02	0.04	0.02	0.01	
5	0.01	0.02	0.02	0.04	0.03	
Σ	0.31	0.62	0.73	0.29	0.39	
Indirect backward linkages						
1	1.09	0.19	0.22	0.09	0.12	
2	0.17	1.42	0.51	0.22	0.28	
3	0.00	0.00	1.00	0.00	0.00	
4	0.01	0.02	0.02	1.01	0.01	
5	0.01	0.02	0.03	0.01	1.02	
Σ	1.28	1.65	1.78	1.33	1.43	

Table A4.6   *continued*

	Agriculture 1	Industry 2	Construction 3	Transport 4	Trade 5	Σ
	Total backward linkages					
1	1.25	0.35	0.36	0.10	0.16	
2	0.31	1.84	1.04	0.44	0.58	
3	0.00	0.00	1.00	0.00	0.00	
4	0.01	0.04	0.06	1.03	0.03	
5	0.02	0.04	0.04	0.05	1.04	
Σ	1.59	2.27	2.50	1.62	1.81	

Source: Our estimates.

Table A4.7   Forward and backward output linkages (India)
(coefficients)

	Agriculture 1	Industry 2	Construction 3	Transport 4	Trade 5	Σ
I. *Forward linkages*						
Direct forward linkages						
1	0.12	0.17	0.01	0.00	0.01	0.32
2	0.06	0.33	0.07	0.04	0.03	0.55
3	0.03	0.13	0.00	0.01	0.03	0.20
4	0.02	0.21	0.06	0.02	0.17	0.48
5	0.04	0.24	0.12	0.04	0.10	0.53
Indirect forward linkages						
1	1.04	0.15	0.03	0.02	0.02	1.26
2	0.06	1.28	0.06	0.03	0.04	1.47
3	0.02	0.11	1.03	0.01	0.02	1.19
4	0.05	0.24	0.06	1.03	0.05	1.43
5	0.06	0.25	0.06	0.03	1.05	1.44
Total forward linkages						
1	1.16	0.32	0.04	0.02	0.03	1.58
2	0.13	1.61	0.13	0.08	0.07	2.02
3	0.05	0.23	1.03	0.03	0.05	1.39
4	0.07	0.45	0.13	1.05	0.22	1.92
5	0.10	0.49	0.18	0.07	1.14	1.98
II. *Backward linkages*						
Direct backward linkages						
1	0.12	0.10	0.02	0.01	0.02	
2	0.11	0.33	0.34	0.29	0.06	
3	0.01	0.03	0.00	0.02	0.02	
4	0.01	0.03	0.04	0.02	0.06	
5	0.03	0.11	0.25	0.11	0.10	
Σ	0.27	0.61	0.65	0.46	0.25	

continued on page 268

Table A4.7   *continued*

	Agriculture 1	Industry 2	Construction 3	Transport 4	Trade 5	Σ
	Indirect backward linkages					
1	1.04	0.09	0.08	0.07	0.02	
2	0.10	1.28	0.27	0.22	0.09	
3	0.01	0.02	1.03	0.02	0.01	
4	0.01	0.04	0.04	1.03	0.02	
5	0.04	0.12	0.12	0.09	1.05	
Σ	1.21	1.54	1.55	1.44	1.19	
	Total backward linkages					
1	1.16	0.20	0.10	0.08	0.04	
2	0.21	1.61	0.61	0.51	0.15	
3	0.02	0.05	1.03	0.04	0.02	
4	0.02	0.07	0.09	1.05	0.07	
5	0.07	0.22	0.38	0.20	1.14	
Σ	1.48	2.15	2.20	1.89	1.43	

Source: Our estimates.

Table A4.8   Forward and backward employment linkages (China) (coefficients)

	Agriculture 1	Industry 2	Construction 3	Transport 4	Trade 5	Σ
I. *Forward linkages*						
	Direct forward linkages					
1	1,263.0	0.0	0.0	0.0	0.0	
2	0.0	113.2	0.0	0.0	0.0	
3	0.0	0.0	174.7	0.0	0.0	
4	0.0	0.0	0.0	356.0	0.0	
5	0.0	0.0	0.0	0.0	341.3	
	Indirect forward linkages					
1	310.7	81.8	18.9	3.2	11.5	426.2
2	185.5	94.8	25.9	7.2	19.5	332.8
3	0.0	0.0	0.0	0.0	0.0	0.0
4	161.6	92.5	34.1	10.7	18.4	317.3
5	109.5	49.3	11.4	7.9	14.0	192.0
	Total forward linkages					
1	1,573.7	81.8	18.9	3.2	11.5	1,689.2
2	185.5	207.9	25.9	7.2	19.5	446.0
3	0.0	0.0	174.7	0.0	0.0	174.7

Table A4.8 *continued*

	Agriculture 1	Industry 2	Construction 3	Transport 4	Trade 5	
4	161.6	92.5	34.1	366.7	18.4	673.2
5	109.5	49.3	11.4	7.9	355.3	533.3

II. *Backward linkages*

Direct backward linkages

	Agriculture 1	Industry 2	Construction 3	Transport 4	Trade 5	
1	1,263.0	0.0	0.0	0.0	0.0	
2	0.0	113.2	0.0	0.0	0.0	
3	0.0	0.0	174.7	0.0	0.0	
4	0.0	0.0	0.0	356.0	0.0	
5	0.0	0.0	0.0	0.0	341.3	

Indirect backward linkages

	Agriculture 1	Industry 2	Construction 3	Transport 4	Trade 5	
1	310.7	438.6	460.7	121.1	208.2	
2	34.6	94.8	118.1	49.9	65.7	
3	0.0	0.0	0.0	0.0	0.0	
4	4.3	13.3	22.3	10.7	8.9	
5	6.1	14.6	15.3	16.3	14.0	
Σ	355.7	561.3	616.4	198.0	296.8	

Total backward linkages

	Agriculture 1	Industry 2	Construction 3	Transport 4	Trade 5	
1	1,573.7	438.6	460.7	121.1	208.2	
2	34.6	207.9	118.1	49.9	65.7	
3	0.0	0.0	174.7	0.0	0.0	
4	4.3	13.3	22.3	366.7	8.9	
5	6.1	14.6	15.3	16.3	355.3	
Σ	1,618.7	674.4	791.1	554.0	638.1	

Source: Our estimates.

Note: The direct forward employment effect is the same as direct backward employment effect since labour is assumed to be homogeneous.

Table A4.9   Forward and backward employment linkages (India) (coefficients)

	Agriculture 1	Industry 2	Construction 3	Transport 4	Trade 5
I. *Forward linkages*					
Direct forward linkages					
1	1,603.7	0.0	0.0	0.0	0.0
2	0.0	301.7	0.0	0.0	0.0
3	0.0	0.0	520.1	0.0	0.0

continued on page 270

Statistical Appendix

Table A4.9 *continued*

	Agriculture 1	Industry 2	Construction 3	Transport 4	Trade 5	
4	0.0	0.0	0.0	757.9	0.0	
5	0.0	0.0	0.0	0.0	367.8	
Indirect forward linkages						Σ
1	262.0	97.7	19.7	15.4	11.9	406.7
2	202.1	184.0	69.9	59.3	25.8	541.0
3	87.2	70.8	13.4	20.9	18.2	210.6
4	113.6	136.6	65.6	39.5	79.7	435.0
5	153.3	146.9	94.4	50.4	53.0	498.0
Total forward linkages						
1	1,865.7	97.7	19.7	15.4	11.9	2,010.4
2	202.1	485.7	69.9	59.3	25.8	842.7
3	87.2	70.8	533.5	20.9	18.2	730.7
4	113.6	136.6	65.6	797.4	79.7	1,192.9
5	153.3	146.9	94.4	50.4	420.8	865.8
II. *Backward linkages*						
Direct backward linkages						
1	1,603.7	0.0	0.0	0.0	0.0	
2	0.0	301.7	0.0	0.0	0.0	
3	0.0	0.0	520.1	0.0	0.0	
4	0.0	0.0	0.0	757.9	0.0	
5	0.0	0.0	0.0	0.0	367.8	
Indirect backward linkages						
1	262.0	314.2	165.4	130.2	68.4	
2	62.8	184.0	182.8	155.3	45.9	
3	10.4	27.1	13.4	21.0	12.4	
4	13.5	52.1	65.4	39.5	54.1	
5	26.8	82.6	138.7	74.2	53.0	
Σ	375.4	660.0	565.6	420.2	233.8	
Total backward linkages						
1	1,865.7	314.2	165.4	130.2	68.4	
2	62.8	485.7	182.8	155.3	45.9	
3	10.4	27.1	533.5	21.0	12.4	
4	13.5	52.1	65.4	797.4	54.1	
5	26.8	82.6	138.7	74.2	420.8	
Σ	1,979.1	961.7	1,085.8	1,178.1	601.6	

Source: Our estimates.

Note: The direct forward employment effect is the same as the direct backward employment effect since labour is assumed to be homogeneous.

Table A6.1   Provincial *per capita* income (China) (yuan)

Province	Per capita income				
	1957	1971	1981	1985 (1981 price)	1987 (current price)
	(current price)				
Beijing	235	594	–	–	2,413
Tianjin	447	784	1,270	1,718	2,264
Hebei	128	207	361	547	791
Shanxi	146	225	376	621	707
Inner Mongolia	164	255	318	507	701
Liaoning	304	436	836	1,215	1,510
Jilin	175	276	418	655	1,016
Heilongjiang	261	382	587	761	1,136
Shanghai	654	1,407	2,501	3,416	3,816
Jiangsu	118	228	494	833	1,251
Zhejiang	136	–	462	822	1,241
Anhui	114	163	304	471	681
Fujian	138	169	349	510	815
Jiangxi	136	212	325	452	619
Shandong	101	185	404	610	935
Henan	98	154	287	331	641
Hubei	146	216	414	660	925
Hunan	112	193	340	463	699
Guangdong	144	208	461	677	1,098
Guangxi	–	–	275	344	519
Sichuan	104	153	282	418	602
Guizhou	87	132	203	320	465
Yunnan	108	153	262	386	525
Tibet	–	–	–	–	598
Shaanxi	124	210	294	446	607
Gansu	112	204	297	456	631
Qinghai	166	269	333	519	756
Ningxia	120	231	333	488	664
Xinjiang	246	229	400	602	853
China	144	233	410	605	872

Sources: China Statistical Press (ed.), *Guomin houru Tongji Ziliao Huibian* (Compendium of National Income Statistics, 1949–85), Beijing, 1987; and *Statistical Yearbook of China*, 1989.

Notes: (1) Data refer to yearly income.
(2) – = not available.

Table A6.2   State *per capita* income (India) (1970–71 prices)

State	Per capita domestic product (Rs)			
	1970–71	*1981–82*	*1985–86*	*1987–88*
Andhra Pradesh	585	721	743	–
Assam	535	534	604	655
Bihar	402	432	486	472
Gujarat	829	989	862	853
Haryana	877	1,081	1,217	–
Himachal Pradesh	678	722	788	–
Jammu and Kashmir	548	638	673	–
Karnataka	641	717	698	776
Kerala	594	629	614	–
Madhya Pradesh	484	531	623	633
Maharashtra	783	985	1,029	1,159
Orissa	478	564	–	498
Punjab	1,070	1,454	1,621	1,755
Rajasthan	651	577	663	583
Tamil Nadu	581	674	979	915
Uttar Pradesh	486	516	587	–
West Bengal	722	750	858	898
All India Average	633	720	798	–

Source: Government of India, Central Statistical Organisation (CSO), *Estimates of State Domestic Product, 1970–71 – 1987–88, 1989*, National Accounts Statistics, 1987 and 1990.

Notes: (1) Data refer to yearly income.
(2) – = not available.

Table A6.3   Provincial *per capita* consumption (China) (yuan)

Province	Per capita consumption				
	1957	1971	1981	1985 (1981 price)	1987 (current price)
	(current price)				
Beijing	202	247	–	–	1,038
Tianjin	188	265	566	765	907
Hebei	103	137	231	344	575
Shanxi	96	126	256	361	411
Inner Mongolia	123	149	315	439	492
Liaoning	174	208	425	554	752
Jilin	122	187	342	491	639

Table A6.3   *continued*

Province	Per capita consumption				
	1957	1971	1981	1985 (1981 price)	1987 (current price)
		(current price)			
Heilongjiang	180	258	380	502	641
Shanghai	278	348	–	–	1,214
Jiangsu	83	132	295	440	589
Zhejiang	101	–	285	430	613
Anhui	–	–	–	–	428
Fujian	111	137	263	391	519
Jiangxi	101	158	–	–	425
Shandong	77	107	263	358	465
Henan	74	95	201	296	350
Hubei	117	130	240	391	528
Hunan	85	121	–	–	447
Guangdong	119	160	325	467	651
Guangxi	–	–	214	286	372
Sichuan	83	120	218	326	425
Guizhou	75	110	–	–	355
Yunnan	85	119	–	–	360
Tibet	–	–	–	–	498
Shaanxi	104	137	252	360	413
Gansu	100	124	–	–	405
Qinghai	–	–	–	–	552
Ningxia	99	160	–	–	477
Xinjiang	198	202	359	471	611

Source: As for Table A6.1.

Notes: (1) Data refer to yearly consumption.
(2) – = not available.

Table A6.4   State *per capita* consumption (India) (Rs at 1973–74 prices)

State	Year		
	1972	1977	1983
Andhra Pradesh	53.8	65.1	75.9
Assam	50.2	49.2	57.4
Bihar	46.8	45.9	45.3
Gujarat	58.8	63.3	72.6
Haryana	83.5	75.1	83.0
Karnataka	56.6	57.9	65.3

continued on page 274

Table A6.4 *continued*

State	Year		
	1972	*1977*	*1983*
Kerala	51.5	63.0	73.0
Madhya Pradesh	51.5	52.5	59.5
Maharashtra	45.7	64.6	61.0
Orissa	47.9	50.5	52.8
Punjab	88.8	93.0	93.2
Rajasthan	69.3	97.1	81.3
Tamil Nadu	50.9	53.6	56.7
Uttar Pradesh	53.3	59.6	60.1
West Bengal	42.0	43.6	46.9
All India	53.0	59.1	61.7

Source: *National Sample Survey (NSS) data*, taken from N. Kakwani and
    K. Subbarao, *Poverty and its Alleviation in India*, paper prepared for
    a World Bank/IFPRI Poverty Research Conference, Arlie House,
    Virginia, October 1989.

Note: Data refer to monthly consumption.

Table A6.5   Agricultural output by province (China) (percentages)

Province	Year			
	1957	*1971*	*1981*	*1985*
	(at current price)		*(at 1981 price)*	
Beijing	13.99	12.55	–	–
Tianjin	10.78	8.95	9.42	9.59
Hebei	53.87	44.63	42.74	47.58
Shanxi	48.91	42.46	36.53	36.80
Inner Mongolia	55.39	51.93	47.58	43.98
Liaoning	21.57	19.10	18.71	17.82
Jilin	39.47	36.43	38.06	37.47
Heilongjiang	45.22	–	29.84	30.42
Shanghai	4.51	5.03	–	–
Jiangsu	56.32	45.03	40.57	39.92
Zhejiang	56.28	–	43.93	38.21
Anhui	70.84	–	58.75	52.57
Fujian	58.36	55.23	48.34	47.61
Jiangxi	61.69	52.74	54.17	51.79
Shandong	59.81	46.53	47.79	49.78
Henan	53.34	51.10	52.58	62.82
Hubei	54.32	50.46	42.30	36.32
Hunan	65.22	53.54	52.36	49.47

Table A6.5   *continued*

Province	Year			
	1957	1971	1981	1985
	(at current price)		(at 1981 price)	
Guangdong	55.32	46.46	43.12	39.88
Guangxi	–	–	55.00	48.04
Sichuan	62.36	55.85	51.83	47.26
Guizhou	64.23	54.62	52.34	48.38
Yunnan	61.15	60.07	52.35	47.99
Tibet	–	–	–	–
Shaanxi	56.81	43.15	42.61	38.89
Gansu	50.33	23.93	31.51	30.63
Qinghai	61.52	44.88	36.58	30.15
Ningxia	78.10	40.55	43.20	39.12
Xinjiang	56.76	48.21	46.97	48.06

Source: China Statistical Press (ed.), *Guomin Shouru Tongji Ziliao Huibian* (Compendium of National Income Statistics), 1949–85, Beijing, 1987.

Table A6.6   Agricultural output by state (India) (1970–71 prices) (percentages)

State	1970–71	1981–82	1985–86	1987–88
Andhra Pradesh	56.6	49.4	41.0	–
Assam	61.4	56.3	–	45.0
Bihar	58.0	44.1	45.4	43.7
Gujarat	48.0	42.1	30.0	14.2
Haryana	64.7	49.6	48.2	–
Himachal Pradesh	57.0	50.9	44.7	–
Jammu and Kashmir	56.5	49.4	46.6	–
Karnataka	54.2	46.1	40.1	38.1
Kerala	49.4	38.9	38.9	–
Madhya Pradesh	59.7	49.2	45.2	39.6
Maharashtra	28.4	27.4	23.5	20.9
Orissa	65.5	64.6	65.0	57.2
Punjab	58.3	50.8	52.1	51.8
Rajasthan	61.0	51.0	52.4	45.8
Tamil Nadu	39.3	30.5	23.2	19.5
Uttar Pradesh	60.0	53.3	49.3	–
West Bengal	43.5	40.5	42.2	41.5

Source: Government of India, Central Statistical Organisation, *Estimates of State Domestic Product*, 1970–71 – 1987–88, 1989, National Accounts Statistics, 1987 and 1990.

Notes: (1) Agriculture = agriculture + forestry + fishing.
(2) – = not available.

Table A6.7   Industrial output by province (China) (percentages)

Province	Year			
	1957	1971	1981	1985
	(current price)		(1981 price)	
Beijing	47.5	70.1	–	–
Tianjin	56.8	73.4	66.2	43.9
Hebei	20.2	32.7	39.7	34.9
Shanxi	26.3	41.6	47.3	40.5
Inner Mongolia	21.2	28.5	34.9	33.2
Liaoning	56.1	63.2	52.8	52.8
Jilin	37.4	49.6	46.3	45.0
Heilongjiang	33.2	56.9	55.4	54.0
Shanghai	60.4	81.9	–	–
Jiangsu	23.1	37.7	43.6	43.9
Zhejiang	18.3	–	38.6	40.3
Anhui	12.8	50.3	26.6	28.8
Fujian	21.5	25.0	30.6	31.8
Jiangxi	18.0	25.0	27.1	29.2
Shandong	23.4	41.1	36.3	33.9
Henan	13.9	33.2	30.9	41.0
Hubei	20.2	31.0	38.9	43.8
Hunan	13.9	29.4	31.2	32.8
Guangdong	22.2	31.3	31.0	34.2
Guangxi	–	–	28.1	30.2
Sichuan	18.7	23.7	31.1	33.2
Guizhou	15.1	25.9	29.9	31.6
Yunnan	19.2	21.1	28.7	31.0
Tibet	–	–	–	–
Shaanxi	18.4	37.0	39.9	39.4
Gansu	13.6	58.0	45.6	42.8
Qinghai	11.1	31.4	32.8	32.4
Ningxia	8.6	33.9	34.3	35.5
Xinjiang	12.5	28.1	30.5	29.9

Source: As for Table A6.1.

Notes: (1) The data represent Chinese national income which is closest to the Indian concept of State domestic product.
(2) – = not available.

Table A6.8   Industrial output by state (India) (percentages, 1970–71 prices)

State	Year			
	1970–71	*1981–82*	*1985–86*	*1987–88*
Andhra Pradesh	10.2	12.9	15.1	–
Assam	11.7	13.5	–	11.4
Bihar	15.4	18.5	16.5	12.4
Gujarat	18.0	19.4	22.5	28.3
Haryana	11.2	15.9	16.4	–
Himachal Pradesh	5.6	6.3	7.2	–
Jammu and Kashmir	6.0	7.7	9.2	–
Karnataka	16.7	22.2	23.6	23.4
Kerala	13.5	17.0	15.5	–
Madhya Pradesh	12.3	17.1	18.6	14.1
Maharashtra	28.2	30.4	32.0	32.5
Orissa	10.2	10.5	6.7	8.6
Punjab	8.8	12.1	11.3	10.6
Rajasthan	9.0	11.6	11.9	8.5
Tamil Nadu	21.5	25.5	23.8	21.5
Uttar Pradesh	9.7	12.8	17.5	–
West Bengal	20.1	18.5	15.2	14.1

Source: Government of India, Central Statistical Organisation, *Estimates of State Domestic Product, 1970–71, 1987–88, 1989*, National Accounts Statistics, 1987 and 1990.

Table A6.9   Agricultural workers by province (China)

Province	Number of agricultural workers (000)[1]		Share[2] (%)	
	1981	*1986*	*1981*	*1986*
Beijing	63	72	1.83	1.81
Tianjin	36	45	1.42	1.61
Hebei	237	209	4.77	3.60
Shanxi	90	85	2.82	2.16
Inner Mongolia	318	356	11.74	10.63
Liaoning	448	454	5.50	4.78
Jilin	216	243	6.28	5.16
Heilongjiang	1,122	1,082	16.70	13.61
Shanghai	229*	176	–	3.52
Jiangsu	397	402	5.88	4.93
Zhejiang	138	144	3.62	3.25
Anhui	211	209	5.90	4.78
Fujian	175	168	7.22	5.92

continued on page 278

Table A6.9   *continued*

Province	Number of agricultural workers $(000)^1$		Share[2] (%)	
	1981	1986	1981	1986
Jiangxi	376	373	2.52	10.60
Shandong	189	167	3.50	2.57
Henan	180	180	3.62	2.91
Hubei	600	601	11.29	9.41
Hunan	367	403	8.60	8.18
Guangdong	977	973	14.41	12.38
Guangxi	247	235	9.50	8.27
Sichuan	215	220	2.89	2.56
Guizhou	80	73	4.31	3.53
Yunnan	232	232	9.86	8.63
Tibet	27	10	15.43	6.29
Shaanxi	92	91	3.10	2.60
Gansu	109	108	6.06	5.19
Qinghai	70*	51	–	7.98
Ningxia	75	71	15.37	12.22
Xinjiang	1,065	975	42.08	35.55

Sources: *Statistical Yearbook of China* (SYC), 1981, p. 116 and SYC, 1987, p. 96.

Notes:
1. Agricultural workers include workers in state-owned units and workers in collective units. No data are available on family farms which form the bulk of the agricultural workforce since the introduction of the agricultural responsibility system.
2. These shares are low because of the incompleteness of data.
* State sector only.

Table A6.10   Agricultural workers by state: India (percentages)

State	Total number of workers (000)		Share (%)	
	1971	1981	1971	1981
Andhra Pradesh	13,215	16,297	73.4	72.0
Assam	6,916	–	–	–
Bihar	14,553	16,577	83.0	79.9
Gujarat	5,673	6,861	67.6	62.5
Haryana	1,772	2,260	66.8	61.7
Himachal Pradesh	990	1,078	77.5	73.3
Jammu and Kashmir	982	1,162	71.5	63.9

Table A6.10   *continued*

State	Total number of workers (000)		Share (%)	
	1971	1981	1971	1981
Kerala	3,449	3,454	55.5	50.9
Madhya Pradesh	12,405	15,651	81.1	78.1
Maharashtra	12,226	15,495	66.5	63.8
Karnataka	7,210	9,397	70.8	68.8
Orissa	5,452	6,657	79.6	77.1
Punjab	2,488	2,908	63.6	59.0
Rajasthan	6,180	7,498	76.8	71.8
Tamil Nadu	9,501	12,101	64.4	63.6
Uttar Pradesh	21,319	24,311	78.0	75.0
West Bengal	7,590	8,974	61.4	58.2
Arunachal Pradesh	216	235	80.3	75.1
India Total	125,057	153,049	69.3	68.8

Source: Government of India, Registrar General, *Census of India*, 1971 and 1981.

Note: Agricultural workers = cultivators + agricultural labourers + workers in fishing, hunting, forestry, etc.

Table A6.11   Industrial workers by province (China)

Province	Number of industrial workers (000)		Share (%)	
	1981	1986	1981	1986
Beijing	1,056	2,028	37.30	34.38
Tianjin	895	1,972	46.13	42.81
Hebei	1,728	4,631	42.24	17.15
Shanxi	1,276	2,881	49.26	23.76
Inner Mongolia	740	1,471	34.51	17.09
Liaoning	2,856	6,219	49.38	34.56
Jilin	1,227	2,562	43.38	26.19
Heilongjiang	2,055	3,997	41.91	30.31
Shanghai	1,971	3,953	54.17	51.50
Jiangsu	1,938	9,237	45.52	26.69
Zhejiang	946	6,052	42.10	25.53
Anhui	1,007	2,842	39.28	11.30
Fujian	651	1,725	36.92	14.50

continued on page 280

Table A6.11   *continued*

Province	Number of industrial workers (000)		Share (%)	
	1981	1986	1981	1986
Jiangxi	954	2,338	39.40	14.67
Shandong	1,792	5,880	43.64	15.72
Henan	1,721	4,298	42.27	11.78
Hubei	1,533	4,097	36.36	17.56
Hunan	1,314	4,023	39.51	14.21
Guangdong	1,493	4,942	29.50	15.73
Guangxi	715	1,356	33.14	7.15
Sichuan	2,453	5,760	42.55	10.82
Guizhou	578	1,527	37.65	11.03
Yunnan	671	1,280	32.66	7.32
Tibet	19	33	11.65	3.07
Shaanxi	1,132	2,335	45.33	16.33
Gansu	640	1,166	39.70	12.10
Qinghai	148	261	31.15	13.79
Ningxia	160	250	37.64	13.65
Xinjiang	398	680	17.58	12.00

Sources: *Statistical Yearbook of China*, 1981, 1987.

Table A6.12   Industrial workers by state (India)

State	Industrial workers (000)			Share (%)		
	1961	*1971*	*1981*	*1961*	*1971*	*1981*
Andhra Pradesh	2,291	1,724	2,381	6.37	3.96	6.28
Assam	384	184	–	3.23	1.23	–
Bihar	1,484	1,145	1,659	3.19	2.03	4.48
Gujarat	1,092	1,047	1,725	5.29	3.92	14.80
Jammu and Kashmir	129	94	208	3.60	2.03	–
Kerala	1,018	1,007	1,133	5.97	4.69	16.61
Madhya Pradesh	1,178	1,120	1,752	3.61	2.67	5.29
Tamil Nadu	2,055	2,023	2,948	6.07	4.89	14.09
Maharashtra	2,136	2,440	3,462	5.36	4.81	13.28
Karnataka	1,130	1,090	1,731	4.76	3.70	10.15
Orissa	617	457	670	3.49	2.07	4.78
Punjab	895	442	650	7.97	3.24	13.47
Rajasthan	770	570	1,025	3.79	2.20	8.36
Uttar Pradesh	2,602	2,002	2,942	3.51	2.25	6.89
West Bengal	1,319	1,855	2,717	3.75	4.16	14.74
Haryana	–	269	475	–	2.67	11.35
Himachal Pradesh	–	55	82	–	1.59	–

Sources: Government of India, Registrar General, *Census of India.*

Note: Industrial workers = workers in large-scale manufacturing + workers in household industry + workers in mining.

Table A6.13   Urban population by province (China) (percentages)

Province	Year	
	1981	*1986*
Beijing	55.4	67.1
Tianjin	51.6	70.7
Hebei	9.3	35.8
Shanxi	13.9	56.9
Inner Mongolia	23.4	45.7
Liaoning	33.5	68.9
Jilin	29.6	63.5
Heilongjiang	31.7	61.1
Shanghai	57.7	63.3
Jiangsu	12.3	32.8
Zhejiang	10.8	43.7
Anhui	9.5	29.2
Fujian	12.2	43.7
Jiangxi	12.0	29.3
Shandong	7.7	57.2
Henan	7.8	21.4
Hubei	13.3	47.2
Hunan	9.7	32.9
Guangdong	12.7	59.0
Guangxi	8.2	38.1
Sichuan	9.2	27.3
Guizhou	8.9	30.0
Yunnan	8.3	28.9
Tibet	8.6	12.3
Shaanxi	12.6	39.5
Gansu	11.4	39.3
Qinghai	17.0	33.9
Ningxia	15.1	40.1
Xinjiang	22.4	43.2

Source: *Statistical Yearbook of China*, 1981, 1986.

Table A6.14   Urban population by state (India)

State	Urban population (million)			Share of urban in total population (%)		
	1961	*1971*	*1981*	*1961*	*1971*	*1981*
Andhra Pradesh	6.28	8.40	12.49	17.44	19.31	23.32
Assam	0.91	1.47	2.05	7.37*	9.20*	10.30*
Bihar	3.91	5.63	8.72	8.43	9.99	12.47
Gujarat	5.32	7.50	10.60	25.77	28.09	31.10
Haryana	1.31	1.77	2.83	17.23	17.65	21.90
Himachal Pradesh	0.18	0.24	0.32	6.34	6.94	7.47
Jammu and Kashmir	0.59	0.86	1.26	16.57	18.61	21.03
Karnataka	5.26	7.12	10.73	22.30	24.30	28.89
Kerala	2.56	3.47	4.77	15.08	16.25	18.74
Madhya Pradesh	4.63	6.78	10.59	14.30	16.28	20.29
Maharashtra	11.16	15.71	21.99	28.22	31.16	35.03
Orissa	1.11	1.84	3.11	8.97	8.39	11.79
Punjab	2.57	3.22	4.47	23.06	23.76	26.62
Rajasthan	3.28	4.54	7.21	16.28	17.62	21.04
Tamil Nadu	8.99	12.47	15.95	26.69	30.27	32.95
Uttar Pradesh	9.48	12.39	19.90	12.85	14.03	17.95
West Bengal	8.54	10.97	14.44	24.45	24.76	26.45
All India	78.94	109.11	159.72	17.98	19.91	23.31

Sources: Government of India, Ministry of Health and Family Welfare, *Health Information of India, 1987*, pp. 10–15, for 1961, 1971 and 1981; and *ESCAP, Population of India, Country Monograph No. 10*, UN, New York, 1982, p. 56.

Note: * combined figures for Assam and Meghalaya.

Table A6.15   Rate of literacy by province (China): number of
illiterates/semi-literates per 1,000 population (age 12 years and over)

Province	Literacy rate (1986)
Beijing	125.0
Tianjin	140.0
Hebei	225.0
Shanxi	181.0
Inner Mongolia	225.0
Liaoning	130.0
Jilin	163.0
Heilongjiang	162.0
Shanghai	144.0
Jiangsu	273.0
Zhejiang	243.0
Anhui	337.0
Fujian	265.0
Jiangxi	222.0
Shandong	281.0
Henan	271.0
Hubei	235.0
Hunan	178.0
Guangdong	168.0
Guangxi	176.0
Sichuan	236.9
Guizhou	323.0
Yunnan	339.0
Tibet	518.0
Shaanxi	247.9
Gansu	350.0
Qinghai	320.0
Ningxia	290.0
Xinjiang	211.0

Source: *Statistical Yearbook of China*, 1986, p. 79.

Table A6.16   Rate of literacy by state: India (percentage of literates to total population)

State	Literacy rate	
	1971	*1981*
Andhra Pradesh	24.6	29.9
Assam	28.1	–
Bihar	19.9	26.2
Gujarat	35.8	43.7
Haryana	26.9	36.1
Himachal Pradesh	31.9	42.5
Jammu and Kashmir	18.6	26.7
Karnataka	31.5	38.4
Kerala	60.4	70.4
Madhya Pradesh	22.1	27.9
Maharashtra	39.2	47.2
Manipur	32.9	41.3
Meghalaya	29.5	34.1
Nagaland	27.4	42.6
Orissa	26.2	34.2
Punjab	33.7	40.9
Rajasthan	19.1	24.4
Sikkim	17.7	34.0
Tamil Nadu	39.4	46.8
Tripura	31.0	42.1
Uttar Pradesh	21.7	27.2
West Bengal	33.2	40.9
All India	29.4	36.2*

Source: Government of India, Registrar General, *Census of India*, 1981, New Delhi.
* Excludes Assam.

Table A7.1 Tractor area, power-irrigated area and fertiliser consumption by province (China)

Province	Tractor-ploughed area (%)			Power-irrigated area (%)			Fertiliser consumption (tons per 1,000 ha)		
	1981	1985	1988	1982	1985	1988	1981	1985	1988
Beijing	75.4	49.7	71.8	82.0	83.1	84.0	237.8	674.7	1,004.0
Tianjin	82.1	53.7	91.2	100.0	100.0	98.9	86.3	454.7	558.9
Hebei	48.7	32.2	53.1	85.0	89.6	91.7	110.0	551.1	565.4
Shanxi	37.8	48.2	52.6	69.3	72.0	73.5	70.4	412.2	337.3
Inner Mongolia	20.8	17.8	29.2	49.2	54.5	59.8	16.0	119.8	111.5
Liaoning	51.5	50.6	63.2	81.7	82.4	83.1	169.8	737.7	519.5
Jilin	34.3	34.1	39.9	58.1	58.6	61.8	76.9	391.7	348.5
Heilongjiang	66.5	61.4	59.7	68.6	57.7	53.8	40.8	122.1	71.6
Shanghai	90.4	44.7	88.4	100.0	100.0	100.0	482.0	1,041.7	2,250.7
Jiangsu	63.7	37.9	76.8	92.6	92.1	60.2	270.0	820.3	1,325.2
Zhejiang	50.2	16.4	45.0	75.4	76.0	66.4	344.0	757.2	1,904.9
Anhui	18.8	11.8	38.0	70.1	65.3	71.0	162.3	648.4	813.5
Fujian	31.2	13.5	31.6	20.9	21.2	16.6	302.6	882.3	1,376.6
Jiangxi	23.6	8.5	24.1	31.7	20.6	21.8	148.4	351.1	563.6
Shandong	59.0	40.8	70.7	83.6	84.8	86.4	202.7	693.4	863.2

Henan	36.0	21.4	52.9	75.8	75.1	72.2	115.8	567.1	689.2
Hubei	29.8	7.9	25.3	60.6	59.0	61.2	153.9	528.2	1,015.7
Hunan	15.0	4.6	18.0	47.3	37.0	77.3	248.1	494.3	943.5
Guangdong	27.9	12.8	29.4	24.7	26.3	32.0	269.4	639.4	1,107.9
Guangxi	24.4	10.5	25.6	18.8	16.7	18.0	169.3	512.7	590.5
Sichuan	11.0	4.4	8.8	20.4	20.3	22.5	181.2	500.8	756.7
Guizhou	0.7	0.09	0.6	19.5	13.7	11.4	118.8	296.9	312.8
Yunnan	6.8	4.1	11.7	13.5	12.5	13.7	90.6	389.3	371.4
Tibet	24.2	10.0	8.0	5.2	6.0	8.5	8.9	119.0	49.5
Shaanxi	28.0	24.9	42.8	63.3	61.8	63.2	70.7	373.5	454.2
Gansu	13.8	16.0	19.6	33.1	28.7	34.9	36.4	208.3	129.5
Qinghai	25.8	25.7	27.9	13.5	14.0	10.7	53.1	235.5	98.6
Ningxia	18.5	21.2	32.3	12.9	15.2	20.1	48.8	280.2	325.4
Xinjiang	63.6	65.9	68.3	7.6	8.4	9.4	38.1	184.4	120.9

Sources: *Statistical Yearbook of China*, 1981 and 1989; and *Agriculture Yearbook of China*, 1986.

Notes: (1) Consumption of fertilisers per 1,000 ha is calculated by dividing the total consumption of fertilisers by total sown/cultivated area;

(2) Share of power-irrigated area is total power-irrigated area divided by total irrigated area; and

(3) Total tractor-ploughed area is percentage of total sown/cultivated area.

Table A7.2 Power-irrigated area, agricultural consumption of electricity and fertiliser consumption by state (India)

State	Power-irrigated area (%) 1982–83[1]	Agricultural consumption of electricity (%)		Fertiliser consumption (ton per 1,000 ha) 1985–86
		1981–82	1985–86	
Andhra Pradesh	4.9	16.5	27.0	112.4
Assam	–	1.3	0.9	7.3
Bihar	29.7	10.9	14.2	53.2
Gujarat	13.2	16.2	16.7	100.7
Haryana	45.7	38.6	40.3	94.5
Himachal Pradesh	6.4	2.1	3.7	23.0
Jammu and Kashmir	0.6	5.6	5.8	34.9
Karnataka	0.1	7.1	17.2	78.9
Kerala	–	3.5	2.7	194.4
Madhya Pradesh	1.9	7.8	8.7	23.4
Maharashtra	–	12.6	17.5	49.0
Manipur	–	8.5	3.0	–
Meghalaya	–	0.03	0.1	–
Nagaland	–	–	–	–
Orissa	1.9	2.2	3.3	20.3
Punjab	57.4	3.6	36.0	204.0
Rajasthan	5.2	32.9	29.0	16.4
Sikkim	–	–	–	–
Tamil Nadu	6.3	27.1	26.7	149.3
Tripura	–	7.9	15.9	–
Uttar Pradesh	54.4	33.3	32.2	103.8
West Bengal	32.1	1.1	1.7	76.3
All India	26.7	15.7	19.8	–

Sources: Government of India, Ministry of Agriculture, *Agricultural Statistics at a Glance*, New Delhi, 1988, and *Indian Agriculture in Brief*, New Delhi, 1986.

Notes: 1. Area under tubewell irrigation.
   – = not available.

Table A7.3 R&D expenditure and scientists/engineers per 1,000
population by province (China)

Province	R&D expenditure per capita (yuan) 1986	Scientists and engineers per 1,000	
		1981	1986
Beijing	301.13	3.41	9.32
Tianjin	68.67	1.80	1.98
Hebei	5.22	0.48	0.22
Shanxi	14.10	0.62	0.38
Inner Mongolia	8.81	0.68	0.35
Liaoning	25.69	1.02	0.71
Jilin	15.73	0.87	0.60
Heilongjiang	12.73	0.92	0.46
Shanghai	128.69	2.23	3.46
Jiangsu	12.55	0.44	0.39
Zhejiang	7.41	0.35	0.26
Anhui	3.90	0.34	0.15
Fujian	6.81	0.46	0.25
Jiangxi	5.72	0.45	0.19
Shandong	7.15	0.38	0.17
Henan	5.55	0.35	0.17
Hubei	8.98	0.67	0.31
Hunan	7.33	0.45	0.21
Guangdong	9.94	0.40	0.25
Guangxi	4.87	0.44	0.17
Sichuan	10.59	0.47	0.29
Guizhou	5.35	0.45	0.19
Yunnan	8.29	0.44	0.24
Tibet	8.91	0.67	0.17
Shaanxi	23.59	0.78	0.74
Gansu	14.05	0.60	0.40
Qinghai	20.16	0.94	0.63
Ningxia	16.83	0.77	0.54
Xinjiang	13.11	0.92	0.42
China	14.17	0.57	0.43

Sources: For R&D expenditure, *Statistical Yearbook of China*, 1987, p. 702;
and for scientists and engineers, *Statistical Yearbook of China*,
1981, p. 464, and 1987, p. 705.

Table A7.4   R&D expenditure in industry by State in India

State	Total R&D expenditure 1984–85 1986–87 (Rs 100 thousand)		Per capita expenditure 1984–85 1986–87 (Rs)	
	1984–85	1986–87	1984–85	1986–87
Andhra Pradesh	4,201.87	5,795.92	7.36	9.78
Assam	107.03	282.51	0.49	1.25
Bihar	2,801.93	3,930.81	3.73	5.01
Gujarat	2,765.99	3,919.44	7.57	10.33
Haryana	987.52	1,665.21	6.96	11.14
Karnataka	9,117.74	9,706.42	22.82	23.33
Kerala	430.75	482.34	1.59	1.72
Madhya Pradesh	292.28	370.55	0.52	0.63
Maharashtra	10,194.68	15,761.97	15.10	22.47
Orissa	333.33	274.92	1.19	0.94
Punjab	351.26	472.29	1.95	2.53
Rajasthan	568.44	920.87	1.51	2.32
Tamil Nadu	2,601.94	3,864.78	5.08	7.31
Uttar Pradesh	1,177.47	1,203.00	0.99	0.97
West Bengal	2,187.74	3,102.86	3.75	5.11
Total	39,141.61	54,259.79	5.39	7.03

Source: Government of India, Department of Science and Technology, *Research and Development in Industry 1986–87*, New Delhi, October 1988.

Note: R&D expenditure includes expenditures by public sector, private sector and small-scale industrial units.

Table A8.1   Doctors and health workers per 1,000 population by province (China)

Province	Doctors per 1,000				Health workers per 1,000		
	1978	1981	1984	1989	1981	1984	1988
Beijing	3.3	4.2	4.4	4.7	9.0	9.4	10.5
Tianjin	2.0	3.0	3.2	4.0	7.2	7.4	7.6
Hebei	1.0	1.2	1.3	1.0	2.5	2.8	2.9
Shanxi	1.45	1.75	1.8	2.09	3.8	4.1	4.5
Inner Mongolia	2.0	1.68	1.76	2.0	4.09	4.3	4.5
Liaoning	1.54	1.67	0.65	2.19	4.75	5.14	5.6
Jilin	1.41	1.61	1.70	2.0	4.21	4.55	4.8
Heilongjiang	1.45	1.63	1.69	2.04	4.32	4.58	4.9
Shanghai	3.05	3.78	3.98	4.54	8.25	8.46	9.1
Jiangsu	1.0	1.08	1.21	1.5	2.69	2.86	3.1

Table A8.1   *continued*

Province	Doctors per 1,000				Health workers per 1,000		
	1978	*1981*	*1984*	*1989*	*1981*	*1984*	*1988*
Zhejiang	0.87	0.95	1.07	1.38	2.53	2.85	2.9
Anhui	1.0	0.86	0.88	1.0	2.23	2.35	2.4
Fujian	0.90	0.90	0.97	1.21	2.42	2.68	2.9
Jiangxi	1.0	1.12	1.19	1.0	2.75	2.95	3.1
Shandong	0.58	0.92	1.00	1.27	2.40	2.59	2.9
Henan	0.62	0.92	1.05	1.21	2.20	2.49	2.6
Hubei	1.13	1.37	1.43	1.63	3.52	3.75	3.9
Hunan	1.0	1.15	1.22	1.3	2.61	2.75	2.9
Guangdong	0.95	1.08	1.16	1.31	2.99	3.19	3.2
Guangxi	1.0	0.96	1.10	1.0	2.04	2.31	2.6
Sichuan	1.02	1.11	1.22	1.42	2.61	2.8	2.8
Guizhou	1.0	0.92	0.98	1.0	2.44	2.59	2.7
Yunnan	1.01	1.14	1.22	1.42	2.39	2.5	2.7
Tibet	1.92	2.15	2.03	2.20	3.76	3.55	3.3
Shaanxi	1.0	1.43	1.55	2.0	3.07	3.37	3.7
Gansu	1.19	1.34	1.33	1.48	2.78	2.87	3.2
Qinghai	1.0	2.09	1.99	2.0	4.45	4.48	4.7
Ningxia	1.44	1.56	1.47	1.94	3.39	3.69	4.0
Xinjiang	1.4	1.76	1.86	2.3	4.83	5.05	5.3
China	1.08	1.25	1.34	–	–	–	3.4

Sources: *Statistical Yearbook of China (SYC)*, 1981 and 1985; and State Statistical Bureau: *Li Shi Tong Ji Zi Liao Hui Bian, 1949–1989* (A Compilation of Historical Statistics).

Note: – = not available.

Table A8.2   Doctors and health assistants per 1,000 population by state: India

State	Doctors per 1,000			Health assistants per 1,000		
	1981	*1986*	*1988*	*1981*	*1986*	*1988*
Andhra Pradesh	0.078	0.480	0.510	0.513	0.060	–
Assam	0.075	0.134	–	0.255	0.038	0.038
Bihar	0.190	0.171	–	0.222	0.029	–
Gujarat	0.342	0.253	0.300	0.396	0.050	0.063
Haryana	0.160	0.164	–	0.302	0.053	0.048
Himachal Pradesh	0.124	0.116	0.210	0.252	0.107	0.132
Jammu and Kashmir	0.133	0.105	0.536	0.868	0.030	–

continued on page 292

Table A8.2   *continued*

State	Doctors per 1,000			Health assistants per 1,000		
	1981	1986	1988	1981	1986	1988
Karnataka	0.102	0.109	0.649	1.120	0.133	–
Kerala	0.388	0.174	–	0.203	0.032	–
Madhya Pradesh	0.080	0.138	0.148	2.107	0.051	0.048
Maharashtra	0.484	0.578	0.602	0.439	0.071	0.085
Manipur	0.289	–	–	–	–	0.085
Meghalaya	0.142	–	0.182	–	–	–
Nagaland	0.279	–	–	–	–	–
Orissa	0.101	0.156	0.168	0.270	0.064	0.060
Punjab	0.172	0.182	0.178	0.483	0.117	–
Rajasthan	0.092	0.090	0.294	–	0.052	0.051
Sikkim	0.243	–	–	–	–	0.029
Tamil Nadu	0.129	0.138	0.826	–	0.031	–
Tripura	0.172	–	0.236	–	–	–
Uttar Pradesh	0.054	0.242	0.064	–	0.067	0.074
West Bengal	0.443	0.482	0.468	–	0.033	–

Source: Government of India, Ministry of Health and Social Welfare, *Health Information of India*.

Note: Data may not be comparable due to incompleteness.
    – = not available.

Table A8.3   Number of doctors by state (India) (Census data)

Province	1961	1971	1981
Andhra Pradesh	25,995	43,441	51,378
Assam	7,265	10,957	–
Bihar	22,174	27,922	44,041
Gurajat	8,407	19,461	30,791
Haryana	–	21,399	17,947
Himachal Pradesh	109	3,193	4,517
Jammu and Kashmir	1,113	4,549	6,644
Kerala	18,052	25,679	29,185
Madhya Pradesh	9,477	20,846	34,593
Maharashtra	9,136	35,215	61,932
Karnataka	18,581	18,952	30,368
Orissa	5,734	9,634	11,183
Punjab	19,218	13,650	27,255
Rajasthan	2,177	15,447	26,357
Uttar Pradesh	29,766	52,760	95,556

Table A8.3   *continued*

Province	1961	1971	1981
Tamil Nadu	–	32,346	41,077
West Bengal	31,265	49,096	50,764
Arunachal Pradesh	–	177	474
All India	242,292	420,947	588,177

Source: Government of India, Registrar General, *Censuses of India*, 1961, 1971 and 1981.

Table A8.4   Hospitals and hospital beds per 1,000 population by province (China)

Province	Hospitals per 1,000 population			Hospital beds per 1,000 population		
	1981	*1986*	*1988*	*1981*	*1986*	*1988*
Beijing	0.044	0.038	0.040	3.3	4.2	4.5
Tianjin	0.043	0.034	0.036	2.6	3.3	3.6
Hebei	0.082	0.057	0.059	1.7	1.9	2.1
Shanxi	0.094	0.093	0.094	2.8	3.2	3.4
Inner Mongolia	0.094	0.087	0.086	2.5	2.5	2.7
Liaoning	0.048	0.048	0.050	3.2	3.8	4.3
Jilin	0.056	0.056	0.056	2.8	3.2	3.4
Heilongjiang	0.054	0.048	0.048	2.8	2.9	3.0
Shanghai	0.034	0.034	0.037	4.3	4.4	4.7
Jiangsu	0.041	0.039	0.039	1.9	2.1	2.2
Zhejiang	0.091	0.078	0.078	1.6	1.8	2.0
Anhui	0.064	0.061	0.057	1.5	1.6	1.7
Fujian	0.044	0.041	0.042	1.8	1.9	2.0
Jiangxi	0.066	0.063	0.062	2.1	2.2	2.2
Shandong	0.034	0.034	0.034	1.6	1.7	1.9
Henan	0.034	0.034	0.034	1.5	1.8	2.0
Hubei	0.038	0.036	0.038	2.4	2.3	2.4
Hunan	0.081	0.072	0.070	2.1	2.1	2.2
Guangdong	0.041	0.035	0.032	1.7	1.8	1.8
Guangxi	0.034	0.035	0.035	1.3	1.5	1.6
Sichuan	0.104	0.078	0.077	1.8	1.8	1.7
Guizhou	0.162	0.111	0.125	1.4	1.5	1.6
Yunnan	0.057	0.051	0.052	1.9	2.0	2.1
Tibet	0.284	0.192	0.222	2.6	2.4	2.3
Shaanxi	0.108	0.080	0.080	2.0	2.2	2.3
Gansu	0.087	0.070	0.071	1.7	1.9	2.0

continued on page 294

Table A8.4   *continued*

Province	Hospitals per 1,000 population			Hospital beds per 1,000 population		
	1981	1986	1988	1981	1986	1988
Qinghai	0.139	0.110	0.111	2.9	3.4	3.3
Ningxia	0.079	0.065	0.046	1.8	2.1	2.2
Xinjiang	0.069	0.069	0.071	3.7	3.9	4.1
China	0.081	0.056	0.056	2.02	2.18	2.3

Sources: *Statistical Yearbook of China (SYC)*, 1981 and 1987; and *Li Shi Tong Ji Zi Liao Hui Bian 1949–1989* (A Compilation of Historical Statistics).

Table A8.5   Hospitals and hospital beds per 1,000 population by state (India)

State	Hospitals			Hospital beds		
	1981	1986	1988	1981	1986	1988
Andhra Pradesh	0.011	0.010	–	0.628	0.609	–
Assam	0.005	0.005	0.008	0.476	0.507	0.605
Bihar	0.003	0.003	–	0.320	0.359	–
Gujarat	0.024	0.037	0.039	0.934	1.046	1.180
Haryana	0.006	0.005	0.004	0.552	0.512	0.476
Himachal Pradesh	0.012	0.014	0.013	0.742	0.862	0.846
Jammu and Kashmir	0.005	0.007	–	0.656	1.094	–
Karnataka	0.006	0.006	0.006	0.793	0.769	0.782
Kerala	0.029	0.012	0.070	1.682	1.918	2.547
Madhya Pradesh	0.005	0.005	0.006	0.317	0.347	0.362
Maharashtra	0.015	0.022	–	1.103	1.309	–
Orissa	0.011	0.010	0.010	0.834	0.437	0.427
Punjab	0.015	0.014	–	0.407	0.808	–
Rajasthan	0.006	0.006	0.006	0.479	0.499	0.486
Tamil Nadu	0.011	0.008	0.007	0.834	0.861	0.863
Uttar Pradesh	0.006	0.006	–	0.407	0.373	–
West Bengal	0.007	0.007	0.006	0.883	0.893	0.856

Sources: For health data, *Health Information of India, 1982*, p. 91, 1987, pp. 141–2 and 1989, p. 139. For population estimates for 1986, A. N. Agarwal, H. O. Varma, R. C. Gupta, *India – Economic Information Yearbook, 1988–89*, New Delhi, National Publishing House, 1988, p. 63; and for population estimates for 1988, Reserve Bank of India, *Report on Currency and Finance, 1987–88*, vol. II, Statistical Statements, Bombay, 1989.

Table A8.6   *Per capita* public health expenditure by province (China, 1981)

Province	Total public expenditure* (million yuan)	Per capita public expenditure (yuan)
Beijing	92.32	10.2
Tianjin	84.61	11.1
Hebei	149.33	2.8
Shanxi	86.00	3.4
Inner Mongolia	89.71	4.7
Liaoning	195.42	5.5
Jilin	116.71	5.2
Heilongjiang	146.57	4.5
Shanghai	114.50	9.8
Jiangsu	190.74	3.2
Zhejiang	136.87	3.5
Anhui	123.04	2.4
Fujian	109.48	4.3
Jiangxi	105.16	3.2
Shandong	237.54	3.2
Henan	198.13	2.7
Hubei	163.03	3.4
Hunan	161.59	3.0
Guangdong	218.49	3.7
Guangxi	105.15	2.9
Sichuan	260.88	2.6
Guizhou	79.35	2.8
Yunnan	105.53	3.3
Xizang	31.60	16.9
Shaanxi	114.04	4.0
Gansu	67.86	3.5
Qinghai	34.67	9.1
Ningxia	26.93	7.1
Xinjiang	79.32	6.0
Total	3,624.57	3.6

Source: * Data taken from Jamison *et al.*, *CHINA – The Health Sector*, World Bank, Washington DC, 1984, Vol. II, Statistical data, Table E-7. It includes recurrent plus capital expenditure but excludes government insurance.

Table A8.7   *Per capita* public health expenditure by state (India) (Rs)

Province	Per capita public expenditure		
	1977–78	*1981–82*	*1985–86*
Andhra Pradesh	17.0	22.51	39.08
Assam	12.0	19.38	44.93
Bihar	8.0	14.49	23.79
Gujarat	18.0	26.71	44.45
Haryana	19.0	37.10	60.05
Himachal Pradesh	–	101.29	133.08
Jammu and Kashmir	44.0	94.72	156.10
Karnataka	16.0	21.00	34.24
Kerala	23.0	35.61	45.36
Madhya Pradesh	14.0	23.05	40.67
Maharashtra	19.0	33.26	63.43
Orissa	13.0	22.18	33.32
Punjab	26.0	32.55	55.37
Rajasthan	23.0	37.22	65.87
Tamil Nadu	16.0	30.10	47.57
Uttar Pradesh	9.0	14.38	26.51
West Bengal	16.0	27.78	37.54
All India	16.0	29.86	46.23

Sources: *Health Information of India, 1987*, p. 73, and 1988, pp. 66–7. For 1977–8, data are taken from Raj Krishna, The Centre and the Periphery – Interstate Disparities in Economic Development, in *Facets of India's Development – G.L. Mehta Memorial Lectures*, Bombay 1986, p. 51.
– = not available.

Table A9.1 Population by educational attainment by province (China, 1982) (percentages)

Province/region/municipality	Illiterates/semi-literates	Primary school leavers	Junior secondary	Senior secondary	College graduates
China	23.5	35.4	17.8	6.6	0.4
Shanxi	24.7	32.7	19.4	7.9	0.6
Guizhou	32.1	28.8	11.4	3.0	0.3
Henan	26.9	31.2	19.2	6.3	0.2
Yunnan	33.7	29.3	10.2	2.8	0.2
Guangxi	17.2	38.8	15.7	6.5	0.3
Gansu	34.9	27.7	12.2	6.3	0.4
Sichuan	23.4	41.4	15.5	4.0	0.3
Anhui	33.4	29.7	14.2	4.0	0.3
Ningxia	28.9	25.7	15.5	5.3	0.5
Jiangxi	22.0	38.6	13.3	5.5	0.3
Tibet	51.8	16.5	3.6	1.2	0.4
Quinghai	31.9	25.7	14.0	5.1	0.7
Hunan	17.6	43.0	17.3	6.5	0.3
Inner Mongolia	22.4	32.8	19.3	7.5	0.4
Fujian	26.3	36.3	12.6	5.7	0.5

continued on page 298

Table A9.1 continued

Province/region/municipality	Illiterates/semi-literates	Primary school leavers	Junior secondary	Senior secondary	College graduates
Hebei	22.3	36.4	19.3	7.5	0.3
Xinjiang	20.9	33.8	17.5	6.4	0.5
Shanxi	18.0	38.8	21.9	7.4	0.4
Shandong	28.0	33.7	17.7	5.9	0.3
Jilin	16.2	36.0	20.9	10.8	0.6
Hubei	23.3	35.6	18.7	7.5	0.4
Guangdong	16.4	40.6	16.9	7.9	0.4
Zhejiang	24.2	39.4	17.8	5.2	0.3
Jiangsu	27.2	32.6	20.1	7.0	0.5
Heilongjiang	16.1	35.5	22.2	9.4	0.5
Liaoning	12.9	35.7	27.6	9.3	0.7
Beijing	12.4	26.2	29.1	17.6	3.6
Tianjin	13.9	30.8	28.5	13.3	1.6
Shanghai	14.3	25.2	28.0	20.3	2.4

Source: State Council Population Census Office and SSB Population Statistics Division, *Zhongguo Disanci Renkuo Pucha de Zhuyao Shuzi.* Cited in John S. Aird, 'The Preliminary Results of China's 1982 Census', *China Quarterly*, No. 96, December 1983.

Table A9.2 Population by educational attainment by state (India, 1981) (percentages)

State	Illiterates	Primary school	Junior secondary	Senior secondary	Graduates & above
India	63.8	10.9	4.2	1.5	1.40
Andra Pradesh	70.0	11.3	3.3	1.2	1.06
Bihar	73.8	5.1	4.2	0.99	0.81
Gujarat	56.3	11.8	6.0	1.0	1.53
Haryana	63.9	10.4	4.6	1.34	1.39
Himachal Pradesh	57.5	14.31	4.4	1.09	1.21
Jammu and Kashmir	73.3	7.1	3.8	1.43	1.38
Karnataka	61.5	12.2	4.8	1.37	1.37
Kerala	29.6	23.2	6.4	1.39	1.38
Madhya Pradesh	70.2	7.6	1.44	1.72	1.16
Maharashtra	52.8	13.8	6.29	1.43	1.82
Manipur	58.6	9.6	4.85	2.04	1.97
Meghalaya	65.9	9.7	2.84	0.89	1.19
Nagaland	57.4	11.9	3.87	0.90	0.77
Orissa	65.8	9.5	2.26	0.60	0.74
Punjab	59.1	12.8	6.2	1.76	1.72
Rajasthan	75.6	6.9	1.9	1.49	1.07
Sikkim	65.8	11.7	2.5	0.94	0.94
Tamil Nadu	53.2	16.3	6.7	1.34	1.26
Tripura	57.9	10.7	3.1	1.75	1.02
Uttar Pradesh	72.8	7.6	2.8	1.74	1.36
West Bengal	59.1	15.3	4.0	1.95	1.95
Arunachal Pradesh	79.2	4.7	2.0	0.63	0.79

Source: Government of India, Registrar General, *Census of India*, 1981, Series I, Social and Cultural Tables, Part IV A, New Delhi, December 1987.

Table A9.3   Per capita public expenditure on education by state (India)

State	Per capita public expenditure (Rs)		
	1977–78	*1981–82*	*1985–86*
Andhra Pradesh	33.0	61.1	101.1
Assam	27.0	53.2	99.7
Bihar	18.0	40.1	64.3
Gujarat	39.0	69.9	147.2
Haryana	35.0	71.5	199.9
Himachal Pradesh	–	113.0	180.6
Jammu and Kashmir	50.0	88.3	145.9
Karnataka	40.0	59.4	109.3
Kerala	64.0	105.5	148.4
Madhya Pradesh	26.0	44.2	82.2
Maharashtra	39.0	71.2	120.5
Orissa	30.0	50.6	76.7
Punjab	50.0	80.3	146.2
Rajasthan	35.0	51.1	99.1
Tamil Nadu	35.0	61.2	108.4
Uttar Pradesh	25.0	34.3	64.3
West Bengal	30.0	58.8	97.3
All India	33.0	57.7	100.4

Sources: Government of India, *A Handbook of Educational and Allied Statistics*, Ministry of Education and Culture, New Delhi and *Selected Educational Statistics*, 1985–6, Department of Education, 1987. For 1977–8, data are taken from Raj Krishna, 'The Centre and the Periphery – Interstate Disparities in Economic Development', in *Facets of India's Development – G.L. Mehta Memorial Lectures*, Bombay, 1986.

Table A9.4 Primary and secondary school enrolment rates by state (India)

State	Primary			Secondary (Junior)		
	1970	*1978*	*1985*	*1970*	*1978*	*1985*
Andhra Pradesh	66.2	77.1	99.0	22.7	27.7	30.8
Assam	66.6	72.2	89.8	34.8	37.4	65.9
Bihar	56.4	75.9	80.3	22.6	28.4	30.7
Gujarat	81.3	99.8	109.4	36.1	46.7	59.7
Haryana	59.9	71.9	86.2	42.2	44.7	55.3
Himachal Pradesh	80.1	122.9	109.1	47.1	57.0	85.9
Jammu and Kashmir	59.2	66.9	78.1	34.3	37.9	46.8
Karnataka	84.7	90.9	80.7	32.1	37.9	69.0
Kerala	119.0	90.5	108.9	63.5	90.5	95.1
Madhya Pradesh	53.7	60.3	95.2	25.3	29.2	44.8
Maharashtra	86.4	107.1	117.3	40.9	45.5	63.7
Manipur	132.5	115.7	121.4	45.5	55.5	70.9
Meghalaya	97.5	118.0	101.6	24.3	41.0	56.5
Nagaland	139.5	124.8	122.6	52.6	54.5	53.9
Orissa	64.6	80.5	93.0	20.2	27.4	37.3
Punjab	76.5	109.6	97.4	46.9	59.0	59.7
Rajasthan	46.5	52.3	78.5	22.4	27.2	38.3
Sikkim	–	122.5	128.3	–	27.8	54.5
Tamil Nadu	96.9	110.4	130.6	45.8	50.7	73.8
Tripura	75.2	78.7	114.9	34.6	34.8	49.1
Uttar Pradesh	90.8	67.0	60.4	35.7	34.7	40.7
West Bengal	76.7	71.7	113.6	34.4	30.5	59.3
Arunachal Pradesh	33.1	71.8	84.9	11.5	19.9	47.1

Sources: Government of India, Ministry of Education, *A Handbook of Educational and Allied Statistics*, New Delhi (September 1983 (for data for 1970–71 and 1978–79); and A. N. Agarwal, H. O. Varma and R. C. Gupta, *India – Economic Information Yearbook, 1988–89*, New Delhi, 1988 (for data for 1985–86).

Table A9.5   Number of primary schools per 1,000 population by province (China)

Province	1961	1971	1978	1985 Total	Rural	Urban
Beijing	0.466	0.596	0.553	0.422	1.025	0.119
Tianjin	–	0.157	0.471	0.408	1.134	0.102
Hebei	0.937	0.958	0.889	0.889	1.003	0.473
Shanxi	1.408	1.768	1.386	1.613	2.057	0.241
Inner Mongolia	0.819	0.815	0.700	0.777	1.036	0.250
Liaoning	0.376	0.757	0.507	0.431	0.666	0.144
Jilin	0.493	1.046	0.953	0.479	0.596	0.324
Heilongjiang	0.483	0.889	0.937	0.548	0.810	0.175
Shanghai	0.496	0.431	0.344	0.262	0.492	0.112
Jiangsu	0.675	0.782	0.684	0.547	0.608	0.314
Zhejiang	0.776	–	1.195	0.906	1.195	0.199
Anhui	0.418	1.135	1.111	0.716	0.823	0.262
Fujian	0.707	1.140	1.238	0.980	1.246	0.216
Jiangxi	1.013	1.592	1.561	1.134	1.430	0.159
Shandong	0.855	1.143	1.108	0.923	0.901	1.183
Henan	0.482	0.658	0.696	0.543	0.629	0.175
Hubei	0.651	1.057	0.787	0.690	0.760	0.483
Hunan	0.902	0.993	0.990	0.908	1.009	0.556
Guangdong	0.654	0.701	0.526	0.472	0.568	0.190
Guangxi	–	–	0.400	0.384	0.412	0.377
Sichuan	0.539	1.028	1.005	0.832	0.947	0.265
Guizhou	0.265	1.104	1.509	0.904	1.117	0.179
Yunnan	0.748	1.691	2.182	1.717	2.012	0.342
Tibet	–	–	–	1.243	1.287	1.506
Shaanxi	0.922	1.506	1.428	1.293	1.556	0.430
Gansu	0.584	1.419	1.820	1.244	1.483	0.274
Qinghai	0.561	1.084	1.787	1.045	1.241	0.515
Ningxia	0.579	1.027	1.549	1.050	1.374	0.237
Xinjiang	0.312	0.703	0.792	0.598	0.765	0.251

Sources: China State Education Commission, *Achievement of Education in China, Statistics, 1949–1983*, Beijing, 1984; and *Achievement of Education in China, Statistics, 1980–1985*, Beijing, 1986.

Table A9.6   Number of secondary schools per 1,000 population by province (China)

Province	1961	1971	1978	1985 Total	Junior secondary school	Senior secondary school .
Beijing	0.055	0.092	0.124	0.090	0.058	0.031
Tianjin	–	0.041	0.144	0.093	0.062	0.031
Hebei	0.032	0.295	0.334	0.111	0.097	0.013
Shanxi	0.040	0.062	0.587	0.180	0.163	0.017
Inner Mongolia	0.015	0.050	0.199	0.102	0.079	0.022
Liaoning	0.028	0.090	0.112	0.068	0.053	0.014
Jilin	0.021	0.102	0.106	0.087	0.069	0.018
Heilongjiang	0.025	0.099	0.140	0.087	0.062	0.025
Shanghai	0.038	0.086	0.104	0.070	0.043	0.027
Jiangsu	0.033	0.097	0.101	0.100	0.083	0.017
Zhejiang	0.020	–	0.109	0.080	0.065	0.014
Anhui	0.016	0.056	0.083	0.081	0.068	0.012
Fujian	0.022	0.041	0.049	0.043	0.026	0.016
Jiangxi	0.027	0.088	0.097	0.077	0.059	0.017
Shandong	0.019	0.187	0.242	0.117	0.106	0.010
Henan	0.020	0.338	0.379	0.123	0.108	0.013
Hubei	0.020	0.134	0.215	0.113	0.098	0.015
Hunan	0.025	0.081	0.250	0.092	0.076	0.016
Guangdong	0.025	0.055	0.048	0.069	0.052	0.016
Guangxi	–	–	0.065	0.066	0.052	0.013
Sichuan	0.013	0.065	0.079	0.057	0.044	0.012
Guizhou	0.009	0.019	0.103	0.049	0.035	0.014
Yunnan	0.010	0.018	0.049	0.051	0.036	0.015
Tibet	–	–	–	0.028	0.020	0.007
Shaanxi	0.026	0.071	0.271	0.103	0.080	0.022
Gansu	0.016	0.037	0.065	0.068	0.044	0.024
Qinghai	0.017	0.024	0.222	0.106	0.060	0.045
Ningxia	0.019	0.113	0.198	0.105	0.072	0.033
Xinjiang	0.028	0.068	0.159	0.157	0.099	0.058

Source: *Statistical Yearbook of China*, 1986.

Table A9.7 Number of primary and secondary schools per 1,000 population by state (India)

State	Primary			Junior secondary			Senior Secondary		
	1970	1977	1985	1970	1977	1985	1970	1977	1985
Andhra Pradesh	0.846	0.767	0.723	0.071	0.084	0.095	0.066	0.067	0.080
Assam	1.202	1.162	1.179	0.209	0.201	0.219	0.091	0.092	0.109
Bihar	0.826	0.774	0.663	0.143	0.298	0.155	0.045	0.046	0.046
Gujarat	0.402	0.326	0.319	0.392	0.387	0.413	0.084	0.089	0.071
Haryana	0.416	0.424	0.348	0.075	0.062	0.076	0.096	0.094	0.122
Himachal	1.082	1.085	1.462	0.213	0.239	0.211	0.125	0.148	0.170
Jammu and Kashmir	1.047	1.164	1.166	0.312	0.356	0.325	0.120	0.134	0.121
Karnataka	0.736	0.637	0.606	0.367	0.335	0.346	0.067	0.068	0.093
Kerala	0.318	0.285	0.248	0.118	0.112	0.104	0.065	0.068	0.088
Madhya Pradesh	0.882	1.060	1.092	0.139	0.175	0.213	0.039	0.041	–
Maharashtra	0.562	0.543	0.544	0.330	0.272	0.233	0.102	0.097	0.097
Manipur	2.288	2.606	1.708	0.355	0.287	0.280	0.113	0.177	0.210
Meghalaya	2.478	2.739	2.748	0.206	0.302	0.397	0.079	0.128	0.179
Nagaland	1.601	1.552	1.380	0.596	0.394	0.372	0.107	0.144	0.120
Orissa	1.256	1.265	1.297	0.189	0.258	0.288	0.048	0.080	0.126
Punjab	0.533	0.610	0.673	0.077	0.108	0.078	0.097	0.114	0.124
Rajasthan	0.756	0.628	0.716	0.078	0.159	0.207	0.039	0.057	0.054
Tamil Nadu	0.629	0.950	1.270	0.142	0.139	0.327	0.063	0.060	0.145
Tripura	0.881	0.584	0.559	0.140	0.121	0.109	0.056	0.065	0.049
Uttar Pradesh	0.699	0.812	0.854	0.098	0.150	0.143	0.038	0.071	0.075
West Bengal	0.803	0.639	0.610	0.066	0.110	0.135	0.094	0.045	0.019
Arunachal Pradesh	–	0.805	0.837	–	0.062	0.065	–	0.094	0.092

Source: Government of India, Ministry of Education, A Handbook of Educational and Allied Statistics, New Delhi, several years.
 – = not available.

Table A9.8 Pupil–teacher ratios in schools by province (China)

Province	Primary				Secondary							
					Junior				Senior			
	1960	1970	1978	1985	1960	1970	1978	1985	1960	1970	1978	1985
Beijing	31	30	21	17	23	21	20	14	20	21	20	12
Tianjin	–	32	19	18	–	20	18	11	–	20	19	10
Hebei	37	30	29	24	24	20	18	16	22	20	21	14
Shanxi	32	29	28	21	21	21	18	17	20	21	21	15
Inner Mongolia	35	32	23	18	23	22	21	18	21	22	19	15
Liaoning	35	30	27	22	23	23	22	17	20	23	20	14
Jilin	34	30	26	22	24	23	20	17	19	23	22	14
Heilongjiang	35	29	26	22	23	30	19	17	19	30	17	14
Shanghai	40	25	17	17	24	16	17	12	21	16	18	11
Jiangsu	29	32	32	26	29	25	24	20	24	25	22	15
Zhejiang	34	31	28	26	27	21	22	22	21	21	20	17
Anhui	30	27	29	27	25	22	24	22	18	22	22	15
Fujian	36	28	27	27	23	21	22	21	21	21	22	15
Jiangxi	35	29	26	27	24	22	21	21	20	22	20	16
Shandong	36	28	27	23	25	19	17	17	23	19	21	16
Henan	37	32	26	24	24	21	16	16	20	21	23	15
Hubei	30	28	27	24	24	20	19	18	22	20	20	14

continued on page 306

306

Table A9.8 continued

| Province | Primary | | | | Secondary | | | | | | | |
| | | | | | Junior | | | | Senior | | | |
	1960	1970	1978	1985	1960	1970	1978	1985	1960	1970	1978	1985
Hunan	31	30	29	25	28	22	21	18	24	22	20	17
Guangdong	36	26	28	25	25	23	20	20	21	23	20	16
Guangxi	38	25	26	25	20	31	20	17	17	31	22	13
Sichuan	37	29	33	31	22	27	25	20	17	27	21	14
Guizhou	34	27	27	28	24	19	26	21	25	19	20	16
Yunnan	37	29	26	30	27	23	22	20	26	22	21	16
Tibet	–	–	26	15	–	5	18	14	–	–	58	10
Shaanxi	34	30	26	22	28	28	21	19	23	28	22	16
Gansu	39	29	29	22	26	25	23	21	26	25	24	18
Qinghai	40	23	25	22	20	28	22	18	19	28	20	16
Ningxia	40	26	28	29	24	19	27	20	27	19	24	18
Xinjiang	34	25	24	20	26	14	20	16	16	14	16	14
China	35	29	28	25	25	22	20	18	21	23	21	15

Sources: China State Education Commission, *Achievement of Education in China – Statistics, 1949–1983*, Beijing, 1984; and *Achievement of Education in China, Statistics, 1980–1985*, Beijing, 1986.

Table A9.9   Pupil–teacher ratios in schools by state (India)

State	Primary			Junior secondary			Senior secondary		
	1970–71	1978–79	1985–86	1970–71	1978–79	1985–86	1970–71	1978–79	1985–86
Andhra Pradesh	39	47	56	31	34	42	18	24	32
Assam	42	33	45	25	24	30	23	23	28
Bihar	39	40	48	33	35	40	29	29	34
Gujarat	37	40	40	37	38	40	27	26	26
Haryana	41	40	45	31	33	35	31	27	34
Himachal Pradesh	28	31	38	20	23	19	25	26	30
Jammu and Kashmir	32	26	29	23	20	22	22	19	21
Karnataka	42	45	40	39	45	43	23	25	26
Kerala	39	40	33	33	28	32	27	28	28
Madhya Pradesh	33	35	43	27	26	28	23	23	n.a.
Maharashtra	33	39	39	34	35	38	25	28	24
Manipur	22	16	20	22	19	18	20	22	20
Maghalaya	36	32	30	19	17	16	26	20	25
Nagaland	42	21	22	17	16	11	24	20	7
Orissa	33	36	39	16	17	32	19	18	17
Punjab	38	41	39	30	25	17	32	22	23
Rajasthan	30	39	46	23	27	31	21	21	20
Sikkim	–	23	15	–	19	19	–	20	22
Tamil Nadu	34	38	43	32	37	43	24	25	28
Tripura	36	32	40	26	22	30	20	21	28
Uttar Pradesh	52	37	41	31	22	23	29	29	35
West Bengal	36	36	39	28	41	45	28	22	32
Arunachal Pradesh	20	31	49	16	20	38	16	19	10
All India	38	38	41	30	32	35	25	25	27

Source: Government of India, Ministry of Education, *A Handbook of Educational and Allied Statistics*, New Delhi.

Notes: (1) Sikkim was not part of India in 1970–71. Hence no data.
(2) n.a. = not available.

Bibliography

Irma Adelman, 'Beyond Export-led Growth', *World Development*, September 1984.

Irma Adelman and Cynthia Taft Morris, *Economic Growth and Social Equity in Developing Countries*, Stanford, Stanford University Press, 1973.

A. N. Agarwal, H. O. Varma and R. C. Gupta, *INDIA – Economic Information Yearbook, 1988–89 and 1990–91* New Delhi, National Publishing House, 1988 and 1991.

P. Aguignier, 'Regional Disparities since 1978', in S. Feuchtwang, A. Hussain and T. Pairault (eds), *Transforming China's Economy in the Eighties, Vol. II, Management, Industry and the Urban Economy*, Boulder, Westview and London, Zed Books, 1988.

I. J. Ahluwalia, *Industrial Growth in India*, Delhi, Oxford University Press, 1985.

Isher Judge Ahluwalia, 'Industrial Growth in India – Performance and Prospects, *Journal of Development Economics*, vol. 23, 1986.

Isher Judge Ahluwalia and C. Rangarajan, 'A Study of Linkages Between Agriculture and Industry: The Indian Experience', in Jeffrey G. Williamson and Vadiraj R. Panchmukhi (eds), *The Balance Between Industry and Agriculture in Economic Development, Vol. 2, Sector Proportions*, London, Macmillan Press, 1989.

Aqueil Ahmad, 'Science and Technology in Development – Policy Options for India and China', *Economic and Political Weekly (Review of Agriculture)*, 23–30 December 1978.

Aqueil Ahmad, 'Toward Closer Links between Science and Society in India – A Futuristic Formula', *Technological Forecasting and Social Change*, vol. 25, 1984.

Iftikhar Ahmed and Vernon Ruttan (eds), *Generation and Diffusion of Agricultural Innovations: The Role of Institutional Factors*, Aldershot, Gower, 1988.

Almanac of China's Economy, 1981.

Samir Amin, *Unequal Development*, New York, Monthly Review Press, 1976.

Samir Amin, *Imperialism and Unequal Development*, New York, Monthly Review Press, 1977.

S. Anand and S. M. R. Kanbur, 'Inequality and Development – A Critique', a paper presented at the 25th Anniversary Symposium of Economic Growth Center, Yale University , 11–13 April, 1986.

S. Anand and S. M. R. Kanbur, 'The Kuznets Process and the Inequality–Development Relationship', Discussion Paper No. 249, Economics Department, Essex University, August 1984.

James E. Anderson, *Public Policymaking*, New York, Holt, Rinehart Winston, 1977, chapter 6 on 'Impact'.

Ronald Anderson, 'Health Status Indices and Access to Medical Care', *American Journal of Public Health*, vol. 68, no. 5, May 1978.

N. H. Antia, 'An Alternative Strategy for Health Care', *Economic and Political Weekly*, 21–28 December 1985.

N. H. Antia, 'The Mandwa Project: An Experiment in Community Participation', *International Journal of Health Services*, vol. 18, no. 1, 1988.

Erik Baark, 'The Technology Policy Reforms in China 1980–85: Concepts, Incentives, and Actors', Institute of Economics and Planning, Roskilde University Centre, *Working Paper No. 5/86*, April 1986.

Erik Baark, *Know-how as a Commodity: Contracts and Markets in the Diffusion of Technology in China*, RPI, University of Lund, 1986.

Erik Baark, *High Technology Innovation at the Chinese Academy of Sciences*, Institute of Economics and Planning, Roskilde University Centre, Denmark, September 1987.

Amaresh Bagchi, 'Decade of Economic Reform in China – A Retrospect', *Economic and Political Weekly*, 24 June 1989.

Amiya Kumar Bagchi, 'On the Political Economy of Technological Choice and Development', *Cambridge Journal of Economics*, vol. 2, no. 2, 1978.

A. K. Bagchi, *Public Intervention and Industrial Restructuring in China, India and Republic of Korea*, New Delhi ILO/ARTEP, 1987.

A. K. Bagchi, *Demand and Technology in India's Industrial Growth*, Calcutta (undated).

Debabar Banerji, *Health and Family Planning Services in India*, New Delhi, Lok Paksh, 1985.

Judith Banister, 'China: Recent Trends in Health and Mortality', *CIR Staff Paper No. 23*, Center for International Research (CIR), US Bureau of the Census, Washington DC, July 1986.

Judith Banister, *China's Changing Population*, Stanford, Stanford University Press, 1987.

Judith Banister and Samuel H. Preston, 'Mortality in China', *Population and Development Review*, vol. 7, no. 1, March 1981.

B. Bannerjee and J. B. Knight, 'Caste Discrimination in the Indian Labour Market', *Journal of Development Economics*, April 1985.

Pranab Bardhan, 'On Life and Death Questions', *Economic and Political Weekly*, Special Number, August 1974.

Pranab Bardhan, 'Little Girls and Death in India', *Economic and Political Weekly*, 4 September 1982.

Pranab Bardhan, *The Political Economy of Development in India*, Oxford, Basil Blackwell, 1984.

Pranab Bardhan, *Land, Labour and Rural Poverty*, Oxford, Oxford University Press, 1984.

P. K. Bardhan and T. N. Srinivasan (eds), *Poverty and Income Distribution in India*, Calcutta, Statistical Publishing Society, 1974.

Pranab K. Bardhan and T. N. Srinivasan (eds), *Rural Poverty in South Asia*, New York, Columbia University Press, 1988.

Pranab K. Bardhan, 'Agrarian Class Formation in India', in Bardhan and Srinivasan (eds), 1988, ibid.

Pranab K. Bardhan, 'Sex Disparity in Child Survival in Rural India', in Bardhan and Srinivasan (eds).

P. K. Bardhan, A. Vaidyanathan, Y. Alagh, G. S. Bhalla and A. Bhaduri, *Labour Absorption in Indian Agriculture – Some Exploratory Investigations*, Bangkok, ILO/ARTEP, 1978.

A. Barnabas, *Social Change in a North Indian Village*, Indian Institute of Public Administration, New Delhi, 1969.

Marianne Bastid, 'Chinese Educational Policies in the 1980s and Economic Development', *China Quarterly*, no. 98, June 1984.

Robert H. Bates, *Markets and States in Tropical Africa – The Political Basis of Agricultural Policies*, Berkeley, University of California Press, 1981.

Jere R. Behrman and Anil B. Deolalikar, 'Health and Nutrition', in H. B. Chenery and T. N. Srinivasan (eds), *Handbook on Economic Development*, vol. I, Amsterdam, North-Holland Publishing Co., 1988.

Bela Belassa, 'China's Economic Reforms in a Comparative Perspective', *Development Research Department Discussion Paper (Report No. DR 177)*, World Bank, Washington DC, April 1986.

Charles Bettelheim, 'Economic Reform in China', *Journal of Development Studies,* July 1988.

Amit Bhaduri, *Macroeconomics – The Dynamics of Commodity Production*, London, Macmillan Press, 1986.

Amit Bhaduri, *Alternative Development Strategies and the Poor*, paper presented at the ILO/SAREC Workshop on the Interrelationship between Macroeconomic Policies and Rural Development. Geneva, 11–13 December 1989.

M. R. Bhagavan, 'Capital Goods Sector in India', *Economic and Political Weekly,* 9 March 1985.

M. R. Bhagavan, 'A Critique of India's Economic Policies and Strategies', *Monthly Review*, New York, July–August 1987.

M. R. Bhagavan, *Technological Advance in the Third World – Strategies and Prospects*, London, Zed Books Press, 1990.

Jagdish Bhagwati, 'Education, Class Structure and Income Equality', *World Development*, May 1973.

J. N. Bhagwati and P. Desai, *INDIA: Planning for Industrialisation, and Trade Policies since 1951*, London, Oxford University Press, 1970.

J. Bhagwati and Sukhamoy Chakravarty, 'Contributions to Indian Economic Analysis: A Survey', *American Economic Association, Supplement to American Economic Review,* September 1969.

A. S. Bhalla, 'From Fel'dman to Mahalanobis in Economic Planning', *Kyklos*, March 1965.

A. S. Bhalla, 'Technological Transformation in China', *Economia Internazionale*, February–May 1984.

A. S. Bhalla, *Economic Transition in Hunan and Southern China*, London, Macmillan Press, 1984.

A. S. Bhalla, 'Rural–Urban Disparities in India and China', *World Development*, August 1990.

A. S. Bhalla, 'Computerisation in Chinese Industry', *Science and Public Policy*, August 1990.

A. S. Bhalla and Yue Ma, 'Sectoral Interdependence in the Chinese Economy in a Comparative Perspective', *Applied Economics*, August 1990.

A. S. Bhalla, 'Access to Health Services', *Journal of International Development*, July 1991.

G. S. Bhalla and D. S. Tyagi, *Patterns in Indian Agricultural Development – A District Level Study*, New Delhi, Institute for Studies in Industrial Development, 1989.

Sheila Bhalla, 'Agricultural Growth – Role of Institutional and Infrastructural Factors', *Economic and Political Weekly*, 5 and 12 November 1977.

Surjit S. Bhalla and Prem S. Vashistha, 'Income Distribution in India: A Reexamination', in Bardhan and Srinivasan (1988).

Krishna Bharadwaj, 'Regional Differentiation in India – A Note', *Economic and Political Weekly*, Annual Number, 1982.

N. J. Bhatia, 'Trends in Credit-Deposit and Investment+Credit Deposit Ratios of Scheduled Commercial Banks, 1969–'85, *Reserve Bank of India Bulletin*, May 1987.

B. B. Bhattacharya and Hanumantha Rao, *Agriculture–Industry Interrelations: Issues of Relative Prices and Growth in the Context of Public Investment*, paper presented at the VIIIth World Economic Congress of the International Economic Association, New Delhi, December 1986.

Nikhilesh Bhattacharya, G. S. Chatterjee and Padmaja Pal, 'Variations in Level of Living Across Regions and Social Groups in India', in Bardhan and Srinivasan (eds), 1988.

I. Z. Bhatty *et al.*, *Focus on Some Major Imbalances in the India Economy*, paper for the Annual Day of the National Council of Applied Economic Research, New Delhi, 5 April 1986.

Ashish Bose and P. B. Desai (eds), *Studies in Social Dynamics of Primary Health Care*, Delhi, Hindustan Publishing Corporation, 1983.

Samuel Bowles, *Class Power and Mass Education*, Cambridge, Mass. Harvard University, October 1971 (mimeo).

Samuel Bowles, 'Education, Class Conflict and Uneven Development', in J. Simmons (ed.), *Education Dilemma*, Oxford, Pergamon Press, 1980.

Hubert O. Brown, 'Primary Schooling and the Rural Responsibility System in the People's Republic of China', *Comparative Education Review*, August 1986.

J. Bruno, 'Populism and Health Policy: The Case of Health Volunteers in India', *Social Science and Medicine*, vol. 20, 1985.

V. Bulmer-Thomas, *Input–Output Analysis in Developing Countries*, Chichester, John Wiley and Sons, 1982.

Fox Butterfield, *China Alive in the Bitter Sea*, New York Times Books, 1982.

William A. Byrd and Lin Qingsong (eds), *China's Rural Industry: Structure, Development and Reform*, Oxford, Oxford University Press, 1990.

T. Byres, 'Of Neo-Populist Pipe Dreams: Daedalus in the Third World and the Myth of Urban Bias', *Journal of Peasant Studies*, vol. 6, no. 2, January 1979.

T. J. Byres, 'The New Technology, Class Formation and Class Action in the Indian Countryside', *Journal of Peasant Studies*, July 1981.

R. H. Cassen, *India: Population, Economy, Society,* London, Macmillan, Press, 1978.

Central Institute of Educational Research, *China's Educational Sciences*, Beijing, 1986.

Sukhamoy Chakravarty, *Development Planning: The Indian Experience*, Oxford, Clarendon Press, 1987.

Jyotiprakash Chakravartya, 'Credit and Agrarian Backwardness: Results of a Field Survey', *Economic and Political Weekly* (Review of Agriculture), March 1982.

Anand Chandavarkar, 'The Financial Pull of Urban Areas in LDCs – The

Phenomenon of Urban Bias in its Financial Aspects and Some Possible Correctives', *Finance and Development*, June 1984.

Nirmal Kumar Chandra, 'Education in China: From the Cultural Revolution to Four Modernisations', *Economic and Political Weekly*, Annual Number, May 1987.

Boudhayan Chattopadhyay, S. C. Sharma and Aswini K. Ray, 'Rural/Urban Terms of Trade, Primary Accumulation and the Increasing Strength of the Indian Farm Lobby', in Boudhayan Chattopadhyay and Pierre Spitz (eds), *Food Systems and Society in Eastern India: Selected Readings*, Geneva, UNRISD, 1987.

T. N. Chaturvedi (ed.), 'Educational Policy and Implementation', Special Number, *Indian Journal of Public Administration*, July–September 1986.

Pramit Chaudhri, *The Indian Economy: Poverty and Development*, London, Crosby Lockwood Staples, 1978.

Kuan-I Chen and J. S. Uppal (eds), *Comparative Development of India and China*, New York, Free Press, 1971.

Lincoln Chen, 'Coping with Economic Crisis: Policy Development in China and India', *Health Policy and Planning*, vol. 2, no. 2, 1987.

Kuan Chen, Gary H. Jefferson, Thomas G. Rawski, Hongchang Wang and Yuxin Zheng, 'New Estimates of Fixed Investment and Capital Stock for Chinese State Industry', *China Quarterly*, June 1988.

Kuan Chen, Hongchang Wong, Yuxin Zheng, Gary Jefferson and Thomas G. Rawski, 'Productivity Change in Chinese Industry: 1953–1985', *Journal of Comparative Economics*, December 1988.

Pi-Chao Chen and Chi-Hsien Tuan, 'Primary Health Care in Rural China: Post-Mao Developments', *Social Science and Medicine*, no. 17, 1983.

H. B. Chenery and T. Watanabe, 'International Comparisons of the Structure of Production', *Econometrica*, no. 4, 1958.

Hollis Chenery *et al.*, *Redistribution with Growth*, London, Oxford University Press, 1974.

Hollis Chenery, Sherman Robinson and Moshe Syrquin, *Industrialisation and Growth – A Comparative Study*, Oxford, Oxford University Press, 1986.

Hollis Chenery and Moises Syrquin, with the assistance of Hazel Elkington, *Patterns of Development, 1950–1970*, New York, Oxford University Press, 1975.

China State Education Commission, *Achievement of Education in China, Statistics, 1949–1983*, Beijing, 1984.

China State Education Commission, *Achievement of Education in China, Statistics, 1980–85*, Beijing, 1986.

China State Planning Commission Centre of Economics and Forecasting and China State Statistical Bureau: *Input–Output Table of China, 1981* (translation by China Statistical Information and Consultancy Services Centre, Honolulo, East-West Center, East-West Population Institute – distributed by the University of Hawaii, Honolulu, 1987).

China State Statistical Bureau, *Statistical Yearbook of China*, several years.

China State Statistical Bureau, *Agricultural Yearbook of China*, several years.

China State Statistical Bureau, *A Survey of Income and Expenditure of Urban Households in China*, Beijing, 1985.

'China's Economy', *The Economist*, London, 1 August 1987.

S. L. Chopra and O. N. S. Chauhan, 'Emerging Patterns of Political Leadership in India', *Journal of Constitutional and Parliamentary Studies*, vol. IV, no. 1, 1970.

Gregory C. Chow, *The Chinese Economy*, New Jersey, World Scientific, 1987.

Colin Clark, 'Economic Development of Communist China', *Journal of Political Economy*, April 1976.

John Connell *et al.*, *Migration from Rural Areas – The Evidence from Village Studies*, Delhi, Oxford University Press, 1976.

Richard Conroy, 'Recent Issues and Trends in Chinese Policy Towards Science and Technology', *Australian Journal of Chinese Affairs*, no. 6, 1981.

Richard Conroy, 'China's Local Scientific Research Sector: Its Role, Impact and Future Prospects', *Australian Journal of Chinese Affairs*, no. 7, 1982.

Richard Conroy, 'Technological Innovation in China's Recent Industrialisation', *China Quarterly*, March 1984.

Richard Conroy, 'Technological Change and Industrial Development', in G. Young (ed.), *China's Modernisation: The Latest Phase*, London, Croom Helm, 1984.

Richard Conroy, 'Laissez-faire Socialism? Prosperous Peasants and China's Current Rural Development Strategy', *Australian Journal of Chinese Affairs*, no. 12, 1984.

Richard Conroy, 'The Disintegration and Reconstruction of the Rural Science and Technology System – Evaluation and Implications' in Ashwani Saith (ed.), *The Re-emergence of the Chinese Peasantry – Aspects of Rural Decollectivisation*, London, Croom Helm, 1987.

S. Corbridge, 'Urban Bias, Rural Bias and Industrialisation: An Appraisal of the Work of Michael Lipton and Terry Byres', in J. Harriss (ed.), *Rural Development Theories of the Peasant Economy and Agrarian Change*, London, Hutchinson, 1982.

Elisabeth Croll, *The Family Rice Bowl – Food and the Domestic Economy in China*, UNRISD, Geneva, 1982.

Elisabeth Croll, *Food Supply in China and the Nutritional Status of Children*, Geneva UNRISD/UNICEF, 1986.

Clive Crook, 'Plain Tales of License Raj', in A Survey of India, *The Economist*, 4–10 May 1991.

Yueli Cui (ed.), *Public Health in the People's Republic of China*, People's Medical Publishing House, Beijing, 1986.

Yannian Dai, 'Dealing With Unfair Income Gaps', *Beijing Review*, 15–21 August 1988.

Ajit K. Das Gupta and Jandhyala, B. G. Tilak, 'Distribution of Education among Income Groups: An Empirical Analysis', *Economic and Political Weekly*, 13 August 1983.

Monica Das Gupta, 'Informal Security Mechanisms and Population Retention in Rural India', *Economic Development and Cultural Change*, October 1987.

Biplab Das Gupta, *Agrarian Change and the New Technology in India*, Geneva, UNRISD, 1977.

Anil G. Deolalikar and Anant K. Sundaram, 'Technology Choice, Adaptation and Diffusion in Private and Stateowned Enterprises in India', in Jeffrey James (ed.), *The Technological Behaviour of Public Enterprises in Developing Countries*, London, Routledge, 1989.

Robert F. Dernberger (ed.), *China's Development Experience in Comparative Perspective*, Cambridge, Mass., Harvard University Press, 1980.

Robert Dernberger and Richard Eckaus, *Financing Asian Development, Vol. 2, China and India*, Asian Agenda Report Series, no. 8, Lanham, MD, University Press of America, New York, The Asia Society, 1988.

Ashok V. Desai, 'The Origin and Direction of Industrial Research and Development in India', Centre for Development Studies (Trivandrum), *Working Paper No. 84*, February 1979.

Ashok V. Desai, 'Factors Underlying the Slow Growth of the Indian Industry', *Economic and Political Weekly*, Annual Number, vol. XVI, nos. 10–12, 1981.

A. V. Desai, 'The Slow Rate of Industrialisation: A Second Look', *Economic and Political Weekly*, Annual Number, 1984.

Ashok V. Desai, 'Technology Acquisition and Applications: Interpretations of the Indian Experience', in Robert E. Lucas and Gustav F. Papanek (eds), *The Indian Economy – Recent Developments and Future Prospects*, Delhi, Oxford University Press, 1988.

Sudha Deshpande and L. K. Deshpande, 'Census of 1981 and the Structure of Employment', *Economic and Political Weekly*, 1 June 1985.

P. N. Dhar, 'The Political Economy of Development in India', *Indian Economic Review*, January–June 1987.

P. N. Dhar, 'The Indian Economy – Past Performance and Current Issues' in Lucas and Papanek, 1988.

Ravindra H., Dholakia, 'Regional Aspects of Industrialisation in India', *Economic and Political Weekly*, 18 November 1989.

Jack Diamond, 'Inter-Industry Indicators of Employment Potential', *Applied Economics*, vol. 7, 1975.

Xue Dixin and others (eds), *China's Search for Economic Growth – The Chinese Economy since 1949*, Beijing, New World Press, 1982.

E. D. Domar, 'A Soviet Model of Growth', in *Essays in the Theory of Growth*, New York, 1957.

Amitav Krishna Dutt, 'Sectoral Balance – A Survey', *WIDER Working Papers, WP. 56*, Helsinki, March 1989.

Alexander Eckstein, *China's Economic Development – The Interplay of Scarcity and Ideology*, Ann Arbor, University of Michigan Press, 1975.

Howard S. Ellis (ed.), *Economic Development for Latin America*, Proceedings of a Conference held by the International Economic Association, London, Macmillan Press, 1961.

Arghiri Emmanuel, *Unequal Exchange – A Study of Imperialism of Trade*, New York, Monthly Review Press, 1972.

M. Engelborghes-Bestels, 'The New Man or a Lost Generation? Education in the Four Modernisations Programme of the PRC', *Issues and Studies*, September 1985.

Joseph P. Farrell, 'Educational Expansion and the Drive for Social Equality', in P. Altbach, R. Arnove and G. Kelly (eds), *Comparative Education*, London, Macmillan Press, 1982.

Stephan Feuchtwang, Athar Hussain and Thierry Pairault (eds), *Transforming China's Economy in the Eighties,* Vol. I on 'The Rural Sector, Welfare and Employment' and Vol. II on 'Management, Industry and the Urban Economy', Boulder, Westview and London, Zed Books, 1988.

A. G. Frank, 'The Development of Under-development', in R. I. Rhodes (ed.), *Imperialism and Underdevelopment,* New York, Monthly Review Press, 1970.

Francine Frankel, *Indian Political Economy, 1947–1977,* Princeton, Princeton University Press, 1978.

Dong Fureng, 'Relationship Between Accumulation and Consumption' in Xu Dixin and others (eds), *China's Search for Economic Growth – The Chinese Economy since 1949* Beijing, New World Press, 1982.

J. van der Gaag, 'Commune Health Care in Rural China', PHN *Technical Note, GEN-20, Population, Health and Nutrition Department,* World Bank, Washington DC, October 1983.

M. V. Gadgil, 'Agricultural Credit in India: A Review of Performance and Policies', *Indian Journal of Agricultural Economics,* July-September 1986.

John Gardner, 'Educated Youth and Urban–Rural Inequalities, 1958–66', in John W. Lewis (ed.), *The City in Communist China,* Stanford, Stanford University Press, 1971.

John Gardner, 'New Directions in Educational Policy', in Jack Gray and Gordon White (eds), *China's New Development Strategy,* London, Academic Press, 1982.

Ajit Kumar Ghose, 'The New Development Strategy and Rural Reforms in Post-Mao China', in Keith Griffin (ed.), *Institutional Reforms and Economic Development in the Chinese Countryside,* London, Macmillan Press, 1984.

Ajit Kumar Ghose, 'The People's Commune, Responsibility Systems and Rural Development in China, 1965–1984', in Ashwani Saith (ed.), *The Re-emergence of the Chinese Peasantry – Aspects of Rural Decollectivisation,* London, Croom Helm, 1987.

A. K. Ghose, 'Rural Poverty and Relative Prices in India', *Cambridge Journal of Economics,* vol. 13, 1989.

Sidney Goldstein, 'Economic Growth in China – New Insights from the 1982 Census', *Papers of the East–West Population Institute, No. 93,* July 1985.

C. Gopalan, 'The Mother and Child in India', *Economic and Political Weekly,* 26 January 1985.

Government of India, Census of Population, 1981, Series 1, India, Paper 2 of 1983, Key Population Statistics based on 5 per cent Sample Data, New Delhi, 1983.

Government of India, Central Statistical Organisation, *Monthly Abstract of Statistics,* New Delhi.

Government of India, Central Statistical Organisation, *National Accounts Statistics,* several years.

Government of India, Central Statistical Organisation, *Basic Statistics Relating to the Indian Economy, 1950–51/1980–81,* New Delhi, 1982.

Government of India, Central Statistical Organisation, *Directory of Manufacturing Establishments Survey, 1984–85,* Summary Results, New Delhi (draft, undated).

Government of India, Central Statistical Organisation, *Estimates of State*

Domestic Product, 1970–71 – 1985–86, New Delhi, June 1987.

Government of India, Central Statistical Organisation, *Annual Survey of Industries, 1983–84,* Summary of Results for Factory Sector, New Delhi, 1987.

Government of India, Directorate General of Health Services, *Health Information of India,* several years.

Government of India, Ministry of Agriculture, *Indian Agriculture in Brief,* 21st edition, New Delhi, 1986.

Government of India, Ministry of Agriculture, *Agricultural Statistics at a Glance,* New Delhi, November 1988.

Government of India, Ministry of Education and Culture, *A Handbook of Educational and Allied Statistics,* several years.

Government of India, Ministry of Finance, *Economic Survey of India,* New Delhi, several years.

Government of India, Ministry of Finance, *Report of the Economic Advisory Council on the Current Economic Situation and Priority Areas for Action (Chakravarty Report),* New Delhi, December 1989.

Government of India, Ministry of Human Resources Development, Department of Education, *National Policy on Education,* New Delhi, May 1986.

Government of India, Ministry of Human Resources Development, Department of Education, *National Policy on Education – Programme of Action,* New Delhi, August 1986.

Government of India, Ministry of Human Resources Development, *Towards an Enlightened and Humane Society* (Report of the Committee for Review of National Policy on Education 1986), Government of India Press, Faridabad, 1991.

Government of India, Office of the Registrar General, *Survey on Infant Mortality and Child Mortality,* New Delhi, 1979.

Government of India, Planning Commission, *Second Five-Year Plan,* New Delhi, 1956.

Government of India, Planning Commission, *A Technical Note on the Sixth Plan of India (1980–'85),* July 1981.

Government of India, Planning Commission, *The Seventh Five Year Plan, 1985–90,* Vol. I, New Delhi, October 1985.

Government of India, Planning Commission, *A Technical Note on the Seventh Plan of India, 1985–90,* New Delhi, 1986.

Government of India, Planning Commission, *Approach to the Eighth Five Year Plan (1990–95),* New Delhi, May 1990 (draft).

Government of India, Reserve Bank of India, *Report of Currency and Finance,* Bombay, several years.

Government of India, Reserve Bank of India, *Capital Formation and Savings in India,* 1950–51 to 1979–80, Bombay, 1982.

Jack Gray and Gordon White (eds), *China's New Development Strategy,* London, Academic Press, 1982.

Keith Griffin, 'The International Transmission of Inequality', *World Development,* March 1974.

Keith Griffin, 'Efficiency, Equality and Accumulation in Rural China – Notes on the Chinese System of Incentives', in Jonathan Unger (ed.), *China's Rural Institutions and the Question of Transferability,* Oxford, Pergamon Press, 1980.

Keith Griffin (ed.), *Institutional Reform and Economic Development in the Chinese Countryside,* London, Macmillan Press, 1984.

Keith Griffin, *World Hunger and the World Economy,* London, Macmillan Press, 1987.

Keith Griffin, *Alternative Strategies for Economic Development,* London, Macmillan Press, 1989.

Keith Griffin and Ashwani Saith, '*The Pattern of Income Inequality in Rural China'*, Asian Employment Programme Working Papers, Bangkok, ARTEP/ILO, July 1980.

Keith Griffin and Ashwani Saith, *Growth and Equality in Rural China,* Bangkok, ILO/ARTEP, 1981.

Keith Griffin and Jeffrey James, *The Transition to Egalitarian Development,* London, Macmillan Press, 1981.

Keith Griffin and John Knight (eds) 'Human Development in the 1980s and Beyond, Special Number, *Journal of Development Planning,* no. 19, 1989.

Merilee S. Grindle (ed.), *Politics and Policy Implementation in the Third World,* Princeton, Princeton University Press, 1980.

Yu Guangyuin (ed.), *China's Socialist Modernisation,* Beijing Foreign Language Press, 1984.

I. S. Gulhati and K. K. George, 'Interstate Redistribution Through Budgetary Transfers', *Economic and Political Weekly,* vol. 13, no. 11, 1978.

Anupam Gupta, *Overall Rate of Growth and Sectoral Rates of Growth – A Study of Instability in Economic Development,* paper presented at the VIIIth World Economic Congress of the International Economic Association, New Delhi, 1–5 December 1986.

Suraj B. Gupta, 'Credit Policy in India – A Critical Review', Department of Economics, Delhi School of Economics, *Working Paper no. 274,* Delhi, August 1985.

Ahsanul Habib, Charles Stahl and Mohammad Alauddin, 'Inter-Industry Analysis of Employment Linkages in Bangladesh', *Economics of Planning,* vol. 19, no. 1, 1985.

Steven Haggblade and Peter Hazell, 'Agricultural Technological and Farm – Non-farm Linkages', *Agricultural Economics,* no. 3 (1989).

Scott Halstead *et al.* (eds), *Good Health at Low Cost,* Conference Report, Rockefeller Foundation, New York, 1985.

B. Harriss, 'Rural–Urban Economic Transactions: A Case Study from India and Sri Lanka', in S. W. R. de Samarasinghe (ed.), *Agriculture in the Peasant Sector of Sri Lanka,* Peradeniya Ceylon Studies Seminar, 1976.

J. Harriss, *Rural Development: Theories of Peasant Economies and Agrarian Change,* London, Hutchinson, 1982.

J. Harriss and Mick Moore, 'Development and the Rural–Urban Divide', Special Issue, *Journal of Development Studies,* April 1984.

J. N. Hawkins, *Education and Social Change in PRC,* New York, Praeger Publishers, 1983.

Donald Hay and Shujie Yao, *Determinants of Productive Efficiency in Chinese Manufacturing Enterprises, 1980–1987,* paper submitted to International Conference on the Chinese Economy, Shenzhen, January 1990.

Donald Hay and Shujie Yao, *A Review of Economic Reforms and Trends of Industrial Development in China, 1978–1988,* Institute of Economics and Statistics, Oxford, May 1990 (mimeo).

Yujiro Hayami, *Agricultural Protectionism in the Industrialised World – The Case of Japan,* paper prepared for a Conference held at the East-West Centre, Honolulu, 17–21 February 1986.

Peter B. Hazell and Steven Haggblade, 'Rural–Urban Growth Linkages in India', World Bank, Agriculture and Rural Development Department, *Working Papers WPs. 430,* Washington DC, May 1990.

Gail Henderson, *Increased Inequality in Health Care: Fact or Fiction?,* paper prepared for the Conference on 'Social Consequences of the Chinese Economic Reforms', Fairbank Center for East Asian Research, Harvard University, 13–15 May 1988.

John Vernon Henderson, 'International Experience in Urbanisation and its Relevance for China', *World Bank Staff Working Papers, No. 759,* Washington DC, 1986.

Ronald J. Herring and Rex M. Edwards, 'Guaranteeing Employment to the Rural Poor: Social Functions and Class Interests in the Employment Guarantee Scheme in Western India', *World Development,* vol. II, no. 7, July 1983.

Alan R. Hinman and Robert L. Parker, 'Costs of Care', *American Journal of Public Health,* September 1982, vol. 72, supplement.

K. N. Hiriyanniah and K. Ramachandran, 'India', in UNESCO, *The Drop-Out Problem in Primary Education – Some Case Studies,* Regional Office for Education in Asia and the Pacific, Bangkok, 1984.

Albert O. Hirschman, *The Strategy of Economic Development,* New Haven Yale University Press, 1958.

Albert O. Hirschman, 'A Dissenter's Confession: The Strategy of Economic Development Revisited', in Gerald M. Meier and Dudley Seers (eds), *Pioneers in Development,* New York, Oxford University Press, 1984.

Samuel P. S. Ho, 'The Asian Experience in Rural Non-agricultural Development – its Relevance for China', *World Bank Staff Working Papers No. 757,* Washington DC, 1986.

William C. Hsiao, 'Transformation of Health Care in China', The *New England Journal of Medicine,* 5 April 1984.

William C. Hsiao, *The Incomplete Revolution – China's Health Care System under Market Socialism,* paper prepared for the Conference on the Social Consequences of the Chinese Economic Reforms, Fairbank Center for East Asian Research, 1988.

Teh-wei Hu, 'Health Care Services in China's Economic Development', in Robert F. Dernberger (ed.), *China's Development Experience in Comparative Perspective*.

Athar Hussain, 'Science and Technology in the Chinese Countryside' in Denis Fred Simon and Merle Goldman (eds), *Science and Technology in Post-Mao China,* Cambridge, Mass., Harvard University Press, 1989.

Athar Hussain and Ehtisham Ahmad, *Public Action for Social Security in China,* paper prepared for a Workshop on Social Security in Developing Countries, London School of Economics, July 1988.

Athar Hussain and Nicholas Stern, *On the Recent Increase in Death Rates in China,* London School of Economics, 1988 (mimeo).

Athar Hussain and Nicholas Stern, *Macroeconomic Consequences of the Chinese Enterprise Reforms,* paper prepared for the Seminar on 'Development Experience in Large Economies: China and India – Reform and Modernisation', 15 to 17 January 1990, New Delhi,

Indian Institute of Public Opinion, 'The Course of State Incomes, 1960–1968, Unequal Growth in Indian States', *Quarterly Economic Report*, April 1969.

S. Ishikawa, *Economic Development in Asian Perspective*, Economic Research Series No. 8, Institute of Economic Research, Hitotsubashi University, 1967.

S. Ishikawa, 'China's Economic System Reform: Underlying Factors and Prospects', *World Development*, August 1983.

Shigeru Ishikawa, *Socialist Economy and the Experience of China – A Perspective on Economic Reform*, Alexander Eckstein Memorial Lecture, 18 March 1985.

S. Ishikawa, 'Technology Imports and Indigenous Technology Capacity in China', *ILO/WEP Working Paper Series, WEP/2–22 WP. 185*, January 1988.

Rizwanul Islam (ed.), *Strategies for Alleviating Poverty in Rural Asia*, Bangkok, ILO/ARTEP, 1985.

Rizwanul Islam, 'Growth of Rural Industries in Post-Reform China: Patterns, Determinants and Consequences', *Development and Change*, October 1991.

Jeffrey James, *Improving Traditional Rural Technologies*, London, Macmillan Press, 1989.

Dean T. Jamison *et al.*, *CHINA: The Health Sector*, World Bank, Washington DC, 1984.

Alain de Janvry and Frank Kramer, 'Limits of Unequal Exchange', *The Review of Radical Political Economics*, vol. II, no. 4, Winter 1979.

Alain de Janvry and K. Subbarao, *Agricultural Price Policy and Income Distribution in India*, Delhi, Oxford University Press, 1986.

Prem Shankar Jha, *INDIA – A Political Economy of Stagnation*, Delhi, Oxford University Press, 1980.

Yang Jianbai and Li Xuezeng, 'The Relation between Agriculture, Light Industry and Heavy Industry in China', *Social Sciences in China*, June 1980.

Chen Jiyuan, 'Technological Renovation and the Restructuring of the Economy', *Social Sciences in China*, Summer 1985.

Leroy P. Jones, 'The Measurement of Hirschmanian Linkages', *Quarterly Journal of Economics*, May 1976.

George Joseph, *International Trade in an Unequal World – A Survey of Different Theories and Their Empirical Potential*, Department of Econometrics and Social Statistics, University of Manchester, 1985 (mimeo).

M. Ann Judd, James K. Boyce and Robert E. Evenson, 'Investing in Agricultural Supply: The Determinants of Agricultural Research and Extension Investment', *Economic Development and Cultural Change*, October 1986.

G. K. Kadekodi, 'The Cost of a Balanced Diet', in R. Sinha *et al.*, *Poverty, Income Distribution and Employment – A Case Study of India*, Glasgow/Delhi Oxford Project Report 1978, Part II (mimeo).

A. Kahlon and D. Tyagi, 'Intersectoral Terms of Trade', *Economic and Political Weekly*, 27 December 1980.

A. S. Kahlon and D. S. Tyagi, *Agricultural Price Policy in India*, New Delhi, Allied Publishers Private Ltd., 1983.

Michal Kalecki, 'Problem of Financing Economic Development in a Mixed Economy', in *Essays on Developing Economies*, Hassocks, Harvester Press Ltd, 1976.

Michal Kalecki, *Essays on Developing Economies*, ibid.

Massoud Karshenas, 'Intersectoral Resource Flows and Development: Lessons of Past Experience', *ILO/WEP Working Paper Series, WEP 10–6, WP. 99*, Geneva, June 1989.

N. Keyfitz, 'Development and Elimination of Poverty', *Economic Development and Cultural Change*, April 1982.

Azizur Rehman Khan and Eddy Lee (eds), *Agrarian Policies and Institutions in China after Mao*, Bangkok, ILO/ARTEP, 1983.

Azizur Rahman Khan and Eddy Lee (eds), *Poverty in Rural Asia*, Bangkok, ILO/ARTEP, 1985.

M. E. Khan and C. V. S. Prasad, *Health Financing in India: A Case Study of Gujarat and Maharashtra*, Operations Research Group, Baroda, India, 1985.

Peter Kilby and Bruce F. Johnston, *Agriculture and Structural Transformation – Economic Strategies in Late-Developing Countries*, New York, Oxford University Press, 1975.

A. Kohli, *The State and Poverty in India: The Politics of Reform*, Cambridge, Cambridge University Press, 1987.

Reeitsu Kojima, 'China's New Agricultural Policy', *The Developing Economies*, December 1982.

Bruce Koppel, 'Janus in Metropolis: An Essay in the Political Economy of Urban Resources', *Developing Economies*, Tokyo, March 1986.

Rajni Kothari, 'Masses, Classes and the State', *Economic and Political Weekly*, 1 February 1986.

Richard C. Kraus, *Class Conflict in Chinese Socialism*, New York, Columbia University Press, 1981.

Raj Krishna, 'The Centre and the Periphery – Inter-state Disparities in Economic Development', in *Facets of India's Development – G. L. Mehta Memorial Lectures*, Bombay, Indian Institute of Technology, 1986.

Raj Krishna, 'Intersectoral Equity and Agricultural Taxation in India', *Economic and Political Weekly*, Special Number, August 1972.

June Kronholz, 'City Limits: China's Controls Curb Third World Curse of Urban Sprawl', *The Wall Street Journal*, 14 June 1983.

Yak-Yeow Kueh, 'China's New Agricultural Policy Program: Major Economic Consequences, 1979–1983', *Journal of Comparative Economics*, December 1984.

Y. Y. Kueh, 'China's Food Balance and the World Grain Trade, Projections for 1985, 1990, and 2000', *Asian Survey*, December 1984.

Y. Y. Kueh, 'Economic Planning and Local Mobilisation in Post-Mao China', *Research Notes and Studies, No. 7*, Contemporary China Institute, School of Oriental and African Studies, University of London, 1985.

Y. Y. Kueh, 'The Maoist Legacy and China's New Industrialisation Strategy', *China Quarterly*, September 1989.

Gopalakrishna Kumar, 'On Prices and Economic Power: Explaining Recent

Changes in Intersectoral Relations in the Indian Economy,' *Journal of Development Studies*, October 1988.

Gopalakrishna Kumar, 'Gender, Differential Mortality and Development – The Experience of Kerala', *Cambridge Journal of Economics*, December 1989.

C. I. Kurian, 'Indian Economy in the 1980s and on to the 1990s', *Economic and Political Weekly*, 15 April 1989.

Simon Kuznets, 'Economic Growth and Income Inequality', *American Economic Review*, vol. 65, no. 1, 1955.

Simon Kuznets, 'Quantitative Aspects of Economic Growth of Nations: V-Long-term Trends in Capital Formation Proportions: International Comparisons for Recent Years', *Economic Development and Cultural Change*, July, 1960, Part II.

Jocelyn Kynch and Amartya Sen, 'Indian Women: Well Being and Survival', *Cambridge Journal of Economics*, September–December 1983.

Deepak Lal, 'Agricultural Growth, Real Wages, and the Rural Poor in India', *Economic and Political Weekly* (Review of Agriculture), 26 June 1976.

Jacques Lamontagne, 'Educational Development in the PRC: Regional and Ethnic Disparities', *Issues and Studies*, September 1986.

David M. Lampton, 'Health, Conflict and the Chinese Political System', *Michigan Papers in Chinese Studies No. 18*, Ann Arbor, Michigan University, 1974.

David M. Lampton, 'Performance and the Chinese Political System – A Preliminary Assessment of Education and Health Policies', *China Quarterly*, September 1978.

David M. Lampton (ed.), *Policy Implementation in Post-Mao China*, Berkeley, California University Press, 1987.

Nicholas R. Lardy, *Economic Growth and Distribution in China*, Cambridge, Cambridge University Press, 1978.

Nicholas Lardy, 'Regional Growth and Income Distribution in China', in Robert F. Dernberger (ed.), *China's Development Experience in Comparative Perspective*.

Nicholas Lardy, *Agriculture in China's Modern Economic Development*, Cambridge, Cambridge University Press, 1983.

Nicholas Lardy, 'Agricultural Prices in China', *World Bank Staff Working Papers, No. 606*, 1983

Nicholas R. Lardy, 'Consumption and Living Standards in China, 1978–83', *China Quarterly*, December 1984.

T. H. Lee, *Intersectoral Capital Flows in the Economic Development of Taiwan, 1895–1960*, Ithaca, Cornell University Press, 1971.

John W. Lewis, *Leadership in Communist China*, Ithaca, Cornell University Press, 1963.

W. A. Lewis, 'Development with Unlimited Supplies of Labour', *The Manchester School*, May 1954.

W. A. Lewis, 'Unlimited Labour: Further Notes', *The Manchester School*, January 1958.

Chengrui, Li, 'Economic Reform Brings Better Life', *Being Review*, 22 July 1985.

Wei Lining and Li Yongzeng, 'Education in China: The Past Four Years', *Beijing Review*, 24 January 1983.

Johannes F. Linn, *Cities in the Developing World – Policies for the Equitable and Efficient Growth*, New York, Oxford University Press, 1983.

M. Lipton, 'Strategy for Agriculture: Urban Bias and Rural Planning', in Paul Streeten and Michael Lipton (eds), *The Crisis of Indian Planning*, Oxford, Oxford University Press, 1968.

M. Lipton, 'Transfer of Resources from Agriculture to Non-agricultural Activities: The Case of India', *Communication Series No. 109*, Institute of Development Studies, 1972.

Michael Lipton, 'Agricultural and Non-agriculture in Institutional Credit – A Note', *Economic and Political Weekly*, 25 September 1976.

M. Lipton, *Why Poor People Stay Poor: Urban Bias in World Development*, London, Temple Smith, 1977.

Michael Lipton, 'Agricultural Finance and Rural Credit in Poor Countries', in Paul Streeten and Richard Jolly (eds), *Recent Issues in World Development – A Collection of Survey Articles*, Oxford, Pergamon Press, 1981.

M. Lipton, 'Why Poor People Stay Poor', Sixth Vikram Sarabhai Memorial Lecture, Indian Institute of Management, Ahmedabad; reprinted in J. Harriss (ed.), *Rural Development: Theories of Peasant Economy and Agrarian Change*.

M. Lipton, 'Urban Bias Revisited', *Journal of Development Studies*, April 1984.

Michael Lipton with Richard Longhurst, *New Seeds and Poor People*, London, Unwin Hyman, 1989.

I. M. D. Little, *Economic Development – Theory, Policy and International Relations*, New York, Basic Books, 1982.

William T. Liu, *China's Statistical Abstract*, Boulder, Praeger Publishers, 1988.

Robert E. B. Lucas and Gustav F. Papanek (eds), *The Indian Economy – Recent Developments and Future Prospects*, Delhi, Oxford University Press, 1988.

Thomas P. Lyons, 'Interprovincial Trade and Development in China, 1957–1979', *Economic Development and Cultural Change*, January 1987.

Thomas P. Lyons, 'Interprovincial Disparities in China: Output and Consumption, 1952–1987', *Economic Development and Cultural Change*, April 1991.

John T. Macree, 'A Clarification of Chinese Development Strategy since 1949', *Developing Economies*, September 1979.

P. C. Mahalanobis, 'Some Observations on the Process of Growth of National Income', *Sankhya*, September 1953.

P. C. Mahalanobis, 'The Approach of Operational Research to Planning in India', *Sankhya*, December 1955.

T. Maitra, B. Dev and N. Bhattacharya, 'An Inquiry on the Distribution of Public Education and Health Services in West Bengal', *Sankhya* (Series C), June 1974.

Wilfred Malenbaum, 'India and China: Contrasts in Development Performance', *American Economic Review*, June 1959.

Wilfred Malenbaum, 'Modern Economic Growth in India and China: The Comparison Revisited, 1950–1980', *Economic Development and Cultural Change*, October 1982.

Wilfred Malenbaum, 'A Gloomy Portrayal of Development Achievements and Prospects – China and India', *Economic Development and Cultural Change*, January 1990.

Markos J. Mamalakis, 'The Theory of Sectoral Clashes', *Latin American Research Review*, vol. 4, no. 3, 1969.

Markos J. Mamalakis, 'The Theory of Sectoral Clashes and Coalitions Revisited', *Latin American Research Review*, vol. 6, no. 3, 1971.

Zedong, Mao, 'On the Ten Major Relationships' in *Selected Works of Mao*, vol. V, Peking, Foreign Language Press, 1956.

R. M. Maru, 'The Community Health Volunteer Scheme in India', *Social Science and Medicine*, vol. 17, 1983.

Nobuo Maruyama, 'The Mechanism of China's Industrial Development – Background to the Shift in Development Strategy', *Developing Economies*, December 1982.

Ashok Mathur, 'Regional Development and Income Disparities in India: A Sectoral Analysis', *Economic Development and Cultural Change*, April 1983.

Bruce McFarlane, 'Political Economy of Class Struggle and Economic Growth in China, 1950–1982', *World Development*, August 1983.

James McGilvray, 'Linkages, Key Sectors and Development Strategy', in Wassily Leontief (ed.), *Structure, System and Economic Policy*, Cambridge, Cambridge University Press, 1977.

Gerald M. Meier and Dudley Seers (eds), *Pioneers in Development*, New York, Oxford University Press, 1984.

John W. Mellor, 'Accelerated Growth in Agricultural Production and the Intersectoral Transfer of Resources', *Economic Development and Cultural Change*, October 1973.

John W. Mellor, *The New Economics of Growth – A Strategy for India and the Developing World*, Ithaca, Cornell University Press, 1976.

Jagannath Mishra and Chakradhar Sinha (eds), *Planning and Regional Development in India*, New Delhi, Gaurav Publishing House, 1985.

A. Mitra, *Terms of Trade and Class Relations*, London, Frank Cass, 1977.

Ashok Mitra (ed.), *China: Issues in Development*, New Delhi, Tulika, 1988.

A. Mody, 'Resource Flows Between Agriculture and Non-agriculture in India, 1950–1970', *Economic and Political Weekly*, Annual Number, March 1981.

A. Mody, 'Rural Resources Generation and Mobilisation', *Economic and Political Weekly*, Annual Number, March 1983.

A. Mody, S. Mundle and K. N. Raj, 'Resource Flows from Agriculture: A Comparative Analysis of Japan and India', in K. Ohkawa and G. Ranis (eds), *Japan and Developing Countries*, Basil Blackwell, 1984.

J. A. Mollet, 'Agricultural Investment and Economic Development – Some Relationships', *Outlook on Agriculture*, vol. 11, no. 1, 1982.

Gavin Mooney, *Economics, Medicine and Health Care*, Sussex, Wheatsheaf Books, 1986.

David Morawetz, *Twenty-Five Years of Economic Development, 1950 to 1975*, Baltimore, Johns Hopkins Press, 1977.

M. Mukhopadhyay, 'Human Development Through Primary Health Care: Cases from India', in D. Morley *et al.* (eds), *Practising Health for All*, Oxford, Oxford University Press, 1983.

Sudhir K. Mukhopadhyay, 'Factors Influencing Agricultural Research and Technology: A Case Study of India', in Ahmed and Ruttan (eds), 1988.

Sudipto Mundle, *Surplus Flows and Growth Imbalances – The Intersectoral Flow of Real Resources in India, 1951–1971*, Delhi, Applied Publishers Ltd., 1981.

Sudipto Mundle, 'The Agrarian Barrier to Industrial Growth', *Journal of Development Studies*, October 1985.

Sudipto Mundle, 'Land, Labour and the Level of Living in Rural Bihar', in Khan and Lee (1983).

Sudipto Mundle, 'Land, Labour and the Level of Living in Rural Punjab', in Khan and Lee (1983).

Philip Musgrave, 'Measurement of Equity in Health', *World Health Statistics Quarterly*, vol. 39, no. 4, 1986.

Moni Nag, 'Impact of Social and Economic Development on Mortality: A Comparative Study of Kerala and West Bengal', *Economic and Political Weekly*, Annual Number, May 1983.

Moni Nag, 'Political Awareness as a Factor in Accessibility of Health Services – A Case Study of Rural Kerala and West Bengal', *Economic and Political Weekly*, 25 February 1989.

D. M. Nanjundappa, 'Rural–Urban Conundrum in Indian Planning', *Indian Economic Journal*, April–June 1982.

National Council of Applied Economic Research (NCAER), *Household Income and its Disposition*, New Delhi, 1980.

NCAER: *Focus on Some Major Imbalances in the Indian Economy*, paper for the Annual Day of the NCAER, New Delhi, April 5, 1986. (mimeo).

NCAER: *Changes in the Household Income, Inter-class Mobility and Income Distribution in Rural India – A Longitudinal Study*, 1970–71/1981–82, New Delhi, 1986 (mimeo).

NCAER: *Changes in the Structure of Household Income and Distribution of Gains in the Rural Household Sector – An All-India Temporal Analysis*, New Delhi, 1987 (mimeo).

Barbara A. Newman and Randall J. Thomson, 'Economic Growth and Social Development: A Longitudinal Analysis of Causal Priority', *World Development*, 1989.

Peter Nolan, 'Inequality of Income Between Town and Countryside in PRC in the mid-1950s', *World Development*, vol. 7, 1979.

Peter Nolan and Gordon White, 'Economic Distribution and Rural Development in China: The Legacy of the Maoist Era?', in Frances Stewart (ed.), *Work, Income and Inequality – Payment Systems in the Third World*, London, Macmillan Press, 1983.

Peter Nolan and Gordon White, 'Urban Bias, Rural Bias, or State Bias? Urban–Rural Relations in Post-revolutionary China', *Journal of Development Studies*, April 1984.

Peter Nolan and Suzanne Paine, 'Towards an Appraisal of the Impact of Rural Reform in China, 1975–85', *Cambridge Journal of Economics*, March 1986.

R. Nurkse, *Problems of Capital Formation in Underdeveloped Countries*, Oxford, Basil Blackwell, 1953.

OECD, *Agriculture in China – Prospects for Production and Trade*, Paris, 1985.

Suzanne Paine, 'Balanced Development: Maoist Conception and Chinese Practice', *World Development*, April 1976.

Suzanne Paine, 'Development with Growth – A Quarter Century of Socialist Transformation in China', *Economic and Political Weekly*, Special Number, August 1976.

Suzanne Paine, 'Reflections on the Presence of Rural or Urban Bias in China's Development Policies, 1949–1976', in Jonathan Unger (ed.), *China's Rural Institutions and the Question of Transferability*, Oxford, Pergamon Press, 1980.

Suzanne Paine, 'Spatial Aspects of Chinese Development – Issues, Outcomes and Policies, 1949–'79', *Journal of Development Studies*, January 1981.

G. Palma, 'Dependency: A Formal Theory of Underdevelopment or a Methodology for the Analysis of Concrete Situations of Underdevelopment', *World Development*, nos 7/8, 1978.

V. R. Panchumukhi, 'Linkages in Industrialisation – A Study of Selected Developing Countries in Asia', *Journal of Development Planning*, vol. 19, no. 1, 1985.

P. G. K. Panikar, 'Health Care System in Kerala', in Scott B. Halstead, Julia A. Walsh and Kenneth S. Warren (eds), *Good Health at Low Cost*.

P. G. K. Panikar, 'Financing Health Care in China: Implications of Some Recent Developments', *Economic and Political Weekly*, 19 April 1986.

P. G. K. Panikar and C. R. Soman, *Health Status of Kerala – Paradox of Economic Backwardness and Health Development*, Centre for Development Studies, Trivandrum, India, 1984.

W. Parish, 'Egalitarianism in Chinese Society', *Problems of Communism*, January–February 1981.

William L. Parish and Martin King Whyte, *Village and Family in Contemporary China*, Chicago, University of Chicago Press, 1978.

William L. Parish and Martin King Whyte, *Urban Life in Contemporary China*, Chicago, University of Chicago Press, 1984.

Robert L. Parker and Alan R. Hinman, 'Use of Health Services', *American Journal of Public Health*, vol. 72, Supplement, 1982.

Surendra J. Patel, 'India's Regression in the World Economy', *Economic and Political Weekly*, 28 September 1985.

Surendra J. Patel, 'Indian Economy at the Dawn of 21st Century', *Mainstream*, 22 February 1986.

Surendra J. Patel, 'Main Elements in Shaping Future: Technology Policies for India', *Economic and Political Weekly*, 4 March 1989.

Utsa Patnaik, 'Output and Marketable Surplus of Agricultural Products: Contributions by Cultivating Groups, 1960–'61', *Economic and Political Weekly* (Review of Agriculture), December 1975.

People's Republic of China, *China Agriculture Yearbook*, Beijing Agricultural Publishing House, 1986, 1987.

People's Republic of China, Ministry of Education, *Achievement of Education in China – Statistics, 1949–1983*, Beijing, 1984.

People's Republic of China, *Achievement of Education in China, Statistics, 1980–1985*, Beijing, 1986.

Dwight Perkins, *CHINA – Asia's Next Economic Giant*, Seattle, University of Washington Press, 1986.

Dwight Heald Perkins, 'Reforming China's Economic System', *Journal of Economic Literature*, June 1988.

Dwight H. Perkins and Moshe Syrquin, 'Large Countries: The Influence of Size', in Hollis Chenery and T. N. Srinivasan (eds), *Handbook of Development Economics*, vol. II, North-Holland, Amsterdam, 1989.

Dwight Perkins and Shahid Yusuf, *Rural Development in China*, Baltimore, Johns Hopkins Press, 1984.

Alan Piazza, 'Trends in Food and Nutrient Availability in China, 1950–81', *World Bank Staff Working Paper No. 607*, September 1983.

Shen Ping-yu, *The Role of the Informal Sector in China's Urban Development – Case Studies of Changshu City and Linhuai Town*, paper presented at the Round Table Conference on the Informal Sector in the Economy of Small Cities, West Berlin, 17–27 February 1985.

Brahm Prakash, Yash Aggarwal, N. V. Verghese and L. S. Ganesh, 'Planning Education for the Future: Developments, Issues and Choices', National Institute of Educational Planning and Administration (NIEPA), *Occasional Papers No. 16*, New Delhi, 1988.

Brahm Prakash and Yash Aggarwal, 'Selected Issues for Implementing New Educational Policy', *Indian Journal of Public Administration*, July–September 1986.

Pradhan H. Prasad, 'On Regional Inequalities in India', *Economic and Political Weekly*, 13 August 1988.

Nicholas Prescott and Dean Jamison, 'Health Sector Finance and Expenditures in China', *PHN Technical Notes, GEN 14*, Population, Health and Nutrition Department, World Bank, Washington DC, May 1983.

Nicholas Prescott and Dean T. Jamison, 'The Distribution and Impact of Health Resource Availability in China', *International Journal of Health Planning and Management*, vol. I, 1985.

S. H. Preston, *Mortality Patterns in National Populations*, New York, Academic Press, 1976.

David F. Pyle, 'From Pilot Project to Operational Program in India: The Problems of Transition', in Grindle (ed.), *Politics and Policy Implementation in the Third World*.

Progress Report on the SPARK Programme for 1988, SSTC, Beijing 1989.

P. Radhakrishnan, 'Land Reform: Rhetoric and Reality', *Economic and Political Weekly*, 24 November 1990.

K. N. Raj, 'Linkages in Industrialisation and Development Strategy: Some Basic Issues', *Journal of Development Planning*, no. 8, 1975.

K. N. Raj, 'Agricultural Growth in China and India: Role of Price and Non-price Factors', *Economic and Political Weekly*, 15 January 1983.

K. R. Ranadive, 'Town and Country in Economy in Transition', *Artha Vijnana*, September 1987.

C. Rangarajan, 'Agricultural Growth and Industrial Performance in India: A Study of Interdependence', *Research Report No. 33*, International Food Policy Research Institute (IFPRI), Washington DC, 1982.

C. Rangarajan, 'Industrial Growth – Another Look', *Economic and Political Weekly*, Annual Number, April 1982.

Gustav Ranis and John C. H. Fei, *Development of the Labour Surplus Economy – Theory and Policy*, Illinois, Richard D. Irwin, Inc., 1964.

Gustav Ranis, Robert L. West, Mark W. Leiserson and Cynthia Taft Morris (eds), *Comparative Development Perspectives*, Boulder, Westview Press, 1984.

Gustav Ranis and Frances Stewart, 'Rural Linkages in the Philippines and Taiwan', in Frances Stewart (ed.), *Macroeconomic Policies for Appropriate Technology in Developing Countries*, Boulder, Westview Press, 1987.

C. H. Hanumantha Rao, *Technological Change in Indian Agriculture: Emerging Trends and Perspectives*, Presidential Address, the Golden Jubilee Conference of the Indian Society of Agricultural Economics, Bombay, 4–7 December 1989.

V. K. R. V. Rao, 'Urban Bias and Rural Development', *Indian Economic Review*, vol. 15, no. 1, 1980.

P. N. Rasmussen, *Studies in Intersectoral Relations*, Amsterdam, North Holland, 1957.

Nikalantha Rath, 'Prices, Costs of Production and Terms of Trade in Indian Agriculture', *Indian Journal of Agricultural Economics*, October–December 1985.

Thomas G. Rawski, *Economic Growth and Employment in China*, New York, Oxford University Press, 1979.

Bruce Reynolds (ed.), *Chinese Economic Reforms: How Far, How Fast?*, New York, Academic Press, 1988.

P. J. Richards and M. Leonor, *Education and Income Distribution in Asia*, London, Croom Helm, 1981.

Barry Richman, 'Chinese and Indian Development – An Inter-disciplinary Environmental Analysis', *American Economic Review, Papers and Proceedings*, May 1975.

James Riedel, 'A Balanced Growth Version of the Linkage Hypothesis: A Comment', *Quarterly Journal of Economics*, May 1976.

Carl Riskin, *China's Political Economy – The Quest for Development Since 1949*, New York, Oxford University Press, 1987.

Carl Riskin, 'Feeding China: The Experience Since 1949', *WIDER Working Papers, WP. 27*, Helsinki, November 1987.

Lord Robbins, 'Equality as a Social Objective', in Lord Robbins, *Politics and Economics – Papers in Political Economy*, London, Macmillan Press, 1963.

Denis A. Rondinelli, 'The Urban Transition and Agricultural Development: Implications for International Assistance Policy', *Development and Change*, April 1986.

P. N. Rosenstein Rodan, 'Problems of Industrialisation in Eastern and Southeastern Europe', *Economic Journal*, June–September 1943.

P. N. Rosenstein Rodan, *Notes on the Theory of the 'Big Push'*, Cambridge Mass., MIT Center for International Studies, March 1957.

D. B. Rosenthal, *The Expansive Elite: District Policies and State Policymaking in India*, Berkeley, University of California Press, 1977.

Lloyd I. Rudolph and Susanne Hoeber Rudolph, *In Pursuit of Lakshmi – The Political Economy of the Indian State*, New Delhi, Orient Longman, 1987.

Ashok Rudra, 'Technology Choice in Agriculture in India over the Past

Three Decades', in Frances Stewart (ed.), *Macropolicies for Appropriate Technology in Developing Countries*, Boulder, Westview Press, 1987.

A. J. Saich, *Reform in Post-Mao China: A Study of the Civilian Science and Technology Sector*, Leiden, February 1986.

Ashwani Saith, 'Contrasting Experiences in Rural Industrialisation: Are the East Asian Successes Transferable?', *Asian Employment Programme Working Papers*, New Delhi, ARTEP/ILO, September 1986.

Ashwani Saith (ed.), *The Re-emergence of the Chinese Peasantry – Aspects of Rural Decollectivisation*, London, Croom Helm, 1987.

Ashwani Saith, *Development Strategies and the Rural Poor*, paper presented at the ILO/SAREC Workshop on the Interrelationship Between Macroeconomic Policies and Rural Development, Geneva, 11–13 December 1989.

David E. Sanger, 'China Plans to Shut Down Redundant Firms', *International Herald Tribune*, Zurich, 29 August 1989.

B. N. Sarkar, 'Interstate Disparities in Education', in Jandhyala B. Tilak (ed.), *Education and Regional Development*, New Delhi, Yatan Publications, 1986.

Atul Sarma and Kewal Ram, 'Income, Output and Employment Linkages and Import Intensities of Manufacturing Industries in India', *Journal of Development Studies*, January 1989.

J. S. Sarma, *Agricultural Policy in India – Growth with Equity*, Ottawa, IDRC, 1982.

Ranjit Sau, 'Some Aspects of Intersectoral Resource Flow', *Economic and Political Weekly*, August 1974.

Ranjit Sau, *India's Economic Development – Aspects of Class Relations*, New Delhi, Orient Longman Ltd, 1981.

Bernard Schaffer, 'Towards Responsibility: Public Policy in Concept and Practice', in E. J. Clay and B. B. Schaffer (eds), *Room for Manouever – Explanation of Public Policy Planning in Agricultural and Rural Development*, London, Heinemann Educational Books, 1984.

Tibor Scitovsky, 'Equity', in Tibor Scitovsky, *Papers on Welfare and Growth*, Stanford, Stanford University Press, 1964.

Amartya Sen, *Poverty and Famines: An Essay on Entitlement and Deprivation*, Oxford, Clarendon Press, 1981.

Amartya Sen, 'Development: Which Way Now?', *Economic Journal*, December 1983.

Amartya K. Sen, 'Family and Food: Sex Bias in Poverty', in T. N. Srinivasan and P. K. Bardhan (eds), *Rural Poverty in South Asia*, New York, Columbia University Press, 1988.

Amartya Sen, 'Development as Capability Expansion', *Journal of Development Planning*, no. 19, 1989.

Amartya Sen, 'The Concept of Development', in H. C. Chenery and T. N. Srinivasan (eds), *Handbook of Development Economics*, vol. I, Amsterdam, North Holland, 1988.

Amartya Sen and Sunil Sen Gupta, 'Malnutrition of Rural Children and the Sex Bias', *Economic and Political Weekly*, Annual Number, May 1983.

Amartya Sen and Jean Drèze, *Hunger and Public Action*, Oxford, Clarendon Press, 1989.

C. Seshadri, 'Equality of Educational Opportunity: Some Issues in Indian Education', *Comparative Education*, October 1976.

C. H. Shah, 'Taxation and Subsidies on Agriculture – A Search for Policy Options', *Indian Journal of Agricultural Economics*, July–September 1986.

Helen Shapiro and Lance Taylor, 'The State and Industrial Strategy', *World Development*, June 1990.

John B. Sheahan, 'Alternative International Economic Strategies and their Relevance for China', *World Bank Staff Working Papers, No. 759*, Washington DC, 1986.

S. L. Shetty, 'An Intersectoral Analysis of Taxable Capacity and Tax Burden', *Indian Journal of Agricultural Economics*, July–September 1971.

S. L. Shetty, 'Structural Retrogression in the Indian Economy', *Economic and Political Weekly*, Annual Number, 1978.

Susan L. Shirk, 'Educational Reform and Political Backlash: Recent Changes in Chinese Educational Policy', *Comparative Education Review*, June 1979.

Mark Sidel, 'University Enrolment in the People's Republic of China, 1977–1981: The Examination Model Returns', *Comparative Education*, vol. 18, no. 3, 1982.

J. Simmons (ed.), *The Education Dilemma*, Oxford, Pergamon Press, 1980.

Hans Singer, 'Balanced Growth in Economic Development: Theory and Practice', in E. Nelson (ed.), *Economic Growth – Rationale, Problems, Cases*, Austin, University of Texas Press, 1960.

Ajit Singh, 'The World Economy and the Comparative Economic Performance of Large Semi-industrial Countries – A Study of India, China and the Republic of Korea', *Asian Employment Programme Working Papers*, Bangkok, ARTEP/ILO, September 1985.

R. Sinha, Peter Pearson, Gopal Kadekodi and Mary Gregory, *Income Distribution, Growth and Basic Needs in India*, London, Croom Helm, 1979.

R. K. Sinha, 'Regional Imbalance and Fiscal Equalisation in India', in Mishra and Sinha, 1985.

Ronald Skeldon, 'On Migration Patterns in India During the 1970s', *Population and Development Review*, December 1986.

G. W. Skinner, 'Rural Marketing in China: Repression and Revival', *China Quarterly*, September 1985.

Vaclav Smil, 'Food Production and Quality of Diet in China', *Population and Development Review*, March 1986.

South Commission, '*The Challenge to the South*', Report of the South Commission, Oxford, Oxford University Press, 1990.

Daniel Southerland, 'Beijing Reinforces Central Planners' Role and Extends Austerity', *International Herald Tribune*, Zurich, 2–3 December 1989.

T. N. Srinivasan, 'Neoclassical Political Economy, the State and Economic Development', *Asian Development Review*, Manila, vol. 3, no. 2, 1985.

T. N. Srinivasan, 'Economic Liberalisation in China and India: Issues and an Analytical Framework', *Journal of Comparative Economics*, September 1987.

Nirankar Srivastav and R. R. Barthwal, 'Measurement of Sectoral Income and Employment Multiplier for the Economy of Uttar Pradesh: An

Application of Semi-closed Input-Output Model', *Indian Journal of Economics*, October 1985.

Ravi Srivastava, *Planning and Regional Disparities in India*, paper presented at the Conference on 'The State and Development Planning in India', School of Oriental and African Studies, London, 21–24 April 1989.

State Statistical Bureau, Department of Population Statistics, *The 1982 Population Census of China*, Major Figures, 1982.

State Statistical Bureau, *Statistical Yearbook of China*, several years.

Benedict Stavis, 'Making Green Revolution: The Politics of Agricultural development in China', *Rural Development Monograph No. 1*, Ithaca, Cornell University Rural Development Committee, 1974.

Ben Stavis, 'Agricultural Performance and Policy: Contrasts with India', *Social Scientist*, May/June 1977.

N. Stern, 'The Economics of Development: A Survey', *Economic Journal*, September 1989.

Frances Stewart, *Technology and Underdevelopment*, London, Macmillan Press, 1977.

Frances Stewart, *Planning to Meet Basic Needs*, London, Macmillan Press, 1985.

Frances Stewart and Paul Streeten, 'New Strategies for Development: Poverty, Income Distribution and Growth', *Oxford Economic Papers*, November 1976.

Bruce Stone, 'Relative Prices in the Peoples' Republic of China: Rural Taxation through Public Monopsony', in John W. Mellor and Raisuddin Ahmed (eds), *Agricultural Price Policy for Developing Countries*, Baltimore, Johns Hopkins Press, 1988.

Paul Streeten, 'Unbalanced Growth', *Oxford Economic Papers*, June 1959.

Paul Streeten, *The Frontiers of Development Studies*, London, Macmillan Press, 1972.

Paul Streeten *et al.*, *First Things First: Meeting Basic Human Needs in Developing Countries*, London, Oxford University Press, 1976.

Paul Streeten, 'Development Dichotomies', *World Development*, October 1983.

'Structure of China's Domestic Consumption', *World Bank Staff Working Papers, No. 755*, 1985.

K. Subbarao, *Some Aspects of Access to Education in India*, paper prepared for a Workshop on Poverty in India held at Queen Elizabeth House, Oxford, October 1987.

K. Subbarao, 'Improving Nutrition in India', *World Bank Discussion Papers, No. 49*, Washington DC, December 1989.

K. K. Subramanian, 'Foreign Technology in the Four Modernisations of China', *Economic and Political Weekly*, 15 June 1985.

K. Sundaram and S. D. Tendulkar, 'Poverty Reduction and Redistribution in Sixth Plan – Population Factor and Rural–Urban Equity', *Economic and Political Weekly*, 17 September 1983.

K. Sundaram, *Agriculture–Industry Interrelation, Issues of Migration*, paper presented at the VIIIth World Economic Congress of the International Economic Association, New Delhi, December 1986.

R. M. Sundrum, *Growth and Income Distribution in India – Policy and*

Performance Since Independence, New Delhi, Sage Publications, 1987.

Gerald E. Sussman, 'The Pilot Project and the Choice of an Implementing Strategy: Community Development in India', in Grindle (ed.), *Politics and Policy Implementation in the Third World*.

Subramanian Swamy, *Economic Growth in China and India, 1952–1970 – A Comparative Appraisal*, Chicago, University of Chicago Press, 1973.

Subramanian Swamy, *Economic Growth in China and India – A Perspective By Comparison*, New Delhi, Vikas Publishing House Private Ltd, 1989.

On-Kit Tam, 'The Development of China's Financial System', *Australian Journal of Chinese Affairs*, no. 17, January 1987.

On-Kit Tam, 'Rural Finance in China', *China Quarterly*, March 1988.

Jeffrey R. Taylor and Karen A. Hardee, *Consumer Demand in China – A Statistical Fact Book*, Boulder (Colorado), Westview Press, 1986.

'Technology Transfer to Rural Areas', *Beijing Review*, no. 25, 22 June 1987.

R. Thamarajakshi, 'Intersectoral Terms of Trade and Marketed Surplus Produce, 1951–52 to 1965–66', *Economic and Political Weekly*, 28 June 1969.

R. Thamarajakshi, 'Role of Price Incentives in Stimulating Agricultural Production', in D. Ensminger (ed.), *Food Enough or Starvation for Millions*, New Delhi, Tata McGraw-Hill, 1977.

Colin Thirtle, 'Induced Innovation Theory and Agricultural Development in LDCs – An Appraisal', *Manchester Working Papers in Agricultural Economics, WP. 88/03*, Manchester, 1988.

Stig Thogersen, 'China's Senior Middle Schools in a Social Perspective. A Survey of Yantai District', *China Quarterly*, March 1987.

Gene Tidrick, 'Productivity Growth and Technological Change in Chinese Industry', *World Bank Staff Working Papers, No. 761*, Washington DC, 1986.

Jandhyala B. G. Tilak, 'Educational Finances in India', *Indian Journal of Public Administration*, July–September 1986, Special Number on 'Educational Policy and Implementation'.

Jandhyala B. G. Tilak (ed.), *Education and Economic Development*, New Delhi, Yatan Publications, 1986.

Jandhyala B. G. Tilak, *The Economics of Inequality in Education*, New Delhi, Sage Publications, 1987.

C. Peter Timmer, 'The Agriculture Transformation', in H. B. Chenery and T. N. Srinivasan (eds), *Handbook of Development Economics*, vol. I.

Michael P. Todaro and Jerry Stilkind, *City Bias and Rural Neglect: The Dilemma of Urban Development*, New York, Population Council, 1981.

James Tong, *Interprovincial Variations in Health Care Services in the People's Republic of China, 1979–1982*, paper prepared for the Annual Meeting of the Association of Asian Studies, Boston, 10–12 April 1987.

John Toye, *Dilemmas of Development – Reflections on the Counter-Revolution in Development Theory and Policy*, Oxford, Basil Blackwell, 1987.

John Toye, 'Political Economy and the Analysis of Indian Development', *Modern Asian Studies*, February 1988.

Shu-ki Tsang, *Problems of Monetary Control for a Socialist Developing*

Economy under Reform – The Case of China, Working Paper Series, Hong Kong Baptist College, June 1989.

Meenakshi Tyagarajan, 'Deposits with Commercial Banks – Profile', *Economic and Political Weekly*, 23 October 1982.

D. S. Tyagi, 'Domestic Terms of Trade and their Effect on Supply and Demand of Agricultural Sector', *Economic and Political Weekly* (Review of Agriculture), 28 March 1987.

United Nations, *Yearbook of National Accounts Statistics*, several years.

UNCTAD, *Technology Issues in the Capital Goods Sector: The Experience of the People's Republic of China*, Geneva, 1984 (UNCTAD/TT/57).

UNDP, *Human Development Report 1990*, New York, Oxford University Press, 1990.

UNESCO, *The Drop-Out Problem in Primary Education – Some Case Studies*, Bangkok, 1984.

UNIDO, *INDIA New Dimensions of Industrial Growth*, Oxford, Basil Blackwell, 1990.

United Nations Pacific Centre for Transfer of Technology, *Technology Policies and Planning – Peoples' Republic of China*, Country Studies Series, Bangalore, India, 1986.

United States Congress, Joint Economic Committee, *China Under the Four Modernisations*, Part I, Selected Papers, Washington DC, US Government Printing Office, 13 August 1982.

H. Uzawa, 'On a Two-Sector Model of Economic Growth', *Review of Economic Studies*, October 1961.

Leela Visaria, 'Infant Mortality in India – Level, Trends and Determinants', *Economic and Political Weekly*, 24 August 1985.

V. S. Vyas and George Mathai, 'Farm and Non-farm Employment in Rural Areas: A Perspective for Planning', *Economic and Political Weekly*, Annual Number, February 1978.

V. S. Vyas *et al.*, 'Indian Agriculture at 2000: Strategies for Equity', *Economic and Political Weekly*, Annual Number, March 1981.

Robert Wade, 'The Market for Public Office: Why the Indian State is not Better at Development', *World Development*, vol. 13, no. 4, 1985.

Kenneth R. Walker, 'China's Rural Economic Development', *China Quarterly*, September 1989.

George C. Wang (ed.), *Economic Reform in the PRC*, Boulder, Westview Press, 1982.

Tuoyu Wang, 'Regional Imbalances' in William A. Byrd and Lin Oingsong (eds), *China's Rural Industry*.

J. Warford, *Financing Rural Health Care*, Inter-regional Seminar on Primary Health Care, Yexian County, Shandong Province, World Bank, Washington DC, April 1980.

A. Watson, 'Agriculture Looks for "Shoes that Fit": The Production Responsibility System and its Implications', *World Development*, vol. II, no. 8, 1983.

Thomas E. Weisskopf, 'The Relevance of the Chinese Experience for Third World Economic Development', *Theory and Society*, (Special Issue on Actual Socialisms), March 1980.

Thomas E. Weisskopf, 'China and India: Contrasting Experiences in Economic Development', *American Economic Review*, Papers and Proceedings, May 1975.

Wang Weizhi, 'A Preliminary Analysis of the Death Rate in China', in Li Chengrui *et al.* (eds), *A Census of One Billion People*, Population Census Office, State Statistical Bureau, Beijing, 1987.

Liang Wensen, 'Balanced Development of Agriculture and Industry', in Xue Dixin and others, 1982.

Willem F. Wertheim and Matthias Steifel, *Production, Equality and Participation in Rural China – Reflections on a Field Trip in September/October 1979*, Geneva, UNRISD, 1982.

G. White, 'Higher Education and Social Redistribution in a Socialist Society – The Chinese Case', *World Development*, vol. 9, no. 2, 1981.

Gordon White, 'Urban Employment and Labour Allocation Policies', in Stephan Feuchtwang and Athar Hussain (eds), *The Chinese Economic Reforms*, London, Croom Helm, 1983.

Gordon White, 'Riding the Tiger: Grass Roots Rural Politics in the Wake of the Chinese Economic Reforms', in Saith, 1987.

Thomas B. Wiens, 'Price Adjustment, the Responsibility System and Agricultural Productivity', *American Economic Review*, Papers and Proceedings, May 1983.

Thomas B. Wiens, 'Issues in Structural Reforms of Chinese Agriculture', in Reynolds, 1988.

Jeffrey G. Williamson, 'Regional Inequality and the Process of National Development – A Description of the Patterns, *Economic Development and Cultural Change*, Part II, July 1965.

Marvin E. Wolfgang (Special Editor), *China in Transition – The Annals of the American Academy of Political and Social Science*, November 1984.

Lung-fai Wong, *Agricultural Productivity in the Socialist Countries*, Boulder, Westview Press, 1986.

Lung-fai Wong, *Agricultural Productivity in China and India: A Comparative Analysis*, paper prepared for a Symposium on Feeding the People of China and India, Chicago University, 15 February 1987.

WHO, 'Methodology of Nutrition Surveillance', *Technical Report Series, No. 593*, Geneva, 1976.

World Bank, *CHINA: Socialist Economic Development*, three volumes, Washington DC, 1983.

World Bank, *Situation and Prospects of the Indian Economy – A Medium-term Perspective*, Washington DC, 16 April 1984.

World Bank, *CHINA: Long-Term Development Issues and Options*, Baltimore, Johns Hopkins University Press, 1985.

World Bank, *CHINA: Issues and Prospects in Education* (Annex I to World Bank, *CHINA: Long-Term Development Issues and Options*), Washington DC, 1985.

World Bank, *CHINA: Economic Structure in International Perspective* (Annex 5 to *CHINA: Long-Term Development Issues and Options*).

World Bank, *Agriculture to the Year 2000* (Annex 2 to *CHINA: Long-Term Development Issues and Options*), Washington DC, 1985.

World Bank, *Economic Models and Projections* (Annex 4 to *CHINA: Long-Term Development Issues and Options*) Washington DC, 1985.

World Bank, *Financing Education in Developing Countries – An Exploration of Policy Options*, Washington DC, 1986.

World Bank, *CHINA – Management and Finance of Higher Education*, Washington DC, 1986.

World Bank, *Financing Health Services in Developing Countries: An Agenda for Reform*, Washington DC, 1987.

World Bank, *India: Poverty, Employment and Social Services*, Washington DC, 1989.

World Bank, *India: Recent Developments and Medium Term Issues*, Washington DC, 1989.

World Bank, *World Development Report*, New York, Oxford University Press (several years).

Wang Yalin and Li Jinrong, 'Urban Workers' Housework – Investigative Report', *Social Sciences in China*, June 1982.

Shujie Yao, 'Chinese Agricultural Policies and the Grain Problem', unpublished M. A. Econ. Dissertation, University of Manchester, August 1987.

Shujie Yao and David R. Colman, 'Chinese Agricultural Policies and Agricultural Reforms', *Oxford Agrarian Studies*, vol. 18, no. 1, 1990.

Shao Yinong, *The Chinese Health System*, London, Office of Health Economics, 1988.

Pan A. Yotopoulos and Jeffrey B. Nugent, 'Balanced Growth Version of the Linkage Hypothesis: A Test', *Quarterly Journal of Economics*, May 1973.

Pan A. Yotopoulos and Jeffrey B. Nugent, 'In Defense of a Test of the Linkage Hypothesis', *Quarterly Journal of Economics*, May 1976.

Pan A. Yotopoulos and Lawrence J. Lau, 'A Test for Balanced and Unbalanced Growth', *Review of Economics and Statistics*, November 1970.

Graham Young, 'Control and Style: Discipline and Inspection Commissions Since the 11th Congress', *China Quarterly*, March 1984.

Mary Young, 'The Barefoot Doctor: Training, Role, Future', PHN *Technical Note, GEN-19*, Population, Health and Nutrition Department, World Bank, Washington DC, May 1984.

Mary E. Young and Andre Prost, 'Child Health in China', *World Bank Staff Working Papers No. 767*, Washington DC, 1985.

Ma Yuanling, *Modern Plant Biotechnology and Structure of Rural Employment in China*, paper prepared for the ILO Technology and Employment Branch, Geneva, ILO 1989 (draft).

S. Akbar Zaidi, 'The Urban Bias in Health Facilities in Pakistan', *Social Science and Medicine*, vol. 20, no. 5, 1985.

Zheng Zonghan, 'On Small Towns', *Social Sciences in China*, no. 4, 1983.

Yuyan Zhang, 'Economic System Reform in China', *WIDER Working Papers, WP 55*, Helsinki, March 1989.

Han Zongli, 'An Inquiry into Investment in Universalising Primary Education', *Chinese Education*, vol. XVII, no. 3, Fall 1984.
David Zweig, 'Context and Content in Policy Implementation: Household Contracts and Decollectivisation, 1977–1983', in David M. Lampton, *Policy Implementation in post-Mao China*, Berkeley, California University Press, 1987.

Author Index*

---

* This index also refers to the Bibliography which includes items not cited in the text but which were found useful as background material.

Subject Index